VM/CMS
Handbook

Howard W. Sams & Company
Hayden Books

Related Titles

Advanced C Primer++
Stephen Prata, The Waite Group

C with Excellence:
Programming Proverbs
Henry F. Ledgard with John Tauer

C Programmer's Guide
to Serial Communications
Joe Campbell

Microsoft® C Programming
for the IBM®
Robert Lafore, The Waite Group

C Primer Plus,
Revised Edition
Mitchell Waite, Stephen Prata,
and Donald Martin, The Waite Group

Programming in C
Stephen G. Kochan

Topics in C Programming
Stephen G. Kochan and Patrick H. Wood

C Programming Techniques for the
Macintosh®
Zigurd Mednieks and Terry Schilke

MS-DOS® Bible
Steven Simrin, The Waite Group

Discovering MS-DOS®
Kate O'Day, The Waite Group

MS-DOS® Developer's Guide
John Angermeyer and Kevin Jaeger,
The Waite Group

Tricks of the MS-DOS® Masters
John Angermeyer, Rich Fahringer,
Kevin Jaeger, and Dan Shafer, The Waite Group

Inside XENIX®
Christopher L. Morgan, The Waite Group

UNIX® Primer Plus
Mitchell Waite, Donald Martin,
and Stephen Prata, The Waite Group

UNIX® System V Primer,
Revised Edition
Mitchell Waite, Stephen Prata,
and Donald Martin, The Waite Group

UNIX® Communications
Bryan Costales, The Waite Group

UNIX® Shell Programming
Stephen G. Kochan and Patrick H. Wood

UNIX® System Security
Patrick H. Wood and Stephen G. Kochan

UNIX® System Administration
David Fieldler and Bruce H. Hunter

Exploring the UNIX® System
Stephen G. Kochan and Patrick H. Wood

UNIX® Text Processing
Dale Dougherty and Tim O'Reilly

Advanced UNIX® —
A Programmer's Guide
Stephen Prata, The Waite Group

UNIX® Shell Programming Language
Rod Manis and Marc Meyer

UNIX® System V Bible
Stephen Prata and Donald Martin,
The Waite Group

Tricks of the UNIX® Masters
Russell G. Sage, The Waite Group

Turbo C Programming for the IBM
Robert Lafore, The Waite Group
(forthcoming)

Quick C Programming
Carl Townsend
(forthcoming)

VM/CMS Handbook

for Programmers, Users, and Managers

Howard Fosdick

HAYDEN BOOKS

A Division of Howard W. Sams & Company
4300 West 62nd Street
Indianapolis, Indiana 46268 USA

Dedication
"Forward, Rozinante!"

FIRST EDITION
FIRST PRINTING—1987

International Standard Book Number: 0-672-46790-9
Library of Congress Catalog Card Number: 87-60538

Acquisitions Editor: *Terese Zak*
Manuscript Editor: *Albright Communications, Inc.*
Interior Designer: *T. R. Emrick*
Illustrator: *Ralph E. Lund*
Cover Art: *Meridian Design Studio Inc.*
Compositor: *Shepard Poorman Communications Corp.*

Printed in the United States of America

Contents

Section 3: The Virtual Machine Environment

Section 4: CMS Communications and Commands

Section 5: Program Development with VM/CMS

Section 6: VM/CMS Command Languages

Section 7: VM/CMS Software

Section 8: VM/CMS and the Future

Preface

The subject of this book is the Virtual Machine/Conversational Monitor System (VM/CMS), a popular name for the licensed program product operating system, Virtual Machine/System Product (VM/SP). The book has two purposes. The first is to give you an understanding of the VM/CMS environment by describing the software components which comprise VM/CMS and analyzing the functions and relationships of those components. This book is *not* strictly confined to the VM/SP operating system licensed program product; it presents the *typical VM/CMS environment.* Its wider purview includes separately purchased software products that are often encountered in VM/CMS shops (for example, the SCRIPT text formatter and the SQL/DS database management system). The intent is a practical overview of the total VM/CMS environment as it is perceived by its users.

The second goal of this book is to enable you to interact with VM/CMS immediately. Brief, practical tutorials present minimal command subsets for each software component. With this book in hand, you can gain immediate "hands-on" capability at your VM-based terminal or PC. For those who require more information, the last subsection of each chapter tells what resources are available.

Only certain topics are included in the "minitutorials." The basis for selection is breadth of use. Those software components of the VM/CMS environment that are most widely used receive the most coverage; those that are not so prevalent are only briefly mentioned. In this way, this book presents a "real world" handbook for VM/CMS. Guidelines for selectivity are not based, a priori, on the formal design of the operating system itself; they are derived from how people actually perceive and use the VM/CMS computing environment.

This book is written for all users of VM/CMS. For the nontechnical reader, it describes the components within VM/CMS, their functions and purposes. It provides overviews of the software products that are commonly found in VM/CMS environments. For the technically oriented, this book includes extensive examples showing how to use VM/CMS commands and facilities. After working with this book, you'll know how to interact with VM/CMS and you'll feel confident about using the vendor's reference manuals. Please feel free to contact me through the publisher with your comments and suggestions regarding the VM/CMS operating system.

Howard Fosdick

Acknowledgments

I wish to thank Terry Anderson, Stewart Berman, Brian Delaney, Gary Guth, George Lales, Brian Maron, Patricia Slaymaker, and Michael Thommes for reading this book and providing expert criticism. Their contributions greatly improved the quality of this book.

I thank Gary DeWard Brown, Rita Carney, Harvey Deitel, Ernest Leatherman, and Hillis Griffin for their support.

I especially thank Dennis Beckley and Priscilla Polk for their constructive criticism and friendly encouragement. The technical insight Dennis and Priscilla have contributed to this and my past efforts has been critical to the quality of this work.

Trademarks

All terms mentioned in this book that are known to be trademarks or service marks are listed below. In addition, terms suspected of being trademarks or service marks have been appropriately capitalized. Howard W. Sams & Co. cannot attest to the accuracy of this information. Use of a term in this book should not be regarded as affecting the validity of any trademark or service mark.

AT&T is a registered trademark of American Telephone and Telegraph
IBM is a registered trademark of International Business Machines Corporation
IBM PC is a registered trademark of International Business Machines Corporation
IBM XT is a registered trademark of International Business Machines Corporation
IBM AT is a registered trademark of International Business Machines Corporation
IBM 9370 is a registered trademark of International Business Machines Corporation
MS-DOS is a registered trademark of Microsoft Corporation
UNIX is a registered trademark of AT&T
CP/M is a registered trademark of Digital Research Inc.
UTS is a registered trademark of Amdahl Corporation
VAX/VMS is a registered trademark of Digital Equipment Corporation
ORACLE is a registered trademark of Oracle Corporation
ADABAS is a registered trademark of Software Ag
INQUIRE is a registered trademark of Infodata Systems Inc.
NOMAD2 is a trademark of D & B Computing Systems

Introduction

The VM/CMS operating system provides one of the outstanding growth stories of the 1980s. During 1985 alone, VM/CMS usage increased 111% on large mainframes and 54% on smaller mainframes.* VM/CMS (also referred to as VM/SP, VM, or CMS) is rising to new prominence among operating systems.

What VM/CMS characteristics prompt this explosive growth?

- VM/CMS is highly interactive, and its design better addresses the need for online computing than do IBM's traditional mainframe operating systems of the OS and DOS families.

- VM/CMS supports an outstanding program development environment through its terminal monitor, CMS. CMS features interactive program development, and it even enables you to encode and test programs for subsequent execution under OS and DOS operating systems.

- VM/CMS is the only major operating system capable of simultaneously supporting multiple operating systems on the same computer. These "guest" operating systems include those in the OS, DOS, UNIX, PICK, and VM/CMS families.

- VM/CMS has been found to be easier to use than other operating systems by both programmers and nontechnical users alike.

IBM has reacted strongly to VM/CMS's demand-pull sales success. First, IBM termed the operating system "strategic." Long the least promoted of IBM's mainframe operating systems, VM/CMS achieves strategic importance as its sales surpass those of MVS/TSO and DOS/VSE. Second, IBM transported VM/CMS to the PC/370 family of microcomputers in a version called Virtual Machine/Personal Computer (VM/PC). Third, IBM chose VM/CMS as the primary operating system for its 9370 superminicomputers. Thus, VM/CMS plays a prominent role across the spectrum of computers, from micro to mini to mainframe.

With VM/CMS emerging as one of the handful of widely used operating systems, it becomes ever more important for computer professionals to familiarize themselves with this system. VM/CMS has burst out of its previously limited markets in engineering, scientific programming,

---

* "Users Keep Turning on to IBM's VM Operating System," *InformationWEEK* (July 8, 1985): 36-43.

and academia. It is now widely used in business, data processing, and general-purpose computing. Programmers, analysts, software engineers, and other technical professionals greatly enhance their personal marketability by learning VM/CMS. Managers need to understand VM/CMS's strengths and weaknesses as an operating environment in order to better appraise its future in their plans. Increasing numbers of end-users also wish to tap the power of VM/CMS and learn how it can help them in their jobs.

Organization

This book is organized as follows: Section 1 introduces VM/CMS, its history and evolution. It describes what an operating system is and what you can accomplish using this one. This section also shows how to log onto VM/CMS systems.

Section 2 describes how to enter and change information in CMS files and teaches a functional subset of commands for the XEDIT editor. It also illustrates CMS commands to copy, rename, erase, compare, and print files. Many of the commands from a textual document output formatter program product called SCRIPT are demonstrated.

Section 3 presents several conceptual views of the VM/CMS operating system. It explains the principles of the "virtual machine" design underlying VM/CMS. This section teaches you how to control and dynamically reconfigure your own virtual machine.

Section 4 further explores CMS capabilities and treats several aspects of CMS use in detail. Among its topics is an introduction to the CMS HELP Facility, a complete online help system within CMS.

Section 5 demonstrates how to use CMS to develop programs targeted for final execution under VM/CMS, OS, and DOS operating systems.

Section 6 introduces the CMS command procedure languages. These languages allow you to issue operating system commands under programmatic control. This section describes the pre-eminent VM/CMS command language, REXX.

Section 7 provides overviews of several of the predominant add-on products available for use under CMS. Since there are hundreds of such products, this section restricts discussion to those most widely used at VM/CMS sites.

Finally, section 8 discusses VM/CMS and the future. As part of this discussion, the microcomputer variant of the operating system, VM/PC, is described. This section also summarizes the relative strengths and weaknesses of the VM/CMS environment. Final comments sketch the probable future role of VM/CMS among operating systems and in the marketplace.

Releases of VM/SP

All examples in this book were machine-tested under VM/SP. Various releases of the operating system are mentioned where appropriate. In an introductory book such as this, the differences between recent releases of the operating system are relatively insignificant, so this book applies to all recent releases of the operating system.

Figures

This book contains extensive in-text examples and illustrations. These examples are models for your own online experience with the operating system. Consider this book your companion while exploring VM/CMS on a terminal or personal computer, and adopt your own most effective approach to learning this important operating system.

Screen displays and coding examples are photographically reproduced in this book. Screen displays may appear slightly different on your terminal, depending on such factors as terminal type and model, the number of lines displayable on the screen, and your VM/SP release.

References to the Vendor's Manuals

This book complements the vendor's reference manuals. It orients you to the functions of VM/CMS software components and packages and shows how these pieces fit together and are actually used within the VM/CMS environment. The book illustrates those commands and facilities that are most immediately useful to the typical VM/CMS user. It prioritizes and selects from the myriad details packed into the reference manuals to provide an efficient and balanced approach to learning VM/CMS.

Each chapter provides references to vendor's manuals for further information. The titles of these manuals are generally stable, but the manual order numbers sometimes change. Refer to: *IBM System/370, 30XX, and 4300 Processors Bibliography, GC20-0001; IBM Marketing Publications KWIC Index, G320-1621;* and *IBM Software Directory, GB21-9949,* for the latest manual references and order numbers when necessary.

SECTION 1

Introducing VM/CMS

- Operating Systems and VM/CMS
- VM/CMS Concepts
- A First Terminal Session

CHAPTER 1

Operating Systems and VM/CMS

What Is an Operating System?

An *operating system* is a computer program designed to control the operation of a computer so that it is used efficiently and effectively by programmers and other users. Operating systems provide the software buffer between the physical hardware comprising the computer and the user programs that run on the hardware. Sometimes operating systems are referred to as *control programs.* This term is particularly descriptive because, in a real sense, an operating system controls the resources of the computer.

The resources under control of the operating system vary, depending upon the physical configuration of the machine at hand. Often they include:

processor(s), the part of the computer which actually executes the instructions in computer programs

main storage, the memory that holds programs while they run

secondary storage, devices such as disks and tapes, which provide long-term storage for large amounts of data and programs

input and output devices, the printers, computer terminals, card readers, card punches, and other devices that permit communication between the human users of the computer and the programs run on the computer

The two broad purposes of an operating system are: to optimize and monitor performance of the computer, by allocating appropriate hardware resources to programs which run on the machine; and to simplify the use of the machine, by providing an intelligent software interface between user programs and actual hardware devices, such as disks, terminals, and printers.

The operating system functions as a control program to the physical hardware of the computer system, as diagrammed in figure 1-1. Programs run on the computer are scheduled by the operating system and executed under its direction. The operating system oversees the set-up, execution, and termination of every program run on the machine. In this manner, the control program assures the orderly operation of the computer and its hardware. The programs that run under the auspices of the operating system are called *application programs* or *user programs*.

Figure 1-1
The Operating
System Controls
Computer
Resources

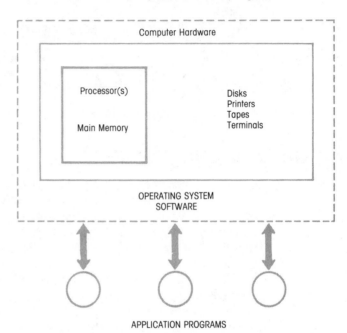

APPLICATION PROGRAMS

Figure 1-2 offers another view of this same principle, this time from the viewpoint of you, the individual terminal user, interacting with the computer through the operating system. A special part of the operating system called the *terminal monitor* reads and interprets the commands you enter through the terminal keyboard. This monitor program assumes full responsibility for interacting with you at the terminal and for carrying out whatever tasks you want performed. You can interact only with the monitor portion of the operating system, or with some other program that the control program permits to run and interact with terminal users. Should you interact with some application program other than the terminal monitor through your terminal, remember that this program still runs under the control of the operating system.

Introducing VM/CMS

Virtual Machine/Conversational Monitor System (VM/CMS) is a general-purpose operating system that runs on mainframes, minicomputers, and

Figure 1-2
Users Interact with
Operating System
through Terminal
Monitor

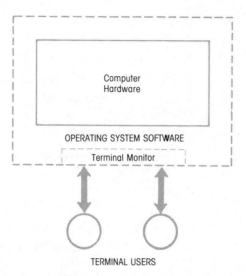

microcomputers. This system is called Virtual Machine/System Product (VM/SP) in the vendor's reference manuals, and also is referred to as VM or VM/370.

Given the vital role of operating systems in modern computers, it comes as no surprise that there exist dozens of these control programs. Besides VM/CMS, the most popular are Microsoft Disk Operating System (MS-DOS), Control Program for Microprocessors (CP/M), Multiple Virtual Storage (MVS), Disk Operating System/Virtual Storage Extended (DOS /VSE), UNIX, and PICK. Each control program has its own unique strengths and weaknesses, since many of these systems were designed with quite different purposes in mind. For example, MS-DOS and CP/M were developed for single-user microcomputers. On the other end of the spectrum, MVS evolved to provide control of large, general-purpose main-frame computers. This operating system handles terminals supporting dozens of concurrent users while simultaneously running large noninteractive programs referred to as "batch jobs." Needless to say, MVS is quite different in both function and design than microcomputer-oriented operating systems like MS-DOS and CP/M. These differences are so pronounced that they extend to the interaction of the individual terminal user with the computer environment. To use a terminal on a computer system, you must be familiar with the terminal monitor commands for that computer's operating system, and these commands differ for each of the operating systems previously mentioned.

As a general-purpose operating system, VM/CMS can support effectively a wide variety of computer-based activities. It is especially well suited for:

- end-user computing, the use of computer terminals by people who are not computer specialists

- interactive computing, the use of computer resources by users of online terminals
- mainframe-based office automation
- providing compatibility between mainframes and microcomputers
- supporting large numbers of terminal users on IBM (and look-alike) mainframes
- program development
- providing compatibility with the other families of operating systems supported by IBM
- providing an environment where other operating systems, as well as VM/CMS, can run simultaneously on a single computer

The VM operating system was developed originally for control of the mainframes IBM designed in the mid-1960s, the IBM 360 series of computers. The distinguishing feature of the 360 series was the then-revolutionary concept that a computer program should be able to run on several computers of different sizes and capabilities without alteration.

VM was developed as an experimental system at the IBM Cambridge Scientific Center in 1964. Within a few years, early forms of VM, CP-40 and CP-67, were running on versions of the IBM 360/40 and 360/67 computers.

This internal IBM developmental activity resulted in the first major commercial offering of the VM/CMS operating system in 1972. Called VM /370, this version coincided with IBM's announcement of its new 370 series of mainframe computers.

VM has a number of different versions, introduced at different times. As table 1-1 shows, there have been several major versions of mainframe VM/CMS, including VM/370, VM/SP, and VM/XA. These versions of the VM operating system are related historically and functionally.

Table 1-1
VM/CMS
Operating System

Acronym	Full Name	Comments
VM/XA	Virtual Machine/Extended Architecture	Further evolution of VM/SP
VM/SP	Virtual Machine/System Product	Sometimes followed by a release number, e.g., VM/SP 4
VM/370	Virtual Machine/370	The original version of mainframe VM
VM/E	Virtual Machine/Entry	An entry-level version of VM for smaller mainframes
VM/IS	Virtual Machine/Integrated System	Another entry-level version of VM introduced with the 9370 series of superminicomputers
VM/PC	Virtual Machine/Personal Computer	A version of VM for microcomputers

Figure 1-3 demonstrates that mainframe VM/CMS has evolved into a more powerful operating system over time. VM/E and VM/IS are versions of the system specifically adapted for use on entry-level mainframes. They are designed as simple starter systems for new or smaller mainframe installations.

Figure 1-3
The Evolution of VM

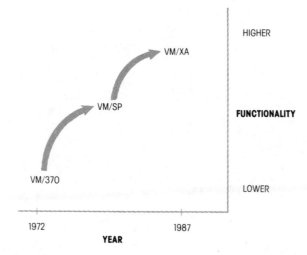

VM/PC is the variant of VM/CMS specifically tailored for use on microcomputer members of the IBM PC family. Example machines on which VM/PC runs include the AT/370 and XT/370, in their several versions. These machines are standard personal computers with a few special circuit boards inserted into their card slots.

From the standpoint of terminal users and programmers, all the versions of VM/CMS appear similar. The commands you enter at the terminal are the same, regardless of which version of VM is used. The exception to this general rule is that the more sophisticated or newer versions of the operating system provide more commands than the earlier versions. Since this book introduces only the most important commands, the material it presents is generically appropriate regardless of the version of VM you use. The one exception is VM/PC, which differs in slight but important ways from the other versions of this operating system. VM/PC runs on single-user computers which have a very different hardware architecture than the mainframes which the other versions of VM control. The ways in which VM/PC differs from the rest of the VM/CMS family will be described in chapter 26.

The computer hardware supported by the VM family of operating systems is illustrated in figure 1-4. VM runs on all models of IBM mainframe computers and on their look-alikes vended by the plug-compatible mainframe manufacturers.

Figure 1-4
VM/CMS Supports
Mainframe and
Microcomputer
Hardware

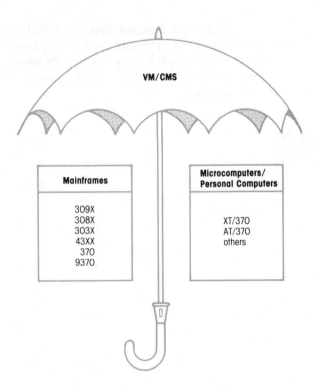

What You Can Do with VM/CMS

This book concentrates on those tasks that terminal users most commonly perform. It also describes how to use other facilities that are typically available on computers running the VM/CMS operating system, but which are not technically part of the operating system itself. You will learn how to:

- enter and change data and programs
- format and print such data files as memos, papers, and other documents
- command the system to execute its many utility functions, such as those that copy, move, sort, and compare data files
- communicate messages and files to other computer users
- enter, compile, test, and run programs (assuming you already know a programming language)
- seek explanatory or "help" information through the terminal
- write programs consisting of VM/CMS commands in one of the "command procedure languages" of the operating system

These tasks are merely a sampling of what can be accomplished with VM/CMS, but will serve as a nucleus upon which to build your understanding.

Test Your Understanding

What are the purposes of an operating system? List the hardware resources controlled by operating systems.

What is a terminal monitor? How does the terminal monitor relate to the operating system and the terminal user(s)?

For what kinds of computing is VM/CMS best suited?

List the major acronyms associated with the VM/CMS operating system. On what kinds of computers do these versions of the operating system run? Determine the release of VM/CMS to which you have access.

What activities can you accomplish using a VM/CMS terminal?

CHAPTER 2

VM/CMS Concepts

VM/CMS Components

VM consists of a number of software components. The two major parts are the *Control Program (CP)* and the *Conversational Monitor System (CMS)*.

The Control Program is the component closest to the hardware on which the operating system runs. In its intimate relationship with the computer hardware resources, CP is responsible for the control of hardware-specific operations, such as causing the printer to print a data file, or directing a disk drive to read and send specified data to the computer's main memory. CP's operations are low-level and complex. One would need knowledge of computer hardware to understand how it performs many of its functions. This book is introductory and therefore does not explore many detailed aspects of VM's CP. But because CP's design underlies certain key VM concepts, the next subsection of this chapter treats these critical characteristics on a conceptual level. Section 3 in this book further explores the Control Program and introduces basic CP commands.

The Conversational Monitor System is the terminal monitor. CMS commands permit you to run application programs; enter data into the system and change data; print files on the printer; read information from tapes and disks; communicate messages and files to other computer users; enter, compile, test, and run programs; and perform many other computer-based tasks. CMS is the part of VM with which terminal users interact most.

CP and the Virtual Machine Concept

From the nature of its functions, it is obvious that CP is a complicated program. However, it is possible and desirable to understand CP on a conceptual level. The Control Program has certain characteristics which render VM unusual among operating systems, providing capabilities which few other operating systems offer. Understanding them leads to the most effective use of VM/CMS.

Chief among CP's characteristics is a process called *virtualization*, making a single real computer appear to be multiple computers. Those computers that result from this software illusion are referred to as *virtual machines*.

Since each virtual machine appears to be a complete computer, each requires an operating system to control it, the same as any real computer system.

The effects of CP are illustrated in figure 2-1. This diagram shows a computer system consisting of a processor, main memory, disks, tapes, printers, and computer terminals. With VM's CP running on this computer, controlling its operations, the real computer is made to appear as if it actually consists of a number of computers. Each of these computers can consist of the same kinds of hardware resources that comprise the real computer on which they are based. The hardware resources comprising each of these virtual machines is under the control of CP and, ultimately, under the control of the system administrators of the VM-based system.

Figure 2-1
Control Program
Creates Virtual
Machines

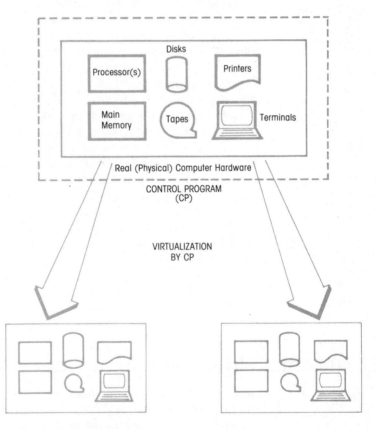

Figure 2-2 provides another view of CP's virtualization of the computer it controls. Part A shows that mainframe machine hardware requires control by an operating system. (For more detail, refer back to figure 1-1.) Part B expands upon this concept, diagramming the situation where VM is involved. The operating system immediately controlling the mainframe hardware is the CP portion of the VM operating system. CP virtualizes that hardware, making it appear as a number of complete illusionary computer systems, in this case, three virtual machines.

Figure 2-2
Control Program
Virtualizes
Machine
Hardware

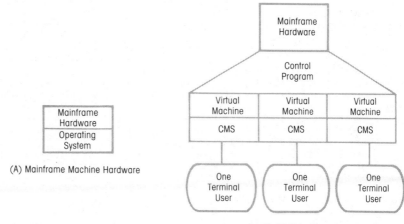

(A) Mainframe Machine Hardware

(B) CP Virtualization

Recall that each of the virtual machines, simulating an actual computer system, requires its own operating system. In figure 2-2(B), each virtual machine does, in fact, have its own operating system. This operating system is CMS, actually a single-user, interactive operating system. It is designed specifically to function in the virtual machine environment created by CP.

Each virtual machine controlled by CMS supports one terminal user. Thus, in a VM/CMS environment, all terminal users believe that they have their own computers at their disposal. These computers may consist of a computer console (the terminal), a processor, main memory, secondary storage on disks and tapes, a printer, a card reader, a card punch, and possibly other devices. All terminal users also believe they have their own operating systems at their disposal, that is, their own copies of CMS. They control their operating systems by issuing commands at their terminals, which CMS considers their computer consoles. This is analogous to the manner in which any large computer operating system is controlled by a system administrator through a specially designated console terminal.

Figure 2-3 offers another diagrammatic view of the same situation, showing that the real computer resources—disks, tapes, etc.—are virtualized by CP so that they support many virtual machines. The users of these virtual machines all consider that they have their own computers consisting of these resources. Each virtual machine can be configured differently. In this figure, the real computer hardware consists of a processor, main memory, four disks, two tape drives, three terminals, and one printer. The first of the two virtual machines is configured so that it appears to consist of a processor, 512 kilobytes (512K) of main memory, a terminal console, four disks, and a printer. The second virtual machine differs from the first, containing a processor, 1024K of main memory, a terminal console, two disks, a tape drive, and a printer. Since virtual machines appear to be true computer systems to their operating systems, there is no reason they could not be configured individually.

Figure 2-3
Virtual Machines
Configured
Differently from
Real Machine

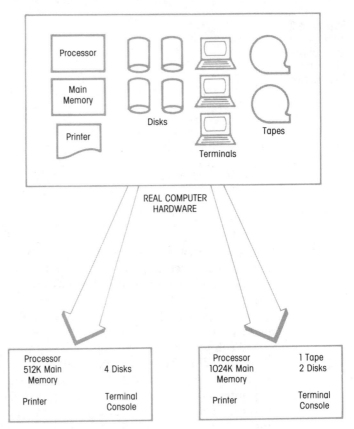

Guest Operating Systems

If the virtual machines that CP manufactures appear real, can CP support operating systems *other* than CMS on its virtual machines? The answer is "yes." One of VM's most unusual characteristics is that it acts as a *host* operating system, supporting a number of *guest operating systems* on its virtual machines.

A guest operating system is a full-fledged operating system that may control a real computer system in its own right, but that, in the VM environment, actually runs on one of the virtual machines created by CP.

In figure 2-4, CP virtualizes the computer hardware and creates several virtual machines. The operating system for two of these virtual machines is CMS. Each of the three other virtual machines in the picture is controlled by a different guest operating system. One runs DOS/VSE, the second runs MVS, and the third is controlled by IX/370 (a version of the UNIX operating system).

Figure 2-4
Control Program
Supports Guest
Operating Systems

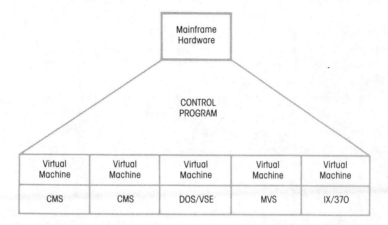

Much of this book is devoted to demonstrating how you use the CMS operating system commands from a terminal. But how would you use DOS /VSE, MVS, or IX/370? The answer is: exactly the way you would use these systems if they were running on their own real computer instead of the CP-provided virtual machine in the VM environment. For example, the terminal monitor program associated with the MVS operating system is called Time Sharing Option (TSO). You interact with MVS/TSO running on a virtual machine in a VM/CMS environment in the same manner as you would interact with this operating system if it were running on its own physical computer. Using this virtual machine guest operating system under VM is the same as using it on a real machine without VM.

This book teaches you how to interact with CMS, because this is the operating system commonly used by terminal users in a VM environment. CMS predominates because it is highly efficient at controlling online terminals, and because it provides certain programming compatibility features with many of the other operating systems that may run as guests in the VM environment.

Figure 2-5 shows some of the operating systems that may run under VM in the VM environment. These operating systems are categorized into five families: the OS, DOS, VM, UNIX, and PICK classes of operating systems. Each family consists of numerous versions and releases of operating systems. Table 2-1 lists just a few of the better-known operating systems in each class. Note that throughout this book, we refer generically to the first two groups of operating systems listed in this table as OS and DOS operating systems.

Figure 2-5
VM Supports Five
Major Families of
Operating Systems

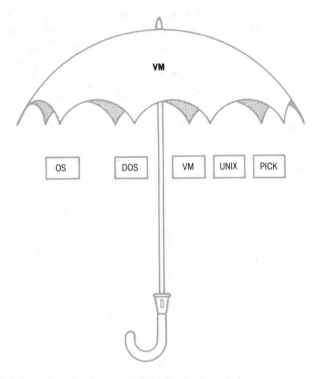

Table 2-1
Families of
Operating Systems
That Run under
VM

OS	DOS	UNIX	VM	PICK
MVS/XA	DOS/VSE	IX/370	CMS	PICK
MVS (OS/VS2)	DOS/VS	VM/IX	RSCS	
OS/VS1	DOS	UTS UNIX	VM	
OS/MVT				
OS/MFT				
OS/PCP				

UTS UNIX and PICK are products of independent vendors.
Not all guests run under all versions of VM.
This list is representative only; it is not a complete listing.

The fourth category of operating systems listed in Table 2-1 is labelled VM, which includes CMS and the Remote Spooling Communication Subsystem (RSCS), a software component of the VM/CMS operating system. RSCS is actually another special-purpose operating system that runs under CP in its own virtual machine as part of the VM environment. Also in this list is VM/CMS. Since CP faithfully reproduces a real machine environment in the form of a virtual machine, VM may run under itself!

Remember that guest systems are operating systems capable of controlling a real machine which may also run on a VM virtual machine. For example, the OS and DOS families of operating systems listed in Table 2-1 are all guest operating systems. However, while the operating systems, IX

/370, RSCS, and CMS are optionally generated and run in the VM environment, they are technically not guest operating systems because they cannot run independent of VM on a real computer.

The VM/CMS operating system's support for the virtual machine concept and guest operating systems has important implications. For example, the virtual machine concept heavily influences how you as a terminal user employ CMS. Your interaction with CMS is predicated on the virtual machine concept. Through your virtual computer console (your terminal) you control your own virtual machine as part of your interaction with the CMS system.

VM/CMS's support for guest operating systems is one of the primary advantages to this operating system. It means that one computer system can support several operating systems *simultaneously,* a feat that none of the other major operating systems can accomplish. VM/CMS is unique among the predominant operating systems in its ability to support multiple guest operating systems.

The ability to run multiple operating systems on a single host computer leads to these advantages:

- An installation gains the advantages inherent in running each of several operating systems at the same time on a single computer. Different computer users work with the operating systems they prefer. For example, on the same physical computer, scientific users work with UNIX on one virtual machine, while data processing personnel work with MVS/TSO on another virtual machine.

- An installation can run a test version of an operating system (or one of its subsystems) on the computer at the same time that it runs a production version of the same system.

- An installation can run different versions of the same operating system on the same computer, for example, in testing updates to the operating system or in problem resolution situations.

- Virtual machines (and operating system environments) can be defined with very different characteristics than the actual underlying physical hardware configuration.

- Many of the difficult problems associated with conversion from one operating system to another or from one version of an operating system to another are ameliorated in a VM environment.

- The virtual machine concept provides a very high degree of security and privacy across virtual machines.

VM/CMS's ability to run other operating systems as guests is one of the premier features leading to its recent popularity. The concepts of the virtual machine environment are presented in much greater detail in section 3 of this book. But first, the next several chapters teach you how to log onto VM/CMS, create files with the system editor, and manipulate those files with basic CMS commands.

For Further Information

VM/CMS components, the virtual machine concept, and the operating system's support of guest operating systems are surveyed in the introductory manual, *VM/SP Introduction*. For Release 3 of VM/CMS, the order number for this manual is *GT00-1349*. For Release 4, use the manual reference number of *GC19-6200*.

The manual, *VM/SP General Information, GC20-1838*, provides a basic understanding of VM/CMS and what it can do. This manual contains a high-level synopsis of the operating system's design and features.

Several operating systems textbooks contain sections which introduce VM/CMS, its history, purposes, and strengths, and describe the general design of this operating system. Among these, *An Introduction to Operating Systems* by Harvey M. Deitel (Addison-Wesley, 1984) analyzes the basic concepts of the VM/CMS architecture. This introduction imparts a comparative sense of the operating system's strengths and possible future. *Operating Systems* by Stuart E. Madnick and John J. Donovan (McGraw-Hill, 1974) also summarizes VM/CMS in terms of its virtual machine philosophy.

Several papers on VM/CMS have appeared in the *IBM Systems Journal* since its introduction. For example, R.J. Creasy relates VM's history in "The Origin of the VM/370 Time-Sharing System," *IBM Systems Journal* (25:5, 1981). "A Virtual Machine Time-Sharing System," by R.A. Meyer and L.H. Seawright, *IBM Systems Journal* (9:3, 1970) provides background on VM/CMS from its early days. And, *IBM Systems Journal* (18:1, 1979) contains several technical papers on VM.

Test Your Understanding

What are the two major components of the VM/SP operating system, and what are their roles?

What does it mean to say that Control Program "virtualizes" the computer hardware? Must the resources of a virtual machine match those of the underlying physical computer?

What is a guest operating system? Is CMS a guest operating system?

What families of operating systems run under VM/SP?

What are the advantages of running multiple operating systems concurrently on the same physical computer? Discuss what benefits your site could gain through such an approach.

CHAPTER 3

A First Terminal
Session

This chapter describes how to gain access to a VM/CMS-based computer,
how to start the CMS operating system on your own virtual machine, and
how to exit the system. The best way to learn this material is by experience, by sitting at your computer terminal and working through the book
examples as they are discussed. This chapter assumes you have access to a
full-screen display terminal.

    Commands you *enter* at your terminal are in computer typeface in
this book. Portions of the commands entered exactly as shown are printed
in upper case. Parts of commands printed in lower case indicate that you
are to replace the lowercase portion of the command with the appropriate
information. VM/CMS accepts either lowercase or uppercase commands as
valid.

    All messages *output* by VM/CMS to the display terminal are set off
with a corner bracket.

Logging onto VM/CMS

Most computer operating systems require terminal users to *log on*. This
procedure consists of those commands entered through the terminal in
order to gain access to the computer.

    To log onto VM/CMS, you need to get these two items of information
from your system administrator or project leader: a user identification code
(*userid*) and the password associated with your userid.

    A computer terminal that is physically connected to a computer run-
ning VM/CMS will usually display a VM or company logo on its display
screen when it is turned on. Remove this logo by pressing the ENTER key,
located on the right-hand side of most computer terminal keyboards. Once
the logo has been removed, enter:

```
LOGON userid
```

As with all the commands in this book, you must press the ENTER key after typing in the command to send it from the display terminal to the computer itself. The system responds with the message:

```
ENTER PASSWORD:
```

Type your password, then press the ENTER key. This password may not appear on the screen as you type it. This is a security measure designed to prevent other people from seeing your password. If you enter an incorrect password (for example, from a typing error) you receive a message similar to this:

```
PASSWORD INCORRECT - REINITIATE LOGON PROCEDURE
```

In this instance, restart the logon sequence by entering the LOGON command with your userid.

As with most commands in the VM environment, the LOGON command can be abbreviated. You could enter:

```
L userid
```

and receive the exact same result as you did when typing the full form of the LOGON command. This book uses the full form of all commands for clarity. As you become an expert user, you will naturally tend to use the abbreviated forms.

On some systems, you can enter the userid and password on the same line:

```
L userid password
```

Whether you can do this on your system depends on how the system administrators have set up your local VM environment.

Once you have logged onto CP, you need to establish CMS as the operating system (terminal monitor) for your virtual machine. Enter this command:

```
IPL CMS
```

IPL stands for *initial program load*, and refers to how you start an operating system from a *systems console,* the master terminal that controls the operating system. The `IPL CMS` command serves to load and start the CMS operating system in your virtual machine.

In response to the `IPL` command, you receive a message similar to the following. (You may have to press the **ENTER** key one extra time in order to receive this message.)

```
R; T=0.01/0.01 10:12:34
```

This response is called the *ready message,* or *prompt.* It shows that CMS is up and waiting for you to enter a command. The `R;` means that CMS is ready for the next command. The first series of numbers tells how much time it took VM to perform the last task you gave it, and the second set of numbers indicates the present time of day.

If you don't want all the numbers trailing the ready message, you can eliminate them by entering:

```
SET RDYMSG SMSG
```

This command tells CMS to set the ready message to the short form. Now you will only see `R;` as your prompt from the system.

Occasionally, you will see a number in parentheses following the `R;` prompt. This number is called a *return code.* A nonzero return code from CMS indicates the failure of the command you last entered. Failed CMS commands also typically display explanatory error messages as well as nonzero return codes.

Once you receive the `R;` prompt, you have started CMS and are ready to enter CMS commands. Remember that prior to issuing the `IPL` command, you have not established an operating system on your virtual machine. The `LOGON` command is actually entered to the Control Program, and is a CP command. It is possible that your system administrator set up your userid with *automatic IPL.* That is, your userid may have been set up for you so that the `LOGON` command to CP results in automatic issuance of the `IPL CMS` command. In this case, no harm is done should you enter the `IPL CMS` command yourself anyway. The `IPL CMS` command must be entered at some point in order to establish a CMS environment. It need only be entered once in any terminal session.

There are, thus, two environments under VM/CMS of which you should be aware. The first is CP, the one you are in until you enter the `IPL CMS` command (assuming you do not have automatic IPL). You know you are in contact with CP when the status message in the lower right-hand side of the screen says **CP READ**. Also, if you press the **ENTER** key, you will receive the indicator **CP**. CP has its own set of commands, some of which are rather advanced and are not much used by the majority of terminal users. This book discusses only those CP commands that are important for general use.

Once you **IPL CMS**, you are in the CMS environment, the one in which most terminal users work. Now you can enter CMS commands, such as the **SET RDYMSG SMSG** command shown above.

If you press the **ENTER** key with no preceding command in the CMS environment, the response on the screen is **CMS**. This indicates that you are in communication with CMS. Thus, if you are ever in doubt as to whether you are communicating with CP or CMS, merely press the **ENTER** key. The system response of either **CP** or **CMS** will tell you which environment you are in.

As in the CP environment, CMS always displays a *status message* in the lower righthand corner of the screen. Table 3-1 lists common CMS notices and their interpretations.

Table 3-1
Common CMS
Status Messages

Message	Meaning
VM READ	CMS is waiting for you to enter a command.
RUNNING	CMS is either working on the last command you entered, or is waiting for you to enter another command.
MORE . . .	CMS has filled up the display screen with information, and has more to display. Press the CLEAR key to see this information immediately. Otherwise, you have sixty seconds in which to view the current screen. Then, CMS automatically displays the next screen of information. To hold the current screen beyond the sixty-second limit, press the ENTER key.
HOLDING	The present screen display will remain until you press the CLEAR key.

To exit the system, enter the **LOGOFF** command:

    LOGOFF

You are now finished with your terminal session.

LOGON Procedure Summary

To summarize the logon process, clear the system logo from the display screen by pressing the **ENTER** key. Then enter the CP command:

    L userid

where `userid` is the user identification code assigned you by your system administrator. CP will prompt you for your password, which you enter. Then, enter:

    IPL CMS

You should now receive the CMS ready message, which starts with the symbol `R;` . If you do not receive the `R;` prompt, and the status message says `VM READ`, press the **ENTER** key to receive the ready message.

You are now ready to enter CMS commands, coverage of which begins in the next section of this book. When you are finished with your terminal session, enter this command:

    LOGOFF

For Further Information

If you have any difficulty with the **LOGON** procedure, ask a colleague or your system administrator for assistance. It is possible that your VM system is set up so that there are special installation-dependent considerations of which you must be aware.

Basic information concerning logging on to VM/CMS terminals is found in several of the IBM VM/CMS reference manuals. The simplest explanation is located in the *VM/SP CMS Primer, SC24-5236*. The *VM /SP CMS User's Guide, SC19-6210*, also covers this topic.

Comprehensive information concerning both logging on and use of the various terminal devices connected to VM/CMS computers is contained in *VM/SP Terminal Reference, GC19-6206*. This manual includes explanations of error messages that may be encountered during the logon procedure.

Test Your Understanding

Get a userid and password from your VM/CMS system administrator. Practice logging onto the system. What happens if you enter an invalid password?

Does your userid have automatic IPL? Find out by determining if you must enter the **IPL CMS** command yourself after logging on.

List the status indicators that display in the lower right-hand corner of your display screen. What do they mean?

At any time, how can you determine whether you are in direct communication with CP or CMS?

Creating, Changing, Manipulating, and Printing Files

- VM/CMS Editors
- File-Editing Subcommands
- File Manipulation via CMS Commands
- Formatting Files for Printing

CHAPTER 4

VM/CMS Editors

A computer *file* is a collection of information in machine readable form. Memos, notes, papers, documents, programs, and data for program processing all are contained and stored in computer files.

A *text editor,* or *editor,* is a computer program with which terminal users interact in order to create, alter, and add to data contained in files. Under CMS, an editor program is entered by a simple command naming the editor and the file to create or update. The terminal user then has a variety of commands, known as *editor subcommands,* through which the information of a file can be entered and altered.

CMS offers several different editors. Your system administrator chooses the editors available on your particular system, but most VM/CMS systems provide two or more. The most common editors are listed in table 4-1.

The *CMS Editor* was originally developed for typewriter-like terminals. This editor is *line-oriented.* That is, the terminal user works with or sees only a single line of file data at a time. This editor is relatively inefficient for terminal users who have screen-based display terminals at their disposal. The CMS Editor is older and less powerful than other commonly available VM/CMS editors, and it is not much used.

Edgar, also known as *Display Editing System,* is superior to the CMS Editor in that it is a *full-screen editor,* allowing the user to view and manipulate files in units of a full screen of information at one time. Edgar is a relatively powerful and easy-to-use editor, but its use has largely been superseded by the XEDIT editor.

XEDIT, or the *System Product Editor,* is the "official" editor of VM /CMS. XEDIT is full-screen and quite powerful. This section of the book concentrates on introducing XEDIT and its many subcommands for creating and altering files.

The full name of the *ISPF Editor* is *Interactive System Productivity Facility Editor.* ISPF Edit is the primary editor used in the OS (MVS/TSO)

Table 4-1
Common VM/CMS
Editors

Name	Other Names	Enter via This Command		Comments
CMS Editor	CMS EDIT	EDIT	fn ft fm	Line-oriented; older; less powerful, not much used
Edgar	DES; Display Editing System	EDGAR	fn ft fm	Full-screen
XEDIT	System Product Editor	XEDIT	fn ft fm	Full-screen; powerful; the "official" system editor
ISPF Editor	Interactive System Productivity Facility; ISPF Edit; SPF Editor; ISPF/PDF	ISPF		Full-screen; powerful; widely used with OS systems; ISPF supports full-screen access to system utilities as well as an editor

Where fn, ft, and fm stand for the filename, filetype, and filemode, respectively, of the file to edit.

operating system environment. ISPF is also sometimes used with the DOS/VSE operating system. Availability of the ISPF Editor for the VM/CMS environment under CMS provides a high degree of compatibility with those other operating systems. For example, a programmer or user who is experienced with ISPF under the MVS/TSO or DOS/VSE operating systems could use ISPF under CMS without any retraining.

In addition to its editing capabilities, ISPF supports access to system utilities. Through ISPF panels, terminal users can: compile, test, and debug programs; perform CMS file management functions; and issue CMS commands directly.

The ISPF Editor and its associated features compose Interactive System Productivity Facility/Program Development Facility (ISPF/PDF), a program product purchased and installed separately from VM/CMS. Section 7 of this book describes the ISPF program products available for VM/CMS.

CMS File-Naming Conventions

In order to use any editor, it is important to understand the CMS file identification conventions. Under CMS, *file identifiers* consist of three parts: *filename, filetype,* and *filemode.* The filename and filetype portions of the unique file identifier must each be from one to eight characters long. Allowable characters include letters of the alphabet (both uppercase and lowercase), digits (0 through 9), and a few special characters.

You may give a file any filename and filetype you wish. However, by convention, the filetype is often assigned a name that signifies the kind of data contained in the file. Programs that process that data file then know what kind of information it contains. This convention also helps *you* remember the kinds of data your files contain.

Table 4-2 lists just a few of the common filetypes that have special significance under CMS. Many of these filetypes will only be of concern when and if you program.

Table 4-2
VM/CMS Filetypes

Filetype	Meaning
ASSEMBLE	Assembly language program statements
BASIC	BASIC language program statements
COBOL	COBOL language program statements
EXEC	Command procedure language statements
FORTRAN	FORTRAN language program statements
HELP . . .	Files beginning with these four characters support the CMS-provided HELP facility
LISTING	Output file produced by a language processor
LOADLIB	Library members created by the link editor
MACLIB	Library members containing macro definitions or copy files
MEMO	A memo
MODULE	Nonrelocatable executable programs
NAMES	A file of users' names used in communication between terminal users
NOTE	A note communicated between CMS terminal users
NOTEBOOK	A collection of notes communicated between CMS terminal users
PASCAL	Pascal language program statements
PLI, PLIOPT	PL/I language program statements
SCRIPT	A textual document ready for print formatting by the SCRIPT document processor
SYNONYM	A table of synonyms for CMS commands and user-written EXEC and MODULE files
TEXT	Relocatable object code created by language processors
TXTLIB	Library members containing relocatable object code
VSBASIC	VS BASIC language program statements
XEDIT	XEDIT macro definitions

The filemode portion of a CMS file name consists of a letter of the alphabet and a digit. These are referred to, respectively, as the *filemode letter* and the *filemode number*. The filemode portion of a file name carries special meaning as to the location and nature of the file. The meaning of the filemode is explored later in chapter 15. For now, note that many CMS commands do not require you to specify the filemode. When you don't specify a letter and number, it normally defaults to filemode A1.

Creating a File

This subsection, and all other portions of this book illustrating editing under CMS, refers to the XEDIT editor.

To create a new file using XEDIT, enter:

```
XEDIT  fn  ft   fm
```

where `fn`, `ft`, and `fm` refer to the filename, filetype, and filemode, respectively. Remember that you do not have to specify the filemode. The default, A1, is fine for all the editing examples in this book.

Let's try creating a new file and entering data into it. After logging on and IPL'ing CMS, enter this command:

```
XEDIT  LEARNING  SCRIPT  (NOPROFILE
```

This CMS command starts XEDIT. Since the file identifier is new, XEDIT creates a new file with this name. If a file with the file name specified already exists on your virtual machine, then XEDIT assumes update of that existing file and displays it for editing. Notice that the filemode is not specified and thus defaults to **A1**.

The final parameter, **(NOPROFILE**, is a *command option*. Command options are additional information that modify the manner in which a CMS command functions. They are recognized by the fact that they always follow a left parenthesis after the command. A right parenthesis to enclose the one or more options specified is acceptable, but unnecessary.

The option **NOPROFILE** on the **XEDIT** command simply ensures that you enter the editor in its "native" state. That is, if your system administrator has set up special, installation-dependent characteristics for your use of the XEDIT editor, this option overrides them. This ensures that you can follow the XEDIT example terminal sessions in this section.

After you enter the above command, a screen similar to that depicted in figure 4-1 appears. The first line of this screen shows the file name of the file being created (or edited), **LEARNING SCRIPT A1**. The **SIZE=0** notation tells how many lines of data are in the file. Since no data has yet been entered into this new file, this value is currently 0. The message **CREATING NEW FILE:** is an editor message declaring just that. Editor messages appear at this location in response to many editor subcommands.

In the middle of the screen appear the notations ***** TOP OF FILE ***** and ***** END OF FILE *****. This is where you enter information into the file. No data is presently displayed here because none has yet been entered.

In the bottom left-hand corner of the screen is the notation: **====>**. This arrow signifies the *command line*, the location where the terminal user enters editor subcommands. The cursor presently rests at this position. Type in the word **INPUT** and press the **ENTER** key.

Now the cursor is immediately below the ruler or *scale* in the middle of the screen. You are now in *input mode*, the editor mode in which you

Figure 4-1 Creating a File

```
LEARNING SCRIPT    A1  V 132   TRUNC=132 SIZE=0 LINE=0 COL=1 ALT=0
CREATING NEW FILE:




===== * * * TOP OF FILE * * *
     !...+....1....+....2....+....3....+....4....+....5....+....6....+....7...
===== * * * END OF FILE * * *


====> _
                                                      X E D I T   1 FILE
```

enter new data into the file. The editor indicates this by the message **INPUT
MODE:** in the message area, and a similar message at the bottom of the
screen. Type in the first line of information shown in figure 4-2:

This really isn't as bad as I thought

Figure 4-2 Entering Data in Input Mode

```
 LEARNING SCRIPT    A1  V 132   TRUNC=132 SIZE=9 LINE=0 COL=1 ALT=0
[INPUT MODE:




* * * TOP OF FILE * * *
!...+....1....+....2....+....3....+....4....+....5....+....6....+....7....+....
This really isn't as bad as I thought
it might be.
Editors are not hard to learn,
that is assuming you practice.
Knowledge is an acquired trait,
but wisdom must be earned.
test line 1 for block shift
test line 2 for block shift
test line 3 for block shift_
====> * * * INPUT ZONE * * *
                                                   INPUT-MODE 1 FILE
```

At the end of the line, press the tab key (on the right-hand side of
most keyboards) to move the cursor to the start of the next input line.
When you have filled the screen with the information of figure 4-2, the
next line contains the message ***** INPUT ZONE ***** at the command line

arrow. To continue entering data at this point, press the **ENTER** key. The data you have entered in the file moves upward on the display screen, leaving room for more input data below. Enter these last lines:

```
test line 4 for block shift
test line 5 for block shift
I'm almost done,
one more line,
now I am!
```

After you have entered all this data, press the **ENTER** key twice. This takes you out of the editor's data input mode, and moves the cursor back down to the command area. You are now in the editor's other mode of operation, the *edit mode*. In edit mode, the cursor rests on the command line, and you enter various edit subcommands in order to modify and alter the data you have entered into the file. Figure 4-3 pictures how the file appears after you have entered the data shown and pressed the **ENTER** key twice.

Figure 4-3 After Data Entry

```
 LEARNING SCRIPT    A1   V 132   TRUNC=132 SIZE=14 LINE=14 COL=1 ALT=14
 XEDIT:
 ===== Knowledge is an acquired trait,
 ===== but wisdom must be earned.
 ===== test line 1 for block shift
 ===== test line 2 for block shift
 ===== test line 3 for block shift
 ===== test line 4 for block shift
 ===== test line 5 for block shift
 ===== I'm almost done,
 ===== one more line,
 ===== now I am!
       !...+....1....+....2....+....3....+....4....+....5....+....6....+....7...
 ===== * * * END OF FILE * * *




 ====>  _
                                                    X E D I T   1 FILE
```

Full-Screen Editing

Once you have entered data into the file, you can alter it in several ways. One of the easiest ways is simply to move the cursor to the proper place in the data and type over that information. You move the cursor within the display screen by pressing one of the four cursor control keys, a group of four keys clustered together on the keyboard and marked with arrows showing the directions they move the cursor. Move the cursor over the data you wish to change and overtype that information.

You can also use the *delete key* to remove characters of data. On most terminals, the delete key is signified on the keyboard by the proofreader's symbol for deletion, a lowercase letter "a" with a squiggly mark through it. Move the cursor to the letter(s) you wish to delete, and press the delete key once to remove each character. Notice that the other characters on the screen move left to take the place of the deleted characters.

The *insert key* is denoted on the keyboard as a lowercase letter "a" with a caret over it, and is located near the delete key. To insert one or more letters, move the cursor up to the line on which the data will be inserted, and position the cursor where those characters will be placed. Now press the PA2 key. This key removes any trailing spaces at the end of the subject line. With most mainframe editors, the spaces following the characters on a line are also considered characters and must be removed before you can insert additional characters on the line. After pressing the PA2 key, press the insert key. Now type whatever characters you wish. When you are finished, press the RESET key to exit the character insertion mode. Notice that if you entirely fill up the line with characters during insertion, the keyboard jams to inhibit further insertions. If this happens, press the RESET key to unlock the keyboard.

What if you wish to insert or delete characters on the first few lines of data we entered earlier? You need some way to display that data on the screen. The answer is the PF7 key, which scrolls the display upward, or toward the beginning of the file. Press the PF7 key now and see how the data is scrolled. Press the PF8 key to scroll the data downward, toward the end of the file. Even with a large file, you can always view any part by repeatedly pressing these scrolling keys.

Line-Oriented Editing

Besides inserting and deleting individual characters, you will want to be able to add, delete, move, and copy lines of file data. In looking at the file, notice the five equal signs ===== positioned at the left of each line of data. You can enter *prefix commands* on any of these lines to alter the file. Like other XEDIT commands, prefix commands can be entered in either upper or lower case. For example, move the cursor over the prefix command area for this line:

```
=====  it might be.
```

and type a letter **A** over the prefix area:

```
a==== it might be.
```

The **A** stands for the prefix **ADD** command. It inserts a blank line immediately after the subject line where you may add a line of information. It is important to note that, like all prefix commands, you can type the **A** *anywhere* over the five equal signs comprising the prefix command area. The editor knows how to recognize your prefix command.

With the prefix **ADD** command, you can also precede (or follow) the **A** with a number indicating how many lines you wish to add following the line you have indicated. The editor provides the number of blank lines that you indicate for your input data.

The **DELETE** prefix area command allows you to delete one or more lines of information. A letter **D** in the prefix area of a line deletes that line. A letter **D** preceded or followed by a number deletes the number of lines indicated, starting with the marked line. For example:

```
=d3== it might be.
```

deletes the line indicated and the two lines immediately following it.

You can also delete a block of lines, by denoting the block with the symbols **DD**. For example,

```
===== This really isn't as bad as I thought
==dd= it might be.
===== Editors are not hard to learn,
===== that is assuming you practice.
===== Knowledge is an acquired trait,
=dd== but wisdom must be earned.
===== test line 1 for block shift
```

The lines within the **DD** symbols (inclusive) are deleted from the file, yielding:

```
===== This really isn't as bad as I thought
===== test line 1 for block shift
```

When using such a prefix area *block command*, you can scroll the screen display after entering the first **DD** symbol, if necessary, in order to properly enter the second **DD** symbol.

The prefix **COPY** command allows you to copy individual lines, a group of lines, or a block of lines from one place in the file to another. In a manner similar to the **ADD** and **DELETE** prefix commands, you mark a line you wish to copy by overtyping the prefix area with a letter **C**. Then locate the line after which you wish to copy the subject line, and mark its prefix area with a letter **F**:

```
===== Editors are not hard to learn,
==c== that is assuming you practice.
===== Knowledge is an acquired trait,
==f== but wisdom must be earned.
===== test line 1 for block shift
```

This results in:

```
===== Editors are not hard to learn,
===== that is assuming you practice.
===== Knowledge is an acquired trait,
===== but wisdom must be earned.
===== that is assuming you practice.
===== test line 1 for block shift
```

You can copy a group of lines by preceding or following the **C** with the number of lines to copy:

```
===== Editors are not hard to learn,
==c2= that is assuming you practice.
===== Knowledge is an acquired trait,
f==== but wisdom must be earned.
===== test line 1 for block shift
```

produces:

```
===== Editors are not hard to learn,
===== that is assuming you practice.
===== Knowledge is an acquired trait,
===== but wisdom must be earned.
===== that is assuming you practice.
===== Knowledge is an acquired trait,
===== test line 1 for block shift
```

You specify a block of lines to copy by enclosing that copy block within a pair of CC symbols. The copy includes the lines marked with the CC symbols. Remember that you can scroll, if necessary, in order to position the second set of CC symbols.

Should you change your mind about the block copy (or any other prefix subcommand), enter the word RESET at the command line arrow. The RESET subcommand removes any subcommand letters presently in the prefix area when the command is not yet completed.

Besides denoting a line which the copied line, group of lines, or block of lines must follow F, you can also specify a line which the copied line(s) precede by marking that line with a letter P (preceding):

```
===== This really isn't as bad as I thought
===p= it might be.
=cc== Editors are not hard to learn,
===== that is assuming you practice.
===cc Knowledge is an acquired trait,
===== but wisdom must be earned.
```

results in:

```
===== This really isn't as bad as I thought
===== Editors are not hard to learn,
===== that is assuming you practice.
===== Knowledge is an acquired trait,
===== it might be.
===== Editors are not hard to learn,
===== that is assuming you practice.
===== Knowledge is an acquired trait,
===== but wisdom must be earned.
```

The MOVE prefix command works exactly the same as the copy subcommand, except that the indicated line, group of lines, or block of lines is relocated within the file. Unlike a COPY subcommand, the MOVE subcommand does not leave the source lines in their original position. The MOVE prefix subcommand is requested via the letter M, optionally preceded or followed by a number of lines to move, or by the block move symbols MM. Thus, one can move an individual line of data, a group of lines, or a block of lines.

```
===== Editors are not hard to learn,
===p= that is assuming you practice.
m==== Knowledge is an acquired trait,
```

yields:

```
=====  Editors are not hard to learn,
=====  Knowledge is an acquired trait,
=====  that is assuming you practice.
```

Here is an example of a block move:

```
=====  This really isn't as bad as I thought
===p=  it might be.
=mm==  Editors are not hard to learn,
=mm==  that is assuming you practice.
=====  Knowledge is an acquired trait,
=====  but wisdom must be earned.
```

results in:

```
=====  This really isn't as bad as I thought
=====  Editors are not hard to learn,
=====  that is assuming you practice.
=====  it might be.
=====  Knowledge is an acquired trait,
=====  but wisdom must be earned.
```

The **DUPLICATE** prefix subcommand is denoted by the quotation mark symbol ". Duplicating a line means that a replication of the original line appears immediately after that line:

```
=====  that is assuming you practice.
"====  Knowledge is an acquired trait,
=====  but wisdom must be earned.
```

produces:

```
=====  that is assuming you practice.
=====  Knowledge is an acquired trait,
=====  Knowledge is an acquired trait,
=====  but wisdom must be earned.
```

You can duplicate a group of lines by preceding or following the quotation mark with a digit. When duplicating a block of lines, enclose them within pairs of quotes "". For example:

```
===== This really isn't as bad as I thought
="''== it might be.
==="" Editors are not hard to learn,
===== that is assuming you practice.
```

produces:

```
===== This really isn't as bad as I thought
===== it might be.
===== Editors are not hard to learn,
===== it might be.
===== Editors are not hard to learn,
===== that is assuming you practice.
```

Test the duplication subcommand so that you see how it operates analogously to the other prefix area subcommands of the editor.

One can shift an individual line, a group of lines, or a block of lines a specified number of column positions to the right or to the left by using the > and < symbols. For example, this prefix subcommand shifts this line three column positions to the right:

```
===== that is assuming you practice.
==>3= Knowledge is an acquired trait,
===== but wisdom must be earned.
```

producing:

```
===== that is assuming you practice.
=====    Knowledge is an acquired trait,
===== but wisdom must be earned.
```

Similarly, here is an example of a six-column block shift to the left:

```
===== test line 1 for block shift
=<<6= test line 2 for block shift
===== test line 3 for block shift
=<<== test line 4 for block shift
===== test line 5 for block shift
```

After the shift, you have:

```
===== test line 1 for block shift
===== ine 2 for block shift
===== ine 3 for block shift
===== ine 4 for block shift
===== test line 5 for block shift
```

The six letters of the affected lines are lost! If you attempt to shift data to the left of the first column, you lose some of it. Similarly, it is possible to lose data if you shift it beyond the right column position in a file.

The final prefix subcommand in this brief XEDIT introduction is the subcommand to set the current line position. The concept of the editor's *current line* means that, at any time, one line is designated as the current line in the file. The relative position of this line affects the operation of editor subcommands with respect to the file data. The current line always appears highlighted immediately above the scale in the middle of the screen display. (Remember that the scale is not itself part of the file; it is only displayed for your convenience in judging column positions when editing.)

To alter the current line, merely enter a slash / in the prefix area of the line you wish to designate as the new current line. The display is immediately altered so that the new current line appears highlighted above the scale.

Remember, you input additional data into the file by entering the **INPUT** edit subcommand on the command line. How does the editor determine where to input the new data? The **INPUT** subcommand clears the screen for additional input data *right after the current line.* You tell the editor where to input new information by:

1. designating the line after which to insert information by marking its prefix area with the / (current line) symbol

2. taking the cursor down to the command line area, either through pressing the tab key on the right-hand side of most keyboards, or, by pressing the **PF12** key. Then, enter the **INPUT** subcommand. Remember you exit data input mode by pressing the **ENTER** key twice.

Leaving the Editor

After creating a data file, leave the editor by entering the subcommand FILE on the command line. This saves the file on disk storage for future use.

If you do *not* wish to save the edited file, enter the subcommand QUIT on the command line. If you entered or altered data in the file, the editor will prompt you to ask if you are certain you do not want to save any file updates made during the editor session. If you do not, enter QQUIT on the command line. Otherwise, entering FILE at this point retains your data and updates for future use.

Thus, the subcommand FILE saves your newly created or altered file for future editing and/or other use. The QUIT / QQUIT subcommand combination will either totally eliminate any newly created file, or will revert any pre-existing file back to its state prior to the start of the current editing session.

Leaving the editor returns you to the CMS command environment.

For Further Information

The *VM/SP CMS User's Guide, SC19-6210*, contains information on CMS file naming conventions.

The manual, *VM/SP: System Product Editor User's Guide, SC24-5220*, explains how to use the XEDIT editor.

Test Your Understanding

Describe the purposes of editor programs. What can you accomplish by using them? What editors are typically available in VM/CMS environments? What editors are accessible on your system?

What are the three parts of CMS file names, and what does each part mean? What would you expect the contents of a file having the filetype of COBOL to be?

Using the XEDIT editor, create a new file named `MYFILE SCRIPT A1`. Be sure to specify the `NOPROFILE` option when entering the editor. Using the editor `INPUT` subcommand, enter several lines of information into the file.

Use the insert, delete, and cursor keys to insert and delete characters from lines of information in the file. Enter more lines of data into the file through the `INPUT` subcommand and practice scrolling the screen display by the `PF7` and `PF8` program function keys.

Practice the `ADD, DELETE, COPY, MOVE,` and `DUPLICATE` prefix commands while editing a file. Use these commands to operate upon a single line, a group of lines, and a block of lines within the file.

Discuss the concept of the current line. How do you set the current line?

When you are through practicing file editing, enter the `FILE` subcommand to save your file. How do you return to editing this file? How would you exit the editor if you did not want to save the file?

CHAPTER 5

File-Editing Subcommands

Chapter 4 discussed the concept of an editor and introduced various features of the most popular VM/CMS editor program, XEDIT. This chapter continues the demonstration of XEDIT, concentrating on subcommands that are entered at the command line. As before, the goal is to render you functional with the editor; there are many more editor features and subcommands than described in this book. It is expected that you read this chapter while sitting at a display terminal and try commands as they are presented. Practice is the best teacher, particularly when using a new editor.

Scrolling

The previous chapter introduced the concept of *scrolling*, adjusting the screen display area so that the desired portion of a large file is displayed. The two *Program Function* (PF) keys, PF7 and PF8, scroll the screen up and down (toward the beginning, and toward the end) of the file, respectively. The UP and DOWN subcommands may also be entered at the command line:

    UP n

scrolls the screen upward n lines. The current line is reset, as appropriate. The DOWN subcommand works similarly:

    DOWN 4

scrolls four lines toward the end of the file.

The subcommands TOP and BOTTOM, entered at the command line, scroll immediately all the way to the beginning or the end of the file, respectively. Most users enter only the abbreviation for BOTTOM, B. BOTTOM is particularly useful when adding lines to the end of a file. Enter B in the command line, then type INPUT to append new data.

Similarly, issue the **TOP** and **INPUT** subcommands to enter new lines before the first line of a file.

Remember, you can also scroll by entering the current line subcommand, designated by a slash (/), in the prefix area of any visible line.

The command line subcommands **LEFT** and **RIGHT** scroll the screen left or right n columns:

```
LEFT 5
```

scrolls the screen five columns to the left.

Finally, you can scroll the display as the result of a **LOCATE** subcommand. This subcommand's general format is:

```
LOCATE  target
```

The `target` portion of the subcommand can be specified in various ways. One method is to name a *search string*. The search string is a group of characters enclosed by *delimiters,* which can be any character that does not appear in the search string. For example, if the search string does *not* contain a slash, you can enclose it within slashes. **LOCATE** searches for the first occurrence of the search string on a line following the current line. For example:

```
LOCATE  /test/
```

searches for the first occurrence of the character string `test` in any line of the data file following the current line.

You can search backward, toward the top of the file, by preceding the search string by a hyphen –. Entering:

```
LOCATE  -/Knowledge/
```

searches backward for the last occurrence of the letters `Knowledge` prior to the current line. The **LOCATE** subcommand sets the current line as appropriate, if the search succeeds. If the search string is not found, the editor displays a message declaring **TARGET NOT FOUND** in the message area. In this case, the current line is set past the last line in the file for forward searches, and before the first line in the file for backward searches.

Whether the **LOCATE** subcommand is case-sensitive in its character string searches depends on the setting of the XEDIT **CASE** option. You can determine the current **CASE** setting by entering the subcommand **QUERY CASE** on the command line. In the response, **I** stands for **IGNORE**, which means that the editor ignores case differences in string searches and letters match regardless of their capitalization. A response which includes an **R** means that the editor **RESPECT**s case in searches, that is, that an uppercase letter does not match its lowercase equivalent in string comparisons.

Two other parameters on the **CASE** option are **UPPERCASE** and **MIXED**. **UPPERCASE** indicates that all characters you enter are automatically translated to upper case, while `MIXED` means that you can type both lowercase and uppercase letters into the file.

Use the editor `SET` subcommand with the `CASE` option to establish any of these parameters. For example, enter:

```
SET CASE UPPERCASE IGNORE
```

to enforce translation to upper case and to ignore case differences when specifying string targets in subcommands like `LOCATE`. Or, enter:

```
SET CASE MIXED RESPECT
```

to permit entry of both uppercase and lowercase letters into a file, and to respect case differences in character string searches.

Finding and Changing Character Strings

The previous discussion demonstrated how to locate a search string, a group of contiguous characters. The `CHANGE` subcommand also refers to strings enclosed in delimiters, in this case to locate and change the subject string.

Among the several formats of the `CHANGE` subcommand, this one alters a string in the current line to another string. The first string specified is the search string, the second, its intended replacement:

```
CHANGE  /you/that you/
```

entered in the command area with this current line:

```
===== that is assuming you practice.
      !...+....1....+....2....+....3....+....4....+....5....+...
```

yields:

```
===== that is assuming that you practice.
      !...+....1....+....2....+....3....+....4....+....5....+...
```

The first occurrence of the string you is replaced with the string **that you**.

To change *all* occurrences of a search string in a file, enter this form of the `CHANGE` subcommand:

```
CHANGE  /searchstring/newstring/  *  *
```

Before you use this command, make sure that the current line precedes the first line in the file by issuing the TOP subcommand. Remember that CHANGE always starts with the current line. The two asterisks, separated by spaces, indicate that all lines to the end of the file are subject to change, and that all occurrences of the search string in each line are to be altered.

You selectively change the occurrences of a character string in a file to a second string by setting the current line pointer where you want to begin. Then type the CHANGE subcommand in the command area, in this format:

```
CHANGE  /searchstring/newstring/
```

but do *not* yet press the ENTER key. Press the PF5 key. This key locates the first occurrence of the old phrase and moves the cursor underneath it. If you wish to apply the change here, press the PF6 key.

You can indefinitely repeat this process, pressing PF5 to find the search string, and, optionally, PF6 to replace it. In this manner, you can step through the file, finding all occurrences of a specified phrase and selectively altering them to the new phrase.

Joining and Splitting Lines

Other common editing tasks are the joining of two short lines into one, and the splitting of a line in order to enter words into it. Both operations are accomplished through the use of the PF11 key.

To split a line, move the cursor under the character position where you want the split to occur. Then, press PF11. Here, the cursor has been positioned for the split:

```
=====  Knowledge is an acquired trait,
```

Pressing PF11 has this effect:

```
=====  Knowledge is _
=====  an acquired trait,
```

You can now add additional words at the end of the first line.

To join two lines, position the cursor at the end of the data in the first line:

```
===== Knowledge is _
===== an acquired trait,
```

Then press **PF11**. In this example, we have restored the original line through this procedure, with the result:

```
===== Knowledge is an acquired trait,
```

PF Keys and the SET Subcommand

You can list the default settings of the PF keys by entering the editor and typing the subcommand **QUERY PF**. Assuming you entered the editor with the **NOPROFILE** option, you view the default PF key settings for XEDIT in your release of VM/SP. You can change a PF key to any desired setting by issuing this subcommand on the command line:

    SET PFn   subcommand

where n represents the PF key number to set, and subcommand, the name of the edit subcommand setting for that key. For example:

    SET PF1 UP 4

sets the **PF1** key to the **UP** subcommand. Now, whenever you press **PF1**, the **UP 4** subcommand is issued. Note that this PF key setting only remains in effect during the current editing session. When you start your next editing session, the editor's PF key defaults are again in effect. Later in this chapter, we discuss how to reassign your PF keys permanently across sessions.

The **QUERY** and **STATUS** subcommands can provide information on the setting of any of several dozen different editor options. And, the **SET** subcommand offers a method to set many of these editor options. For example, we earlier mentioned that the **QUERY CASE** subcommand allows you to determine whether the letters you enter in the file are automatically changed to upper case. The corresponding **SET CASE** subcommand allows you to either **SET CASE UPPERCASE**, for automatic translation of all letters to upper case, or to **SET CASE MIXED**, for entry of both uppercase and lower-case letters.

Upon entry to the editor, three other PF key settings are especially useful. **PF6** is set to the question mark (?), which has this meaning in the editor: redisplay the most recently executed subcommand in the command line. If you wish, you can then reissue that subcommand by pressing the **ENTER** key.

PF9 immediately reissues the last subcommand entered, and it does not display the subcommand at the command line.

Finally, the **PF1** key enters a HELP facility through which you can get complete information concerning any XEDIT subcommand. Pressing **PF1** alphabetically lists the XEDIT subcommands for which HELP is available. Select an entry from the list by moving the cursor underneath any character of the subcommand on which you need HELP. Pressing the **ENTER** key then displays the desired information. Return to the HELP menu by pressing **PF3**, and to XEDIT, by pressing **PF3** again.

Chapter 14 presents a complete tutorial on the CMS HELP facility and how to use it.

Tabs

Any good computer-based editor offers the functional equivalent of typewriter tab keys. In XEDIT, these tab settings are automatically set to certain default values, based on the filetype of the file you edit. For example, for a file identifier with filetype of COBOL, tabs are set for columns 1, 8, 12, and other positions appropriate for editing COBOL programs. The SCRIPT filetype of the editing example of the preceding chapter has default tab settings every fifth column, starting with the first column. (The SCRIPT filetype indicates that a file contains a textual document.)

To tab while in the editor's input mode, press the **PF4** key. This moves the cursor to the next tab position.

To view the present tab settings, enter the subcommand **QUERY TABS**. You can set the tabs by entering:

```
SET   TABS   n1 n2 n3 ...
```

on the command line, where the list of numbers following the keyword **TABS** indicates where you desire the settings. For example:

```
SET   TABS   10   20
```

sets tabs at column positions 10 and 20.

Entering the subcommand **MODIFY TABS** displays the current settings for you. You then directly overtype them, and press the **ENTER** key, thereby setting new tab positions.

Tabbing is particularly useful when entering tabular, or columnar, data. Information such as this list of students and their grades is amenable to this approach to data entry. Merely issue the command SET TABS 1 18 31 prior to entering the sample data, then use the PF4 key to tab as required:

```
=====   NAME:          GRADE:      TERM GRADE:
=====
        !...+....1....+....2....+....3....+....4....+....5...
===== Maalmers, B.     73          C
===== Daed S. Luap     65          D
===== George, G.       93          A
===== Frederick, T.    73          C
```

Another useful subcommand for working with tabular data is the SORT subcommand. It enables you to sort lines into either ascending or descending order, as based on the computer's collating (character-ordering) sequence. An example is:

SORT * 18 19 1 15

The asterisk * prompts the editor to begin sorting with the line after the current line, and sort all subsequent lines to the end of the file. It sorts lines in the default sequence of ascending order. The two pairs of numbers 18, 19 and 1, 15 each specify the starting and ending columns for a sort field. Thus, this example sorts the lines with students and their grades in order of ascending grade, and within grade, in order of ascending last name:

```
=====   NAME:          GRADE:      TERM GRADE:
=====
        !...+....1....+....2....+....3....+....4....+....5...
===== Daed S. Luap     65          D
===== Frederick, T.    73          C
===== Maalmers, B.     73          C
===== George, G.       93          A
```

The SORT subcommand is extremely useful in data entry. Enter the data in any order you choose, then use the SORT subcommand to order it after it has all been entered. This relieves you of the need to enter ordered data.

Power Typing

XEDIT provides other input conveniences in addition to tabbing. *Power typing* refers to the ability to enter text rapidly without concern about the line-oriented arrangement of words on the display screen. Power typing offers an alternative method of data input to the INPUT subcommand. To enter information after the current line via power typing mode, enter the subcommand **POWERINP**, abbreviated **POW**, in the command line. As with the **INPUT** subcommand, the screen parts to allow data entry. Now, enter the text *without* regard to the ends of lines on the screen display. Do not be concerned if words are split across lines. Separate sentences that are to appear on a new line by entering a pound symbol #, as shown in figure 5-1.

Figure 5-1   XEDIT's Power Typing Feature

```
POWER     SCRIPT   A1     * * * P O W E R    T Y P I N G * * *      ALT=0
* * * TOP OF FILE * * *
This is an example text file which was entered in XEDIT's "power typing" mode.
In this mode, you don't worry about where the end of a line occurs, or even whet
her you have split words across lines -- XEDIT puts split words back together wh
en you exit power typing mode.  #Note also, that sentences that begin on a new l
ine can be preceded by the "pound sign," and XEDIT dutifully starts these senten
ces on new lines._
```

As with data entry in input mode, press the **ENTER** key once to gain more screen space for data entry, and press the **ENTER** key twice to exit power typing textual input mode.

After scrolling to the top of the file, the data will appear as illustrated in figure 5-2. Words are rejoined and the sentences preceded by pound symbols are placed on separate lines.

Figure 5-2   Power Typing after Text Entry

```
POWER     SCRIPT   A1   V 132   TRUNC=132 SIZE=7 LINE=0 COL=1 ALT=7




=====  * * * TOP OF FILE * * *
      !...+....1....+....2....+....3....+....4....+....5....+....6....+....7...
=====  This is an example text file which was entered in XEDIT's "power typing"
=====  mode.  In this mode, you don't worry about where the end of a line
=====  occurs, or even whether you have split words across lines -- XEDIT puts
=====  split words back together when you exit power typing mode.
=====  Note also, that sentences that begin on a new line can be preceded by
=====  the "pound sign," and XEDIT dutifully starts these sentences on new
=====  lines.
=====  * * * END OF FILE * * *

====>  _
                                                    X E D I T  1 FILE
```

Power typing mode permits skilled typists to rapidly enter textual information.

Recovery

One concern in data entry and editing is the possibility of losing data due to a system outage. XEDIT offers a number of mechanisms to ensure that you never accidentally lose data due to system problems.

Chapter 4 described the functions of the FILE, QUIT, and QQUIT subcommands. The SAVE subcommand preserves the current state of your edited file, but unlike FILE, SAVE allows you to continue in the editing session.

The SET AUTOSAVE subcommand is another extremely important and highly recommended subcommand for avoiding loss of data. Issue this command in this format:

```
SET  AUTOSAVE  n
```

where n is a number stating that after every n number of alterations to your file, the editor should save the file on your behalf. This is done automatically, without any interruption to the editing session. For example:

```
SET  AUTOSAVE  15
```

specifies that the file will automatically be saved each time you have altered or entered 15 lines of data. The editor saves your updated file to a new file having a number as its filename and AUTOSAVE as its filetype.

The important point to remember about the SET AUTOSAVE subcommand is that its default setting is OFF. If you want it active, you *must* issue this subcommand, and preferably at the beginning of each editing session. There is a way around this inconvenience of re-entering this subcommand each time you enter the editor. A special file of editor subcommands is automatically executed each time you enter the XEDIT editor. This file is named by the special CMS file name of:

```
PROFILE  XEDIT
```

With the editing knowledge you now have, you could create a file with this name and enter subcommands such as SET AUTOSAVE and your favorite PF key settings into it. Then, the next time you enter the editor, enter:

```
XEDIT  fn  ft
```

excluding the NOPROFILE option suggested in chapter 4. NOPROFILE is a special option that tells the editor not to execute its PROFILE XEDIT subcommand file. The NOPROFILE option was originally suggested so that you would not unknowingly execute an *edit profile* set of commands that would make the function of your editor appear different than that shown in these examples. Section 6 of this book describes CMS features that allow you to create very powerful PROFILE files of subcommands, and it includes a sample PROFILE XEDIT file.

Copying One File into Another

The XEDIT editor provides for copying all or part of one file into a specified position in the file being edited. In other words, you can combine files or parts of files as desired.

The XEDIT GET subcommand is the mechanism through which inclusion of one file into another is accomplished. GET always copies the lines of the file you specify after the current line; always set the current line to properly reflect where you want to copy the data.

The simplest form of the GET subcommand is:

```
GET   fn   ft   fm
```

where fn, ft, and fm are replaced by the filename, filetype, and filemode of the file you wish copied into the file you are editing. As on the XEDIT command, these examples leave off the filemode reference, since we assume it is A1. Thus, a command line entry such as this:

```
GET   LEARNMOR   SCRIPT
```

copies the entire contents of the file LEARNMOR SCRIPT after the current line in the file being edited.

Another form of the GET subcommand states that only part of the file referred to in the GET subcommand will be copied into the file being edited. This form of the subcommand specifies the number of the first line of the file to be copied, and the number of lines of data to include. For example:

```
GET   LEARNMOR   SCRIPT   1   20
```

copies the first 20 lines of the file LEARNMOR SCRIPT into the current file after the current line, while this command:

```
GET   LEARNMOR   SCRIPT   10   15
```

tells XEDIT to copy 15 lines from the file LEARNMOR SCRIPT, starting with the tenth line of that file. Again, these lines are placed immediately after the current line of the file being edited.

What happens if you do not know the initial line number and the number of lines to copy? In this case, make use of the editor's ability to edit another file. Simply enter a subcommand to edit the second file on the command line:

```
XEDIT   fn   ft
```

where fn and ft specify the file from which you will copy one or more lines. This subcommand puts you into editing mode with the specified file. Entering the subcommand SET NUMBER ON in the command line area replaces the equal signs of the prefix area with line numbers. After you determine the group of lines you want to copy, make the first one the current line. Then enter:

    PUT   n

where n represents the number of lines to copy from the visible file, starting with the current line.

Now enter the **QUIT** subcommand, and the first file will reappear on the screen. Enter:

    GET

in the command line, with no filename, and the lines you specified are copied after the current line.

Suppose you are editing the file **LEARNING SCRIPT**, and you wish to copy part of the file **LEARNMOR SCRIPT** into **LEARNING SCRIPT**. Unfortunately, you do not know the exact lines to copy without viewing them first. First, enter:

    XEDIT   LEARNMOR   SCRIPT

in the command line area. This places you into edit with the file **LEARNMOR SCRIPT**. View the file as desired, and then make the first line to copy into the file **LEARNING SCRIPT** the current line. You can do this by entering a slash in the prefix area for that line. After this is accomplished, enter the subcommand **SET NUMBER ON** in the command line. This makes it easier to judge the number of lines involved in the copy operation:

```
00012 this line will not be copied
00013 this is the first line copied
      !...+....1....+....2....+....3....+....4....+....5...
00014 this is the second line copied
00015 this is the last line copied
00016 this line will not be copied
```

Assuming that line 13 above is the first line to copy, you have properly positioned it as the current line in the file. Assuming further that you've decided to copy line 13 and the next two lines into the original file **LEARNING SCRIPT**, enter:

    PUT   3

in the command line area. Now that the lines to copy have been specified, enter **QUIT** to return to editing the file **LEARNING SCRIPT**. Set the current line so that it represents the line in this file after which you want the copied lines to appear. Then enter:

GET

and the lines specified earlier are copied after the current line. As in all editor copy operations, the original contents of the file from which the lines are copied are unaltered.

Editing Multiple Files and the Split Screen Feature

The preceding section illustrated that the editor provides the ability to edit more than one file without having to completely exit editing of the first file. You initiate editing of a second file (and subsequent files) simply by entering the XEDIT subcommand in the command line area. Every time this is done, the new subject file appears for editing. The file currently displayed for editing is referred to as the *current file.*

When you enter the XEDIT subcommand, if the file name specified refers to a pre-existing file, the editor permits viewing and update of that file. If the file name provided is new, the editor creates a new file with the name you give it.

When you have finished viewing or editing the file named in the last XEDIT subcommand, save or exit that file using the normal subcommands of FILE or QUIT, respectively. The editor returns you to editing the file you were working with when you entered the XEDIT subcommand on the command line.

This concept of editing one or more additional files without completing the editing of an original file allows for rapid and convenient editing of several files. Its use in the copying of lines from one file into another provides just one concrete example of its value.

A similar editor feature permits display of different edited files on the same display device simultaneously, or, the display of different parts of the same file. Thus, you can view and edit different files or different parts of the same file at the same time on your display screen.

To split the screen horizontally into two editing areas, enter the SET SCREEN subcommand in the command line. For example:

```
SET  SCR  2
```

divides the display into two logical screens, one on top of the other. Figure 5-3 illustrates how this provides two different views of the same file for editing. Note that any editing command entered in half the display area for one view of the file will naturally be reflected in the other view, if appropriate.

To vertically partition the display into two components, enter:

```
SET  SCR  2  V
```

Figure 5-4 shows how this subcommand partitions the screen into two vertical display areas.

Figure 5-3   Two Views of One File under XEDIT

```
POWER      SCRIPT    A1   V 132   TRUNC=132 SIZE=7 LINE=0 COL=1 ALT=0




===== * * * TOP OF FILE * * *
      !...+....1....+....2....+....3....+....4....+....5....+....6....+....7...
===== This is an example text file which was entered in XEDIT's "power typing"
===== mode.  In this mode, you don't worry about where the end of a line
===== occurs, or even whether you have split words across lines -- XEDIT puts
====> _
                                                          X E D I T  1 FILE
POWER      SCRIPT    A1   V 132   TRUNC=132 SIZE=7 LINE=0 COL=1 ALT=0




===== * * * TOP OF FILE * * *
      !...+....1....+....2....+....3....+....4....+....5....+....6....+....7...
===== This is an example text file which was entered in XEDIT's "power typing"
===== mode.  In this mode, you don't worry about where the end of a line
===== occurs, or even whether you have split words across lines -- XEDIT puts
====>
                                                          X E D I T  1  FILE
```

Figure 5-4   Vertical Split Screen within XEDIT

```
POWER      SCRIPT    A1   V 132   TRUNC=132  POWER      SCRIPT    A1   V 132   TRUNC=132







===== * * * TOP OF FILE * * *        ===== * * * TOP OF FILE * * *
      !...+....1....+....2....+....3...      !...+....1....+....2....+....3...
===== This is an example text file whic ===== This is an example text file whic
===== mode.  In this mode, you don't wo ===== mode.  In this mode, you don't wo
===== occurs, or even whether you have  ===== occurs, or even whether you have
===== split words back together when yo ===== split words back together when yo
===== Note also, that sentences that be ===== Note also, that sentences that be
===== the "pound sign," and XEDIT dutif ===== the "pound sign," and XEDIT dutif
===== lines.                            ===== lines.
===== * * * END OF FILE * * *           ===== * * * END OF FILE * * *

====> _                                 ====>
```

Whether you split the screen display horizontally or vertically, **SET SCREEN** options provide for specification of the relative sizes of the screen windows. The **SIZE** option allows you to create screen displays with the number of lines you indicate, while the **WIDTH** option permits specification of the number of columns each vertical screen contains.

The **SET SCREEN 1** subcommand returns the editor to its original state of one logical display screen.

The editor's split screen option may, at first, appear complicated. However, it is a very powerful feature, one that most users soon find indispensable. You may wish to practice entering the **XEDIT** subcommand in the command line while editing a file at this time. Be sure to try the split screen feature as well.

For Further Information

Perhaps the single most useful editor subcommand is **HELP**. Entering **HELP** and the name of a subcommand on which you need information on the command line immediately presents relevant explanatory information on the screen. For example:

    HELP   INPUT

immediately provides access to online information concerning the **IN-PUT** subcommand. Exit back to the editor by pressing the **PF3** key.

You can also press the **PF1** key at any time in the editor. This displays a menu of editor subcommands. You pick one for further explanation by moving the cursor under your selection and pressing the **ENTER** key. After viewing the explanation, return to the **HELP** subcommand menu by pressing **PF3**, or, to the editing session by pressing **PF4**.

After gaining some experience with XEDIT, you will find that the online HELP facility provides all the information you normally require in working with the editor. Nevertheless, the vendor's manuals provide worthwhile tutorial and reference information.

The manual, *VM/SP Terminal Reference, GC19-6206,* describes the physical attributes of most kinds of terminals. It tells where the cursor, program function, program attention, character insert, character delete, attention, tab, **CLEAR**, **RESET**, and **ENTER** keys are located. Use this manual if you have difficulty finding keys used by the editor.

The manual, *VM/SP: CMS Primer, SC24-5236,* provides a very brief and simple introduction to the XEDIT editor. It is oriented toward users with little or no previous experience with computer-based editing.

The manual, *VM/SP: System Product Editor User's Guide, SC24-5220,* similarly offers a tutorial on XEDIT, and assumes you are a data processing or computer professional and have used other computer-based editors. This manual is most useful for its frequent reproductions of screen displays in illustrating the effects of editor subcommands. It presents equivalent tutorial material for those using typewriter-like terminals. It also includes a selection of advanced topics of interest to those with substantial XEDIT experience.

The final manual of importance is *VM/SP: System Product Editor Command and Macro Reference, SC24-5221.* As an editor reference manual, this book provides an alphabetical listing of all editor subcommands and all their options, including those for the **QUERY**, **STATUS**, and **SET** subcommands. It is intended for users who are comfortable with the XEDIT editor, and is useful for providing details on specific commands or questions you may have concerning their use.

As you gain experience with XEDIT, you may want to refer to these manuals to learn advanced editor features. Remember that this chapter covered only the basics: when you are ready, inspect the vendor's manuals to learn of more advanced editor features that can increase your editing productivity.

Test Your Understanding

Edit a textual data set. Enter the QUERY CASE subcommand. Does the editor respect or ignore the case of letters? Practice finding a character string containing both lowercase and uppercase letters through the LOCATE subcommand. Now SET CASE to the other setting and try the LOCATE subcommand again. Do you still find the character string?

Globally change all occurrences of a textual string within the file. Inspect each character string prior to altering it.

You want to insert several words within the middle of a line. Accomplish this through use of the program function keys.

Set PF2 to the QUERY PF subcommand. Now enter that subcommand by pressing PF2. Are all your other program function keys set to their editor defaults?

Using the editor's HELP function, access information on the editor's CLOCATE subcommand from within the editor. How does the CLOCATE subcommand differ from the LOCATE subcommand?

Edit a new file and set the tabs to columns 1, 25, and 50. Enter your friend's last names, first names, and gender into these columns. After you have entered data for several people, sort the table by last name using the SORT subcommand. Note that CMS also offers a SORT command. Could you have sorted the table with the CMS SORT command rather than the XEDIT SORT subcommand? Which command would you prefer to use and why?

Create a new file and enter several lines of information through power typing. Do you find power typing faster for data entry than the editor INPUT subcommand? Do you think its advantages depend on whether you know how to touch type?

Copy the first ten lines of another file onto the end of the file in which you entered information through power typing. Now split the screen display into two parts, and display the same ten lines from within both files simultaneously. How independent are the two file displays? How independent are the two displays if both portions of the screen display different parts of the same file?

CHAPTER 6

File Manipulation via CMS Commands

You now know how to use XEDIT to enter and alter information into permanent disk storage. As you enter data for storage, you continually create files. It soon becomes obvious that you require a group of commands to manage your files. For example, as you generate new files, you may want to list which files you have in storage. Or, you may forget the name of a particular file and need to search for it.

You might also wish to rename files, delete old or obsolete files, make additional copies of files, and print files. These file operations are required by the users of any computer system and CMS provides a powerful group of commands to perform these functions. This chapter discusses these CMS file-manipulation commands. As always, the discussion is based on examples; practice these commands on your terminal as they are demonstrated.

Listing File Names

Two commands list the names of files on disk storage. LISTFILE is one of them. Often abbreviated LISTF, its simplest format is:

        LISTFILE   fn   ft   fm

Substitute explicit filenames, filetypes, or filemodes for fn, ft, and fm to display the files matching those specifications. An asterisk in any part of the full file name matches all files. For example:

        LISTF   *   SCRIPT

lists all your CMS SCRIPT files. It results in a listing similar to this, assuming you have created three SCRIPT files with these names:

```
LEARNING   SCRIPT   A1
LEARNIN2   SCRIPT   A1
TEMP       SCRIPT   A1
R;
```

Since the filemode is omitted, the command only lists those files on the user's A-disk.

Coding an asterisk preceded by any number of characters in any part of the file name results in listing those names that begin with the specified characters:

```
LISTF  TEST*  COBOL
```

lists all the COBOL programs whose filenames begin with the letters TEST. An asterisk may also substitute for a group of characters elsewhere in the file name:

```
LISTF  *TEST*  COBOL
```

lists all files whose filename contains the contiguous characters TEST. For example, the response to this command could be:

```
ATEST    COBOL  A1
ATESTB   COBOL  A1
TEST     COBOL  A1
TESTING  COBOL  A1
R;
```

assuming files of these names exist on the user's A-disk. This command lists all your files on all disks:

```
LISTF  *  *  *
```

You might wish to enter this command, just to see what files are on the various disks other than the A-disk. These files include many files you have not created called *system files*. System files are part of the VM/CMS operating system. Notice that when you list more files than can fit on a single screen, you receive the MORE... message in the bottom right-hand corner of the screen. Clear the screen to see the rest of the listing. On most terminals, this is accomplished by pressing the CLEAR and ALT keys together. On other terminals, you only need press the CLEAR key itself.

LISTFILE is a line-oriented command. That is, the system responds to this command by sending back one or more lines of information that are written on the terminal screen. These lines display one after another, immediately underneath the user's LISTFILE command.

As with many of its commands, CMS offers a full-screen counterpart to the `LISTFILE` command. It is called `FILELIST`. This full-screen command clears the screen and then lists the requested files. Use of this command requires a display terminal.

`FILELIST` is abbreviated `FILEL`. `FILELIST` permits selective listing of files in the same manner as does `LISTFILE`. Here are several examples:

`FILEL`

asks for a listing of all files on your A-disk. Entering:

`FILEL TEST  *`

requests a listing of all files on the A-disk with filename `TEST`. The command:

`FILEL  *      PLI`

asks for a listing of all files on the A-disk with filetype `PLI`.

Omission of the filemode means that the A-disk is assumed. Entering a command such as:

`FILEL  *  SCRIPT`

results in a full-screen display such as that shown in figure 6-1. This screen indicates that this user has three SCRIPT files on his or her A-disk.

Figure 6-1   FILELIST Display

```
ZHMF01     FILELIST A0   V 108   TRUNC=108 SIZE=3 LINE=1 COL=1 ALT=0
Cmd    Filename Filetype Fm Format Lrecl      Records      Blocks    Date       Time
       TEMP     SCRIPT   A1 F         80          1           1 10/22/85 19:09:16
_      LEARNIN2 SCRIPT   A1 F         80          3           1 10/22/85 19:08:19
       LEARNING SCRIPT   A1 F         80          3           1 10/22/85 19:07:42




















1= Help      2= Refresh  3= Quit    4= Sort(type)  5= Sort(date)  6= Sort(size)
7= Backward  8= Forward  9= FL /n  10=             11= XEDIT      12= Cursor
====>
                                                    X E D I T   1 FILE
```

The display shows the filename, filetype, and filemode of every file in the selected list. Also, it presents information concerning the internal storage representation of each file in the `FORMAT`, `LRECL`, `RECORDS`, and `BLOCKS` columns. The `DATE` and `TIME` columns tell when the files were last updated. If a file has never been altered, these columns indicate the date and time of its creation.

The PF key settings at the bottom of the screen are very important. **PF7** and **PF8** are used to scroll upward and downward, respectively, through the list. These keys are essential for scrolling when the listing takes up more than a single screen.

PF4, **PF5**, and **PF6** also have preset functions. **PF4** sorts the file list by filename within filetype, while **PF5** sorts the files by date and time, from the newest to the oldest. **PF6** sorts the file listing from the largest file to the smallest.

PF1 is the **HELP** key. Press it to read online tutorial information on the **FILELIST** command, and exit the **HELP** panel by pressing **PF3**. **PF3** is also the key you press to exit the file listing generated through **FILELIST**.

An outstanding feature of the **FILELIST** command is that you can immediately enter the XEDIT editor to display or alter any file in the list simply by taking the cursor down to the line of the file to edit, and pressing the **PF11** key. You enter the XEDIT editor with that selected file. Use XEDIT exactly as shown in earlier chapters. To exit XEDIT, enter the XEDIT subcommand of either **FILE** or **QUIT**, as may be appropriate. The system returns you to the same file listing from which you entered. An asterisk * appears to the left of the file name just edited. This indicates that activity occurred on this file.

You can also enter XEDIT to create a new file through this file listing display. Merely move the cursor to the command line at the bottom of the screen (denoted by the arrow). Type:

```
XEDIT  fn  ft  fm
```

with the name of the new file you wish to create. You enter the editor with this new file. Exiting the editing session with the new file again returns you to the original **FILELIST** display. Notice, however, the name of the new file you created does not yet appear in the file listing. To make it appear, press **PF2**. This is the *refresh* program function key. It "refreshes" the **FILELIST** display with any new information since either **FILELIST** (or refresh) were last issued.

In summary, the **FILELIST** command displays the information provided by the **LISTFILE** command in a full-screen format under control of the **XEDIT** command. You can directly manipulate the display listing via **XEDIT** commands. You can also issue commands to rename, delete, copy, compare, and print files, as described in the next subsection.

Renaming, Deleting, Copying, Comparing, and Printing Files

An important column in the **FILELIST** display of figure 6-1 is labelled **Cmd**. Underneath this column heading, you can enter commands to rename, delete, copy, and compare the files listed.

For example, to change the name of an existing file to a new name, take the cursor down underneath the `Cmd` column to the line of the file to rename. Enter a **RENAME** command in this format:

```
RENAME  /  newfilename  newfiletype  filemode
```

You enter this command right over the information already on the line. The slash / stands for the old file to rename, which is on the line on which the command is entered. You can alter the file's filename or filetype (but not the letter portion of the filemode) through the **RENAME** command. Even though **RENAME** cannot alter the filemode letter, the filemode must still be entered as part of the command.

Figure 6-2 shows an example of renaming the file **LEARNIN2 SCRIPT A1** to **NEWNAME SCRIPT A1**:

Figure 6-2   Entering the RENAME Command

```
ZHMF01     FILELIST A0    V 108    TRUNC=108 SIZE=3 LINE=1 COL=1 ALT=0
Cmd    Filename Filetype Fm Format Lrecl      Records       Blocks    Date      Time
       TEMP     SCRIPT   A1 F         80          1            1  10/22/85 19:09:16
rename / newname script a1_F           80          3            1  10/22/85 19:08:19
       LEARNING SCRIPT   A1 F         80          3            1  10/22/85 19:07:42




1= Help       2= Refresh  3= Quit    4= Sort(type)  5= Sort(date)  6= Sort(size)
7= Backward   8= Forward  9= FL /n  10=            11= XEDIT      12= Cursor
====>
                                                           X E D I T   1 FILE
```

Figure 6-3 shows that after you enter the **RENAME** command and press the **ENTER** key, the system sends the completion message:

```
*        LEARNIN2 SCRIPT A1 ** Discarded or renamed **
```

To see the file properly renamed in the **FILELIST** display, press the **PF2** key. Figure 6-4 shows that this refreshes the display listing the files. What if the **RENAME** command fails? In this case, an asterisk appears

Figure 6-3   System Response to RENAME

```
ZHMF01     FILELIST A0   V 108   TRUNC=108 SIZE=3 LINE=1 COL=1 ALT=3
Cmd    Filename Filetype Fm Format Lrecl     Records      Blocks   Date      Time
       TEMP     SCRIPT   A1 F        80          1           1 10/22/85 19:09:16
 *     LEARNIN2 SCRIPT   A1 ** Discarded  or  renamed **
       LEARNING SCRIPT   A1 F        80          3           1 10/22/85 19:07:42
─




















1= Help       2= Refresh   3= Quit     4= Sort(type)  5= Sort(date)  6= Sort(size)
7= Backward   8= Forward   9= FL /n   10=             11= XEDIT        12= Cursor
====>
                                                            X E D I T    1 FILE
```

Figure 6-4   RENAME after Pressing PF2

```
ZHMF01     FILELIST A0   V 108   TRUNC=108 SIZE=3 LINE=1 COL=1 ALT=8
Cmd    Filename Filetype Fm Format Lrecl     Records      Blocks   Date      Time
 _     TEMP     SCRIPT   A1 F        80          1           1 10/22/85 19:09:16
       NEWNAME  SCRIPT   A1 F        80          3           1 10/22/85 19:08:19
       LEARNING SCRIPT   A1 F        80          3           1 14/22/85 19:07:42




















1= Help       2= Refresh   3= Quit     4= Sort(type)  5= Sort(date)  6= Sort(size)
7= Backward   8= Forward   9= FL /n   10=             11= XEDIT        12= Cursor
====>
                                                            X E D I T    1 FILE
```

underneath the `Cmd` column and is followed by one or more digits. These digits are called *return codes,* and they indicate why the command failed. For example, if you issue a **RENAME** command and forget to enter the filemode, you receive the explanatory error message: `INCOMPLETE FILEID SPECIFIED`. Pressing the **CLEAR** key to return to the file list display shows an asterisk followed by the command return code `*24` indicating the error in the `Cmd` column.

Discarding a file from the system is accomplished in a manner very similar to that of renaming a file. Take the cursor down to the line on which the file you wish to erase from your disk is listed. Enter the command `DISCARD` on that line underneath the `Cmd` column heading.

Figure 6-5 shows elimination of the file `LEARNING SCRIPT A1` from the system.

Figure 6-5   Discarding a File

```
ZHMF01    FILELIST A0   V 108   TRUNC=108 SIZE=3 LINE=1 COL=1 ALT=8
Cmd     Filename Filetype Fm Format Lrecl     Records       Blocks     Date       Time
        TEMP     SCRIPT   A1 F        80         1            1 10/22/85 19:09:16
        NEWNAME  SCRIPT   A1 F        80         3            1 10/22/85 19:08:19
discardEARNING   SCRIPT   A1 F        80         3            1 10/22/85 19:07:42




1= Help      2= Refresh  3= Quit    4= Sort(type)  5= Sort(date)  6= Sort(size)
7= Backward  8= Forward  9= FL /n  10=            11= XEDIT       12= Cursor
====>
                                                        X E D I T   1 FILE
```

The system displays a message such as the one in figure 6-6 to show that the file has been discarded:

```
*       LEARNING   SCRIPT  A1 has been discarded.
```

Pressing **PF2** refreshes the screen and updates the file listing. This is illustrated in figure 6-7.

Be sure you want to permanently delete a file when using `DISCARD`. The file is no longer available after you discard it. The `DISCARD` command is thus useful to thin out your files and eliminate old or obsolete files, but be sure you never again intend to use the file you delete.

Copying a file is accomplished in a manner very similar to renaming a file. Copying a file is useful when you wish to update a file, but still want to keep a copy of the original. It is also useful when you intend to create a new file but wish to use a pre-existing file as a template or model for the new one.

Figure 6-6   System Response to Discarding a File

```
ZHMF01     FILELIST A0    V 108    TRUNC=108 SIZE=3 LINE=1  COL=1 ALT=12
Cmd     Filename Filetype Fm Format Lrecl      Records         Blocks    Date       Time
        TEMP      SCRIPT   A1 F         80           1              1 10/22/85 19:09:16
        NEWNAME   SCRIPT   A1 F         80           3              1 10/22/85 19:08:19
*       LEARNING SCRIPT    A1 has been  discarded.




1= Help        2= Refresh  3= Quit    4= Sort(type)  5= Sort(date)  6= Sort(size)
7= Backward  8= Forward  9= FL /n  10=             11= XEDIT       12= Cursor
====>
                                                             X E D I T   1 FILE
```

Figure 6-7   Discarding a File after Pressing PF2

```
ZHMF01     FILELIST A0    V 108    TRUNC=108 SIZE=2 LINE=1  COL=1 ALT=16
Cmd     Filename Filetype Fm Format Lrecl      Records         Blocks    Date       Time
_       TEMP      SCRIPT   A1 F         80           1              1 10/22/85 19:09:16
        NEWNAME   SCRIPT   A1 F         80           3              1 10/22/85 19:08:19




1= Help        2= Refresh  3= Quit    4= Sort(type)  5= Sort(date)  6= Sort(size)
7= Backward  8= Forward  9= FL /n  10=             11= XEDIT       12= Cursor
====>
                                                             X E D I T   1 FILE
```

To copy a file, move the cursor down to the line showing the name of the file name to copy. Underneath the **Cmd** column, enter this command format:

```
COPYFILE  /  newfilename  newfiletype  newfilemode
```

As with the **RENAME** command, type this information directly over what appears on the screen and press the **ENTER** key. The copy command is performed. Press the PF2 key to see the newly created file included in your screen's file listing.

You can also use the abbreviation for this command, COPY. In this example, we have copied the file on which this information is overtyped into a new file called MYCOPY SCRIPT A1:

```
COPY / MYCOPY SCRIPT A1
```

You can also compare two files for differences through the FILELIST panel display. This is useful in determining if two files are duplicates, or to see how one version of a file differs from a newer, altered copy.

One way to compare two files is to visually inspect each via the XEDIT editor. An easier way is to use the COMPARE command. Take the cursor down to the name of one of the files to compare. Underneath the Cmd column in the display, enter this command:

```
COMPARE   /   secondfilename  secondfiletype  secondfilemode
```

Type this information directly over what appears on the line. The first file involved in the comparison is that named by the line on which you are typing the COMPARE command. The second file in the comparison is that named in the file name you type.

In response to this command, the system displays a message such as this:

```
COMPARING 'LEARNING SCRIPT A1' WITH 'LEARNIN2 SCRIPT A1'.
```

LEARNING SCRIPT A1 is the name of the file over which you've typed the COMPARE command, while LEARNIN2 SCRIPT A1 is the name you've entered.

If the two files differ, those lines that occur in one file (but not the other) are displayed on the screen. Eventually you receive the message: FILES DO NOT COMPARE. . You also receive the message PREMATURE EOF ON FILE 'filename filetype filemode'. if one file is shorter than the other. The file name listed is that of the file having fewer lines. The system displays the continuation message MORE... in the lower right-hand corner of the screen in order to denote the end of the comparison. Press the CLEAR (or CLEAR and ALT keys) to return to the FILELIST display screen.

If the two files are identical, after the COMPARING... message, you will receive the MORE... indicator. Clear the screen to return to the FILE-LIST file listing.

Figures 6-8 through 6-12 show the process and results of comparing the files **LEARNING SCRIPT A1** and **LEARNIN2 SCRIPT A1**. The system responds to the **COMPARE** commands by listing the two lines that occur in one file and not the other. The **PREMATURE EOF ON FILE...** message is not displayed because the files have the same number of lines. The user returns to the **FILELIST** display by pressing the **CLEAR** key.

Figure 6-8 Files for the COMPARE Command

```
 LEARNING SCRIPT    A1  F 80   TRUNC=73 SIZE=3 LINE=0 COL=1 ALT=0
====>
=====
===== first line of data
===== second line of data
===== third line of data
=====




 LEARNIN2 SCRIPT    A1  F 80   TRUNC=73 SIZE=3 LINE=0 COL=1 ALT=0
====>
=====
===== first line of data
===== second line of data is different
===== third line of data
=====
```

Figure 6-9 File Listing before COMPARE

```
ZHMF01    FILELIST A0   V 108   TRUNC=108 SIZE=3 LINE=1 COL=1 ALT=0
Cmd   Filename Filetype Fm Format Lrecl      Records     Blocks   Date      Time
_     TEMP     SCRIPT   A1 F        80          1          1 10/22/85 19:09:16
      LEARNIN2 SCRIPT   A1 F        80          3          1 10/22/85 19:08:19
      LEARNING SCRIPT   A1 F        80          3          1 10/22/85 19:07:42












1= Help      2= Refresh   3= Quit    4= Sort(type)  5= Sort(date)  6= Sort(size)
7= Backward  8= Forward   9= FL /n  10=            11= XEDIT       12= Cursor
====>
                                                    X E D I T   1 FILE
```

Another capability offered through the **FILELIST** command display is the ability to print a file. To do this, merely take the cursor down to the

Figure 6-10   Entering the COMPARE Command

```
ZHMF01    FILELIST A0   V 108   TRUNC=108 SIZE=3 LINE=1 COL=1 ALT=0
Cmd   Filename Filetype Fm Format Lrecl      Records     Blocks   Date     Time
      TEMP     SCRIPT   A1 F         80            1          1 10/22/85 19:09:16
      LEARNIN2 SCRIPT   A1 F         80            3          1 10/22/85 19:08:19
compare / learnin2 script a1_        80            3          1 10/22/85 19:07:42
```

```
1= Help       2= Refresh   3= Quit     4= Sort(type)  5= Sort(date)  6= Sort(size)
7= Backward   8= Forward   9= FL /n   10=             11= XEDIT        12= Cursor
====>
                                                             X E D I T   1 FILE
```

Figure 6-11   System Response to COMPARE

```
COMPARING 'LEARNING SCRIPT A' WITH 'LEARNIN2 SCRIPT A'.
second line of data
second line of data is different
FILES DO NOT COMPARE.


                                                    MORE...
```

Figure 6-12   File Listing after COMPARE

```
ZHMF01    FILELIST A0   V 108   TRUNC=108 SIZE=3 LINE=1 COL=1 ALT=3
Cmd   Filename Filetype Fm Format Lrecl      Records     Blocks   Date     Time
      TEMP     SCRIPT   A1 F         80            1          1 10/22/85 19:09:16
      LEARNIN2 SCRIPT   A1 F         80            3          1 10/22/85 19:08:19
*4    LEARNING SCRIPT   A1 F         80            3          1 10/22/85 19:07:42
```

```
1= Help       2= Refresh   3= Quit     4= Sort(type)  5= Sort(date)  6= Sort(size)
7= Backward   8= Forward   9= FL /n   10=             11= XEDIT        12= Cursor
====>
                                                             X E D I T   1 FILE
```

line of the file to print, underneath the Cmd column. Type the word PRINT on the line showing file name to print. Pressing the ENTER key prints the indicated file.

Figure 6-13 shows how to print two of the files of the original FILE-LIST display of figure 6-1.

Figure 6-13   PRINTing Two Files from FILELIST

```
 ZHMF01    FILELIST A0   V 108   TRUNC=108 SIZE=3 LINE=1 COL=1 ALT=0
Cmd    Filename Filetype Fm Format Lrecl    Records    Blocks    Date      Time
       TEMP     SCRIPT   A1 F       80        1         1 10/22/85 19:09:16
print LEARNIN2 SCRIPT   A1 F       80        3         1 10/22/85 19:08:19
print_LEARNING SCRIPT   A1 F       80        3         1 10/22/85 19:07:42




















1= Help       2= Refresh  3= Quit    4= Sort(type)  5= Sort(date)  6= Sort(size)
7= Backward   8= Forward  9= FL /n   10=            11= XEDIT       12= Cursor
====>
                                                 X E D I T   1 FILE
```

You can print as many files as you like by typing PRINT in front of each on the appropriate line in the Cmd column. However, the files are not printed until you press the ENTER key. Should you want to scroll to another screen in the FILELIST display, be sure to press the ENTER key prior to scrolling to execute the PRINT command. (This rule also applies to the DISCARD command.)

How do you get more than a single printed copy of a file? One way is to enter the PRINT command several times in the Cmd area for that particular file.

Another solution is to take the cursor down to the XEDIT command line, denoted by the arrow in the lefthand corner of the screen. Enter the command:

SPOOL   PRINT   COPY   n

where n is the number of copies you want to result from entering the PRINT command one time. Now all PRINT commands result in n copies being printed. For example, entering:

SPOOL PRINT COPY 3

sets each `PRINT` command to generate three printed copies. Now, when you enter a `PRINT` command, the system responds with a message such as this:

```
PRT FILE 432 FOR USERID COPY 003 NOHOLD
```

`COPY 003` means that three copies of the file have been printed. You must enter:

```
SPOOL   PRINT   COPY   1
```

to reset the number of copies generated by a single `PRINT` command to one.

Line-Oriented CMS Commands

Given the advanced capabilities of the `FILELIST` command, and how easily one can discard, rename, copy, and compare files using its display, you might wonder why anyone would ever use the `LISTFILE` command. There are several reasons:

1. You may not have full-screen capability. For example, typewriter-like terminals do not support full-screen commands.

2. You may be using an older version of CMS that does not offer the full-screen commands.

3. If you are writing a program that issues CMS commands (called a *command procedure*), line-oriented CMS file manipulation commands are more convenient to use than full-screen commands. Section 7 of this book covers command procedures and how to write them.

4. You may be working on a remotely attached terminal where full-screen interaction is painfully slow.

Since there are legitimate reasons not to use `FILELIST`, this chapter subsection presents the CMS line-oriented commands necessary to rename, discard, copy, compare, and print files. These commands are all entered directly to CMS; that is, they are entered as commands when you have the CMS ready `R;` prompt.

The CMS `RENAME` command is used to rename files. Enter it as:

```
RENAME   oldfn   oldft   oldfm   newfn   newft   newfm
```

Like the `RENAME` command entered through the `FILELIST` display, one cannot change the filemode letter through this command. (The filemode letter corresponds to a *virtual disk,* or *minidisk,* under CMS. Use the `COPYFILE` command to move files across minidisks.)

Here's an example of the `RENAME` command:

```
RENAME  MYPROG  DATA  A1  NEWPROG  INPUT  A1
```

The file named `MYPROG DATA A1` has been renamed to `NEWPROG INPUT A1`.

Use the equal sign = in the new file name to keep that part of the newly named file the same as the original file name. For example:

```
RENAME  oldfn  oldft  oldfm  newfn  =  =
```

changes the filename of the file from `oldfn` to `newfn`. The filetype and filemode portions of the file name remain unaltered:

```
RENAME  TESTPROG  COBOL  A1  COBPROG  =  =
```

changes the file name of a COBOL program from `TESTPROG COBOL A1` to `COBPROG COBOL A1`.

The CMS `ERASE` command permanently deletes one (or more) files from your CMS disks. `ERASE` offers the same function as does the `DISCARD` command through `FILELIST`. Enter this command as:

```
ERASE  fn  ft  fm
```

For example:

```
ERASE  OBSOLETE  SCRIPT  A1
```

erases the file named `OBSOLETE SCRIPT A1`. This command:

```
ERASE  *  DATA
```

deletes all files with the filetype of `DATA` on the A-disk. The A-disk is assumed where a filemode is not specified.

Exercise caution when using `ERASE`. Since a single `ERASE` command can delete multiple files, be sure you understand the exact consequences of any `ERASE` command *before* issuing it to CMS.

The CMS `COPYFILE` command provides the ability to copy files, similar to `COPYFILE` entered from within `FILELIST`. In its simplest form, it copies a single file to a new file:

```
COPYFILE  oldfn  oldft  oldfm  newfn  newft  newfm
```

As an example:

```
COPYFILE  TEST1  COBOL  A1  TEST2  COBOL  A1
```

creates an identical copy of **TEST1 COBOL A1** under the name **TEST2 COBOL A1**. Use the equal sign = to avoid typing redundant portions of file names, in a manner similar to that seen earlier in the **RENAME** command:

```
COPYFILE   TEST1   COBOL   A1   TEST2   =   =
```

produces the same result as the previous example above.

If a file exists with the name of the output file identifier specified in the **COPYFILE** command, **COPYFILE** outputs an error message and terminates. This prevents a file from being inadvertently overwritten. In order to override this default, include the **REPLACE** option in the **COPYFILE** command:

```
COPYFILE   TEST1   COBOL   A1   TEST2   COBOL   A1   (REPLACE
```

This replaces the current contents of file **TEST2 COBOL A1** with the data of **TEST1 COBOL A1**. **REPLACE** is the **COPYFILE** default in the event that the output file identification is specified as all equal signs = = = or, in the case that only a single file identification is specified in the **COPYFILE** command.

COPYFILE has numerous options, which can be used to:

- copy only particular records (or lines of data) from within a file
- copy two or more input files into a single output file
- combine two or more files without creating a new file
- modify file record formats (for example, convert a file from variable-length records to fixed-length records)
- translate specified characters to different characters
- convert uppercase letters to lower case, or vice versa

The CMS **COMPARE** command compares two CMS files on a record-by-record (or line-by-line) basis. Like the **COMPARE** command entered under **FILELIST**, any lines that do not match between the two files display on the terminal. For example:

```
COMPARE   EXAMPLE1   SCRIPT   A1   EXAMPLE2   SCRIPT   A1
```

displays those records that vary between these two files.

Note that if many lines are different, the listing could be quite lengthy. An easy way to end the display is to enter the CMS command **HT** (halt typing), when the **MORE...** message is displayed in the bottom right-hand corner of the screen. **HT** immediately terminates the output display of a CMS command at the terminal.

Use the CMS **PRINT** command to print a file:

```
PRINT   MYFILE   TEXTUAL   A1
```

prints the file named `MYFILE TEXTUAL A1`.

Among the several options for this command, the most useful is that for translation of all lowercase letters in the file to uppercase letters before printing. This function is essential when printing a textual document on a printer that only prints uppercase letters.

```
PRINT  MYFILE  TEXTUAL  A1  (UPCASE
```

translates the data of file `MYFILE TEXTUAL A1` to uppercase letters prior to printing. Notice that, as with all CMS commands, the command option is preceded by a left parenthesis. A closing right parenthesis is not necessary.

As with the example shown earlier concerning the `PRINT` command entered via the `FILELIST` screen display, you could enter the command:

```
SPOOL  PRINT  COPY  n
```

prior to any `PRINT` command to alter the number of printed copies a single `PRINT` command generates. Remember that each subsequent `PRINT` command continues to generate n copies of printed output until this command is entered:

```
SPOOL  PRINT  COPY  1
```

Note that `SPOOL` (like the `LOGON`, `LOGOFF`, and `IPL` commands presented in chapter 3) is actually a CP command. CP executes these commands, rather than CMS. This contrasts to all the other commands in this chapter, which are CMS commands. Section 3 of this book further describes the roles of CP and CMS and helps you see why you use certain commands executed by each of these two basic components of VM/CMS. That section also introduces a collection of useful CP commands.

Finally, the CMS `TYPE` command provides a line-oriented display of a CMS file. The `TYPE` command lists either all, or only part, of a file online. Entering:

```
TYPE  MYPROG  BASIC  A1
```

lists the named file on the terminal. The command:

```
TYPE  MYPROG  BASIC  A1  5  10
```

lists records (lines) five through ten of this file at the terminal, while:

```
TYPE  MYPROG  BASIC  A1  5  *
```

lists lines five through the end of the file. If this listing is lengthy, remember that you can terminate its display through entry of the `HT` command.

For Further Information

Further information and more examples of the use of these commands can be found in the vendor's reference manual, *VM/SP CMS Primer, SC24-5236*. This manual provides a simple, example-oriented tutorial on these commands.

Later portions of this book provide further reinforcement of the examples in this chapter. Strive to increase your comfort level with these commands by practicing their use at a CMS terminal.

Be aware that this chapter covers only a core subset of CMS file-oriented commands. And, of those commands discussed, only their more common uses have been described. Complete command information is found in the vendor's CMS reference manual, *VM/SP CMS Command and Macro Reference, SC19-6209*. This manual alphabetically lists each CMS command with exhaustive description of its options. The manual, *VM/SP CMS User's Guide, SC19-6210*, is more approachable for new users. It offers a technical but readable explanation of many CMS commands and their uses.

Test Your Understanding

List all the SCRIPT files on your A-disk through the `LISTFILE` command. Now do the same through the `FILELIST` command. Which listing do you prefer and why?

Using the `FILELIST` display, sort the files on the screen, first by filename within filetype, then by data and time, and finally by size. If you have trouble, press the **PF1** key for help.

Copy the first file in the `FILELIST` display to a new file called `MYTEST SCRIPT A1`. Which command do you use to do this?

Continuing to use the `FILELIST` display, rename the copied file through the `RENAME` command. Now compare it to the original file through the `COMPARE` command. Print three copies of the file through the `PRINT` command. Is there more than one way to accomplish this? Finally, erase the new file through the `DISCARD` command. Once you `DISCARD` a file, can you ever retrieve it again?

Exit the `FILELIST` display and achieve the same results as in the previous two paragraphs through the standard CMS line-oriented commands: `COPYFILE`, `RENAME`, `COMPARE`, `PRINT`, and `ERASE`. Do you prefer working off the `FILELIST` display or the line-oriented commands? Why?

Try to copy a file to the name of an existing file. How does CMS respond? What would you do if you still wanted to perform the copy?

List the contents of a file on the terminal through the CMS `TYPE` command. If the file is lengthy, how could you view only the first few lines?

CHAPTER 7

Formatting Files for Printing

All computer-using organizations need to produce formatted documents. By *format,* we mean that the information stored in a file must be properly arranged when printed. For example, a letter is a particular type of document that requires its own style of formatting for printing. The internal addresses, the date, the salutation, the body of the letter, and the closing all represent parts of the letter that must be properly arranged on the printed page of the final product. A book is another kind of document printed in its own special format with a table of contents, a preface, separate chapters, appendices, and index.

Output formatting capability is an essential feature of word processing. One tool required to support such word processing is an editor program like XEDIT. The other is the text formatting program.

Data processing personnel, secretaries, and managers require text formatting capabilities. Systems analysts use the text formatter in writing feasibility studies, design documents, and project descriptions; programmers employ it in program specifications and documentation.

Because there exists this need to format various kinds of documents for printing, a program product called SCRIPT is often used with VM/CMS to format documents. This product is also known by such names as SCRIPT/VS, SCRIPT/370, Document Composition Facility (DCF), and DCF /SCRIPT.

SCRIPT is *not* part of the VM/CMS operating system itself. It is a separately purchased program product. By providing a text formatter, however, SCRIPT fulfills such an essential function that it has become a de facto standard product available on the great majority of VM/CMS-based computers.

There are several distinct versions of SCRIPT. IBM Corporation presently markets SCRIPT/VS Release 3. This is the product upon which the examples in this chapter are based. It is possible that your computer runs an older version of this same product, in which case you will find that the

SCRIPT commands presented in this chapter are nearly the same as those in your own version of SCRIPT.

There also exists a popular version of SCRIPT available from the University of Waterloo. This package's commands are also similar to those discussed in this chapter. While there are minor incompatibilities between Waterloo SCRIPT and IBM SCRIPT, the languages are, for all practical purposes, similar enough that they can be considered two dialects of the same language.

The first step in using SCRIPT is to enter text into a file using any of the VM/CMS editors. XEDIT can be used for this purpose. In the data file, you imbed commands to the SCRIPT program. These SCRIPT commands convey instructions to the SCRIPT processor concerning the manner in which to format the document for printing. Now, run SCRIPT. This produces a formatted output file without the SCRIPT control words. The formatted output may be either sent directly to a printer, or routed to a disk file for storage and later use.

A SCRIPT file thus consists of two kinds of information: instructions to the SCRIPT processor, known as *control words;* and the actual text of the file. The SCRIPT control words are recognizable because they consist of two letters preceded by a period. They normally begin in the first column position of any line in the file.

Figure 7-1 summarizes the process of document formatting using SCRIPT. The file is created, using a VM/CMS text editor. The appropriate filetype for a document created for SCRIPT processing is `SCRIPT`. After data entry, this file is run through the SCRIPT processor, producing a formatted document. The output of the SCRIPT processor is sent either to the terminal screen, the printer, or a disk file.

Of course, after running a text file through the SCRIPT processor, it's possible that the formatted output does not look as anticipated. That is, you may have misjudged the effects of SCRIPT control words in formatting the output. In this case, go back and alter the original document and its imbedded SCRIPT control words via a text editor. Then, rerun the file through the SCRIPT processor. When the formatted output matches the desired document, you have completed corrections to the control words.

This iterative process of editing the document until the proper output is achieved via SCRIPT is represented in figure 7-1 by the loop arrow. Generally, you'll find SCRIPT control words so easy to use that you can achieve correctly formatted output with only one or two runs of the SCRIPT processor.

The remainder of this chapter introduces the principles of output formatting via SCRIPT by presenting a small subset of the SCRIPT control word commands. This chapter touches only the surface of a very large topic; there are well over one hundred SCRIPT control words. You will learn a core subset of SCRIPT keywords with which you can handle the fundamentals of document formatting. Continued practice with the product and reading the vendor's reference manuals can provide further expertise in document formatting.

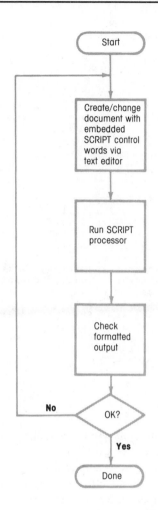

Figure 7-1
Output Formatting
via SCRIPT

Using SCRIPT

Figure 7-2 shows entry of a textual document into a file named **EXAMPLE SCRIPT A1**. After entering this information, and the command, **FILE**, you receive the ready prompt from CMS. At this time, enter this command:

```
SCRIPT  EXAMPLE  (NOPROF
```

The **SCRIPT** command sends this file for processing through the SCRIPT program. The filename of this file is **EXAMPLE**, and its filetype is assumed to be **SCRIPT**.

NOPROF is a SCRIPT command option. Like all CMS command options, this keyword follows a left parenthesis after the command. The parenthesis does not need to be closed with a corresponding right parenthesis. The SCRIPT **NOPROF** option is analogous in function to the **NOPROFILE** option seen earlier in the XEDIT command: it ensures that the

Figure 7-2   Input to SCRIPT

```
EXAMPLE   SCRIPT    A1  F  80   TRUNC=80 SIZE=11 LINE=0 COL=1 ALT=0




=====  * * * TOP OF FILE * * *
       !...+....1....+....2....+....3....+....4....+....5....+....6....+....7...
=====  Job Listing #37 - Wazulu College
=====
=====  Director of Academic Computing
=====
=====  Director of Academic Computing is responsible directly to College
=====  Bursar in providing a quality computing environment supporting
=====  35,000 students.  Applicant must have had at least 40 years computing
=====  experience, of which no less than 38 1/2 have been in a supervisory
=====  capacity overseeing a staff of no less than 500 FTE.  Complete
=====  familiarity with all aspects of mainframes and microcomputers
=====  required.  Salary $14,000 to $16,000 per annum.
=====  * * * END OF FILE * * *


====>  _
                                                         X E D I T   1 FILE
```

results of your own SCRIPT processing match those of this chapter as closely as possible.

The result of SCRIPT processing appears on the terminal for inspection. This output appears similar to that shown in figure 7-3. (It may appear slightly different depending on which version and release of SCRIPT your site has installed.)

Figure 7-3   Output from SCRIPT

```
Job Listing #37 - Wazulu College

Director of Academic Computing

Director  of  Academic  Computing is responsible directly to
College Bursar in providing a quality computing  environment
supporting  35,000  students.    Applicant  must have had at
least 40 years computing experience, of which no  less  than
38  1/2  have  been  in a supervisory capacity overseeing a
staff of no less than 500 FTE.   Complete  familiarity  with
all  aspects  of  mainframes  and  microcomputers  required.
Salary $14,000 to $16,000 per annum.
```

Notice that even though the file did not contain any SCRIPT control words (SCRIPT processor commands), the file has been formatted for printing based on certain SCRIPT defaults. The SCRIPT processor assumes these defaults in the absence of any control word commands to the contrary. Most noticeable among these SCRIPT defaults is justifying the input text at the right margin. SCRIPT inserts spaces between words in the text in order to produce this justification.

Another SCRIPT default automatically numbers pages. This particular version of SCRIPT places the page number in the bottom center of each page, enclosed within two dashes.

Less obvious are the SCRIPT defaults that define placement of the text on the output page. That is, output characteristics such as the size of the page margins and the number of characters per line were determined by SCRIPT defaults. Later, this chapter shows how to alter these defaults.

Figure 7-4 shows the same input document as that of figure 7-2, but this time with several imbedded SCRIPT control words. Each of these control words consists of two letters and begins with a period. Each instructs SCRIPT to take one of the formatting actions listed in table 7-1.

Table 7-1
SCRIPT Formatting
Commands

Control Word	Formatted Result
.ce	Centers one or more lines between the page margins
.cm	Allows insertion of a SCRIPT comment; associated text is not placed into the formatted output
.ds	Double spaces all subsequent lines (single spacing is the SCRIPT default)
.rf	Specifies one or more input lines as a "running footing" to be printed at the bottom of each page in the formatted document
.uc	Underscores and capitalizes one or more input lines
.up	Prints one or more input lines in upper case
.us	Underscores one or more input lines

Figure 7-4 Input to SCRIPT

```
.cm This example uses SCRIPT control words to format the document
.rf cancel

.uc Job Listing #37 - Wazulu College

.ce Director of Academic Computing

.ds
.us Director of Academic Computing
is responsible directly to College
Bursar in providing a quality computing environment supporting
35,000 students.  Applicant must have had at least 40 years computing
experience, of which no less than 38 1/2 have been in a supervisory
capacity overseeing a staff of no less than 500 FTE.  Complete
familiarity with all aspects of mainframes and microcomputers
required.
.up Salary $14,000 to $16,000 per annum.
```

Figure 7-5 shows the tremendous difference even these few SCRIPT control commands make in the formatted output. SCRIPT provides extensive formatting flexibility for very little effort.

Figure 7-5 Output from SCRIPT

```
JOB LISTING #37 - WAZULU COLLEGE
                Director of Academic Computing
Director  of  Academic  Computing is responsible directly to

College Bursar in providing a quality computing  environment

supporting  35,000  students.   Applicant  must have had at

least 40 years computing experience, of which no  less  than

38  1/2  have  been  in a supervisory capacity overseeing a

staff of no less than 500 FTE.  Complete  familiarity  with

all  aspects  of  mainframes  and  microcomputers  required.

SALARY $14,000 TO $16,000 PER ANNUM.
```

The output text is double-spaced. Individual elements of the text are centered, underscored, and capitalized. Note again the use of the SCRIPT default to justify the paragraph on the right side. SCRIPT automatically insures vertically flush left and right margins in the formatted output.

The first line in the input file is merely a SCRIPT comment. SCRIPT interprets the control word .cm (comment) to mean that the contents of the line are to be ignored; text appearing after the .cm command is not placed in the formatted output. Use this control word to imbed whatever commentary you wish in the file.

The .rf (running footing) control word identifies one or more lines of text that are repeated at the bottom of each output page. In this example, the special keyword cancel is used to simply turn off SCRIPT's default running footing of the page number enclosed within dashes. Thus, no running footing appears on the bottom of the output page in figure 7-5.

To identify some other running footing line, you might use the .rf command like this:

```
.rf on
XYZ CORPORATION PROPRIETARY
Unauthorized Duplication Punishable by Applicable Statutes
.rf off
```

This defines two lines of text that will appear on the bottom of subsequent document pages (until overridden by another use of the running footing control word). Note that SCRIPT processes the running footings (and running page headings) prior to processing the text for that page.

Thus, set up the running footing before the pages on which it is to occur, because the footing will not take effect until the next output page is produced. Later, this chapter shows how to make running headings and footings take effect immediately.

The `.uc` control word underscores and capitalizes the words following it on the same line. This control word can also underscore and capitalize any number of lines simply by specifying:

```
.uc n
```

where n is the number of lines to underscore and capitalize. Thus, `.uc 5` underscores and capitalizes the five lines following this command. Omission of n defaults this parameter to 1.

You can also underscore and capitalize an arbitrary number of input lines following this keyword by entering:

```
.uc on
```

and then entering:

```
.uc off
```

when the group of lines to be affected is completed. Thus, you can bracket a group of lines to be underscored and capitalized by these two uses of the `.uc` control word:

```
.uc on
This is the first line to underscore and capitalize.
This is the second.
And this is the last.
.uc off
```

These three lines will be underscored and capitalized. Subsequent lines in the input text are unaffected.

The `.us` (underscore) and `.up` (uppercase) control words are used in a manner similar to `.uc`. Both alter input text by underscoring words or translating to upper case, respectively. Use them as you would use `.uc`. Either place a group of words to alter on the same input line as the control word, specify the number of lines of input text to alter by a numeric operand following the control word, or enclose one or more lines to alter between the control words with the `on` and `off` operands. Thus, `.us 5` underscores the five lines of input text following the command, and `.up on` and `.up off` can enclose any number of lines of text to be printed in upper case.

In the example, the text to be affected by the `.us` and `.up` control words was placed on the same lines as those control words. Since no blank lines occur between the altered text and that which follows, SCRIPT formats both altered and unchanged text into a single paragraph. Placing text on the same line as its control word is an easy way to show exactly which words in the input text will be altered by SCRIPT in the output.

The `.ce` control word centers text in the output document. It is used in the same way as are `.uc`, `.us`, and `.up`. You can therefore: place the text to center on the same line as the `.ce` command, as in the example; specify that a number of lines following the `.ce` command should be centered; or, enclose a group of lines to center between a pair of `.ce on` and `.ce off` control words.

Finally, the `.ds` control word double spaces all subsequent lines in the input. It allows you to enter single-spaced text and easily convert it to a double-spaced document upon formatting. The SCRIPT default is single spacing, so you must specify `.ds` if you want double-spaced output. You can intersperse `.ds` and `.ss` (single spacing) as desired. In this example:

```
.ds
(first section of text)
.ss
(second section of text)
.ds
(third section of text)
```

all the text in the first section will be double-spaced. The second block of text will be single-spaced, and the third section of text is double-spaced. Use of these SCRIPT commands allows you to alter the line spacing in an output document at will.

Indents, Justification, Boxes, and Imbedded Files

In figure 7-6, the first new control word is `.in` (indent). As used here, `.in` indents all subsequent input text twenty positions. This effectively indents the two titles following this control word. The next occurrence of the indent keyword, `.in -20`, resets the left margin displacement twenty positions to the left, thereby restoring the original setting.

The indent control word with 0 as its operand:

```
.in 0
```

could also be used to restore the original left margin. It cancels the effect of any outstanding `.in` control word.

The `.sk` (skip) and `.sp` (space) control words occur several times in the input document. Each places a specified number of blank lines in the output document:

```
.sk 4
```

places four blank lines in the output. The operand to either `.sk` or `.sp` is multiplied by the line spacing presently in effect. Thus, the above com-

Figure 7-6   Input to SCRIPT

```
.cm Another example of using SCRIPT for document formatting
.rf cancel
.in +20
Wazulu College
.sp 2
Job Listing Booklet
.in -20
.sk
.fo off
The Job Listings in this booklet represent the present personnel
needs of Wazulu College for the 1986/87 academic year.  Applicants
interested in these positions must submit resumes, including complete
salary history and four letters of reference, no later than June 1.
.fo on
.ll 7i
.pa
Job Listing #36 - Wazulu College
.sp
Programmer/Analyst
.sk
Programmer/Analyst is responsible to Director of Academic Computing
in designing programs necessary to support the College's continuing
financial snafu.
.br
Five years experience required in each of the following computer
languages: Assembler, COBOL, PL/I, C, PASCAL, BASIC, RPGII, LISP and
PROLOG; and with each of the following operating systems: VM, MVS, DOS,
UNIX, and MS-DOS.
.br
Alternatively, one PhD or 15 years additional experience may be
substituted for each language proficiency missing from the above list.
.sp 4
.bx left right
.ce on
Salary is $6,000 to $6,400 per annum,
depending upon experience
.ce off
.bx off
.sk 4
.im example
```

mand would produce eight blank lines of output if double spacing were in effect. Where an operand is not provided:

> .sp

it defaults to 1. This command results in a single blank line in the output, assuming single spacing as shown in figure 7-7.

The difference between .sk and .sp is simply that .sp always inserts blank line(s) into the formatted output, and .sk inserts blank line(s) only if they would not occur at the top or bottom of an output page. (In some versions of SCRIPT, .sk inserts blank lines only if they would not occur at the top of a page.)

Following the first instance of the .sk control word in the example, the .fo off command turns off SCRIPT's automatic justification of input

Figure 7-7   Output from SCRIPT

```
                        Wazulu College


                     Job Listing Booklet

The Job Listings in this booklet represent the present personnel
needs of Wazulu College for the 1986/87 academic year.  Applicants
interested in these positions must submit resumes, including complete
salary history and four letters of reference, no later than June 1.


Job Listing #36 - Wazulu College

Programmer/Analyst

Programmer/Analyst is responsible to Director of Academic Computing in
designing  programs  necessary  to  support  the  College's continuing
financial snafu.
Five years experience required  in  each  of  the  following  computer
languages:  Assembler,  COBOL, PL/I, C, PASCAL, BASIC, RPGII, LISP and
PROLOG; and with each of the following  operating  systems:  VM,  MVS,
DOS, UNIX, and MS-DOS.

Alternatively,  one  PhD  or  15  years  additional  experience may be
substituted for each language proficiency missing from the above list.



+------------------------------------------------------------------+
!               Salary is $6,000 to $6,400 per annum,              !
!                     depending upon experience                    !
+------------------------------------------------------------------+



Job Listing #37 - Wazulu College

Director of Academic Computing

Director of Academic Computing  is  responsible  directly  to  College
Bursar  in providing a quality computing environment supporting 35,000
students.   Applicant must  have  had  at  least  40  years  computing
experience,  of  which  no less than 38 1/2 have been in a supervisory
capacity overseeing a staff of  no  less  than  500  FTE.    Complete
familiarity  with  all  aspects  of  mainframes  and  microcomputers
required.  Salary $14,000 to $16,000 per annum.
```

text at the right margin. The text following this control word retains the
ragged right margin of the input text. In the example, text which is not to
be justified is enclosed between the .fo off and .fo on commands. Like
the .ds and .ss keywords, these formatting control words can be interspersed at will throughout the input text. SCRIPT formats even and ragged
right margins as instructed.

One mysterious error beginners often encounter with SCRIPT con-
cerns confusion over SCRIPT's automatic concatenation and justification of
input text. If you enter input text with a ragged right margin:

```
First sentence not to justify.
Second sentence not to justify.
Third and last sentence that is not to be blocked off on right.
```

SCRIPT will format this text into a paragraph with an even right margin:

```
First  sentence not  to justify.   Second sentence not  to
justify. Third and last sentence that is not to be blocked
off on right.
```

To prevent this, you must turn off the formatting mode with the `.fo` off command. This input text would *not* be altered by SCRIPT:

```
.fo off
First sentence not to justify.
Second sentence not to justify.
Third and last sentence that is not to be blocked off on right.
```

Resume concatenation of input lines and justification of output lines at any time with the `.fo` on command.

Alternatively, the `.br` (break) control word can ensure that the line following this command is not concatenated with previous input text:

```
First sentence not to concatenate.
.br
Second sentence not to concatenate.
.br
Third and last sentence that is not to be concatenated.
```

These sentences will *not* be concatenated into a single paragraph with an even right margin due to the presence of the `.br` control word.

A third method to prevent SCRIPT from concatenating sentences into a single blocked paragraph is simply to enter the second (and subsequent) sentences in some character position other than the first one on each line. That is, SCRIPT only concatentates lines when words occur starting in the first character position in each line.

In the document of figure 7-6, the `.ll` (line length) control word occurs after the `.fo` (format) keywords. The `.ll` command sets the width of subsequent output lines. Its use in this example sets a printed width of seven inches `7i` for subsequent output.

The `.pa` (page eject) control word appears next. It forces an immediate skip to a new page in the output. Thus, `Job Listing #36...` occurs on a new page in the output. Specifying this control word with an operand:

```
.pa n
```

sets the page number of the next page as indicated. Thus,

> .pa 4

would skip to a new page and number it as page four.

Toward the end of the input text in the example, the .bx (box) control words cause SCRIPT to automatically draw a box around a block of text. The first occurrence of the .bx keyword begins the box, and the operands left and right cause vertical rules to be drawn at the left and right margins of the page. The .bx off command completes the box and ends the delineation of the text contained within it. The center control words bracket the boxed text, insuring that it is centered within the box.

Finally, the .im (imbed) command causes SCRIPT to process the file that the .im command names as its operand the same as if the text in that file were part of the current file. This instance of the imbed control word refers to the file **EXAMPLE SCRIPT A1** file, the file presented in figure 7-2. SCRIPT processes a file specified through the imbed command exactly as if the text of that file occurred at the point of the imbed control word. The SCRIPT formatting controls in effect apply to the processing against the imbedded file (except as altered by control words in the imbedded file). SCRIPT processing then resumes in the original file immediately following the imbed command.

The imbed command thus provides a powerful way to combine textual documents at the time of SCRIPT processing. One can partition a large document among many separate files and produce combined formatted output through SCRIPT. For example, several people could enter portions of a large document into several different input files. Yet, a single final document could be produced via SCRIPT's imbed feature. Proper use of SCRIPT provides great flexibility in the partitioning and formatting of large documents.

Running Heads, Tabs, and Footnotes

Following a SCRIPT comment identifying the input of figure 7-8, the .rh (running heading) command denotes the heading that will occur on all pages of the output document. The control words .rh on and .rh off surround the line(s) of the page heading. In this example, there will be two lines in the heading. The second of these lines illustrates the .sx (split text) command. This keyword produces output in three parts, each of which is spaced across the output page in the manner shown in figure 7-9. The slashes / in this line indicate the separate portions of the page heading. The option c, which immediately follows the control word .sx in the command, tells SCRIPT *not* to replicate the center page portion of the text Wazulu College. In other words, the center portion of the split text is normally replicated across the center column in the page. The c option prevents this.

The heading generated by the .rh and .rf control words normally

Figure 7-8   Input to SCRIPT

```
.cm A last example of SCRIPT control words

.rh on
Wazulu College Personnel Report
.sx c /S.B.H.E./Wazulu College/1986-87/
.rh off
.rh execute
.cm define equal sign ( = ) as the tab character
.ti = 05
.tp 24 31 38 47

.cm set top page margin to one inch
.tm 1i
.cm set bottom page margin to one inch
.bm 1i
.cm set page length to eleven inches
.pl 11i
.cm set page margins to 6 character positions
.pm 6

.sp 4;.fo on
This document describes in detail Wazulu College's projected personnel
needs during the coming academic year.  It compares the current year's
requirements versus previous years and describes the College's new
hiring philosophy.  The chart on the following page lists the raw
numbers of employees over the past several years and provides a
breakdown by employee type.
.fl on
.sp 4
.us Previous Requirements:  1983    1984    1985    Emp. Type
=42=44=41=:FTE
=121=133=122=:PTE
=11=13=12=:STE
=8=13=10=:GA
.fl off

.fn on
Note: All personnel requirements subject to legislative approval.
Final approval is expected by Christmas 1988.
.fn off
```

occurs for the first time on the first output page following their specification. The .rh execute command tells SCRIPT to make the page heading occur on the present output page. In the example, omission of the .rh execute command would have caused the running heading to appear for the first time only on output pages after its occurrence. Leaving out the .rh execute command in the example would have meant the page headings would only occur in the second output page.

The .ti control word translates the first character specified = into the second character indicated. Here the second character is the hexadecimal value 05. The effect of this command is to make the equal sign a *tab character,* since SCRIPT recognizes the hexadecimal value 05 for this purpose. A tab character on any input line denotes that the other information on that line is to be automatically spaced across the output line by SCRIPT. Thus, the .tp (tab position) command lists a group of vertical column alignments that represent output tab positions. Look at the data that is

Figure 7-9   Output from SCRIPT

```
Wazulu College Personnel Report
S.B.H.E.                      Wazulu College                    1986-87




This document describes in detail Wazulu College's projected
personnel  needs  during  the  coming  academic  year.     It
compares the current  year's  requirements  versus  previous
years  and  describes  the  College's new hiring philosophy.
The chart on the following page lists  the  raw  numbers  of
employees  over  the  past  several  years  and  provides  a
breakdown by employee type.



------------------
Note: All  personnel  requirements  subject  to  legislative
approval.  Final approval is expected by Christmas 1988.


Wazulu College Personnel Report
S.B.H.E.                      Wazulu College                    1986-87



Previous Requirements:    1983    1984    1985    Emp. Type
                           42      44      41       :FTE
                          121     133     122       :PTE
                           11      13      12       :STE
                            8      13      10       :GA
```

separated by equal signs toward the bottom of the input file. Figure 7-9 shows that SCRIPT stripped out the tab characters occurring in the input, and spaced the data items after each tab character to the column positions indicated by the tab position control word. The output demonstrates how SCRIPT's software tabbing feature was employed to create a simple table.

Four control words illustrate how to alter SCRIPT's placement of text on the printed page. One can easily set the top and bottom page margins, the left margin, and even SCRIPT's assumption as to the page length with the control words .tm, .bm, .pm, and .pl respectively.

Figure 7-10 shows the SCRIPT terminology and control words used for different portions of the printed page. Remember, in the absence of these control words, SCRIPT assumes defaults appropriate to the output device type.

After setting the page layout parameters, the .sp (space) control word tells SCRIPT to space four times. The .fo on (format) command turns on SCRIPT's automatic formatting capability for the lines following it. Multiple SCRIPT control words can be placed on a single input line, if separated by a semicolon.

The two occurrences of the .fl (float) control word enclose a group

Figure 7-10
SCRIPT Page
Layout

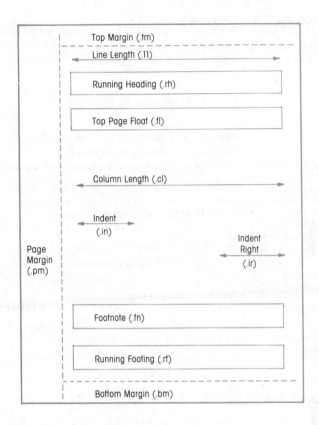

of lines that are kept together and are placed at the top of the next output page. The input lines are "floated" to the top of the next page. This accounts for the appearance of the table at the top of the second output page in figure 7-9.

The .fn (footnote) control words conclude the input file by enclosing a group of lines to appear as a footnote. The output shows that SCRIPT properly places this footnote at the bottom of the page. SCRIPT also prints a line immediately above the footnote, following accepted footnote style.

Advanced SCRIPT Capabilities

Remember, SCRIPT has many more commands than are presented here. Some of the advanced capabilities of SCRIPT include:

- selection of various character fonts (on supporting printers)
- control over page layout (including newspaper-style multiple columns per page)
- automatic creation of a Table of Contents
- building of document indexes

Additional SCRIPT Command Options

The beginning of this chapter described how to execute the SCRIPT processor:

```
SCRIPT  EXAMPLE  (NOPROF
```

against the document file named **EXAMPLE SCRIPT A1**. The SCRIPT processor has two dozen additional options other than **NOPROF**.

The **PRINT** option sends the output from the SCRIPT processor to the printer. Rather than displaying it on the terminal:

```
SCRIPT  EXAMPLE  (PRINT
```

sends the formatted document directly to the printer.

The **FILE** option permits you to direct the output of SCRIPT processing to a CMS file. To use it, specify a filename immediately after the **FILE** option:

```
SCRIPT  EXAMPLE  (FILE(OUTPUT))
```

sends the formatted version of **EXAMPLE SCRIPT A1** to the CMS file named **OUTPUT SCRIPT A1**. Override the default filetype **SCRIPT** and filemode **A1** by specifying them:

```
SCRIPT  EXAMPLE  (FILE(OUTPUT LISTING D1))
```

This example fully qualifies the output file name as **OUTPUT LISTING D1**.

The **CONTINUE** option on the SCRIPT command tells SCRIPT to keep processing even after an error is encountered in the input file. You would normally specify **CONTINUE** when debugging SCRIPT processor commands.

Finally, the **SPELLCHK** option automatically checks the input document for spelling errors. For example, the results of processing the document of figure 7-2 against SCRIPT's spelling checker is depicted in figure 7-11. Notice that what SCRIPT really does is compare each individual word in the input document versus the words contained in its spelling dictionary. Any input words not found in the SCRIPT dictionary are cited as possible spelling errors. From the descriptive information SCRIPT provides, you should be able to determine whether you need to correct a spelling error, or whether SCRIPT merely doesn't recognize a valid word. In the example, SCRIPT does not recognize the name of the college or several valid technical words.

The SCRIPT control word **.du** (dictionary update) provides a way to specify input words to the SCRIPT spelling dictionary for the processing of **a** particular document:

Figure 7-11 Output from SPELLCHK

```
script example (noprof spellchk
SCRIPT/VS RELEASE 3, LEVEL (0.1) - 10/10/86
WORDS NOT FOUND: Wazulu
'EXAMPLE' LINE 1: Job Listing #37 - Wazulu College
WORDS NOT FOUND: Bursar
'EXAMPLE' LINE 6: Bursar in providing a quality computing environment supporting
WORDS NOT FOUND: FTE
'EXAMPLE' LINE 9: capacity overseeing a staff of no less than 500 FTE.  Complete
WORDS NOT FOUND: mainframes
'EXAMPLE' LINE 10: familiarity with all aspects of mainframes and microcomputers


                                                  MORE...
```

```
.du add word1 word2 ... wordn
```

adds words to the SCRIPT dictionary. Adding words to make the example of figure 7-2 run cleanly can be done by placing this line in the beginning of the input document:

```
.du add Wazulu Bursar FTE mainframes
```

These new words are only in effect during the processing of the document in which the `.du` command appears. That is, you have not permanently added words to the SCRIPT spelling dictionary through the `.du` control word.

Generalized Markup Language

In addition to SCRIPT, IBM's DCF program product provides another document formatting language called the Generalized Markup Language (GML). GML control words are referred to as GML *tags*. They are interspersed in an input document in exactly the same manner as SCRIPT control words. However, GML tags begin with a colon **:** and normally end with a period (as opposed to SCRIPT control words, which begin with periods).

Rather than specifying processing actions like SCRIPT control words, GML tags identify particular parts of documents. Then, processing appropriate to that portion of the document occurs in response to the tag. For example, paragraphs are denoted by the **:p.** (paragraph) tag. When DCF encounters this GML tag, it formats the text that follows it as a new paragraph.

The key difference between the GML and SCRIPT is that these two languages embody entirely different approaches to output formatting. GML denotes particular parts of documents (headings, paragraphs, footings, etc.). Documents are formatted according to these identifying tags.

With SCRIPT, the user directs the SCRIPT processor to take specific actions (skipping lines or pages, indenting lines, centering text, etc.).

GML and SCRIPT represent conceptually different approaches to document formatting because GML tags indicate parts of documents while SCRIPT control words specify processing actions.

Each approach has its benefits. GML enables an organization to easily standardize and control its paperwork. The organization can insure that documents of the same kind (internal memos, scientific reports, etc.) match the organization's standards because GML document tags specify processing according to document part and type. Word processing personnel and secretarial staff often find this GML approach easier to understand.

On the other hand, SCRIPT's command-oriented approach appeals to people who want to directly specify format-processing actions. SCRIPT makes relatively complex or unusual formatting requirements easy to achieve. People with technical and programming backgrounds often prefer it to GML.

Neither SCRIPT nor GML appears superior across the board. Both are easy to learn, easy to use, and quite powerful. SCRIPT/VS is more widely used, although GML yields higher productivity.

For Further Information

This chapter provided a simple introduction to document formatting in the VM/CMS environment. It demonstrated the most common product for this purpose, SCRIPT/VS. This introduction covers a small but highly effective subset of the SCRIPT language. Keep in mind that only two dozen (of over 100) SCRIPT commands were presented. The objective is to make you functional as quickly as possible, and put you in the position of being able to use the product and gain "hands-on" experience.

You should now be able to approach the vendor's product reference manuals with confidence. Among these manuals, the *DCF: SCRIPT/VS Text Programmer's Guide, SH35-0069*, provides complete and well-illustrated explanations of the many ways to use SCRIPT control words in document processing. The *DCF: SCRIPT/VS Language Reference, SH35-0070*, alphabetically lists and describes each SCRIPT control word. Using the material of this chapter as a basis, you can now use SCRIPT and refer to these manuals as required to augment your knowledge.

GML is described in other vendor's reference manuals. The *DCF: GML Starter Set User's Guide, SH20-9186*, provides a progressive introduction to the use of GML tags. *DCF: GML Starter Set Reference, SH20-9187*, lists and describes all tags alphabetically. Perhaps the simplest introduction to this topic is found in the *VM/SP CMS Primer, Release 3, SC24-5236*. While very brief, this introduction gives you the flavor of GML tags by presenting a very simple subset. Note that these three manuals also reference several more technical manuals pertaining to advanced GML capabilities.

Test Your Understanding

What is the purpose of text-formatter programs like SCRIPT? How does the function of SCRIPT differ from that of XEDIT?

Enter your own job description into a CMS file. Use SCRIPT control words to center a paragraph title, to underline the job title in the job description, to double space the text, and to underscore and capitalize a portion of the text. Comment your work by using SCRIPT comment control words. Now run the SCRIPT processor on your sample text and display the formatted document on the terminal.

Update your job description by turning off the running footing, adding a running page heading, and single spacing the document. Run the SCRIPT processor twice against the file, printing the formatted output text the first time and writing it to an output file of the name `OUTPUT INFO A1` the second time.

SCRIPT defaults to formatting paragraphs with even margins. How do you override this default? Is there more than one way to accomplish this? Enter a test document in which you vary whether

SCRIPT concatenates and justifies the text. Verify the accuracy of your SCRIPT control words by processing the document through SCRIPT.

Check your spelling in the document via the SCRIPT spelling checker. If your document contains valid words that SCRIPT flags as misspelled, how do you temporarily add words to the SCRIPT dictionary to overcome this?

Look up how to prepare indexes through SCRIPT in the manuals. Do you identify words for indexing?

What are the differences in approach to text formatting between SCRIPT and GML? Do you have access to both languages on your system?

SECTION 3

The Virtual Machine Environment

- Several Views of VM/CMS
- The Virtual Machine Philosophy
- Controlling and Configuring Your Virtual Machine
- Additional Virtual System Resources

CHAPTER 8

Several Views
of VM/CMS

What major components make up CMS and CP? What software is commonly installed in addition to the operating system? What are the roles of common VM/CMS software products and how do they fit together? This chapter shows several conceptual frameworks through which VM/CMS can be considered.

The Software Component View of VM/CMS

One approach to understanding VM/CMS analyzes the software components that comprise the system. Remember, CP manages the physical resources of the real computer system, and CMS is a single-user operating system that runs under CP. Table 8-1 summarizes the roles of these VM /CMS components.

	CP	CMS
Table 8-1 The Roles of CP and CMS	Manages the physical resources of the real computer	A highly interactive, single-user operating system which runs on its own virtual machine
	Creates and maintains virtual machines for software that uses CP's virtual machine facility	Supports file creation and manipulation
	Includes commands for control and modification of virtual machine configurations	Supports many application programs and systems
	Manages input/output requests from virtual machines to real devices	Includes complete set of commands and tools for program development targeted toward multiple operating systems

Each of these two major components consists of logical subcomponents. CP contains the *Inter-User Communication Vehicle* (IUCV) and the *Virtual Machine Communication Facility* (VMCF).

IUCV is that part of CP that manages communications among programs within the VM/SP system. IUCV facilitates communication between different virtual machines on the same physical computer, and between the virtual machines and CP. This latter case represents virtual machine operating system requests for CP system services. For example, virtual machines request console communication services, message system services, and disk input/output (I/O) services.

VMCF enables virtual machines to send and receive data to and from other virtual machines. VMCF is composed of various functions to control and facilitate data transfer.

The CMS component also contains several environments or facilities:

- XEDIT, the System Product Editor
- CMS Batch Virtual Machine Facility
- several command procedure languages, including the System Product Interpreter, REXX
- the system-provided assembly language translator
- the DEBUG environment for debugging assembler language programs
- the CMS/DOS environment for developing and testing programs targeted at DOS operating systems

The CMS Batch Virtual Machine is a CMS facility that allows users to submit *background programs* or *batch* programs for computer processing. Batch programs do not interact with terminal users. Instead, once they are submitted, background jobs run to completion without any further interaction with terminal users. Programs designed for batch processing typically read their input data through such devices as disks, tapes, and card readers, and they produce their outputs on disks, tapes, and printers.

Compilation of a large program exemplifies the utility of the CMS batch machine facility. As a CMS user, you compile a program simply by entering the appropriate language translator command to CMS. However, this "foreground compilation" ties up the terminal. An alternative is to send the compilation task to your system's CMS batch machine facility for background processing. Then, proceed to other work at your terminal. The CMS batch machine returns the compilation results back to you at your CMS virtual machine when the job is completed. Use the CMS batch machine to avoid tying up your terminal during execution of long-running programs.

Command procedure languages are interpreted programming languages that allow you to issue CMS and CP commands. They provide the capability to direct execution of the operating system commands logically. Use command procedures to issue complex or lengthy series of CMS and CP commands automatically, thereby avoiding the tedious and error-prone retyping of these commands.

CMS supplies three command procedure languages: EXEC, EXEC2, and REXX. REXX is the official System Product Interpreter of Release 3 (and later releases) of VM/CMS. Section 6 of this book teaches how to program using REXX.

CMS includes the system assembly language translator and an assembly-level program called DEBUG. You enter the testing environment for assembler programs under CMS by issuing the `DEBUG` command. The DEBUG environment then has its own set of subcommands that help in debugging the assembly program code. Section 5 contains further information on assembly language programming and debugging under CMS.

CMS also includes an environment called CMS/DOS for the development and testing of DOS programs. Chapter 18 describes use of this environment.

Additional VM/SP Components

There are many other software components of a large and complex operating system like VM/CMS. This list of VM/CMS operating system components includes only the software components that actually come with a VM/SP program product license. Typical VM/CMS installations run a number of separately purchased program products as well. These products may either be *system-level,* that is, products that are logical additions or extensions to the VM/SP operating system itself, or they may be *application-level* products. Application-level products run under the auspices of system-level components and often invoke the services provided by the system-level software.

The available literature on VM/CMS does not always make clear that certain separately purchased system-level program products do not come with VM/SP, but must be licensed separately. Confusion centers on these important products:

- RSCS, the Remote Spooling Communications Subsystem
- IPCS, the Interactive Problem Control Subsystem
- VM/Pass-Through Facility
- VM/SP HPO, the VM/SP High Performance Option

In VM/SP Release 3, RSCS is a separately licensed program product that manages data transfer among multiple, distributed VM/CMS-based computers. It provides an easy way for terminal users to send data files and messages to users on other VM/CMS computers. It also helps terminal users print files on remote network printers.

RSCS runs as its own virtual machine, under CP. It is distinguished from IUCV, which is a part of CP, in that RSCS is concerned with connections across more than one physical computer. As part of CP, IUCV handles communications within a single VM/SP-based computer.

Since RSCS facilitates communications between VM/CMS computers, it runs on each computer participating in the RSCS network.

IPCS is a tool for the system administrators and system programmers who oversee and maintain operation of a VM/CMS system. IPCS aids in diagnosing system-level software failures and in problem reporting. The product runs as an application under CMS.

The VM/Pass-Through Facility is a program product that permits terminal users to interactively access different VM/CMS-based computers. VM/Pass-Through does this in such a way that it appears to the CMS user that his terminal is actually attached to the remote VM/CMS system. VM/Pass-Through runs on each computer participating in the network.

The VM/SP High Performance Option makes VM/SP's Control Program more efficient. VM/SP HPO includes a wide range of CP support extensions to enhance VM/CMS operation. It is also a separately purchased program product.

Classifications of VM/CMS Components

There are several different approaches to the classification of VM/CMS software components. The preceding material implicitly describes VM/CMS systems on the basis of which software components are part of the VM/SP program product license itself, and which program products are independently purchased. This is a valid and useful approach because the VM/SP program product constitutes a base level VM/CMS system, a system whose components are common to all VM/SP users. Particular installations may or may not install the separately purchased program products mentioned.

The *program product component view* of VM/CMS yields the classification of VM/CMS software components in table 8-2.

SQL/DS is a complete relational database management system installed on many VM/CMS computers. PROFS is an office-automation system for end users. ISPF and DMS/CMS are programmer support tools. These and other separately purchased program products available for the VM/CMS environment are described in section 7 of this book.

The program product component view of VM/CMS software is rigorous in that one can easily classify a VM/CMS program as either separately licensed or not. However, it is sometimes arguable as to how useful such a classification may be in terms of analyzing the VM/CMS components and their software functions. Another approach to defining VM/CMS components that is just as rigorous is the *virtual machine component view*, categorizing programs by whether they control their own virtual machine. Some program products on VM/CMS-based computers run as their own virtual machine (or operating system) under CP. Others run under the virtual machine controlled by a separate program product, while some merely represent an environment within another program product.

		Separately Licensed Components Installed at Many
	VM/SP Components	**VM/CMS Sites**

Table 8-2
VM/CMS Software
Components

VM/SP Components	Separately Licensed Components Installed at Many VM/CMS Sites

CP
    includes: IUCV and VMCF
CMS
    includes: XEDIT, CMS EDIT
    editors; CMS Batch Machine
    Facility; 3 command procedure
    languages; assembly language
    translator; assembly DEBUG
    environment; CMS/DOS
    environment
	RSCS
	IPCS
	VM/SP HPO
	VM/Pass-Through
	Program language translators like
	   COBOL, PL/I, BASIC, many
	   others
	SCRIPT
	SQL/DS
	ISPF
	DMS/CMS
	PROFS
	Many other program products from
	   IBM and other vendors

For example, VM/CMS software components that run in their own virtual machine include:

- CMS
- RSCS
- SQL/DS
- VM/Pass-Through
- OS operating systems (MVS/XA, MVS/SP, etc.)
- DOS operating systems (DOS/VSE, DOS, etc.)
- UNIX operating systems (IX/370, etc.)
- Other operating systems (PICK, etc.)

Those components that run within the virtual machine of another component are listed in table 8-3.

Figure 8-1 diagrams several VM/CMS software components that run in their own virtual machines. Such components can all be considered operating systems. Some of these cannot exist outside the VM/CMS environment; they can only run in the virtual machine created and maintained by the Control Program component of VM/SP. Examples of these *host-dependent systems* are: CMS, the single-user interactive operating system developed for VM/CMS; RSCS, a single-purpose operating system designed to implement networking between VM/CMS computers; and, SQL/DS, a virtual machine that maintains shared databases between CMS users on a single VM/CMS computer.

Of these host-dependent systems, some are called *service virtual machines,* because they exist simply to provide particular services to other virtual machines. Examples of these are RSCS and SQL/DS.

Table 8-3
VM/CMS Software
Components That
Run within the
Virtual Machine of
Another
Component

Components	Component Relationship
XEDIT, CMS EDIT editors	Part of CMS
CMS Batch Machine Facility	Part of CMS
Command Procedure Languages	Part of CMS
Assembly DEBUG Facility	Part of CMS
Assembly Language	Part of CMS
CMS/DOS	Part of CMS
High-level Programming Language (COBOL, BASIC, PL/I, etc.)	Run under CMS
Many programmer tools like ISPF, DMS/CMS, etc.	Run under CMS
IPCS	Runs under CMS
IUCV	Part of CP
VMCF	Part of CP
VM/SP HPO	Add-in part of CP
Many applications for end-users	Run under CMS

Figure 8-1
VM/CMS
Operating Systems

MACHINE HARDWARE							
CONTROL PROGRAM (CP)							
CMS	RSCS	SQL/DS	MVS/SP	DOS/VSE	VM/SP	IX/370	ETC.

Other software components requiring their own virtual machines under VM/CMS are capable of running in *native mode* on their own computers (without CP). Division of virtual machine operating systems into guest operating systems and host-dependent virtual machines indicates which virtual machine components were designed specifically for the VM/CMS environment. Components created solely for VM/CMS tend to have more narrowly defined functionality than general-purpose operating systems.

Unlike the program product and virtual machine views of VM/CMS software, the level-oriented view cannot rigorously distinguish among VM /CMS components. Classification of components as system- or application-level requires subjective judgments. However, this approach does give an idea concerning the roles of different programs within VM/CMS. Table 8-4 categorizes VM/CMS software by level.

The program product, virtual machine, and level-oriented taxonomies of VM/CMS software are important because, all too often, users proficient in the use of individual VM/CMS components lack conceptual understanding of the overall system. This is to be expected in the case of a large, complex operating system such as VM/CMS. Nevertheless, a high-level overview helps in understanding the system interrelationships that are so important to effective use of VM/CMS.

The next chapter probes the relationship of the virtual machine view of VM/CMS software to CMS. It explains how virtual machine concepts

Table 8-4
Level-Oriented
View of Software
Components

System-level Products	Application-level Products
CP	Programming language translators
CMS	(like COBOL, BASIC, PL/I, etc.)
RSCS	Programmer tools like ISPF
IPCS	and DMS/CMS
VM/Pass-Through	SCRIPT
VM/SP HPO	Many applications oriented
	towards end-users

create the philosophy that underlies the entire CMS system, and relates this understanding to specific CP/CMS commands and their use.

Release 4 of VM/SP

Part of the confusion concerning the roles of different VM/CMS software products is that the classifications of these components have shifted over the various releases of VM/CMS. The above taxonomy is based on Release 3 of VM/SP. Several changes have occurred with Release 4 of VM/SP. First, a new component named Group Control System (GCS) comes with the VM /SP Release 4 license. GCS runs in its own virtual machine as a virtual machine supervisor for a group of communications software components that support full Systems Network Architecture (SNA) capability. SNA is IBM's definition of rules and protocols for the sending of data across computer networks. These networks may be *heterogeneous,* meaning that they consist of geographically distributed systems involving diverse computer hardware and operating systems. Some of the communications components associated with GCS under Release 4 include RSCS, Advanced Communications Function/Virtual Terminal Access Method (ACF/VTAM), and VM SNA Console Support (VSCS).

GCS is host-dependent, and although it is included with the VM/SP Release 4 license, installations may or may not choose to install it. GCS is the umbrella product for a group of related programs implementing SNA under VM/SP.

One other Release 4 VM/SP change of note is that IPCS is now a facility of CMS. The VM/SP product license includes IPCS, and it runs as an application under CMS, as before.

The Environment View of VM/CMS

The component views of VM/CMS classify, through several taxonomies, the software components which comprise VM/CMS at typical installations. The *environment view* looks instead at the logical groupings of commands, or *command sets,* which the terminal user may issue at any particular time. Each environment supports a universe of commands and responds to those commands in a known manner. Certain keys and commands transit terminal users between environments. Environments are also referred to as *modes*.

Figure 8-2 diagrams the major VM/CMS environments, the commands executable in each, and the methods of transition from one environment to another.

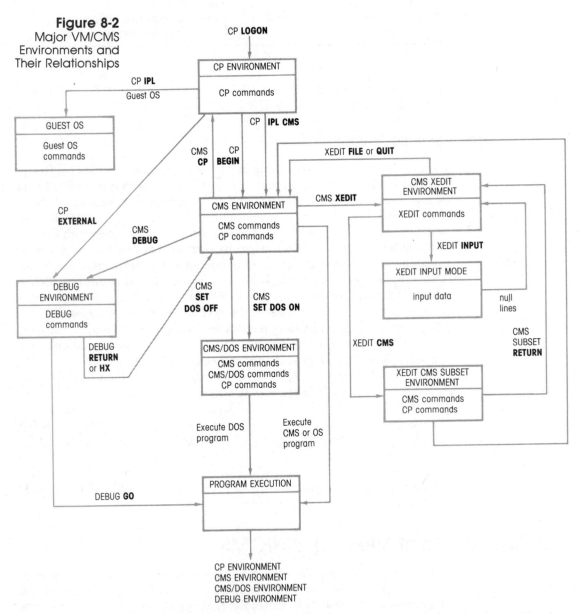

Figure 8-2
Major VM/CMS
Environments and
Their Relationships

You initially gain system access by the CP **LOGON** command. This places you in contact with CP. Here, you may issue any CP commands allowable within your *privilege class*. Privilege classes are groupings of CP commands that enforce a security system. (Some CP commands are highly sensitive and restricted to the system administrators.)

Once in the CP environment, you issue the CP `IPL` command to establish your CMS virtual machine. It might be possible to IPL a guest operating system, such as MVS or DOS/VSE, if the VM/CMS installation has licensed and set up access to these systems. In this book, the assumption is that users IPL the CMS operating system.

Once in CMS, users can issue any CMS command. You can also issue CP commands in one of several ways. One way is to preface the CP command with the letters `CP`:

    CP cp-command

tells CMS to pass the command to CP for execution. The response to the CP command appears on the terminal and is followed by the CMS ready prompt `R;`.

Another way to issue CP commands from the CMS environment is to enter:

    CP

without any CP command. You receive the `CP READ` status message in the bottom right-hand corner of the screen. Now enter any CP commands permitted in your privilege class. Restore your virtual machine to the state it was in prior to the interruption by entering the CP `BEGIN` command:

    BEGIN

A third way to issue CP commands from within CMS is via the `#CP` function:

    #CP cp-command

This places you in direct communication with CP. You can enter any CP command allowed your privilege class. For example, use the `#CP` function to display the current time and date:

    #CP QUERY TIME

The `#CP` function can be entered from many of the other environments shown in figure 8-2 including the CMS/DOS, DEBUG, CMS, XEDIT, and XEDIT CMS SUBSET environments. Use the `#CP` function to issue direct CP commands from any of these environments.

The final way to issue CP commands from within the CMS environment is merely to enter them (without the `CP` prefix or via the `#CP` function). In this method, CMS recognizes that the command you entered is not a valid CMS command, and therefore passes it to CP. However, in order for this to occur, you must have the *implied CP function* (IMPCP) turned on.

Use the CMS `QUERY` command with the `IMPCP` operand to determine the status of the implied CP function:

    QUERY IMPCP

If the response is:

```
IMPCP     = ON
```

your CP commands are automatically passed to CP for execution. If the response is:

```
IMPCP     = OFF
```

issue the CMS `SET` command with appropriate operands to turn on the implied CP function:

    SET IMPCP ON

CMS defaults with the implied CP function `ON` when you IPL.

It is important to realize that although there are several ways to enter CP commands from within the CMS environment, it is not possible to enter CMS commands from within the CP environment. To execute CMS commands, you must first initiate the CMS environment by entering the CP `IPL CMS` command.

From within CMS, the terminal user can enter one of several environments. For example, entering the `XEDIT` command summons XEDIT. Here, you use the XEDIT commands to enter and alter the data of a file.

From within XEDIT, enter the input mode, or XEDIT input environment, by entering the XEDIT subcommand `INPUT`, as demonstrated in chapter 4. Exit the editor's input mode by sending null lines. Now you are back in XEDIT.

From XEDIT, access the CMS Subset environment by entering the XEDIT command `CMS`. The editor responds:

```
CMS SUBSET
```

Now you can enter many CMS commands. The special CMS Subset environment command RETURN returns you to XEDIT. Also, you can enter the immediate command HX (Halt Execution). This aborts the editing session and immediately returns you to CMS.

From within XEDIT, you can also execute a single CMS command by entering it on the XEDIT command line. In this case, prefix the CMS command by the letters CMS.

In addition to entering the various environments associated with the editor environment, you can also execute user-written programs from within the CMS environment. Once program execution begins, you cannot execute CMS or CP commands. However, executing programs can be interrupted by an *attention interruption*. Attention interruptions are either directed at the virtual machine operating system, CMS, or at CP. Pressing the ENTER key changes the CMS virtual machine to VM READ status, at which point commands can be entered. Pressing the PA1 key (or its equivalent on various terminals) results in entry to the CP environment. Here, you can enter CP commands. Resume the interrupted program's execution via the CP BEGIN command:

    BEGIN

Now you are executing the original program under CMS again.

Another environment accessible from CMS is the CMS/DOS environment, which is used to compile, debug, and run programs written for the DOS family of operating systems. It consists of the regular CMS command set plus a group of commands specifically oriented toward the development of DOS-oriented programs. You can also execute CP commands from within CMS/DOS in the same manner as under CMS. Execution of DOS programs under CMS/DOS places you into the program execution environment in the same way as execution of CMS or OS programs does within the CMS environment.

Enter the CMS/DOS environment from CMS by entering the CMS SET command with the DOS ON operands:

    SET DOS ON

Exit of CMS/DOS is accomplished when you IPL CMS again, or by entering:

    SET DOS OFF

The Debug environment is a facility of CMS designed for the testing and debugging of assembly language programs. It supports over a dozen commands that permit inspection of the virtual machine registers and other status indicators during program execution. It facilitates the setting of *breakpoints,* or addresses at which program execution is suspended, so that you can inspect the virtual machine's status in real time.

From CMS, use the CMS DEBUG command to enter the Debug environment. Enter Debug from CP by the command EXTERNAL (assuming an initial IPL to CMS). The CP EXTERNAL command causes an external interrupt to your virtual machine.

Return to the CMS environment from Debug by several methods. Program completion automatically returns you to CMS. Entry of the Debug command HX also returns you to CMS. Finally, if you entered the Debug environment from CMS, the Debug RETURN command brings you back to CMS.

Occasional confusion concerning the many VM/CMS environments is to be expected, but there is an easy way to determine which environment you are in. Simply press the ENTER key (enter a null line). The VM/CMS environment displays its name on the terminal.

For Further Information

Separately purchased software products mentioned in this chapter are individually described in section 7 of this book.

The reference manual, *VM/SP Introduction,* explains the functions of many VM/CMS software components and separately purchased programs on an overview level. Since the components evolve, the reference manual number varies according to the release of VM/SP: Release 4, GC19-6200-3; Release 3, GT00-1349 (formerly GC19-6200-2); Release 2, GQ19-6200; Release 1, GT19-6200.

In addition, the *VM/SP CMS User's Guide, SC19-6210,* contains a chapter entitled "VM/SP Environments and Mode Switching." That chapter presents a complete explanation of the VM/CMS environments and how to switch between them. The *VM/SP Terminal Reference, GC19-6206,* also tells how to switch between VM/CMS command environments.

Test Your Understanding

List the major functions of CP and CMS. Why is this division of functionality appropriate?

What is the function of IUCV within VM/CMS? How is this similar to or different from the role of RSCS?

What is a CMS "environment"? Name several environments within CMS.

Name several software programs that run in their own virtual machine under VM/SP. Which of these are operating systems? Which are "host-dependent" virtual machines? Which are guest operating systems? What does it mean to say that an operating system runs in "native mode"?

Refer to table 8-4. Do you disagree with any of the classifications in the chart?

What are a few of the major differences between VM/SP Release 4 and VM/SP Release 3?

What is GCS? Why is it important to VM/CMS sites?

What are CP command privilege classes? What is their role within VM/CMS?

You want to issue the CP `QUERY TIME` command. Show two ways to do this from within CMS. How would you issue this command from other CMS environments?

From within CMS, turn off the implied CP function. Now issue the CP `QUERY TIME` command. What must you do differently to issue this command properly when the implied CP function is off versus when it is on?

How do you enter the CMS/DOS environment from CMS? How do you exit it? Can you issue CMS commands from within the CMS /DOS environment?

CHAPTER 9

The Virtual Machine Philosophy

The previous chapter considered the total VM/CMS system in terms of both the software components and the operating environments of which it is composed. This chapter further details the virtual machine view of VM /CMS. VM's most fundamental characteristic is its "virtual machine" philosophy, a unique approach to operating system design. The virtual machine principle is responsible for many of VM/SP's strengths as an operating system. For example, VM is unique among major operating systems in supporting guest operating systems and thereby creating a multiple operating system environment on a single computer.

The virtual machine philosophy is directly reflected in how you, as a CMS terminal user, interact with VM/CMS. Understanding virtual machine concepts underlies effective use of this operating system. Many CMS commands relate to virtual machine concepts; certainly, most of the CP commands for general users fall into this category.

CP's Approach to Virtualization

A real computer consists of various hardware resources. Mainframe computers typically include one or more of each of the physical devices listed in table 9-1.

CP virtualizes the real computer into a number of virtual machines. Each virtual machine is the functional equivalent of a real computer. CP makes it appear to the operating system running in each virtual machine that that operating system controls physical (real) devices.

CP virtualizes the processor(s) through a technique called *time slicing*. Time slicing means that each virtual machine receives a portion of the real processor's time. Since CP controls the physical computer, the virtual machines are not even aware of the time slicing. Each virtual machine operat-

Table 9-1
Mainframe
Computer
Hardware

Hardware Component	Function
Processor	Executes instructions of computer programs
Main memory	Internal storage for executing programs and data
System console	Terminal through which system administrators control the system
Card reader	Input device for punched data cards
Card punch	Output device for punching data cards
Printer	Prints output
Disk drive	Magnetic media storage featuring direct data access
Tape drive	Magnetic media storage for volume data storage permitting sequential data access only

ing system runs under the illusion that it is fully in control of the real processor.

Card readers, card punches, and printers are *unit record devices.* They must be dedicated solely to a particular program for the duration of that program's execution. Otherwise, input to (and output from) different programs would be interspersed.

These *dedicated devices* render a multi-user computer system slow and inefficient because programs must wait for access to devices they require. CP circumvents the problems associated with dedicated unit record devices by virtualizing unit record equipment through a technique called *spooling.* Spooling means that output directed to a physical card punch or printer is intercepted by CP's spooling facility. The information sent to a unit record device is collected by the spooling facility and routed to a disk file under CP control. For card readers, spooling means that cards are read into intermediate spool files. CP presents card data to the virtual machine from this virtualized card reader.

Figure 9-1 shows the manner in which CMS commands (**PRINT,** **PUNCH,** and **READCARD**) cause input or output of data. These I/O files are intercepted by CP's spooling facility and collected in CP-controlled queues on disk. (Figure 9-1 represents these intermediate spooling queues as circles.) CP is then free to route the spooled files to the real unit record devices it controls at the appropriate time. CP's spooling facility interfaces with the virtual machine's CMS commands for unit record I/O so that the virtual machine operating system thinks it is communicating with real devices. CP's control of spool files thereby permits shared use of otherwise dedicated unit record devices.

The intermediate spooling of files allows CP to queue and schedule input/output to real unit record devices so that I/O records are not interspersed. CP's spooling technique gives each virtual machine the illusion that it controls real input/output equipment.

CP virtualizes a real disk through a *minidisk,* a portion of a real disk made to appear by CP as a real disk to a virtual machine operating system.

From the operating system viewpoint, CP logically divides each phys-

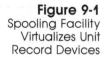

Figure 9-1
Spooling Facility
Virtualizes Unit
Record Devices

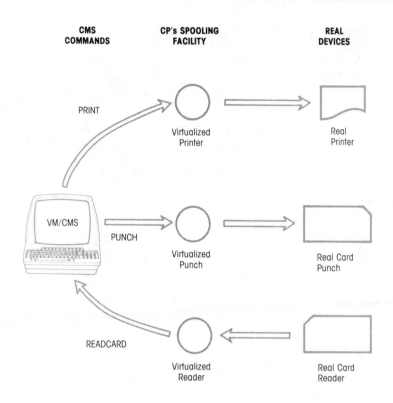

CMS
COMMANDS

CP's SPOOLING
FACILITY

REAL
DEVICES

PRINT

Virtualized
Printer

Real
Printer

VM/CMS

PUNCH

Virtualized
Punch

Real Card
Punch

READCARD

Virtualized
Reader

Real Card
Reader

ical disk drive into one or more minidisks. Since each minidisk appears like a real disk to the virtual machine to which it is assigned, users in different virtual machines may share physical disks with other users without being aware of it.

Finally, CP virtualizes real storage through *virtual storage* techniques. *Real storage* is the memory inside the computer in which executing programs reside, and is also sometimes referred to as *main memory* or *internal memory*.

In its allocation of real storage between virtual machines, CP breaks executing programs and their in-memory data into small units, called *pages*. Not all pages necessary for execution of a program reside in main memory. Instead, disk space is substituted for real memory; disk storage supplies virtual storage. As pages on disk are required in main memory, they are moved into internal memory by CP. This process of moving pages from disk storage to real storage is called *demand paging*.

Thus, CP's virtual storage technique uses both real storage and disk storage to create the illusion that the computer contains more real storage than it actually does. Users can run programs larger than real memory; programmers do not have to segment large programs into overlays in order to fit into real memory. CP's virtual storage concept stretches the real storage available in the computer system in a manner transparent to virtual machine operating systems, terminal users, and application programs.

The CMS Virtual Machine

As a CMS user, you control your own virtual machine, the functional equivalent of a full mainframe computer. Figure 9-2 diagrams a typical CMS virtual machine. You control your virtual machine through your *virtual console,* or terminal, which has many of the capabilities of a mainframe console. Like every virtual device, the virtual console is assigned a virtual address. A *virtual device address* constitutes a unique hexadecimal identifier within your virtual machine. The virtual console is located at virtual device address 009.

Figure 9-2
A Typical CMS
Virtual Machine

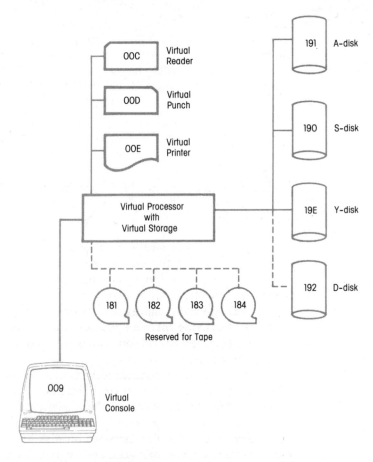

Three unit record devices are attached to the virtual machine. They are the virtual reader, virtual punch, and virtual printer, at virtual device addresses 00C, 00D, and 00E, respectively.

CMS virtual machines normally have at least three minidisks. At virtual addresses 191, 190, and 19E, they are the A-disk, S-disk, and Y-disk, respectively. The A-disk is your "work disk," the minidisk on which you normally enter your files. The S-disk is the CMS system disk, and the Y-disk an extension of it. Some CMS virtual machines also have a D-disk at device address 192, and even other minidisks. A major benefit of the virtual machine philosophy is that different virtual machines are configured in different ways appropriate to their users. Thus, your own virtual machine configuration may vary from the basic CMS configuration presented in figure 9-2.

Table 9-2 lists the basic virtual disk configuration common to most CMS users.

Table 9-2
Virtual Disk
Configuration

Filemode	Minidisk Virtual Address	Minidisk Use
S	190	Operating system minidisk for CMS, CMS resides here
A	191	Primary minidisk for user work
D	192	Additional (optional) minidisk for user work
Y	19E	Extension of the operating system minidisk for additional system files

As the table indicates, the filemode letter portion of CMS file names corresponds to the disk letter of the minidisk on which they reside. For example, this file:

```
testfile   cobol   a1
```

has a filemode letter of **a**, which indicates that the file resides on the virtual disk the CMS user accesses as his A-disk.

A CMS virtual machine may use up to four tape drives at one time. These use reserved virtual device addresses 181, 182, 183, and 184. In order for a CMS virtual machine to use a tape, the tape must be mounted and attached to that virtual machine by the system operator, who is the system administrator or operator of the real VM/SP system (not the terminal users at their CMS virtual consoles).

To request tape usage, you send a message to the system operator. The operator mounts the tape and attaches the device to your virtual machine. You receive a message back to your terminal when this has been accomplished. The CMS commands involved in tape use are described in section 5.

Tape drives, like unit record devices, are inherently dedicated devices. But because of the nature of tape usage, CP does not virtualize tapes through its spooling facility. Instead, tapes are temporarily dedicated (or "attached") to specific virtual machines as requested by their operators (terminal users). When you are through using a tape, you detach the tape drive from your virtual machine so that it is available to other users.

Defining the CMS Virtual Machine

The configuration for a user's virtual machine is initially defined by CP at logon time. CP creates the virtual machine for the user's terminal session as part of the logon process.

After logon, you may also dynamically reconfigure your virtual machine, within certain limits, by issuing CP commands that control the virtual machine environment.

CP initially defines your virtual machine's characteristics at logon time through information contained in the *CP Directory*. A CP Directory entry defines the virtual resources for each user's virtual machine, and the corresponding real resources which underlie them. Log onto CP via a CP **LOGON** statement such as this one:

```
LOGON ZHMF01  MYPASS
```

The userid of **ZHMF01** and the password of **MYPASS** are matched by CP to an entry in the CP Directory (or, the user is denied access). The relevant Directory statement might look similar to this:

```
USER ZHMF01 MYPASS 512K 1M G
```

This identifies the userid and associated password, indicating an initial internal memory allocation of 512 kilobytes and a maximum possible allocation of 1 megabyte. Minimum and maximum storage amounts are specified as a range because, like many characteristics of your CMS virtual machine, you may change them through CP commands entered at your terminal. In other words, though your CP Directory entry initially defines your virtual machine configuration, you may subsequently modify that configuration (within limits) after logging on.

The CP Directory tells CP if you are authorized to use the system, and the initial configuration of your CMS virtual machine.

CP Directory statements include such initial configuration information for the user's CMS virtual machine as virtual machine input/output configuration, associated virtual and real device addresses, virtual processor storage size, disk usage values, and other options.

Here is a simplified example of a CP Directory entry for the userid **ZHMF01**:

```
USER ZHMF01 512K 1M G
        IPL CMS
        CONSOLE 009 3270
        SPOOL 00C 2540 READER *
        SPOOL 00D 2540 PUNCH A
        SPOOL 00E 1403 A
        LINK CMSSYS 190 190 RR
        LINK CMSSYS 19E 19E RR
```

```
MDISK 191 3380 020 004 VMSRES MR
MDISK 193 3380 050 005 VMSEXT MR
```

The **USER** control statement in the CP Directory defines a virtual machine and identifies the directory entry for the specified user. CP uses the userid and password information to identify and verify users logging onto the system.

The **USER** statement also states the allowable virtual storage range for this virtual machine. The **G** states that this user can execute CP commands designed for *general users*. General users issue CP commands that direct their own virtual machine; they cannot execute those CP commands that control the real machine. Separation of CP commands into *command privilege classes* constitutes an important part of VM/SP's security function.

The **IPL** control statement in a CP Directory entry contains the name of the system to be loaded for the terminal user during logon. This causes the automatic IPL referred to in chapter 3. As a user, you override automatic IPL by entering the CP **LOGON** command with the **NOIPL** option:

```
LOGON   userid  NOIPL
```

The CP Directory **CONSOLE** control statement identifies the CMS user's virtual console as at virtual device address **009**, and as of a terminal type which is of the **3270** series of terminals.

The next three **SPOOL** statements specify the unit record devices assigned to the CMS virtual machine. Virtual device addresses of **00C**, **00D**, and **00E** indicate the virtual card reader, virtual card punch, and virtual printer, respectively. The device types are the **2540** reader/punch and the **1403** printer. The device type is followed by the one-character *spooling class*. CP groups spooled files according to logical groupings. All files in a particular spooling class may be processed together and directed to the same real device. CP's spooled virtualization of unit record devices provides great flexibility and power in the disposition of spooled files.

The CP Directory **LINK** control statement makes a minidisk that belongs to another user accessible to this user's CMS virtual machine. These links are established at logon time to two minidisks owned by the userid named **CMSSYS**. Looking at the virtual addresses of these minidisks shows that they are the S-disk and Y-disk. The characters **RR** specify the access mode to these minidisks. Since these are the minidisks on which the operating system resides, the access mode is read-only.

The **LINK** control statement in the CP Directory defines what disks you have access to (that you do not own) at logon time. CP also has a dynamic **LINK** command which you can issue while in CMS to gain access to other users' minidisks after logon. The CP **LINK** command is one of several CP commands which allow you to alter your CMS virtual machine configuration in real time.

Finally, the **MDISK** control statements in the Directory describe minidisks which your CMS virtual machine owns. In this **MDISK** statement:

MDISK 191 3380 020 004 VMSRES MR

191 is the virtual device address, 3380 is a real disk device type, 020 and 004 specify the relative location and size of the minidisk within the real disk, VMSRES is the volume serial number of the real disk, and MR indicates *minidisk ownership,* defined as writable access. Normally, only a single CMS virtual machine running on the real computer owns any minidisk.

Passwords for read- and write-access may also be specified on the MDISK statement. CMS users other than the owner of a minidisk must specify the password to gain the desired access to that minidisk.

Determining Your CMS Virtual Machine Configuration

The virtual machine configuration for each user is initially defined for that user at logon time, based upon that user's configuration information in the CP Directory. CP commands dynamically reconfigure your virtual machine, allowing you to alter its storage capacity or add another minidisk, for example.

The basic CP command to interrogate your virtual machine status and virtual resources is the CP QUERY command. Each of the following CP QUERY command examples is preceded by the letters CP to distinguish it from the CMS commands illustrated extensively elsewhere in this book. Remember, CP is not required as long as the implied CP function is on.

Enter these example commands to see how your virtual machine is configured.

What is the time and date, and how much time have you used during your terminal session:

    CP QUERY TIME

What options are in effect for your virtual console:

    CP QUERY TERMINAL

How many files are spooled for your virtual unit record devices (printer, punch, card reader):

    CP QUERY FILES

What is the status of all your virtual devices:

    CP QUERY VIRTUAL ALL

You can also query individual virtual device status by stating one of these operands in place of ALL, as shown in table 9-3.

Table 9-3
Operands for
Individual Virtual
Device Status

Operand	Display
CHANNELS	Mode of channel operation
GRAF	Status of virtual local display devices
CONSOLE	Status of virtual console
DASD	Status of virtual disks
TAPES	Status of virtual tapes
LINES	Status of virtual communication lines
UR	Status of virtual unit record devices
STORAGE	Size of virtual storage
vaddr	Status of virtual device at virtual device address "vaddr"

What files are in your virtual unit record devices:

```
CP  QUERY  READER
           PRINTER
           PUNCH
```

The vertical alignment of device names indicates that you should select one of them when issuing this command. Here's an example of proper use of this command:

```
CP  QUERY  PRINTER
```

You can also use the abbreviated names for devices, as listed in table 9-4. Thus:

Table 9-4
Device Name
Abbreviations

Device Name	Abbreviations
READER	RDR
PRINTER	PRT
PUNCH	PCH or PUN

```
CP  QUERY  PRT
```

generates the same system response as the previous statement.

Querying a unit record device returns such information as the logon id (userid) of the person who created any spooled file, CP's identification number for the spool file, and the file size. Follow the command with the ALL operand to additionally list the spooled files' filenames and filetypes, date and time of creation, and distribution code. Here's an example:

```
CP  QUERY  PRT  ALL
```

There are many specific operands for querying the status of individual files and groups of files within CP's spooling system. These are covered as necessary during the more detailed discussion of the use of the spooling system in chapter 10.

What are your current PF key settings for the virtual console:

```
CP  QUERY  PF
```

What is your logon id (userid) and the name of your computer (for networking purposes):

```
CP  QUERY  USERID
```

What information is available about the real system processor(s) and your virtual processor identification number: (Table 9-5 shows the interactive queries.)

Table 9-5 Operands for Processor Status	CP Processor QUERY	Result
	CP QUERY PROCESSR	Displays real processor(s) online to VM/SP
	CP QUERY SPMODE	Displays whether VM/SP is in single processor mode
	CP QUERY CPUID	Returns the CPU identification number of your virtual processor

What release of VM/SP is running on the real machine:

```
CP  QUERY  CPLEVEL
```

This command displays the release number of VM/SP, its service level, the time at which it was generated, and the time at which CP was last started.

List the status of the **virtual** system functions you can set:

```
CP  QUERY  SET
```

This command returns the status for some two dozen functions you can set for your virtual machine. An example of these functions is whether or not you receive messages on your virtual console. For this particular function, the CP **QUERY SET** command returns either:

```
MSG ON
```

or

```
MSG OFF
```

to indicate that reception of messages is enabled or disabled. The corresponding CP SET command that allows you to set this function is:

```
CP  SET  MSG   ON
                   OFF
```

Another important function related by the CP QUERY SET command is whether your virtual machine is running in *extended control* (EC) or *basic control* (BC) mode. Extended control is the mode of operation introduced by IBM with the 370 series of computers and virtual storage operating systems in the 1970s. Basic control mode represents the 360 series scheme of control registers. This distinction is important to assembly language programmers who work with their virtual machine on the machine level.

If your virtual machine operates in BC mode, any virtual address up to X'5FF' is valid. Otherwise, you are in EC mode, and any virtual address up to X'FFF' is valid.

Check to see which mode you are in by issuing a CP QUERY command:

```
CP  QUERY  SET
```

Change your mode of operation by entering:

```
CP  SET  ECMODE  OFF
                     ON
```

After entering this command, you receive a response similar to this from the system:

```
CP ENTERED; DISABLED WAIT PSW '00020000 00000000'
```

You now have to IPL your virtual machine again:

```
CP  IPL  CMS
```

Issue the CP **QUERY SET** command again to verify that you have altered your virtual machine's mode of operation.

The CP **QUERY SET** command displays some two dozen other settings concerning the state of your virtual machine. Many of these indicators refer to technical aspects of internal operation. Chapter 11 describes those uses of the CP **SET** command that are most important to general users.

For Further Information

The manual, *VM/SP Introduction,* describes the concepts of this chapter and how they underlie the design of CP and CMS. The order number for this manual varies according to release of VM/SP; see chapter 8 for a list of the manual numbers and their associated VM/SP releases.

The *VM/SP Planning Guide and Reference, SC19-6201,* tells how to set up the Control Program Directory. It lists all Directory statements and their operands along with coding notes.

The *VM/SP CP Command Reference for General Users, SC19-6211,* lists all operands of the CP QUERY and SET commands. As the material in this chapter only constitutes an introduction, see this manual for a more technical explanation of the settable virtual machine functions. The manual also includes sample outputs from all variants of the CP QUERY command along with interpretive information. While not appropriate for an overview, you may find that the detailed descriptions in this manual are exactly what you require to solve specific problems.

Test Your Understanding

Name and describe the techniques through which CP virtualizes the real computer. Your answer should refer to virtualization of processor(s), disks, unit record devices, the system console, and storage.

When you issue the CMS PRINT or PUNCH commands, what really happens? Discuss the concept of spooling in relation to the CMS READCARD command.

What are the major filemode letters within your CMS virtual machine, and what are their meanings? Your A-disk has what virtual address?

Discuss the minidisk concept. What are the differences between minidisks and real disks?

What is the function of a CP Directory entry? What does your own look like? What CMS or CP commands can you issue to determine how many MDISK statements must be in your CP Directory entry?

Enter the CP QUERY VIRTUAL ALL or CP QUERY ALL command. This command provides the basic configuration information for your virtual machine. From the information it provides, what virtual devices are associated with your virtual machine and what are their virtual addresses? What other information is associated with each virtual device? Does the associated information vary depending on device type?

The CP QUERY ALL command also supplies information concerning your current minidisk configuration. To how many cylinders do you have read-write access, and to how many do you have read-only access? Are all the disks you can access of the same device type?

How much virtual storage does your virtual machine have? How can you determine this?

What release and service level of VM/SP runs on your computer? What CP command do you enter to find out?

CHAPTER 10

Controlling and Configuring Your Virtual Machine

The previous chapters developed a virtual machine view of VM/CMS, and examined the operating system architecture in terms of virtual machine principles. This chapter presents CP commands that allow you to direct the operation of your virtual machine and to modify its configuration. With an understanding of the virtual machine concept and a few CP commands, you will find VM/CMS a tremendously rich and flexible software environment in which to work.

Recall that chapter 8 introduced several techniques by which CP commands can be issued from within CMS. Perhaps the easiest way is simply to precede the command with `CP` or `#CP` on the command line.

CP Command Privilege Classes

From what you now know about CP's role in implementing the virtual machine philosophy, you should understand why a security scheme such as CP's command privilege classes is necessary. Clearly, while all users need access to CP commands to control and modify their own virtual machine, only a small group of system administrators should have authority to execute CP commands that direct the real computer's operation. The concept of command privilege classes provides the mechanism through which sensitive CP commands are limited to users of proper security level. Table 10-1 shows how CP commands logically divide into two major groups.

Table 10-1
CP Commands Divide into Two Logical Groupings

Function	Users	CP Privilege Classes
Control of real machine	System administrators	A through F
Control of virtual machine	General users	G

From the viewpoint of the VM/SP system administrators, there exist seven CP command privilege classes. Each is identified by a letter, A through G. A VM/SP user may be assigned to only one privilege class, or to several classes. The CP Directory entry determines the privilege classes for each user.

There also exists one special CP command privilege class called ANY. It consists of a small group of commands which are available to any user, for example, those commands for logging on and logging off VM/SP.

Table 10-2 shows a full list of the CP command privilege classes and their users.

Table 10-2
CP Command
Privilege Classes

Class	User Group
A	Primary system operator
B	System resource operator
C	System programmer
D	Spooling operator
E	Operating system analyst
F	Service representative
G	General user
ANY	Any user
H	IBM reserved

The majority of VM/CMS users are *general users* and are assigned CP command privilege class G. This group includes programmers, analysts, managers, word processing personnel, end-users, and others. These users also issue class ANY commands.

This book is directed toward general use of VM/CMS, and as such, covers only CP commands for the general user. These CP commands enable CMS users to control the resources of their personal CMS virtual machines. All the CP commands you see demonstrated in this book are either privilege class G or ANY.

Privilege classes apply to CP *only.* All CMS users may issue all CMS commands.

Virtual Unit Record Devices

Chapter 9 and figure 9-1 show how CP virtualizes unit record devices through its spooling facility. The spooling facility routes files for input /output through queues maintained by CP.

CP provides powerful commands by which you control the spooling operations of your virtual machine. You use CP spooling commands to change how your system handles data input/output without having to write special programs (or altering existing ones) to do this. The result is an exceptionally flexible system for the CMS user.

CMS Commands That Initiate Spooling

Three basic CMS commands send and receive files to and from virtual unit record devices (and thereby through CP's spooling facility). They are **PRINT**, **PUNCH**, and **READCARD**. **PRINT** sends a file to your virtual printer, **PUNCH** punches a file to your virtual punch, and **READCARD** reads a file onto disk from your virtual card reader.

To print a file enter:

```
PRINT  filename  filetype  filemode  (options
```

where `filename`, `filetype`, and `filemode` name the disk file to print.

PRINT assumes the file to print does not contain carriage control (printer control) characters unless the filetype is **LISTING** or **LIST3800**. If the file contains carriage control characters, indicate this by the **CC** option. When using **CC**, the **HEADER** option creates a page header at the top of the output page which lists the filename, filetype, and filemode.

This example **PRINT** command prints a file with embedded carriage control characters preceded by an appropriate page heading:

```
PRINT  REPORT  DATA  A1  (CC  HEADER
```

Another important **PRINT** option is **UPCASE**. **UPCASE** translates lower-case to uppercase letters prior to printing. This option is critical when your file contains both lowercase and uppercase letters but your physical printer only prints in uppercase.

The CMS **PUNCH** command sends a file to your virtual punch. Its format is:

```
PUNCH  filename  filetype  filemode  (options
```

The most important **PUNCH** option specifies **HEADER** or **NOHEADER**. **HEADER**, which is the default, inserts a control card in front of the punched output. The control record is commonly called a **READ** card and this is its format:

```
:READ filename filetype filemode origin date-written time-written
```

For the file named **TEST2 DATA A1**, the **READ** card might look like:

```
:READ  TEST2    DATA    A1 ZHMF01 02/05/86 06:08:46
```

Remember that **PUNCH** automatically places this initial record in your output file to the virtual punch unless you specify the **PUNCH NOHEADER** option.

The maximum length of **PUNCH** file records is 80 characters. The maximum length for **PRINT** file records varies according to the printer characteristics, with 132 characters (133 including carriage control character) the standard for many printers.

The CMS `READCARD` command reads a file from your virtual card reader and creates a CMS disk file.

It can be entered in two basic forms. First:

```
READCARD  filename  filetype  filemode
```

reads the next spool file in your virtual reader into a CMS disk file named by `filename filetype filemode`. If there is a `READ` control card in the file of the virtual reader, it becomes the first line of data in the newly created disk file. To remove it, go into the editor and edit the disk file.

The other form of `READCARD` is:

```
READCARD  *
```

In this form, `READCARD` determines the disk file name from the `READ` card in the input spool file. The disk file is named according to the information on the `READ` card. If the input deck has no `READ` card, then CMS automatically names the new disk file:

```
READCARD  CMSUT1  A1
```

For both forms of the `READCARD` command, if the file name of the new disk file is the same as an existing disk file name, that existing disk file is replaced. Take care not to lose any existing files by reading in a file that takes the file name of an existing file. Check the incoming file name through the CP `QUERY` command:

```
CP  QUERY  READER  ALL
```

If there is a conflict with an existing file name, either rename the existing file, or use the form of the `READCARD` command that allows you to specify a new name for the incoming disk file. Note that the CP `QUERY` `READER` command does not tell whether `READ` cards are present in files in the virtual reader.

Manipulating Spooled Files

The power of CP's spooling facility lies in your capability to issue CP commands through your virtual console that affect spooled files. For virtual output devices, files sit in the spool queues until finally printed or punched on real devices. For input files in the virtual reader, files remain in the spool queue until you issue commands that alter this, such as `READCARD`. In either case, when the files are queued in the CP-controlled spool facility, you issue CP commands to change their disposition.

CP commands that affect files presently on the spooling queues include: **CHANGE**, **ORDER**, **PURGE**, and **TRANSFER**. In these commands, you refer to spooled files by *spool id, spool class,* and *spool device.*

The spool id is a 4-digit identifier assigned to each spooled file by CP. Spool class, as discussed in chapter 9, is a logical grouping of spooled files, all of which are processed in the same manner. For example, a group of files requiring special forms on the printer may be grouped in a different spooling class than those files which are printed on regular printer paper. Spool device refers to whether the files are directed to the virtual printer, punch, or card reader.

Remember, the CP **QUERY** command supplies information concerning files in the spooling system:

```
CP   QUERY   PRINTER   ALL
CP   QUERY   PUNCH   ALL
CP   QUERY   READER   ALL
```

As an example:

```
CP   QUERY   PRINTER   ALL
```

This command displays information on files that have been sent to the virtual printer, but that have not yet started printing. Output appears similar to this:

```
ORIGINID FILE  CLAS RECRDS CO HLD ROUTE   DATE  TIME  NAME   TYPE  DIST
ZUSERA   0353  A PR 000004 04 USR PRTR06  03/03 22:30 TESTX  DATA  ORNL
ZUSERA   0408  A PR 000011 01 USR PRTR06  03/03 22:33 TEST7  DATA  ORNL
```

In this example, **ORIGINID** is the userid of the user who placed the file in the queue, **FILE** is the spoolid, **CLAS** shows the printer class, **RECRDS** indicates the file's size, **CO** tells how many copies will print, **HLD** shows the hold status, **ROUTE** names the physical printer, **DATE** and **TIME** tell when the file was placed in the queue, **NAME** and **TYPE** give the file's name, and **DIST** is the distribution code.

Until the spooled files are actually processed, use the CP **CHANGE** command to alter the spool file name, spool file type, and the distribution code. This information appears in the first page of printed output. You can additionally change the number of copies that will be printed for a file, the spooling class, and the hold status.

Files in *hold status* remain in the queue and are not released to a real device until their status is altered to *nohold status.* Hold status keeps files in spool queues until you enter CP commands to alter their status.

Here are some examples of the CP **CHANGE** command for spooled printer files:

```
CP  CHANGE  PRINTER  0902  COPY  4
```

prints four copies of the file in the virtual printer spooling queue having the spoolid of 0902.

This command changes the distribution code (printed on the page banner) of all files in the printer queue to ORNL:

```
CP  CHANGE  PRINTER  ALL  DIST  ORNL
```

This command places all files in your virtual printer queue to HOLD status:

```
CP  CHANGE  PRINTER  ALL  HOLD
```

The files will not be released to the real printer via CP until you release them for printing by entering:

```
CP  CHANGE  PRINTER  ALL  NOHOLD
```

This command shows how to change the spooling class of files in the spool queues:

```
CP  CHANGE  PRINTER  CLASS A  CLASS W
```

This changes the disposition of all printer files in spooling class A to class W. Remember that the spooling class represents a logical group of files subjected to the same kind of processing. Spooling classes are single characters, from A to Z, and 0 through 9. Changing classes for the printer files might, for example, direct that they be printed on special forms. This depends on the kinds of processing your installation defines for the different spooling classes.

The CP CHANGE command works similarly for punch and reader files. There exist minor differences in the CHANGE command according to device type, however. For example, the COPY and DIST options do not apply to input files in your virtual card reader.

For any of these CHANGE commands, CP comes back with a message telling the number of files altered. This helps verify that the command had the intended consequences. You might also issue a CP QUERY command for the relevant virtual device to check its spooled files. It is always a good idea to verify the effects of the CP spooling commands unless you are familiar with them:

```
CP  QUERY  device-name  ALL
```

The CP ORDER command allows you to order your spooled files for a particular virtual device. This is useful because the order of the files in the spooling queue is the order in which they are released to real devices. As an example:

```
CP  QUERY  READER  ALL
```

produces a response similar to this:

```
ORIGINID FILE  CLAS RECRDS CO HLD ROUTE  DATE  TIME  NAME   TYPE  DIST
ZUSERA   0511  A PU 000004 01 NOH        03/03 22:04 TEST2  DATA  OR2
ZUSERB   0885  A PU 000011 01 NOH        03/03 22:33 TEST7  DATA  OR2
ZUSERA   0910  A PU 000006 01 NOH        03/03 22:41 TEST1  DATA  OR2
```

You can reorder the spooled files to read them in a different order by subsequent CMS READCARD commands. This command reorders the spooled files by spoolid:

```
CP  ORDER  READER  0885  0910  0511
```

The result is:

```
ORIGINID FILE  CLAS RECRDS CO HLD ROUTE  DATE  TIME  NAME   TYPE  DIST
ZUSERB   0885  A PU 000011 01 NOH        03/03 22:33 TEST7  DATA  OR2
ZUSERA   0910  A PU 000006 01 NOH        03/03 22:41 TEST1  DATA  OR2
ZUSERA   0511  A PU 000004 01 NOH        03/03 22:04 TEST2  DATA  OR2
```

You can reorder by spooling class, too:

```
CP  ORDER  READER  CLASS  W  CLASS  A
```

Now all class W files are processed before class A files.

The CP PURGE command deletes closed spooled files. It purges files from the virtual device spool queues, meaning that those files are never presented to a real device for processing. It deletes these files regardless of their hold status, so long as CP has not yet selected them for processing. The following list shows examples of PURGE commands:

```
CP  PURGE  READER  ALL

CP  PURGE  PUNCH  CLASS  A  CLASS  B

CP  PURGE  READER  0305  0201

CP  PURGE  READER  CLASS  A  0427  0911
```

The first example deletes all files in the virtual reader. The second PURGE command eliminates all class A and class B files from the virtual punch. The third example purges two files from the virtual reader, having spoolids of 0305 and 0201. The final example shows that you can freely intermix spoolids and class operands in the PURGE statement.

You can also include the FORM operand in this command. FORM names consist of from one to eight characters and are defined by system programmers during system generation. You usually associate this operand with the different forms used for printers.

The final CP command that operates on spooled files that have not yet been selected for processing by a real device is TRANSFER. TRANSFER moves spooled files from one user or queue to another. Examples of TRANSFER commands:

```
CP  TRANSFER  PUNCH  ALL  TO  ZUSER  READER

CP  TRANSFER  PUNCH  ALL  FROM  ZUSER  READER

CP  TRANSFER  PUNCH  ALL  TO  *  READER

CP  TRANSFER  READER  CLASS  B  TO  ZUSERB  READER

CP  TRANSFER  READER  CLASS  B  FROM  ZUSERB  READER
```

The simplified format of this CP TRANSFER command is:

```
CP  TRANSFER  PRINTER  spoolid    TO    *       PRINTER
              PUNCH    CLASS c           userid  PUNCH
              READER   FORM form                 READER
                       ALL        FROM  ALL
                                        userid
```

Wherever a virtual device is not specified, it defaults to READER.

Thus, the first TRANSFER example moves all files currently spooled to your virtual punch to the virtual reader of CMS user ZUSER. The second command transfers those files back from ZUSER to your own virtual punch.

The third example transfers all the files spooled to your virtual punch to your virtual machine's reader. The asterisk * denotes your own userid.

The fourth example transfers all your class B reader files to the virtual reader of user ZUSERB. Finally, the last example reclaims those same class B files you sent to user ZUSERB and places them in your own virtual reader. Note that TRANSFER only reclaims closed spool files that you created.

TRANSFER does not transfer spool files between all devices. For example, transfer from print to punch and punch to print queues are flagged as errors.

In addition to altering the characteristics of files that are in CP's spooling queues, you may alter the operation of the spooling facility for your virtual devices. These alterations affect subsequent input/output. They do *not* affect files that have already been spooled.

Thus, you may alter spooling characteristics such as spool file class, distribution code, number of copies, etc., by issuing CP SPOOL commands. These commands affect individual spool files, all the files of a particular spooling class, or all the files spooled for a particular device.

The CP SPOOL command changes spooling characteristics that affect the spooling facility *for files that are subsequently spooled.* It does *not* affect files currently in the spool queues.

The basic format of the CP SPOOL command is:

```
CP  SPOOL  device  operand(s)
```

You can indicate the device in several ways. Table 10-3 shows the options available.

Table 10-3
Examples of
Device References

Reference	Examples
Device name	PRINTER, PUNCH, READER
Device abbreviation	PRT, PUN, RDR
Device virtual address	00E, 00D, 00C
Device virtual address (without leading zeroes)	E, D, C

Rather than illustrating all the SPOOL command operands, here are examples that show the more common uses of SPOOL. All reference the device by the full device name, for clarity:

```
CP  SPOOL  PRINTER  FOR  ZUSER

CP  SPOOL  PUNCH  HOLD

CP  SPOOL  READER  HOLD

CP  SPOOL  PRINTER  TO  ZUSER

CP  SPOOL  PRINTER  TO  *

CP  SPOOL  PRINTER  CLASS  C

CP  SPOOL  PUNCH  COPY  3
```

In the first example, the SPOOL command's FOR operand specifies the userid under which printed or punched output is produced. The new user becomes the owner of the output file because it is printed or punched using his distribution code. (Distribution codes for printed or punched output for each user's CMS virtual machine are defined in that user's CP Directory entry.)

The second example illustrates the HOLD attribute. When HOLD is issued for printer or punch virtual devices, subsequent files sent to those devices are not released to real devices by CP until you specifically release them. The initial status for all virtual devices is NOHOLD. Issue a CP SPOOL command with the NOHOLD operand to change any held device back to NOHOLD operation.

The third example shows that the HOLD operand means something different for virtual readers than it does for virtual printers and punches. For the virtual card reader, HOLD stipulates that reading a file from the reader does *not* result in removal of the file from the reader. Thus, you can issue a SPOOL READER HOLD, with the result that reading in subsequent files from the reader does not eliminate them from the spool queue. The SPOOL command with the NOHOLD operand restores the virtual reader to normal default operation for subsequent spool files.

The next two SPOOL commands illustrate the TO operand, which directs the output to the specified virtual output device (either the printer or punch) to the virtual reader of the specified CMS user. In the first, all subsequent output to the printer is redirected to the virtual reader of the CMS user with the logon id of ZUSER. The second shows use of the asterisk * to stand for your own CMS userid. This example directs all output to your printer to your virtual reader.

The next command changes the class of the virtual printer device. The default spooling classes for each of your devices are initially established in the CP Directory entry defining your virtual machine configuration. Here, subsequent printer output is directed to class C.

The final example produces multiple copies of any file sent to a virtual output device. Each CMS PUNCH command now results in three copies punched on the real device.

While there are many other uses of the CP SPOOL command, the final ones of interest are CONT and NOCONT. CONT permits *spooling continuous,* meaning that all files sent to a virtual output device are concatenated into a single file until a CP CLOSE command is issued, turning off continuous spooling. In this example:

```
CP   SPOOL   PRINTER   CONT
PRINT   TEST1   DATA   A1
PRINT   TEST2   DATA   A1
CP   SPOOL   PRINTER   NOCONT
CP   CLOSE   PRINTER
```

two CMS files, TEST1 DATA A1 and TEST2 DATA A1, are sent to the virtual printer. With continuous spooling initiated by the CP SPOOL command via the CONT operand, these two files are concatenated into one. CP requires that the CLOSE command terminate the concatenated file to release it to the printer. When the two files are printed, they have only a single banner page and are treated like a single printed file.

Here is another example of spooling continuous:

```
CP  SPOOL  PUNCH  TO  *  CONT
PUNCH  TEST1  DATA  A1
PUNCH  TEST2  DATA  A1
CP  SPOOL  PUNCH  NOCONT
CP  CLOSE  PUNCH
```

The two output files are again concatenated into one. If one were to enter a CP **QUERY READER** command following this command sequence, it would reveal a single concatenated file in the virtual reader. One CMS **READCARD** command reads this single concatenated file.

VM/CMS Redirection of I/O

From the conceptual standpoint, the CMS general user redirects I/O through the CP commands controlling the spooling facility. Single commands spool printer output to another user's virtual reader, send punch output to one's own reader, or, redirect printed output to the distribution code of another CMS user. This ability to reroute input/output dynamically is commonly called *redirection of input/output,* a principle of modern operating system design usually associated with the UNIX operating system. UNIX popularized this concept and consciously encourages its use through universal application to all devices and through a simple notation designed for this purpose.

Part of UNIX's success in I/O redirection is its treatment of all devices as *character-oriented:* files are sent to devices as streams of characters. VM/CMS also facilitates redirection of I/O. However, as the discussion in this chapter shows, CP's support for I/O redirection is limited. CP commands inconsistently apply the principles of I/O redirection toward virtual devices; some command operands are valid only for certain devices. In part, this is because VM/CMS treats devices as *record-oriented.* That is, the basic unit of input/ouput is the record. Also, while CP implements I/O redirection through a small group of commands, the system lacks the supporting notation and syntax embodied in UNIX.

While not as universal as UNIX's I/O redirection, VM/CMS's spooling facility is very powerful. The virtual machine concept provides CMS users great flexibility because they control their own virtual machines.

For Further Information

The *VM/SP CMS User's Guide, SC19-6210,* contains a chapter on working with various input/output devices in the VM/CMS environment. It covers both CMS commands for I/O and CP commands to manipulate the underlying virtual devices.

The manual, *VM/SP CMS Command and Macro Reference, SC19-6209,* formally explains commands like **PRINT, PUNCH,** and **READCARD.** Its counterpart for CP commands is *VM/SP CP Command Reference for General Users, SC19-6211.* This is the basic reference manual for the CP commands illustrated in this chapter. Check these sources for full command syntax and explanation of operands.

Try the commands in this chapter online. The commands are so powerful (and idiosyncratic) that online practice is the best way to learn. To view online help for any CP command, enter:

```
HELP  CP  command-name
```

where command-name is the CP command for which you need information. For example, enter:

```
HELP  CP  SPOOL
```

for online explanation of the CP **SPOOL** command. For help with CMS commands, enter:

```
HELP  CMS  command-name
```

Complete information on the CMS Help facility is contained in section 4 of this book.

Test Your Understanding

What is your command privilege class? Does this refer to CMS commands as well as CP commands?

Spool your virtual punch to your virtual reader, and punch a file. What command do you issue to find out if there is a file in your virtual reader? Do messages appear relating to the spooling activity? Once the file is in your virtual reader, read it into a file named **MYINPUT DATA A1** through the CMS **READCARD** command.

Spool another file to your virtual reader. Assuming you want to read this file into the pre-existing CMS file named **MYINPUT DATA A1,** what are your options? Does it matter whether the punched file contains a **READ** card?

Spool several more files to your virtual reader. List the files in the reader through the CP **QUERY** command. Now order the files into the reverse of their original order, and verify this through the CP **QUERY** command.

Issue CP **CHANGE** commands against the reader files. What characteristics can you alter?

Purge the files from your reader, one by one. On the basis of what characteristics can you identify and purge the reader files?

Look in the CP reference manual and determine from and to what devices are CP **TRANSFER** commands valid. Now, spool a file to the virtual reader of another user, and then reclaim the file via the CP **TRANSFER** command. How do you identify the file(s) affected by the **TRANSFER** command, and under what conditions can you transfer back to your reader the file(s) you have sent to another user?

Practice issuing CP **SPOOL** commands in reconfiguring your virtual machine's I/O system. Note that you can display your virtual machine's configuration at any time through the CP **QUERY** command. Does the **SPOOL** command affect any files already spooled to your virtual devices?

Spool three files to your own virtual reader but read the data of all three by a single CMS **READCARD** command.

If you are familiar with PC-DOS (MS-DOS) or a version of UNIX, contrast the redirection of input/output in either of these operating systems to how it is accomplished within VM/CMS.

CHAPTER 11

Additional Virtual System Resources

This chapter continues the discussion of the previous chapter concerning CP commands which modify or reconfigure your CMS virtual machine. While the last chapter focused on the spooling facility and virtual unit record devices, this chapter concentrates on other virtual system resources. These include the virtual console, minidisks, tapes, and virtual storage. All the CP commands presented in this chapter are privilege class G.

Controlling the Virtual Console

The CP SPOOL command also applies to the virtual console. For example, you can spool data displayed on the terminal to your virtual reader through this command:

```
CP  SPOOL  CONSOLE  START  TO  *
```

On the terminal, you operate as before. When you wish to terminate virtual console spooling, enter:

```
CP  SPOOL  CONSOLE  STOP
CP  SPOOL  CONSOLE  CLOSE
```

The CP SPOOL CLOSE command releases the spooled file to your virtual reader. Now you can read it into a disk file through the CMS READCARD command. Note that spooling the virtual console to the reader does not create a READ card in the input deck. You will probably want to specify a file name when reading in a spooled virtual console file through this method:

```
READCARD  CONSOLE  DATA
```

This reads the spool file into a disk file named **CONSOLE DATA A1**.

You can also spool your virtual console to the printer queue and get a copy of your terminal session by issuing:

```
CP  SPOOL  CONSOLE  START
```

Any time you wish to stop spooling and release the spool file for printing, enter:

```
CP  SPOOL  CONSOLE  STOP
CP  SPOOL  CONSOLE  CLOSE
```

You can apply the CP **SPOOL** command to your virtual console with other operands that are valid for printer files including **CLASS**, **COPY**, **CONT**, and **HOLD**.

Reconfiguring with the CP SET Command

As alluded to in chapter 9, the CP **SET** command permits setting of certain virtual console characteristics. For example, you can suppress messages sent from other users (via the CP **MESSAGE** command) and resulting from spooling by:

```
CP  SET  MSG  OFF
```

The system default upon logon is **CP SET MSG ON**.

Other operands of the CP **SET** command dictate whether special messages, warning messages, and informational responses from certain CP commands are received at the virtual console.

You can also set the PF keys on your virtual console to various command strings. Pressing the relevant PF key issues a command, or displays the character string assigned to it on the virtual console. In the latter, you then press the **ENTER** key to issue the command.

To set a PF key to issue a command directly, enter:

```
CP  SET  PF1  IMMED  "#CP QUERY PRINTER ALL
```

Now, when you press **PF1**, it issues the command **#CP QUERY PRINTER ALL**. The **IMMED** operand says that merely pressing the PF key is sufficient to issue the command. Its opposite is **DELAYED**, which displays the character string on the virtual console and requires you to press the **ENTER** key to enter the command. (**DELAYED** is the default.) The quotation mark **"** is the logical escape symbol and is used when you enter a **#CP** function or execute a series of commands via a PF key.

Here's an example that sets a console PF key to execute a CMS command:

```
CP  SET  PF9  IMMED  FILELIST  *  COBOL  A1
```

Pressing **PF9** executes the CMS command FILELIST * COBOL A1. A full-screen display listing your COBOL program source files appears.

A special PF key setting is available through the keyword RETRIEVE. The command:

```
CP  SET  PF12  RETRIEVE
```

means that pressing the **PF12** key redisplays the last line entered in the terminal input area. You may modify it and re-enter the line. This is especially useful in overcoming typing errors.

If you press **PF12** more than once, you will notice that VM/SP remembers several input lines. Exactly how many it remembers depends on their lengths. The input lines are retrieved in reverse chronological order, most recent to oldest. After displaying the oldest one in memory, the system circles back to the most recent.

Another special PF key setting is the COPY operand. To assign the COPY operand to a PF key enter:

```
CP  SET  PF8  COPY
```

If you use a 3270 family display terminal, and it is connected to a nondedicated 3270 display printer attached to the same control unit, pressing **PF8** copies the currently displayed screen to the printer. If the message NOT ACCEPTED appears in the screen status area (in the lower right-hand corner of the display), the printer is either not ready or not available.

In addition to the CP SET command, the CP SCREEN and TERMINAL commands also define characteristics of your virtual console. Assuming that the terminal and its controller support color capabilities, SCREEN allows you to change color and highlighting definitions. The CP TERMINAL command controls several miscellaneous virtual console functions. These include the output line length, character set, logical editing symbols, and other terminal attributes.

Minidisks

The minidisk configuration of your virtual machine is initially defined at logon time. Remember that CP configures your virtual machine based on the CP Directory statements associated with your logon id. The MDISK directory statement defines minidisks which your virtual machine owns. The LINK control statement provides permanent links to minidisks owned by other users. Minidisks defined as part of your virtual machine configuration are accessible every time you log on.

CP offers CMS users the opportunity to dynamically add minidisks to their virtual machine. These additional minidisks are *temporary,* in that they only are accessible after issuing appropriate CP commands. Your access to them remains valid only for the duration of the terminal session.

There are two ways to gain temporary access: CP LINK temporarily accesses minidisks owned by other CMS users. CP DEFINE temporarily gains ownership of minidisks.

The CP LINK command has this format:

```
CP LINK TO userid vaddr1 AS vaddr2 mode PASS=password
```

where userid is the logon id of the CMS user to whose disk you are linking (the owner of the minidisk); vaddr1 is the virtual device address of that minidisk in the CP Directory for that userid; vaddr2 is the virtual address by which this device will be identified in your own configuration.

The MODE operand of the LINK command determines whether the link establishes read-only or write-access. To link to another user's disk, you normally use the read-only access mode R.

CP LINK command access modes consist of either one or two characters. The first character represents the desired access mode, which may be read-only, write, or multiple. The optional second character specifies the alternate access mode if the primary mode request cannot be honored. The secondary access mode may be either read-only or write.

VM/CMS does not guarantee data integrity when multiple users have write-access to a disk, so you should talk to your system administrator about the site-recommended access modes before linking to any disk you do not own with other than read-only access. Table 11-1 lists access modes and their meanings.

	Access Mode	Meaning
Table 11-1 LINK Command Access Modes	R	Read-only access is established to the minidisk if no other user has the disk in write status. (This is the default mode if none is specified.)
	RR	Read-only access is established regardless of whether another user has the disk in write status. This mode assures the link will occur.
	W	Write-access is established only if no other user has a link to the disk.
	WR	Write-access is established if available. If it is not available, then read-only access is given.
	M	Write-access is established only if no other user has write-access to the disk.
	MR	Write-access is established unless another user has write-access to the disk, in which case a read-only link is established.
	MW	Write-access is established in all cases.

Access modes are a complex topic. If you study the manuals on this subject, keep this preeminent VM/CMS rule in mind: *CMS does not protect from loss of data when more than one user tries to write to a single minidisk.* In other words, VM/CMS does *not* provide shared write-access integrity for multiple users to CMS files. The vendor's reference manuals even state that the guaranteed read-only access mode of RR can potentially cause "unpredictable results" because it allows one user to read a disk while another is updating the same disk at the same time. This is very different from the principle of file integrity embodied in such mainframe operating systems as MVS/TSO and DOS/VSE.

A second fundamental rule of the VM/CMS environment: *only one CMS user owns (has write authority) to any minidisk.* Others normally link to the disk in read-only mode.

The final parameter on the CP LINK command is the optional operand PASS=. The password you enter must match that on the owner's MDISK statement in the owner's CP Directory entry. Passwords are specified according to the access mode desired. That is, there may be up to three passwords for any minidisk: the read, write, and multiple passwords. You specify the one appropriate to the kind of link you are establishing. For example, for R access you enter the read password. Note that if your site has installed the Password Suppression Facility, you must enter the password on a separate line after the system prompts you.

Here is an example of the CP LINK command:

```
CP  LINK  TO  ZUSER  191  AS  201  R
```

This command establishes a read-only link to the minidisk of ZUSER, defined in his CP Directory entry as residing at virtual address 191. This is the A-disk of ZUSER. Specification of the link as access mode R is the most conservative approach; the link will only be established if no other user has the minidisk in write status. R linkage assures data integrity for the files on the minidisk.

In your virtual machine, the virtual address for this minidisk is 201. You may only read, not update, files on this linked disk.

After linking to another user's minidisk, you inform CMS of this additional resource through the CMS ACCESS command:

```
ACCESS  vaddr2  filemode
```

where vaddr2 corresponds to the virtual address for this device in your virtual machine that you specified in the CP LINK command, and filemode is the filemode letter you assign this minidisk. To continue the above example of the LINK command:

```
ACCESS  201  E
```

This command indicates to CMS that the minidisk you shared to as your virtual device at virtual address 201 is now your CMS E-disk. All files residing on this disk have the filemode letter of E from the viewpoint of your CMS virtual machine.

When you no longer need access to a minidisk, use the CMS RELEASE

Figure 11-1   Linking to a Minidisk Owned by Another CMS User

```
This figure duplicates a CMS user's terminal session as he requests a
read-only link to another CMS user's A-disk.   Commands you enter are
in  boldface;  system responses are in regular typeface.   The linked
disk is indicated in the lists of disks by an arrow ( <=== ).


R;
CP  QUERY  DASD
DASD 190   3350 PD7137 R/O      50 CYL
DASD 191   3380 PD8008 R/W      10 CYL
DASD 19E   3350 PD7139 R/O      35 CYL
DASD 19F   3350 PD7141 R/O      30 CYL
R;
QUERY  DISK
LABEL  CUU M  STAT CYL TYPE BLKSIZE      FILES   ...
ZHMF01 191 A   R/W 10  3380  4096          254   ...
CMS190 190 S   R/O 46  3350  4096          181   ...
CMS19F 19F Y/S R/O 30  3350  4096          191   ...
CMS19E 19E Z/S R/O 35  3350  4096          292   ...
R;
CP  LINK  TO  ZJCR01  191  AS  201  R
R;
CP  QUERY  DASD
DASD 190   3350 PD7137 R/O      50 CYL
DASD 191   3380 PD8008 R/W      10 CYL
DASD 19E   3350 PD7139 R/O      35 CYL
DASD 19F   3350 PD7141 R/O      30 CYL
DASD 201   3380 PD8045 R/O      10 CYL         <===
R;
QUERY  DISK
LABEL  CUU M  STAT CYL TYPE BLKSIZE      FILES   ...
ZHMF01 191 A   R/W 10  3380  4096          254   ...
CMS190 190 S   R/O 46  3350  4096          181   ...
CMS19F 19F Y/S R/O 30  3350  4096          191   ...
CMS19E 19E Z/S R/O 35  3350  4096          292   ...
R;
ACCESS  201  E
E (201) R/O
R;
```

command to release the device. The **RELEASE** command constitutes the inverse of the CMS **ACCESS** command:

RELEASE E

The inverse of the CP **LINK** command is CP **DETACH**. Detach a device from your virtual machine configuration when you no longer need the link to it:

CP DETACH 201

Note that CMS refers to minidisks by disk letter (or filemode letter), whereas CP uses virtual device addresses. Therefore, the CMS **RELEASE** command references a filemode letter while the CP **DETACH** command disconnects by virtual device address.

Figure 11-1
(cont.)

```
CP   QUERY   DASD
DASD 190   3350 PD7137 R/O      50 CYL
DASD 191   3380 PD8008 R/W      10 CYL
DASD 19E   3350 PD7139 R/O      35 CYL
DASD 19F   3350 PD7141 R/O      30 CYL
DASD 201   3380 PD8045 R/O      10 CYL        <===
R;
QUERY  DISK
LABEL   CUU M   STAT CYL TYPE BLKSIZE    FILES  ...
ZHMF01 191 A    R/W 10  3380  4096        254   ...
ZJCR01 201 E    R/O 10  3380  4096         63   ...     <===
CMS190 190 S    R/O 46  3350  4096        181   ...
CMS19F 19F Y/S  R/O 30  3350  4096        191   ...
CMS19E 19E Z/S  R/O 35  3350  4096        292   ...
R;
RELEASE  E
R;
CP   QUERY   DASD
DASD 190   3350 PD7137 R/O      50 CYL
DASD 191   3380 PD8008 R/W      10 CYL
DASD 19E   3350 PD7139 R/O      35 CYL
DASD 19F   3350 PD7141 R/O      30 CYL
DASD 201   3380 PD8045 R/O      10 CYL        <===
R;
QUERY  DISK
LABEL   CUU M   STAT CYL TYPE BLKSIZE    FILES  ...
ZHMF01 191 A    R/W 10  3380  4096        254   ...
CMS190 190 S    R/O 46  3350  4096        181   ...
CMS19F 19F Y/S  R/O 30  3350  4096        191   ...
CMS19E 19E Z/S  R/O 35  3350  4096        292   ...
R;
CP   DETACH   201
DASD 201   DETACHED
R;
CP   QUERY   DASD
DASD 190   3350 PD7137 R/O      50 CYL
DASD 191   3380 PD8008 R/W      10 CYL
DASD 19E   3350 PD7139 R/O      35 CYL
DASD 19F   3350 PD7141 R/O      30 CYL
R;
QUERY  DISK
LABEL   CUU M   STAT CYL TYPE BLKSIZE    FILES  ...
ZHMF01 191 A    R/W 10  3380  4096        254   ...
CMS190 190 S    R/O 46  3350  4096        181   ...
CMS19F 19F Y/S  R/O 30  3350  4096        191   ...
CMS19E 19E Z/S  R/O 35  3350  4096        292   ...
R;
```

The CP LINK command establishes *temporary access* to a minidisk owned by another CMS virtual machine. By temporary access, we mean that the link lasts for the duration of the terminal session, or until a corresponding DETACH command is issued.

Figure 11-1 shows a complete example of linking and accessing another CMS user's A-disk. The CP command QUERY DASD and the CMS command QUERY DISK are interspersed in the session so that you can see when these operating systems are aware of the disk.

The CP DEFINE command is used to gain temporary ownership of a disk. The CP DEFINE command alters your virtual machine configuration for the terminal session by adding additional resources.

To define a minidisk, enter:

```
CP  DEFINE  Tdisk  AS  vaddr  CYL  nnn
```

Tdisk indicates a real disk device type, for example, T3350 or T3380; vaddr specifies the virtual address of this minidisk in your virtual machine configuration. CYL states that this request is for a minidisk of nnn cylinders in size.

For example, to request a 3380-based minidisk of 10 cylinders at virtual address 204, enter:

```
CP  DEFINE  T3380  AS  204  CYL  010
```

Since this virtual disk is new to your operating system, you must format it for use via the CMS FORMAT command:

```
FORMAT  204  E
```

This example assigns a CMS filemode letter of E to the minidisk at virtual device address 204, and formats it for use. Whenever you format a disk, CMS asks you if you really want to do this since it erases all files on the minidisk. With a newly defined minidisk, you answer YES because you have no files on the disk and you need to format it to use it. You could format a minidisk you have been using for some time, but it is not recommended because it eliminates all files on that minidisk.

The CMS FORMAT command also prompts you to enter a minidisk label. This minidisk name consists of up to six characters. It is the minidisk name which you will see when you enter the CMS command QUERY DISK.

When through with a minidisk gained through CP DEFINE, use the CMS RELEASE and CP DETACH commands to eliminate it from your virtual machine configuration. You can enter both commands together by issuing the RELEASE command with the DET option:

```
RELEASE  vaddr  (DET
```

or, in terms of the previous example:

```
RELEASE  204  (DET
```

Note that the DET operand is *not* an abbreviated form of the word DETACH. The RELEASE command does not work if you enter this operand as DETACH.

Access to Tapes

Remember, tape drives are dedicated devices under VM/CMS. Tape drives are dedicated to individual CMS virtual machines at the request of the CMS users. To add a tape drive to your virtual machine, use the CP **MESSAGE** command to send the system operator a message requesting a tape mount:

```
CP  MESSAGE  userid      messsage-line
             OPERATOR
```

As an example:

```
CP  MESSAGE  OPERATOR  PLEASE MOUNT VOLSER CM948 ON 181
```

The keyword **OPERATOR** directs the message to the system operator, and your message follows this operand. In response to the message, the operator does two things: mounts the tape on an available tape drive; and issues the CP **ATTACH** command to attach the tape drive to your virtual machine.

When the tape is ready, you receive a message like this on your console:

```
TAPE  181  ATTACHED
```

You cannot attach the tape yourself because **ATTACH** is a privilege class B CP command. In this way, the system operators retain control of the tape drives.

You request a tape mount at one of the virtual device addresses: 181, 182, 183, or 184. CMS permits use of up to four tapes at one time. When through with the tape, you should detach the virtual device via the CP **DETACH** command referencing the virtual device address:

```
CP  DETACH  181
```

Virtual Storage

Recall that the CP Directory entry for your CMS virtual machine specified its minimum and maximum virtual storage. Upon logon, you receive the minimum specification as your initial virtual storage allocation. To increase this amount (up to the maximum allowed by your CP Directory entry) use the CP **DEFINE** command:

```
CP  DEFINE  STORAGE  nnnnnK
                     nnM
```

This command causes a *virtual system reset.* In other words, you must IPL your virtual machine again after commanding CP to increase your virtual storage size:

```
CP  DEFINE  STORAGE  1M
```

```
STORAGE = 01024K
CP ENTERED; DISABLED WAIT PSW '00020000 00000000'
```

```
CP  IPL  CMS
```

The first statement increases the virtual storage of your CMS virtual machine to 1 megabyte, a value that must be defined as allowable in your virtual machine's CP Directory entry. The system acknowledges your request and places your virtual machine into a wait state. Enter the CP command IPL to regenerate your CMS virtual machine.

Additional Machine Resources

The CP DEFINE command can help you add other resources to your virtual machine configuration. These resources are temporary: they remain part of your virtual machine's configuration only for the duration of the current terminal session. CP DEFINE allows you to reconfigure your virtual machine to include: virtual printers of many kinds, virtual system consoles, several kinds of virtual punches, virtual communication lines, virtual channels (either selector or block multiplexor), and many models of disks. Remember that the CP DEFINE command is the basic mechanism through which you temporarily add many other kinds of resources to your virtual machine.

While CP DEFINE adds resources to your virtual system, the CP SET command sets many aspects of your virtual machine's operation. CP QUERY indicates the present settings.

Finally, CP lets you affect the status of your virtual devices. Use CP commands such as NOTREADY, READY, and RESET to control virtual device status.

For Further Information

The *VM/SP CMS User's Guide, SC19-6210,* provides both background material and examples of the CMS and CP commands of this chapter. The *VM/SP CMS Command and Macro Reference, SC19-6209,* contains exact command formats and description for the CMS commands introduced here. The *VM/SP CP Command Reference for General Users, SC19-6211,* contains this same detailed information for all CP commands in this chapter, including complete information on the LINK command. This manual covers warnings concerning which modes do not mix and a chart showing the manner in which the system determines which access modes to grant for any LINK command request.

Test Your Understanding

You are testing some CMS commands and you want a written record of what you have done and the command responses. How can you get this log without writing anything down on paper? Demonstrate your ability to do this by recording CMS's response to a QUERY DISK command you issue.

Set PF1 to issue immediately any CP command of your choice and test its operation. Now alter that key setting to DELAYED and again test its operation. For what situations might you prefer keys with DELAYED versus immediate settings?

What are the differences between linking to a minidisk yourself versus having it done for you in your CP Directory entry?

Link to another user's A-disk. Now try to edit a file on that minidisk. Can you do it? What dangers or problems are involved?

What are the differences between linking to and accessing another user's minidisks versus defining a minidisk for your use via the CP DEFINE command?

When do you use the CMS FORMAT command? When could its use be disastrous?

How do you access a tape under CMS? Describe this process and the commands involved.

Determine how much virtual storage your virtual machine has presently. Now, dynamically reconfigure your system to have more virtual storage and verify that you have successfully acquired the extra storage. Are there limits as to how much virtual storage you can access?

What CP command do you issue to gain access to additional virtual printers, system consoles, communication lines, channels, and other resources?

SECTION 4

CMS
Communications
and Commands

- Full-Screen Communications
- Commands Providing Additional Flexibility
- The CMS HELP Facility
- CMS Wrapup

CHAPTER 12

Full-Screen Communications

VM/CMS supports special facilities for communications among CMS computer users. This is important because of the virtual machine philosophy of this operating system. With all users having their own virtual machine, how do they communicate across virtual machines?

Because CMS does not support file-write integrity among multiple CMS users, communications and data sharing under VM/CMS become related issues. VM/CMS includes extensive facilities to permit communications and data sharing, features that provide great flexibility to users.

One facility for communication within VM/CMS consists of a comprehensive set of full-screen CMS communications commands, including NAMES, TELL, NOTE, SENDFILE, and RDRLIST. These five commands comprise the highest level vehicle within VM/CMS for interuser communication. The commands take advantage of full-screen displays, PF keys, and RSCS to permit simple communication between users on the same or different physical computers.

Supporting this nucleus of basic CMS commands are the additional CMS communications commands NAMEFIND, PEEK, RECEIVE, DISK, and RDR. While one need only work with the key five CMS communications commands, these extra commands offer CMS users greater flexibility.

The CP commands of the spooling facility create a second, lower-level facility for communication between VM/CMS users in their redirectability of input/output. The CP commands for linking to other CMS user's minidisks represent a third facility for communication and data sharing within VM/CMS. Finally, there exist numerous separately licensed program products that can be purchased for the VM/CMS environment to enable data sharing between CMS users. These products run in their own virtual machines, and they permit CMS users to access the databases controlled by that virtual machine. Data access is on a record-oriented basis. This class of product includes database management systems (DBMS) available from IBM and other vendors. Chapter 13 discusses the differences between record-oriented data sharing and the three kinds of VM/CMS communication facilities listed above.

Communicating with Other Users

CMS includes a full complement of easy-to-use commands that facilitate communication with other CMS users on the same physical computer, and with CMS users on geographically dispersed computers in a network. This latter capability assumes installation of RSCS on each computer in the network.

The CMS communication facilities send three kinds of communication: *messages,* or single lines of information; *notes,* or brief communications such as interoffice memos; and files, CMS files of arbitrary length.

In order to send these communications to other CMS users, you need to know the userid of the recipient and the *node* of that CMS user.

The node (or *nodeid*) is the identifier for that user's computer. It is only required when communicating across VM/CMS systems in a network.

The CMS NAMES Command

Many of the CMS communication commands are based on the concept of a *names file.* A names file is simply a directory of users to whom you send messages, notes, and files. Each entry in this directory can contain the recipient's userid, node, nickname, name, address, and telephone number.

To create a names file, enter the CMS command:

    NAMES

Filling in the screen in figure 12-1 results in one entry in your names file. This screen requires that you fill in a `Nickname`, which is a name you assign this user and by which you can refer to him or her in the other CMS communication commands. You must also fill in the `Userid`, and the `Node` name (if the user is located on a different physical computer than your own).

You only fill in the `Name`, `Phone`, and `Address` fields if you like. However, they are useful because they're automatically placed in the headings of notes generated through the CMS `NOTE` command.

Usually when using the `NAMES` panel to send notes, copies are automatically kept of all notes you send or receive. These are placed in a file named `ALL NOTEBOOK A0`. If you wish notes passed to/from the CMS user represented by a particular `NAMES` entry placed into a separate file, assign the filename of that file in the upper right-hand corner of the screen, under the fieldname, `Notebook`. Then, all notes to/from this person are kept in the CMS file named `FILENAME NOTEBOOK A0`, where `FILENAME` is the identifier you entered in the `Notebook` field.

The bottom of the `NAMES` command panel shows the functions of PF keys while viewing this screen. Press `PF2` after you've filled in the panel to

Figure 12-1   The NAMES Screen

```
====> ZHMF01    NAMES    <========>  N A M E S   F I L E   E D I T I N G  <====
Fill in the fields and press a PFkey to display and/or change your NAMES file.
Nickname: _          Userid:          Node:          Notebook:
                       Name:
                      Phone:
                    Address:
                           :
                           :
                           :
           List of Names:
                           :
                           :
                           :
You can enter optional information below.  Describe it by giving it a "tag".
Tag:                 Value:
Tag:                 Value:
Tag:                 Value:
Tag:                 Value:
Tag:                 Value:
Tag:                 Value:
Tag:                 Value:



  1= Help       2= Add      3= Quit     4=  Clear      5= Find     6= Change
  7= Previous   8= Next     9=          10= Delete      11=         12= Cursor
====>
                                                          MACRO-READ 1 FILE
```

create an entry in your names file for this person. Press **PF4** to clear the fields so that you can type in another entry. Exit the **NAMES** panel by pressing **PF3**.

Once you have added entries in your names file, you may need to search for specific entries to change or delete them. Bring up the **NAMES** command screen by entering:

NAMES nickname

where nickname is the nickname of the entry to change or delete. Retype any fields for changes, then press **PF6** to alter them in the names file. Or press **PF10** to delete the entry displayed on the screen from the names file.

If you don't know the nickname of the entry to alter, enter:

NAMES

as before. Now fill in any field from the screen, and press **PF5**. The **FIND** function retrieves the first entry from the names file matching the field you specified.

Pressing **PF1**, the Help key, provides online information on how to perform these functions.

You can also scroll through entries in the names file, a full entry (screen) at a time by pressing **PF8** for the next entry, or **PF7** for the previous entry. The information in the "names file" is stored in a CMS file named:

```
userid NAMES AO
```

where userid is your own CMS userid.

Figure 12-2 shows a **NAMES** panel entry for a CMS user with whom you communicate. The **Node** field identifies the name of the computer on which this user works. Leave this field blank if the user uses the same physical computer. (This is the default.) The **Notebook** field indicates that the notes sent to (and received from) this user are placed in a file named **MILESTON NOTEBOOK** on your A-disk. Communicate with this user by either his userid of **ZFLP01** or his nickname of **AARDVARK**.

Figure 12-2   Filling in the NAMES Screen

```
====> ZHMF01    NAMES    <=========>  N A M E S   F I L E   E D I T I N G  <====
Fill in the fields and press a PFkey to display and/or change your NAMES file.
Nickname: aardvark Userid: zflp01    Node: SAND    Notebook: mileston
                   Name: Fillipe Pas
                  Phone: 279-6648
                Address: 1 Milky Way
                      : Villa Park
                      : IL  60181_
                      :
        List of Names:
                      :
                      :
                      :
You can enter optional information below.  Describe it by giving it a "tag".
Tag:               Value:
Tag:               Value:
Tag:               Value:
Tag:               Value:
Tag:               Value:
Tag:               Value:
Tag:               Value:


 1= Help        2= Add      3= Quit     4=  Clear      5= Find      6= Change
 7= Previous    8= Next     9=          10= Delete     11=          12= Cursor
====>
                                                       MACRO-READ 1 FILE
```

The **List of Names** field in the **NAMES** panel supports an important feature. Instead of creating a names file entry for a CMS user, you can enter the **Nickname** field and a list of entries in the **List of Names** field. The list of names may include: the nickname of an entry in the name file; the userid of a CMS user on your physical computer; or an entry in the form of userid **AT** node (for users not on the same physical computer).

In the latter case, userid is the user's logon id and node is the user's computer identifier.

With this use of the **NAMES** panel, you build distribution lists for your notes. By referring to the **Nickname** of a **NAMES** panel that contains a **List of Names**, you send a note to every recipient in the **List of Names** with a single CMS command.

Figure 12-3 illustrates creation of a distribution list. Assuming that entries JOHN, BRYAN, FRED, BARON, SUE, and SHORE represent individual names file entries, table 12-1 shows to whom notes are sent when using the specified nicknames as destinations.

Table 12-1
Distribution of
Notes by
Nickname

Nickname	Chained List of Names	Actual Recipients
STAFF	PROJECTA	JOHN BRYAN FRED
	PROJECTB	BARON SUE SHORE
PROJECTB	PROJECTB	BARON SUE SHORE

Sending a note to STAFF sends notes to JOHN, BRYAN, FRED, BARON, SUE, and SHORE. Sending a note to PROJECTB sends copies to BARON, SUE, and SHORE.

In summary, NAMES panels can be used to enter distribution lists of note recipients. The following demonstrations of CMS commands explain the role of the names file in communications.

Sending Messages

Several CMS commands use the information in the names file to send messages, notes, and files to other CMS users. These users may either work on the same real computer system, or on another physical computer connected to your own via the RSCS network.

The CMS TELL command sends short messages to other CMS users. Its format is:

```
TELL  name  message
```

name may be either:

1. The Nickname field from a names file (This name can refer to a single CMS user, or a group of users, through the List of Names feature of the NAMES panel.)

2. the userid of a CMS user on your own computer

3. in the form userid AT node, where the user is on a different VM /CMS computer connected to your own via RSCS

Figure 12-3 Creating a List of Names

```
 ====> ZHMF01   NAMES    <========>  N A M E S   F I L E   E D I T I N G  <====
Fill in the fields and press a PFkey to display and/or change your NAMES file.
Nickname: PROJECTA Userid:          Node:          Notebook:
                         Name:
                        Phone:
                      Address:
                             :
                             :
                             :
             List of Names: JOHN BRYAN FRED_
                             :
                             :
                             :
You can enter optional information below.  Describe it by giving it a "tag".
Tag:                     Value:
Tag:                     Value:
Tag:                     Value:
Tag:                     Value:
Tag:                     Value:
Tag:                     Value:
Tag:                     Value:



  1= Help        2= Add       3= Quit      4=  Clear        5= Find       6= Change
  7= Previous    8= Next      9=          10= Delete       11=           12= Cursor
 ====>
                                                          MACRO-READ 1 FILE
```

```
 ====> ZHMF01   NAMES    <========>  N A M E S   F I L E   E D I T I N G  <====
Fill in the fields and press a PFkey to display and/or change your NAMES file.
Nickname: PROJECTB Userid:          Node:          Notebook:
                         Name:
                        Phone:
                      Address:
                             :
                             :
                             :
             List of Names: BARON SUE SHORE_
                             :
                             :
                             :
You can enter optional information below.  Describe it by giving it a "tag".
Tag:                     Value:
Tag:                     Value:
Tag:                     Value:
Tag:                     Value:
Tag:                     Value:
Tag:                     Value:
Tag:                     Value:



  1= Help        2= Add       3= Quit      4=  Clear        5= Find       6= Change
  7= Previous    8= Next      9=          10= Delete       11=           12= Cursor
 ====>
                                                          MACRO-READ 1 FILE
```

**Figure 12-3
(cont.)**

```
====> ZHMF01   NAMES    <========>  N A M E S   F I L E   E D I T I N G  <====
Fill in the fields and press a PFkey to display and/or change your NAMES file.
Nickname: STAFF    Userid:          Node:           Notebook:
                    Name:
                   Phone:
                 Address:
                        :
                        :
                        :
         List of Names: PROJECTA PROJECTB_
                        :
                        :
                        :
You can enter optional information below.  Describe it by giving it a "tag".
Tag:                 Value:
Tag:                 Value:
Tag:                 Value:
Tag:                 Value:
Tag:                 Value:
Tag:                 Value:
Tag:                 Value:



1= Help        2= Add      3= Quit     4= Clear      5= Find     6= Change
7= Previous    8= Next     9=         10= Delete    11=         12= Cursor
====>
                                                    MACRO-READ 1 FILE
```

Here's an example:

TELL STAFF   GROUP MEETING AT 3 TODAY ROOM ORNL433

This sends the message GROUP MEETING AT 3 TODAY ROOM ORNL433 to the six members in the list of names associated with the nickname STAFF. Or enter:

TELL ZUSERA   CALL ORNL X-8774 FOR BUG REPORT FAST!!

This sends a message to the CMS user on your physical computer whose logon id is ZUSERA. In this case, the TELL command doesn't take advantage of your names file because the command refers to a userid rather than a nickname.

When using the TELL command, the intended recipient(s) must be logged on the computer to receive your message. Messages that fail must be sent again later, when they have logged on, if you intend to get a CMS message to them via TELL. Check to see if a user is logged on through:

CP QUERY userid

where userid is the user's logon id.

Note that if the intended recipient has specified:

```
CP  SET  MSG  OFF
```

this has the same effect as if the recipient were not logged on.

Sending Notes

The CMS **NOTE** command is more convenient for sending longer messages than **TELL**. The **NOTE** command is often used to send interoffice memos and notices. Like the **TELL** command, **NOTE** uses the names file in directing communications. But unlike **TELL**, recipients do not have to be logged onto the computer when you send the communication. A note is stored in recipients' virtual card readers until they are ready to receive it.

To send a note, enter a CMS **NOTE** command similar to this example:

```
NOTE  name1  name2 ...
```

The one or more names specified as operands in the **NOTE** command may be either nicknames (from the names file), CMS userids, or userid specifications for remote computer users in the form:

```
userid  AT  node
```

These routing destinations present the same possibilities as mentioned earlier with the **TELL** command. You can mix destinations of any format.

Entry of the **NOTE** command:

```
NOTE  AARDVARK
```

displays the **NOTE** command screen of figure 12-4. The system automatically includes headings in your note. These contain the date and time and information from your names file. If you don't like the automatically generated headings, you can alter them merely by overtyping them.

Entering the **NOTE** command places you in XEDIT. You may enter the text of the note through the XEDIT facilities for entry and alteration of data files. Note the PF key settings at the bottom of the screen. All the keys except **PF5** help in editing the note. Press **PF5** when you have completed entry of the note and wish to send it. **PF5** routes copies of the note to the list of users associated with this note when you entered the **NOTE** command. Then, it returns you to CMS.

When editing a note, if you wish to save it and finish later, enter the XEDIT command **FILE** on the command line. To access the note later, enter:

```
NOTE
```

Figure 12-4 The NOTE Screen

```
ZHMF01    NOTE      A0   V 132  TRUNC=132 SIZE=9 LINE=9 COL=1 ALT=0




* * * TOP OF FILE * * *
OPTIONS: NOACK     LOG     SHORT     NOTEBOOK MILESTON



Date: 7 July 1986, 22:51:28 CST
From: ZHMF01   at ORNL
To:   ZFLP01 at SAND

* * * END OF FILE * * *



1= Help       2= Add Line  3= Quit   4= Tab      5= Send      6= ?
7= Backward   8= Forward   9= =      10= Rgtleft 11= Spitjoin 12= Power input
====> _
                                                 X E D I T   1 FILE
```

with no parameters. CMS restores you to editing the partially completed note. The note was not sent; it was stored under the CMS file named:

```
userid NOTE A0
```

where userid is your own logon id.

In entering the **NOTE** command, you can generate a more complete heading by entering the **LONG** option on the **NOTE** command:

```
NOTE  name  (LONG
```

Figure 12-5 shows what the heading looks like for this example:

```
NOTE  AARDVARK  (LONG
```

You may also wish to send complimentary copies of notes to people who aren't the primary recipients. This is analogous to the business practice of "copying" people on interoffice memos. To do this, enter the **NOTE** command with the **CC:** operand. The operands following the **CC:** consist of the same kinds of destinations as the primary **NOTE** command destination specifications:

Figure 12-5   The NOTE Screen with LONG Heading

```
ZHMF01    NOTE      A0  V 132   TRUNC=132 SIZE=9 LINE=9 COL=1 ALT=0




 
 
 
 
* * * TOP OF FILE * * *
OPTIONS: NOACK     LOG    LONG        NOTEBOOK MILESTON



Date: 7 July 1986, 22:51:28 CST
From: ZHMF01    at ORNL
To:   Fillipe Pas              279-6648          ZFLP01    at  SAND
* * * END OF FILE * * *



1= Help        2= Add Line  3= Quit   4= Tab      5= Send     6= ?
7= Backward    8= Forward   9= =      10= Rgtleft 11= Spitjoin 12= Power input
====>  _
                                                  X E D I T   1 FILE
```

NOTE PROJECTA CC: PROJECTB

Figure 12-6 shows the heading that results from this example. The TO: and CC: lists in the note reference the note recipients.

Finally, a copy of each note you send is automatically appended to a file named **ALL NOTEBOOK A0**, separated from the previous note by a line of equal signs. You can always view previously sent notes by entering:

NOTE XEDIT ALL NOTEBOOK

Remember that if you send notes referring to a person in the names file for whom you entered a **Notebook** field, copies of these notes are placed in a **NOTEBOOK** file under the filename you specified. This file also retains copies of notes you receive from that person.

Sending Files

The CMS **SENDFILE** command sends copies of files from your CMS virtual machine to other CMS users. Like the **TELL** and **NOTE** commands, **SENDFILE** communicates with CMS users on other physical computers connected to your own via an RSCS network.

Figure 12-6   The NOTE Screen with CC: Heading

```
ZHMF01    NOTE     A0  V 132  TRUNC=132 SIZE=10 LINE=10 COL=1 ALT=0




* * * TOP OF FILE * * *
OPTIONS: NOACK    LOG    SHORT    NOTEBOOK ALL



Date: 7 July 1986, 22:51:28 CST
From: ZHMF01    at ORNL
To:   JOHN, BRYAN, FRED
cc:   BARON, SUE, SHORE

* * * END OF FILE * * *


1= Help       2= Add Line  3= Quit   4= Tab      5= Send      6= ?
7= Backward   8= Forward   9= =      10= Rgtleft 11= Spitjoin 12= Power input
====>  _
                                                      X E D I T  1 FILE
```

One way to use the **SENDFILE** command is to enter the name of the file to send on the command line. Here is an example:

SENDFILE SAMPLE DATA A1 TO ZUSERA

This sends a copy of the file named **SAMPLE DATA A1** to the CMS user whose logon id is **ZUSERA**. As in the **TELL** and **NOTE** commands, the userid can be specified as a nickname (from your names file), another user's logon id, or a phrase in the form **userid AT note**. **SENDFILE** takes advantage of the names file concept to provide maximum flexibility in defining the destination of the file.

You can also enter **SENDFILE** without any operands:

SENDFILE

This form of the command results in a full-screen display similar to that illustrated in figure 12-7. To send a file via this screen, enter the filename and filetype of the file to send. If the file is not on your A-disk, enter the filemode as well.

Figure 12-7   The SENDFILE Screen

```
----------------   SENDFILE   ----------------

File(s) to be sent    (use * for Filename, Filetype and/or Filemode
                           to select from a list of files)
Enter filename :  _
      filetype :
      filemode :

Send files to  :

Type over YES or NO to change the options:

   NO     Request acknowledgement when the file has been received?

   YES    Make a log entry when the file has been sent?

   YES    Display the file name when the file has been sent?

   NO     This file is actually a list of files to be sent?



   1= Help          3= Quit          5= Send          12= Cursor
====>
                                                   MACRO-READ 1 FILE
```

Now, enter the options to the four yes/no questions. To change any
selection, merely overtype the default. Here are explanations of the four
questions:

> `NO  Request acknowledgment when the file has been received?`

Entering **YES** to this question provides you with an acknowledgment
after the recipient receives your file. The acknowledgment contains the
date and time you sent the file, and the recipient's userid and node.

> `YES  Make a log entry when the file has been sent?`

Answering **YES** to this question ensures that entries are made in a file
named userid `NETLOG AO` each time you send a file; userid refers to your
CMS logon id.

If you answered **YES** to the first question above (the acknowledgment option), then entries are also made in this log file when you receive acknowledgments.

```
YES   Display the file name when the file has been sent?
```

SENDFILE clears the screen and displays the name of the file sent, the userid, and the node of the recipient in response to a **YES** to this question.

```
NO  This file is actually a list of files to be sent?
```

Answering **YES** to this question indicates that you intend to send more than a single file to the recipient(s) via this single **SENDFILE** command.

Once you have chosen answers to the four questions on the **SENDFILE** screen, send the file by pressing **PF5**. This action also exits the **SENDFILE** display. Pressing the **ENTER** key sends the file and retains the **SENDFILE** command screen.

There are two ways to send multiple files to recipient(s). In one method, enter the CMS **FILELIST** command prior to issuing **SENDFILE**. Remember that **FILELIST** displays a file that contains a list of files. When in the **FILELIST** display, save the file listing under any new file name you choose.

Here's an example. Enter:

```
FILELIST  *  DATA  A1
```

This results in a **FILELIST** controlled display of all the files of filetype **DATA** on your screen. As figure 12-8 illustrates, save this display listing by entering the XEDIT command **FILE** on the command line, followed by the file name. Here, the file listing is saved in the CMS file named **SENDME LIST A1**.

Exit the **FILELIST** panel, and enter the **SENDFILE** panel:

```
SENDFILE
```

Figure 12-9 shows that **SENDME LIST A1** has been specified in the file

Figure 12-8   Saving a List of Files from a FILELIST Display

```
ZHMF01    FILELIST AO   V 108   TRUNC=108 SIZE=4 LINE=1 COL=1 ALT=0
Cmd   Filename Filetype Fm Format Lrecl     Records     Blocks    Date      Time
      TEST1    DATA     A1 F       80             1          1 10/22/85 19:11:16
      TEST2    DATA     A1 F       80             3          1 10/22/85 19:09:19
      TEST3    DATA     A1 F       80             3          1 10/22/85 19:08:42
      TEST4    DATA     A1 F       80             5          1 10/22/85 19:07:44




















1= Help       2= Refresh  3= Quit    4= Sort(type)  5= Sort(date)  6= Sort(size)
7= Backward   8= Forward  9= FL /n  10=            11= XEDIT       12= Cursor
====> FILE SENDME LIST A1_
                                                         X E D I T  1 FILE
```

Figure 12-9   Sending a List of Files via the SENDFILE Screen

```
             ---------------- SENDFILE ----------------

File(s) to be sent    (use * for Filename, Filetype and/or Filemode
                          to select from a list of files)
Enter filename : SENDME
      filetype : LIST
      filemode : A1

Send files to : ZUSERA

Type over YES or NO to change the options:

   NO    Request acknowledgement when the file has been received?

   YES   Make a log entry when the file has been sent?

   YES   Display the file name when the file has been sent?

   YES_  This file is actually a list of files to be sent?



   1= Help            3= Quit            5= Send            12= Cursor

====>

                                              MACRO-READ 1 FILE
```

name portion of the **SENDFILE** screen. The answer to the fourth question
on the screen is **YES**, because **SENDME LIST A1** contains a list of files to send.
Press **PF5** or **ENTER** and the files are sent.

Perhaps the easiest way to send multiple files is to enter the `SENDFILE` command:

`SENDFILE`

and prompt `SENDFILE` to provide you with a list of files from which to select those to send. Do this by entering an asterisk * in the filename, filetype, and/or filemode fields at the top of the screen. Figure 12-10 shows entry of an asterisk for the filename. This prompts `SENDFILE` to display a filelist itself, as seen in figure 12-11. Now, enter the letter `S` in front of each file to send, under the `Cmd` column on the lefthand side of the screen. The example in figure 12-12 sends two files. If necessary, you may scroll the screen display via **PF7** and **PF8**. Press **ENTER** to send the files. **PF3** exits you when done.

Figure 12-10   Requesting a Filelist from the SENDFILE Screen

```
---------------- SENDFILE ----------------
File(s) to be sent     (use * for Filename, Filetype and/or Filemode
                            to select from a list of files)
Enter filename : *
      filetype : DATA
      filemode : A1

Send files to  : ZUSERA_

Type over YES or NO to change the options:

   NO     Request acknowledgement when the file has been received?

   YES    Make a log entry when the file has been sent?

   YES    Display the file name when the file has been sent?

   NO     This file is actually a list of files to be sent?



   1= Help          3= Quit          5= Send          12= Cursor

====>
                                              MACRO-READ 1 FILE
```

`SENDFILE` is the most powerful and flexible of the basic CMS communications commands. It allows you to send files of any format and length. On the other hand, the `TELL` command is quickest for short messages, and the `NOTE` command automatically structures interoffice memos and letters.

Figure 12-11   Filelist Displayed from SENDFILE Screen

```
ZHMF01    FILELIST A0   V 108   TRUNC=108 SIZE=4 LINE=1 COL=1 ALT=0
Cmd    Filename Filetype Fm Format Lrecl     Records     Blocks   Date      Time
 —       TEST1    DATA     A1 F       80         1          1 10/22/85 19:11:16
         TEST2    DATA     A1 F       80         3          1 10/22/85 19:09:19
         TEST3    DATA     A1 F       80         3          1 10/22/85 19:08:42
         TEST4    DATA     A1 F       80         5          1 10/22/85 19:07:44




1= Help      2= Refresh  3= Quit    4= Sort(type)  5= Sort(date)  6= Sort(size)
7= Backward  8= Forward  9= FL /n   10=            11= XEDIT       12= Cursor
Type 'S' in front of each file to be sent and press Enter.
====>
                                                     X E D I T  1 FILE
```

Figure 12-12   Sending Two Files from SENDFILE's Filelist Screen

```
ZHMF01    FILELIST A0   V 108   TRUNC=108 SIZE=4 LINE=1 COL=1 ALT=0
Cmd    Filename Filetype Fm Format Lrecl     Records     Blocks   Date      Time
         TEST1    DATA     A1 F       80         1          1 10/22/85 19:11:16
 S       TEST2    DATA     A1 F       80         3          1 10/22/85 19:09:19
 S_      TEST3    DATA     A1 F       80         3          1 10/22/85 19:08:42
         TEST4    DATA     A1 F       80         5          1 10/22/85 19:07:44




1= Help      2= Refresh  3= Quit    4= Sort(type)  5= Sort(date)  6= Sort(size)
7= Backward  8= Forward  9= FL /n   10=            11= XEDIT       12= Cursor
Type 'S' in front of each file to be sent and press Enter.
====>
                                                     X E D I T  1 FILE
```

Receiving Messages, Notes, and Files

Your CMS virtual machine defaults to CP SET MSG ON. Unless you have issued:

        CP SET MSG OFF

you need take no action to receive messages sent to you via the CMS `TELL` command; they appear automatically.

You receive notes and files via the CMS `RDRLIST` command. These communications arrive via your virtual reader. You know that there are one or more files in your reader because when you logon and IPL CMS, a message such as this appears:

```
FILES:  002 RDR, NO PRT, NO PUN
```

Or, you may receive a message that files are in your reader while under CMS. Remember you can check your virtual reader at any time by entering the CP command `QUERY READER`.

To handle the files in your virtual reader, enter this CMS command:

```
RDRLIST
```

The screen of figure 12-13 appears. This display shows the filename and filetype for each file, the spooling class, the sending userid and node, the file status, the number of records in the file, and the date and time the file was sent.

From this screen, you can:

- receive a file (move it from the reader to your A-disk)
- discard a file (permanently delete the file without receiving it)
- "peek" at a file (look at it without removing it from your virtual reader)

To receive a file, take the cursor up to the line listing the file name and press `PF9`. If you receive a message like this:

```
File 'fn ft fm' already exists.--specify 'REPLACE' option.
```

then you already have a file with the same name as the reader file on disk. One approach to resolving this conflict is to replace the old file with the new file from your reader (permanently deleting the old file). Move the cursor up to the line with the file to read underneath the `Cmd` enter area and enter this `RDRLIST` subcommand:

Figure 12-13   The RDRLIST Screen

```
ZHMF01    RDRLIST  A0  V 108   TRUNC=108 SIZE=2 LINE=1  COL=1 ALT=0
Cmd    Filename Filetype Class User  at Node     Hold  Records  Date      Time
       TEST2    DATA     PU A  ZHMF01   ORNL      NOH       3   10/22     20:33
       TEST3    DATA     PU A  ZHMF01   ORNL      NOH       3   10/22     20:33
—




















1=  Help      2= Refresh  3= Quit     4= Sort(type)  5= Sort(date) 6= Sort(user)
7= Backward   8= Forward  9= Receive 10=            11= Peek       12= Cursor
====>
                                                       X E D I T   1 FILE
```

RECEIVE / (REPLACE

The old disk file is replaced by the reader file. An alternative solution is to receive the file from your reader by giving it a new name. Take the cursor to the line containing the file name, and enter this command under the Cmd column:

RECEIVE / NEWNAME NEWTYPE A1

The reader file is moved to disk under the filename NEWNAME NEWTYPE A1.

You receive notes in the same way as other CMS files. Notes have the filetype of NOTE. To receive a note, move the cursor up to the line of the note information and press PF9. The note is added to the file ALL NOTEBOOK A0, unless you specified a special notebook file for notes from this user in your names file. In this case, the note is added to whatever you named the notebook file for communications with this user.

To discard a reader file via the RDRLIST screen, move the cursor underneath the Cmd indicator on the line of the file you want to eliminate. Enter DISCARD, in the same way you would when discarding a disk file through the FILELIST command screen.

You can also view a file from the RDRLIST screen without removing it from your virtual reader. Move the cursor to the line of the file and press the PF11 key. You now view the file under XEDIT control, as shown in figure 12-14.

Figure 12-14   "Peeking" at a File Still in Your Virtual Reader

```
 0215     PEEK     A0  V 80  TRUNC=80 SIZE=3 LINE=0 COL=1 ALT=0
File TEST2 DATA from ZHMF01 at ORNL.  Format is NETDATA.
* * * TOP OF FILE * * *
THIS IS THE FIRST LINE OF DATA IN THE FILE.
THIS IS THE SECOND LINE OF DATA IN THE FILE.
THIS IS THE THIRD AND LAST LINE OF DATA IN THIS FILE.
* * * END OF FILE * * *




















1=  Help      2= Add Line 3= Quit      4= Tab      5= Clocate      6= ?/Change
7= Backward   8= Forward   9= Receive  10= Rgtleft 11= Spltjoin   12= Cursor
====> _
                                                      X E D I T   1 FILE
```

To receive the file you see, press **PF9**. To exit the display, press **PF3**. Exit the **RDRLIST** screen by this same key.

Other useful program function keys under **RDRLIST** include the scrolling keys, **PF7** and **PF8**. You can also sort the reader listing by filetype, date, and userid of origin, by pressing **PF4**, **PF5**, and **PF6**, respectively.

For Further Information

A simple tutorial on the CMS commands for communication is located in the *VM/SP CMS Primer, SC24-5236*. That book covers the commands: NAMES, TELL, NOTE, SENDFILE, RDRLIST, RECEIVE, and CP SET MSG OFF/ON. The discussion is introductory and does not attempt to explain all the command options.

The *VM/SP CMS User's Guide, SC19-6210*, includes a chapter on the CMS communication commands suitable for programmers. Complete details on all CMS commands are found in *VM/SP CMS Command and Macro Reference, SC19-6209*. This contains exact command formats and description for the CMS commands introduced here. Use this manual (and your own online experiments) for the most precise and comprehensive information on how the CMS communications commands work.

Test Your Understanding

What are the basic units of communication under CMS, and what information do you need to know to communicate with other CMS users?

Create a NAMES file having entries for CMS users with whom you communicate. What information must each entry minimally contain? Practice using the PF keys on the NAMES display to scroll through the entries after you have entered them. You might also want to retrieve a particular entry through PF5. Remember that if you need help, you can access help information through PF1.

Use the NAMES command to assign a single name to all the CMS users entered in your NAMES file. Send everybody in the file a one line message. What's the most convenient CMS command for sending this message?

Use the CMS NOTE command to send a brief communication to somebody in your NAMES file. When you send the note, does it refer to a userid or a nickname? What do you do if you later want to look up what the note said?

If recipients are not logged on the computer, do messages sent via the CMS TELL command reach them? How about communications sent via NOTE and SENDFILE? What command do you enter to determine if a particular user is logged on?

Use the CMS SENDFILE command to send a copy of a single file to yourself. Now send yourself multiple files without exiting the SENDFILE panels. Exit the SENDFILE command and enter the RDRLIST command to handle the reader files. Using the RDRLIST panel, discard the first file you sent to yourself. Receive the second one. Given that this file has the same name as an existing file, what are your alternatives?

Practice using the program function keys from the RDRLIST display. Do the keys for sorting the display work the same as from within a FILELIST display?

CHAPTER 13

Commands Providing Additional Flexibility

Chapter 12 described the core group of CMS commands for communication between users. These commands are: NAMES, TELL, NOTE, SENDFILE, and RDRLIST.

This chapter expands that core group of CMS communication commands in describing a variety of other CMS commands. While one can be self-sufficient using only the nucleus commands presented thus far, these additional CMS commands provide greater control and flexibility in communications.

Supportive Commands

The five CMS commands, NAMES, TELL, NOTE, SENDFILE, and RDRLIST, comprise a complete VM/CMS communication system. With the addition of the CP QUERY command, you can communicate within VM/CMS with little knowledge of other commands for this purpose.

There are, however, several other CMS commands designed for communication, including NAMEFIND, PEEK, RECEIVE, DISK, and RDR. Remember, PRINT, PUNCH, and READCARD also transfer information through virtual unit record devices.

The CMS NAMEFIND command displays information from your names file. NAMEFIND is a lower-level facility than the retrieval function supported through the PF5 key in the NAMES command panel.

A names file is a collection of entries, each of which is associated with a nickname. The fields within each names entry are identified by a tag. Example tags are :nick for nickname, and :name for the NAMES command Name field.

List the tags (and the values for each entry) for your names file by entering:

    TYPE userid NAMES

where userid is your logon id.

Enter the NAMEFIND command by specifying a list of tags, one or more of which have associated values. Tags without values indicate the data to retrieve. In this example:

```
NAMEFIND  :NICK JOHN  :NAME  :PHONE
```

the command responds with the NAME and PHONE fields from the names file for the entry having the nickname JOHN.

The CMS PEEK command provides lower-level access to the same "peek" function accessible by the PF11 key from the RDRLIST command screen. To enter PEEK directly, type:

```
PEEK  spoolid
```

where spoolid is the spool identification number assigned the file in the virtual reader by the CP spooling facility. Figure 12-14 illustrates results of "peeking" at a file in the reader. Recall that you can view spoolids for all files in the virtual reader via the CP command CP QUERY READER ALL. Entering PEEK without a spoolid peeks at the "next" file in the virtual reader. CMS's definition of the next file depends on the reader's class, the file classes, and the files' hold statuses.

The CMS RECEIVE command is familiar to you already as that function assigned to the PF9 key when viewing the RDRLIST screen. The basic format of RECEIVE is:

```
RECEIVE  spoolid  filename  filetype  filemode  (options
```

The spoolid operand indicates the spool identification number of the file to receive. It defaults to that of the next accessible file in the virtual reader queue.

Filename, filetype, and filemode define the name the new file is assigned on disk. If they are omitted, the file's present name is used (except for notes, which are added to a file of filetype NOTEBOOK). If you intend to replace an existing file by the RECEIVE file, specify the RECEIVE command REPLACE option.

Several of the options available with RECEIVE correspond to those of the RDRLIST command RECEIVE function. For example, RECEIVE options determine whether the communication is logged and whether an entry is placed in the notebook file.

You can use the CMS DEFAULTS command to establish the default options of the RECEIVE command on your virtual machine. You can also set the default options of most other CMS communication commands via the DEFAULTS command including NOTE, SENDFILE, RDRLIST, PEEK, and TELL. The DEFAULTS command thus represents a way to tailor CMS communication command default options to your liking. Refer to the vendor's manuals for complete details on the DEFAULTS command.

The CMS `RDR` command determines the characteristics of a file in your virtual reader. This is important because, as should be evident by now, CMS provides a host of commands which place files in your virtual reader. `RDR` tells you whether your reader file was placed there as an unnamed file via the `PRINT` command, a `PRINT` file with a name, an unnamed `PUNCH` file, a `PUNCH` file with a `READ` card, a file sent by the `DISK DUMP` command, or whatever. Entering:

    RDR

provides this information for the next accessible file in your virtual reader. Which file CMS considers "next" in the reader depends on the reader's class, the classes of the files in the reader, and whether they are held.

If the reader is empty, `RDR` indicates this by the message `READER EMPTY`. Note that `RDR` reorders the files that are not in hold status according to class.

There is another CMS command (in addition to `PUNCH`) that sends files to your virtual punch. Like `PUNCH`, this command is sometimes used to send files between CMS users. This is the CMS `DISK` command.

In order to spool a file to another CMS user, issue a CP `SPOOL` command to direct your virtual punch to the virtual reader of the other user:

    CP SPOOL PUNCH TO ZUSERA

At this point, use either `PUNCH` or the CMS `DISK` command with the `DUMP` operand to send data to user `ZUSERA`. (If the user works on another physical computer, you can spool files to that user through an RSCS network by using the CP `TAG` command.)

For example, to send the file named `MYFILE DATA A1` via `DISK DUMP` enter:

    DISK DUMP MYFILE DATA A1

After sending the file(s), you may conclude the operation with this command:

    CP SPOOL PUNCH CLOSE

When the file is sent via the CMS `DISK DUMP` command, the user to whom the file has been spooled loads the file through the `DISK` command with the `LOAD` operand:

    DISK LOAD

The recipient cannot assign the file any other name than that it originally had on the sender's system. If a file exists with the same name as that as the input card stream, it is replaced.

What are the differences between spooling files with the CMS `PUNCH`

/READCARD commands versus DISK DUMP/DISK LOAD? First, the PUNCH command restricts the maximum card length to 80 characters, whereas DISK DUMP permits longer record lengths. Secondly, the PUNCH/READCARD combination of commands allows the user to specify the name of the disk file to which the file in his virtual reader will be transferred. The DISK DUMP /DISK LOAD combination of commands do not.

One note of caution: a CMS user cannot use the READCARD command to read a file sent to his virtual reader via DISK DUMP. An attempt to do so results in an error and the destruction of the reader input file. Therefore, if you do not know whether a file was sent to you via the PUNCH or DISK DUMP commands (or even the other CMS commands described in this chapter), use the RDR command to determine how the file was sent.

You may also use the RECEIVE command to read the virtual reader file. RECEIVE knows to call internally the READCARD or DISK LOAD command, as appropriate. The RECEIVE command is generally more convenient than the READCARD or DISK LOAD commands.

The best choice of all is to use the RDRLIST command. Recall that PF9 on that display is set to issue the RECEIVE command for you automatically. RDRLIST is your most automatic choice for receiving notes and files.

It is due to complexities such as these that we recommend using the highest-level commands possible for routine VM/CMS communications, those commands based on the names file concept introduced in chapter 12. Those five core CMS commands provide the most convenience and power. They represent the latter evolution of VM/CMS communication facilities, and are largely built upon the CMS commands examined in this chapter subsection.

Data Sharing Summary

Table 13-1 summarizes VM/CMS facilities and commands for communication and data sharing.

The high-level CMS commands for communications (NAMES, TELL, NOTE, SENDFILE, RDRLIST) utilize the names file and provide maximum convenience in the routing of information. You may use nicknames for easy identification of destinations. Where more than a single physical computer is involved in the communication, these commands employ VM's RSCS facility in a fully transparent manner.

These commands also take advantage of full-screen displays and program function keys. The result is an easy-to-learn and easy-to-use full function system for the sending and receipt of messages, notes, and files.

Supporting this kernel of highest-level CMS commands are the group of commands described in this chapter. These CMS commands provide additional control and flexibility in interuser CMS communication and underlie the five core communication commands.

CP commands represent lower-level control of your virtual machine, giving you effective control of communications through the CP spooling

Table 13-1
VM/CMS
Communication
/Data Sharing
Facilities

Facility	Part of	Unit of Communication	Commands
CMS communication commands	CMS	Messages, notes, files	CMS NAMES, TELL, NOTE, SENDFILE, RDRLIST Also CMS NAMEFIND, PEEK, RECEIVE, RDR, PRINT, PUNCH, DISK, READCARD
CP spooling facility	CP	Files	CP SPOOL, CLOSE, CHANGE, ORDER, PURGE, TRANSFER, TAG Supported by CMS PRINT, PUNCH, DISK, READCARD, etc.
CP messaging	CP	Messages	CP MESSAGE, SMSG
CP minidisk linkage	CP	Minidisk	CP LINK, DETACH, QUERY. CMS ACCESS, RELEASE, QUERY
DBMS in its own virtual machine	Separate program product	Records (sets of records for relational DBMS)	Product-dependent

facility. These CP commands provide some degree of redirectability of I/O. For example, you can direct your printed or punched output to the virtual reader of another user; or, you can alter the distribution of your output so that it is routed to another user.

CP commands like **SPOOL** and **CLOSE** are part of this CP facility for communication, and related CMS commands are those that perform input /output through the virtual devices (**PRINT**, **PUNCH**, **DISK LOAD**, **DISK DUMP**, **READCARD**).

The CP commands also include commands that operate on spooled files. These commands include **CHANGE**, **ORDER**, **PURGE**, and **TRANSFER**.

Along with the CP spooling facility are CP commands for messaging. These include **MESSAGE** and **SMSG**.

The CP commands, especially the CP spooling facility, provide a more complex system for interuser communication and data sharing than the CMS-level facility described above. But the spooling system also lends the low-level power and flexibility that some situations require. Use the CP spooling system when your communication needs cannot easily be satisfied by the higher-level CMS communications facilities.

CP minidisk linkage represents another VM/CMS feature for information sharing. Recall that linkage to another user's minidisk may be accomplished during logon or dynamically. In the former case, linkage is established through your CP Directory entry. In the latter case, you issue the CP `LINK` and CMS `ACCESS` commands described in chapter 11.

The main advantage to this approach is that it operates on a minidisk, rather than a file, basis. You link to a minidisk, meaning that you access whatever files are stored on that minidisk.

The primary disadvantage to minidisk linkage is that VM/CMS does not guarantee file integrity in instances of shared write-access to linked minidisks. In this respect VM/CMS differs from most multi-user operating systems.

The last category of data sharing systems addresses this defect inherent in minidisk linkage. Many file management and database management systems products are available for purchase for the VM/CMS environment. These guarantee data integrity while permitting multiple users write-access. These packages run in their own virtual machines under CP and typically support multi-threaded access to data. They guarantee data integrity in multiple-write situations through their provision of file and record locking.

Packages of this nature include ADABAS, INQUIRE, RAMIS, NOMAD 2, FOCUS, IFS VSAM, and SQL/DS. The key to these products is that they are complete database management systems (with the exception of IFS VSAM). They store, manipulate, and access data in terms of records. As a relational DBMS, SQL/DS additionally permits manipulation of sets of records through its relational language operators. SQL/DS predominates in the marketplace.

Installations buy and install DBMS packages in order to build record-processing systems in the VM/CMS environment. For example, you can develop production data processing systems under VM/CMS using SQL /DS. Such systems are comparable in concept and design to the applications built with IMS/DB-DC or DB2 under the MVS operating system, or with CICS-DL/I or SQL/DS in DOS/VSE environments. Database management systems that run in their own virtual machine are the key ingredient that renders VM/CMS a suitable environment for record-oriented transaction processing. VM/CMS evolved into a full-fledged production database and applications environment with the advent of these DBMS products in the late 1970s and early 1980s.

For Further Information

A simple tutorial on the CMS commands for communication is located in the *VM/SP CMS Primer, SC24-5236.* That book only covers a small subset of CMS communication commands. The discussion is introductory and does not attempt to explain all the command options.

The *VM/SP CMS User's Guide, SC19-6210,* includes a chapter on the CMS communication commands suitable for programmers. Complete details on all CMS commands are found in *VM/SP CMS Command and Macro Reference, SC19-6209.* The *VM/SP CP Command Reference for General Users, SC19-6211,* contains equivalent explanations for CP commands for general users.

Note that if users work on other physical computers, you can spool files to them through an RSCS network by using the CP `TAG` command. See the manual *VM/SP CP Command Reference for General Users, SC19-6211,* for information on using the `TAG` command.

Test Your Understanding

Name a minimal set of CMS commands that provide for most communication needs between CMS users. What features make these commands easier to use than other CMS and CP communication commands?

Practice using the CMS `NAMEFIND` command. The functionality of the `NAMEFIND` command is available from the full-screen panel of which other CMS command?

Practice using the CMS `PEEK` command. The `PEEK` command is accessible, via a PF key, from the full-screen panel of which other CMS command?

Practice using the CMS `RECEIVE` command. The `RECEIVE` command is accessible, via a PF key, from the full-screen panel of which other CMS command?

Spool your virtual punch to your virtual reader. Practice sending files to yourself by the CMS `DISK DUMP/DISK LOAD` commands and then by the CMS `PUNCH/READCARD` commands. Now try to `PUNCH` a file and read it by the `DISK LOAD` command. What happens? Similarly, try to `DISK DUMP` a file and read it via the `READCARD` command. What happens to the file in this case?

Contrast the CMS communication commands, the CP spooling commands, and the CP minidisk linkage commands. When is the use of each most appropriate?

Why do installations purchase DBMS program products that run in their own virtual machine? What is the key advantage to such software?

CHAPTER 14

The CMS HELP Facility

One of CMS's greatest strengths as a terminal monitor is its complete online HELP facility. The HELP facility provides information on commands for all VM/CMS environments. These include:

CMS commands

CP commands

CMS and CP messages

CMS EDIT editor subcommands

XEDIT editor subcommands

DEBUG subcommands

EXEC command procedure statements

EXEC2 command procedure statements

REXX command procedure statements

SQL/DS relational DBMS program product EXECs (present only if SQL/DS is installed on your system)

The HELP facility supports single-command, online access to explanatory and usage information for any command in any of these VM/CMS environments.

The HELP facility promotes self-sufficiency in the VM/CMS operating system. Once you learn its features, you may find it more convenient than referring to printed manuals. The HELP facility fulfills an important role as a tutorial tool as well as an online HELP system.

Design of the HELP Facility

The HELP facility consists of two basic kinds of screen displays: HELP menus and HELP command files.

HELP menus display lists of commands from which you select HELP information. HELP menus group all commands for a particular VM/CMS environment together. Each menu panel lists the commands for a particular VM/CMS environment.

HELP command files comprise the screen displays containing the description, format, operands, usage notes, and system responses for each command. You view this information via the System Product Editor, XEDIT. This means that various XEDIT facilities are available while viewing the command panels. Command explanations are therefore CMS HELP files displayed under the control of the XEDIT editor.

Figure 14-1 shows that the CMS HELP facility forms a three-level hierarchy. The HELP master menu presents you with a list of VM/CMS command environments, from which you select the environment of interest. This displays a second-level HELP menu, a menu which lists all the commands for a specific VM/CMS environment. The commands of each environment are listed alphabetically on these menus. Selecting any command from one of these menus displays that command's HELP file under XEDIT's control.

The key to understanding the HELP facility is that access can occur at any point in the diagram of figure 14-1. That is, you can descend the hierarchy to the HELP file for a particular command. You can also directly access any command or menu panel by a single command. Thus, new users navigate the levels of the HELP hierarchy successively, if necessary, while experienced users with specific questions access HELP for any command through a single CMS command.

Accessing the HELP Facility

The CMS HELP command accesses any panel in the HELP facility. There are several forms of this command:

    HELP

or

    HELP MENU

displays the highest-level HELP menu. This menu appears similar to that depicted in figure 14-2. From this menu, select the environment of the command with which you need help. Notice that each selectable entry on this menu is immediately preceded by an asterisk. This means that these options are themselves menus (rather than command HELP files).

Select an entry by moving the cursor (via the terminal's cursor control keys) underneath any letter of an environment name. Then, press either the PF1 key or the ENTER key.

This displays an environment menu. Environment menus occur as the second tier of the HELP facility hierarchy in figure 14-1.

Figure 14-1
Design of the CMS
HELP Facility

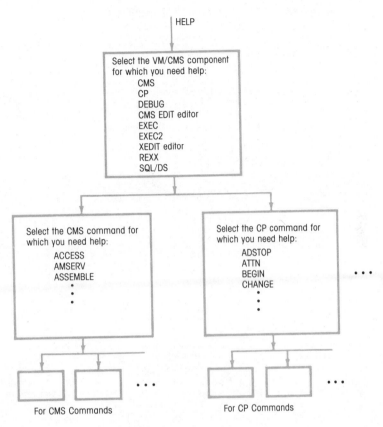

INDIVIDUAL COMMAND HELP FILES

As an example, selecting the CMS environment menu presents a panel similar to that of figure 14-3. This screen alphabetically lists all CMS command HELP files.

Notice that the CMS menu also lists the VM/CMS menus for those environments that are considered subenvironments of CMS itself. These occur first in the selection options. They are preceded by asterisks, since they are menus rather than command HELP files.

Selecting a command from the CMS menu displays that command's HELP information file under XEDIT control. Select an option in the same manner from any HELP menu: move the cursor under your selection and press either the **PF1** or **ENTER** keys.

Direct Command File Access

We describe navigation through the HELP menu hierarchy to familiarize you with the design of the HELP system. Often, you will find it more convenient to access directly either the menu for a particular environment, or the command HELP file itself.

Figure 14-2   The Topmost HELP Facility Menu

```
====> HELP  MENU   <========>  H E L P  I N F O R M A T I O N  <==============

To select HELP information  on one of the following topics,  place the cursor
under any letter of the topic you want.   Then press PF 1 or  the ENTER key.
If you are  using a  terminal that doesn't  have a terminal or PF  keys then you
must type  in the  complete HELP  command with  operands and  options.  Enter
'HELP HELP' to view  the format of the CMS HELP  command.  Note: Message HELP
files are  viewed by keying  in the message  number in the  following manner:
'HELP message number'.

Note: The  SQLDS item  is operational only  if you  have the SQL/Data System
(5748-XXJ) Program Product installed on your system.

*CMS      *Debug    *Exec     *Exec2    *REXX      *SQLDS    *Xedit
*CP       *Edit

1= Help      2= Top      3= Quit   4= Return      5= Clocate       6= ?
7= Backward  8= Forward  9= PFKey 10= Backward 1/2  11= Forward 1/2  12= Cursor
====>
                                                       MACRO-READ 1 FILE
```

Figure 14-3   The CMS HELP Menu

```
====> CMS   MENU   <========>  H E L P  I N F O R M A T I O N  <==============
A file may be selected for viewing  by placing the cursor under any character
of the  file wanted  and pressing  the PF 1 or  ENTER key.   A MENU  file is
indicated when  a name  is preceded  by an asterisk (*).  If you are  using a
terminal that  doesn't have  a  cursor or PF  keys then  you must type  in the
complete HELP  command with operands  and options.  For a  description  of the
operands and options type HELP HELP.

*DEBUG     CP         EXECOS     HX         NAMEFind   READcard   START
*Edit      DDR        EXECUPDT   IDentify   NAMES      RECEIVE    STATE
*EXec      DEBUG      FETch      IMMCMD     NOTE       RELease    STATEW
*EXEC2     DEFAULTS   FILedef    INClude    NUCEXT     Rename     SVCtrace
*REXX      DESBUF     FILELIST   LAbeldef   NUCXDROP   RESERVE    SYNonym
*Xedit     DISK       FINIS      LISTDS     NUCXLOAD   RO         TAPE
ACcess     DISKID     FORMAT     Listfile   NUCXMAP    RSERV      TAPEMAC
AMserv     DLBL       GENDIRT    LISTIO     OPTION     RT         TAPPDS
Assemble   DOSLIB     Genmod     LKED       OSRUN      RUN        TE
ASSGN      DOSLKED    GLobal     LOAD       PEEK       SENDFile   TELL
ATTN       DROPBUF    GLOBALV    LOADLIB    PRint      SENTRIES   TS
CATCHECK   DSERV      HB         LOADMod    PSERV      SET        TXTlib
CMDCALL    Edit       Help       MACLib     PUnch      SETPRT     Type
CMSBATCH   ERASE      HI         MAKEBUF    Query      SO         Update
COMpare    ESERV      HO         MODmap     RDR        SORT       WAITRD
CONWAIT    EXec       HT         MOVEfile   RDRList    SSERV      Xedit
COPYfile   EXECIO

1= Help      2= Top      3= Quit   4= Return      5= Clocate       6= ?
7= Backward  8= Forward  9= PFKey 10= Backward 1/2  11= Forward 1/2  12= Cursor
====>
                                                       MACRO-READ 1 FILE
```

To access the menu for a particular environment directly, enter:

HELP component **MENU**

where `component` is the name of the VM/CMS environment menu to access. For example, to enter the CMS HELP menu of figure 14-3 directly, enter:

```
HELP  CMS  MENU
```

The possible component operands are those shown in figure 14-2. The list might vary slightly at your site, depending on what is installed. For example, `SQLDS` is only a valid component for systems on which the SQL /DS database management system program product has been installed.

Directly access the HELP file for a specific command with this form of the CMS `HELP` command:

```
HELP  component  command-name
```

where `component` names the VM/CMS environment, as before, and `command-name` specifies the command name. For example:

```
HELP  CMS  LISTFILE
```

retrieves the HELP information for the CMS `LISTFILE` command.

If you do not specify a component, CMS is assumed. Thus:

```
HELP  CP  QUERY
```

displays information on the CP `QUERY` command, while:

```
HELP  QUERY
```

brings up the HELP file for the CMS `QUERY` command.

There exist two other significant forms of the `HELP` command. The command:

```
HELP  HELP
```

shows how to use the CMS `HELP` command itself, while:

```
HELP  message-number
```

displays HELP information for either CP or CMS messages. CP and CMS message numbers consist of seven character identifiers of the form:

```
xxxnnnt
```

The first three characters `xxx` are either `DMS` for CMS messages, or `DMK` for CP messages.

The next three characters `nnn` are the numeric digits of the message number.

The last character **t** is a single character indicating the message type. For example, **S** denotes a Severe error.

As an example, entry of the CMS command:

```
HELP  DMS250S
```

provides online description of the CMS error message, **DMS250S**.

The Command HELP Display

To recapitulate, CMS HELP panels are arranged hierachically. Enter the hierarchy at any point through the formats of the CMS HELP command shown in table 14-1.

Table 14-1
Entering CMS HELP
Panels

HELP Command Format	Panel of Entry
HELP MENU	The topmost HELP menu
HELP component MENU	An environment menu
HELP component command-name	A command HELP file

Figure 14-4 contains a sample command display. The HELP file is that of the CMS **CP** command, which allows entry of CP commands from within CMS. This HELP file was accessed by entry of:

```
HELP   CMS   CP
```

or

```
HELP   CP
```

(since the default component is **CMS**), or by selecting the **CP** command from the CMS HELP menu of figure 14-3.

As figure 14-4 illustrates, the command **HELP** information includes a brief description of the command, its formal syntax, an explanation of its operands, usage notes, and system responses.

The PF keys valid during display of the HELP file are enumerated at the bottom of the screen. **PF7**, **PF8**, **PF10**, and **PF11** scroll the file. **PF3** quits the current file, and takes you back to the last panel displayed (up one level in the hierarchical diagram of figure 14-1). **PF4** immediately returns you to CMS.

When viewing any HELP file, pressing the **PA2** key sends a copy of the screen display to the currently spooled printer. After exiting the HELP facility, enter the CP command:

```
CP  SPOOL  PRINTER  CLOSE
```

to close and print the spool file.

Figure 14-4 The CMS CP Command HELP File

```
 ====> CMS  CP <========>  H E L P  I N F O R M A T I O N  <====================
CP

Use  the  CP  command  to  transmit  commands  to  the  VM/SP  control  program
environment without leaving the CMS environment.

The format of the CP command is:

+-------------------------------------------------------------------------+
!  CP   !  ( commandline )                                                !
+-------------------------------------------------------------------------+

where:

commandline
          is any CP command valid for your CP command privilege class.  If this
          field is omitted, you are placed in  the CP environment and may enter
          CP commands  without preceding  each command with  CP.  To  return to
          CMS, issue the CP command BEGIN.

Usage Notes

 1. You must use the CP command to invoke a CP command:

     -  From within a CMS or an EXEC 2 EXEC
     -  If  the  implied  CP (IMPCP)  function is  set  to OFF  for your  virtual
        machine
     -  In a job you send to the CMS batch facility

 2. To enter a CP  command from the CMS environment without  CMS processing the
    command line, use #CP.

 3. When you enter an invalid CP command  following the CP command, you receive
    a return code of -1.  In an EXEC, this return code is +1.

Responses

All responses are  from the CP command  that was issued; the CMS ready message
1=           2= Top      3= Quit   4= Return        5= Clocate       6= ?
7= Backward  8= Forward  9= PFKey 10= Backward 1/2  11= Forward 1/2  12= Cursor
====>
                                                        MACRO-READ 1 FILE
```

Reprinted by permission from *IBM VM/SP CP Command Reference for General Users (SC19-6211-2)*, © 1983 by International Business Machines Corporation.

A major feature of the HELP facility is that you can enter CMS and CP commands directly from the HELP file display, on the command line at the bottom of the screen next to the arrow ====>. This is useful because you can try out the command while viewing its HELP panel. Should you need to try the command more than once, the PF6 key redisplays the last command entered in the command line.

The HELP Facility's Reserved Filetypes

The CMS HELP facility reserves several filetypes for its use. These reserved HELP filetypes constitute useful information if you wish to make copies of the HELP files and/or tailor the system to your own requirements.

All the reserved HELP filetypes are of the general form:

HELPxxxx

where xxxx indicates a group of related commands. Table 14-2 lists HELP filetypes and their uses.

Table 14-2
HELP Filetypes

Filetype	Reserved for
HELPCP	CP commands
HELPCMS	CMS commands
HELPDEBU	DEBUG subcommands
HELPEDIT	CMS EDIT editor subcommands
HELPEXEC	EXEC command processor statements
HELPEXC2	EXEC2 command processor statements
HELPHELP	HELP files for CMS HELP command
HELPMENU	Menus of HELP components
HELPMSG	HELPs for CMS and CP messages
HELPREXX	REXX command processor statements
HELPXEDI	XEDIT subcommands
HELPSET	XEDIT SET subcommands
HELPPREF	XEDIT PREFIX subcommands
HELPSQLD	SQL/DS HELPs (if installed)

For Further Information

The best way to gain familiarity with the CMS HELP facility is simply to use it.

The manual *VM/SP CMS User's Guide, SC19-6210,* contains a highly readable chapter on the CMS HELP facility. It also includes an advanced chapter explaining how installations customize the HELP facility.

Test Your Understanding

For which VM/CMS environments does the HELP facility supply online information? How do you access the top-level HELP panel listing these environments?

How do you directly access the HELP panel for a particular CMS command? How do you directly access the HELP panel for a particular CP command? What information does the HELP panel provide?

It's nine o'clock and your boss or teacher expects you to write a **REXX** command procedure program by noon, but you do not have the **REXX** programmer's manuals. Can you retrieve information on this language online? How?

You execute a CMS program and receive an unexpected error message. How could you find information on the error?

CHAPTER 15

CMS Wrapup

Order of Command Execution

When you enter a command to CMS, that command might be: a CMS command; a CP command; a command to one of the CMS subenvironments like the XEDIT editor; the name of a program to execute; or one of several other kinds of commands. How does CMS know for which part of VM/CMS the command is intended?

Commands entered to a particular VM/CMS environment are assumed executable in that environment. For example, when in XEDIT, you enter XEDIT subcommands.

Figure 15-1 illustrates the *command search order* for commands entered directly to CMS. The search order for commands entered to CMS is:

1. EXEC file search
2. CMS command search
3. MODULE file search
4. CP command search

EXEC files are programs written in one of the command procedure languages of CMS. Command procedures contain CMS and CP commands embedded in logical constructs, and they can call programs written in traditional programming languages like COBOL, Assembler, and PL/I. CMS supports three command procedure languages called EXEC, EXEC2, and REXX. A procedure written in any of these languages for CMS is referred to as an EXEC. Since you can write CMS EXECs yourself, the CMS search order means that any EXEC you write essentially becomes an operating system command. You can regard it as an extension to the operating system because CMS recognizes and executes it as any other CMS command. Section 6 of this book teaches you how to write command procedures.

Figure 15-1
CMS Command
Search Order

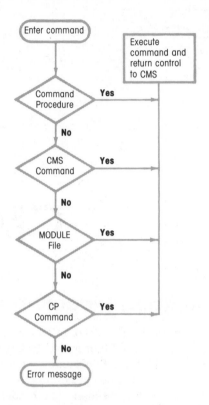

If the command you enter is not an EXEC, CMS then searches for a CMS command to execute. This command might be a *nucleus-extension command,* resident in the *transient area,* or a *nucleus-resident command.* The differences between these kinds of commands are important to systems programmers but are transparent to CMS users.

Next, CMS searches for a MODULE file to execute. Modules are nonrelocatable executable programs on disk, ready to be loaded into virtual storage and executed. Section 5 describes how to convert programs you write in languages like COBOL, Assembler, PL/I, and FORTRAN into MODULE files. CMS modules all have the reserved filetype MODULE.

Much like programs written in command procedure languages, CMS's inclusion of MODULE files in its command search order means that you can effectively extend the operating system and its universe of commands by writing your own. Develop programs that contain new functions and make them into MODULE files on disk, and you have effectively added new CMS functions. The terminal user need only type in the filename of the module to execute it.

If the command you enter does not fall into the above categories, CMS passes it to CP. CP then attempts execution of the command.

The CMS SET command enables you to omit the first and the last steps in the command search order. Enter:

```
SET  IMPEX  OFF
```

and CMS does not consider EXEC files as commands. Now, to execute a command procedure, you must precede it by the CMS command **EXEC**. For example, for a command procedure named **TEST EXEC A1**, you enter:

    TEST

to execute it. If you issued the command **SET IMPEX OFF** to turn off the *implied EXEC function*, you must enter:

    EXEC TEST

to run it. Otherwise, you receive an error.

Similarly, you may omit the final step of the CMS command search order by turning the implied CP function off:

    SET IMPCP OFF

Now CMS generates error messages for commands it does not recognize, rather than passing them on to CP.

By default, CMS initializes the implied EXEC and implied CP functions **ON**. Issue the CMS **QUERY** command at any time to determine their settings:

    QUERY IMPEX
    QUERY IMPCP

Synonyms for Commands

You can establish alternate names for CMS and user-written commands through a table of synonyms. You create this *synonym file* via the XEDIT editor, with filetype **SYNONYM**. Each line of the file contains one command with a synonym by which you can refer to it. Each line is in this format:

    system-command user-synonym count

where **system-command** is either the name of a command procedure, a CMS command, or a **MODULE** file. Thus, you can rename either CMS commands or your own user-written programs and procedures via the **SYNONYM** command. **user-synonym** is the name by which the **system-command** can be executed. **count** specifies the minimum number of characters of **user-synonym** which must be entered in order for CMS to recognize the command. If count is missing, the synonym has no abbreviation (or, "short form"). Here's an example synonym file:

    CL3270 CLS
    LISTFILE DIR
    FILELIST CHKDSK 3

These three lines are saved, for example, in the CMS file named MYSYNS SYNONYM A1. Issuing the CMS SYNONYM command referring to this file:

SYNONYM MYSYNS

establishes these synonyms as valid. Now, you may enter the user-written command CL3270 by entering:

CLS

Invoke the CMS command LISTFILE like this:

DIR

The final synonym associates with the CMS FILELIST command. It may be entered as any variation of the character string CHKDSK, as long as that string consists of at least the first three characters. CHK, CHKD, CHKDS, and CHKDSK are all valid. Of course, you may still use the original command name FILELIST as well as its synonym.

While this example is very simple, it should give you an idea of the power of the SYNONYM command. Here, we have used it to simulate certain MS-DOS (PC-DOS) commands under CMS. The CMS SYNONYM command allows you to modify or tailor your CMS system command names as desired.

Synonyms only last for the duration of the terminal session. You will probably want to include the SYNONYM command in the command procedure that is automatically executed for your virtual machine during the IPL process. This EXEC, with the special reserved file name of PROFILE EXEC, runs every time you logon to CMS. Section 6 shows you how to write a PROFILE EXEC.

CMS File System Summary

CMS file identifiers consist of three parts: filename, filetype, and filemode.

Filetypes describe what kind of information the file contains or how the file is used. The CMS concept of *reserved filetypes* standardizes the filetypes for such common data files as compiler program output listings, textual information, program source code, etc. A summary of many of the CMS filetypes mentioned in this book is contained in table 4-2.

Filemodes consist of a filemode letter and a filemode number. The filemode letter indicates the disk upon which the file resides. For example, a file with a filemode of B1 is stored on the B-disk. Filemode letters range from A to Z.

The letter names of CMS disks are assigned via the CMS ACCESS or FORMAT commands. Remember that certain CMS disks are assigned particular letter names. For example, the A-disk is your primary read-write disk. The letter name of a CMS minidisk is also important in that CMS searches the disks in alphabetical order; this is called the CMS search order. When looking for a file (or command) residing on disk, CMS accepts the first file matching its criteria in the disk search order. Thus, if you enter a CMS command that looks for a file named **FINDME TEST**, CMS will accept the first file matching that name in its search order.

You can also declare a minidisk as an *extension* of another disk. This is accomplished through this form of the CMS **ACCESS** command:

```
ACCESS  201  B/A
```

Extensions are read-only disks that follow their "parent minidisks" in the CMS search order. In this example, the A-disk is the parent minidisk and the B-disk its extension.

Unfortunately, CMS commands are not consistent in the way they handle disk searches for files. Some CMS commands search all the accessed minidisks in the standard search order until the indicated file is located. Other CMS commands search only the A-disk and its extensions. Still other CMS commands do not search an extension when looking for a file. The CMS search order determines the order but not the extent of disk searching. Refer to the CMS reference manuals when you require exact information on how far different CMS commands follow the search order in locating files.

The filemode number of a CMS file indicates the kind of processing for that file. When it is not specified, the filemode number defaults to 1. Since this book is introductory, most of the files to which it refers are of filemode 1 and reside on the primary read-write disk. These files have the filemode **A1**.

Table 15-1 lists CMS filemode numbers and their meanings.

Table 15-1
Filemode Numbers and Their Meanings

Filemode Number	Meaning
0	Indicates private files not listed when another user links read-only to your A-disk (not a complete security function, minidisk passwords are used for security purposes)
1	Indicates read-write files (default filemode number)
2	Identical to filemode 1, but often indicates files shared by users who link to a common minidisk
3	Indicates temporary files only (files erased after they are read)
4	Indicates files in OS-simulated dataset format
5	Identical to filemode 1, but often used to group files logically
6	Indicates files which can be "updated in place" under proper conditions

Tape Handling

CMS supports tape formats generated by its own commands and by other operating systems of the OS and DOS families. *OS operating systems* refer to the family of operating systems designed for large IBM mainframes, and includes MVS/XA, OS/VS2 (MVS), MVT, and others. *DOS operating systems* refer to IBM's family of operating systems for its smaller mainframes, and includes DOS/VSE, DOS/VS, DOSII, and DOS.

VM/CMS features a high degree of compatibility with OS and DOS operating systems. Tape handling is one facet of this compatibility. The CMS TAPPDS command, for example, creates CMS disk files from OS or DOS sequential tape files. It also accepts tapes created from an OS partitioned dataset (PDS). TAPPDS handles tapes used as input or output with several OS utility programs including IEBPTPCH, IEBUPDTE, and IEHMOVE.

The CMS TAPEMAC command provides additional support for OS-created tapes. It builds CMS *macro libraries* (which are similar to OS partitioned datasets) from OS tapes containing unloaded PDSs created by the OS IEHMOVE utility. TAPEMAC therefore loads OS unloaded PDSs to CMS disks as CMS MACLIBs.

Although a comprehensive discussion of these commands is outside the scope of this book, remember that CMS handles tapes created by a variety of OS utility programs, in a variety of formats, and requiring various kinds of tape label processing.

In addition to tape formats supported by OS and DOS operating systems, CMS has its own tape formats. CMS commands for tape manipulation aid you in tape backup, archiving, and minidisk and file transfer.

For example, the CMS DASD Dump Restore (DDR) program allows you to dump, restore, copy, and print minidisks. Use it to:

- dump all or part of the data from disk to tape
- load data to disk from a DDR-created tape
- copy data from one DDR-created tape to another tape (more generally, copy data from one device to another of the same type)
- print DDR-created tape (and disk) records on the virtual printer
- display DDR-created tape (and disk) records on the virtual console

Perhaps the most frequently used CMS command for tape processing is TAPE. This command allows you to perform a number of control operations on tapes mounted on tape drives dedicated to your CMS virtual machine.

The TAPE command also allows you to dump files from disk to tape, and to reload these files to disk. Files processed by the TAPE command are in a unique CMS format.

Table 15-2 illustrates several TAPE command operations through an online dialogue. TAPE DUMP dumps CMS files from disk to tape; TAPE LOAD loads files created via TAPE DUMP back to disk. TAPE SCAN and TAPE SKIP allow you to position the tape.

Table 15-2
TAPE Command
Operations

Terminal Display	Comments
TAPE 181 ATTACHED	Message indicates that the tape is attached.
listfile * assemble a (exec R; cms tape dump TAPE DUMP PROG1 ASSEMBLE A1 DUMPING..... PROG1 ASSEMBLE A1 TAPE DUMP PROG2 ASSEMBLE A1 DUMPING..... PROG2 ASSEMBLE A1 TAPE DUMP PROG3 ASSEMBLE A1 . . .	Prepare to dump all ASSEMBLE files by using the LISTFILE command EXEC option; then execute the CMS EXEC using TAPE and DUMP as arguments. The TAPE command responds to each TAPE DUMP by printing the file identification of the file being dumped.
TAPE DUMP PROG3 ASSEMBLE A1 DUMPING..... PROG9 ASSEMBLE A1 R;	The last file, PROG9 ASSEMBLE, is dumped.
tape wtm R;	TAPE command writes a tape mark to indicate an end of file.
tape dump mylib maclib a DUMPING..... MYLIB MACLIB A1 R;	Two macro libraries are dumped, by specifying the file identifiers.
tape dump cmslib maclib * DUMPING..... CMSLIB MACLIB S2 R;	
tape wtm R;	Another tape mark is written.
tape dump mylib txtlib a DUMPING..... MYLIB TXTLIB A1 R;	A TEXT library is dumped.
tape wtm 2	Two tape marks are written to indicate the end of the tape.
tape rew R;	The tape is rewound.
tape scan (eof 4 SCANNING.... PROG1 ASSEMBLE A1 PROG2 ASSEMBLE A1 PROG3 ASSEMBLE A1 PROG4 ASSEMBLE A1 PROG5 ASSEMBLE A1 PROG6 ASSEMBLE A1 PROG7 ASSEMBLE A1 PROG8 ASSEMBLE A1 PROG9 ASSEMBLE A1	The tape is scanned to verify that all of the files are on it.

Table 15-2 (cont.)

Terminal Display	Comments
END-OF-FILE OR END-OF-TAPE	Tape mark indication.
MYLIB MACLIB A1	
CMSLIB MACLIB S2	
END-OF-FILE OR END-OF-TAPE	
MYLIB TXTLIB A1	
END OF-FILE OR END-OF-TAPE	Two tape marks indicate the end of the tape.
END-OF-FILE OR END-OF-TAPE	
R;	
#cp det 181	The CP DETACH command rewinds and detaches the tape.
TAPE 181 DETACHED	

*******The tape created above is going to be read.*******

Terminal Display	Comments
TAPE 181 ATTACHED	Message indicating the tape is attached.
tape load prog4 assemble	One file is to be read onto disk.
LOADING.....	The TAPE command displays the
PROG4 ASSEMBLE A1	name of the file loaded. Any
R;	existing file with the same filename and filetype is erased.
tape scan	The remainder of the first tape file
SCANNING....	is scanned.
PROG5 ASSEMBLE A1	
PROG6 ASSEMBLE A1	
PROG7 ASSEMBLE A1	
PROG8 ASSEMBLE A1	
END-OF-FILE OR END-OF-TAPE	Indication of end of first tape file.
R;	
tape scan	The second tape file is scanned.
SCANNING....	
MYLIB MACLIB A1	
CMSLIB MACLIB S2	
END-OF-FILE OR END-OF-TAPE	
R;	
tape bsf 2	The tape is backed up and
R;	positioned in front of the last tape file.
tape fsf	The tape is forward spaced past the
R;	tape mark.
tape load (eof 2	The next two tape files are going to
LOADING.....	be read.R;
MYLIB MACLIB A1	
CMSLIB MACLIB A2	
END-OF-FILE OR END-OF-TAPE	
MYLIB TXTLIB A1	
END-OF-FILE OR END-OF-TAPE	
R;	
#cp detach 181	The tape is detached.
TAPE 181 DETACHED	

Table 15-3 lists additional **TAPE** operands and their uses.

	Operand	Action
Table 15-3	BSF	Backspace n tape marks
Additional TAPE	BSR	Backspace n tape records
Operands	ERG	Erase gap
	FSF	Forward n tape marks
	FSR	Forward n tape records
	REW	Rewind tape to load point
	RUN	Rewind tape and unload
	WTM	Write n tape marks

The CMS **MOVEFILE** command, like the **DDR** command, addresses both tape and disk handling functions. With **MOVEFILE**, you can copy sequential disk files to tape and vice versa. More generally, with **MOVEFILE** you can move data from any device supported by CMS to any other device supported by CMS. You can also display tape labels and move labelled tape files. **MOVEFILE** proves especially useful in copying a file from tape to disk when the tape format is unknown.

MOVEFILE requires that you define its input and output files through the CMS **FILEDEF** command. This example copies a tape file to disk:

```
FILEDEF   INPUT   TAP1
FILEDEF   OUTPUT  DISK   NEWFILE   DATA  A1
MOVEFILE  INPUT   OUTPUT
```

TAP1 is the symbolic name for the tape drive you have attached to your virtual system at virtual device address 181. The name of the newly created disk file is **NEWFILE DATA A1**. The **FILEDEF** command allocates the input and output files for the **MOVEFILE** operation.

Immediate Commands

CMS includes ten commands referred to as *immediate commands.* CMS executes these commands as soon as they are entered. Other CMS commands enter a command buffer called the *console stack,* where they await execution. CMS executes immediate commands without routing them through the console stack.

Immediate commands are entered following an *attention interruption* from your terminal. On full-screen display terminals, such as 3270 devices, you only need the **RUNNING** status indicator in the bottom right-hand corner of the screen to enter an immediate command. On typewriter terminals, you press the Attention Key (**PA1** or its equivalent) to signal an attention interruption. After the attention interruption, enter the immediate command.

An example of an immediate command is HT, which halts the output display of an executing program. Sometimes, if the output is coming to the terminal rapidly, you may need to wait until the screen status area indicates the word **MORE...** before you enter the HT command. HT halts a program's output to the terminal display, but allows the program to continue execution. RT (resume typing) resumes the program's terminal output.

Another useful immediate command is HX. HX halts execution of the current program and returns control to CMS. Table 15-4 lists CMS immediate commands.

Table 15-4
CMS Immediate
Commands

Command	Effect
HB	Halt Batch Execution stops execution of a CMS batch virtual machine at the end of the current job.
HI	Halt Interpretation terminates execution of all executing command procedures (EXECs).
HO	Halt Tracing stops recording of trace information during program execution. The program continues execution.
HT	Halt Typing suppresses terminal output by an executing program. The program continues execution.
HX	Halt Execution stops the execution of a currently executing program and returns to the CMS environment.
RO	Resume Tracing resumes recording of trace information suspended by an SO command. The program continues execution.
RT	Resume Typing resumes terminal output from an executing program previously suppressed by an HT command.
SO	Suspend Tracing suspends recording of trace information. Program execution continues.
TE	Trace End stops tracing of command procedures (EXECs).
TS	Trace Start initiates tracing of command procedures (EXECs).

CMS provides several facilities by which you may define your own immediate commands. Issue the CMS **IMMCMD** command from within EXECs in order to establish or cancel immediate commands. Use the **IMMCMD** macro from within assembler language programs to create immediate commands.

For Further Information

In general, the manual *VM/SP CMS User's Guide, SC19-6210*, contains descriptive and tutorial information on all CMS and selected CP commands, and the CMS file system. The *VM/SP CMS Command and Macro Reference, SC19-6209*, provides complete CMS command formats and detailed description.

The discussion on CMS's command search order constitutes a simplified overview of a more complicated topic. If you need more detail on this subject, consult *SC19-6209* and the *VM/SP System Programmer's Guide, SC19-6203*.

Test Your Understanding

List the CMS command search order. How do you include or exclude steps from this sequence?

If you issue a CMS command that searches for the file named **TEST DATA** and you have two files with this name on different minidisks, which file will CMS locate to satisfy the CMS command?

Describe several possible reasons for establishing aliases for CMS and user-written commands. How do you do this? Write and test a sample **SYNONYM** file.

What are the CMS filemode numbers and their uses?

Some major CMS tape-handling commands include: **TAPPDS**, **TAPEMAC**, and **TAPE**. Describe their functions.

Dump a dataset from disk to tape and then load it back to disk from that tape using the **DDR** command. Under what circumstances might you use other CMS commands to perform this task?

Contrast when you would use the CMS **MOVEFILE** command versus the **COPYFILE** command. Do these commands offer overlapping functionality? (Hint: look up both commands in the *VM/SP CMS Command and Macro Reference, SC19-6209*, for full descriptions.)

What is a CMS "immediate command" and how are these commands different from other CMS commands?

Program Development with VM/CMS

- Programming Facilities of CMS
- DOS Programming Facilities of CMS
- Interactive Debugging under VM/CMS
- VSAM Storage and CMS Batch Execution

CHAPTER 16

Programming
Facilities of CMS

CMS is an especially supportive operating system for program development. This chapter shows how to use CMS facilities in the development of
programs for CMS and OS operating systems.

By default, CMS is oriented toward the development of CMS and OS
programs. You enter a special environment called CMS/DOS to develop
DOS operating system programs.

The CMS facilities for CMS and OS programming support a large
variety of language processors, including a "core" group, traditional in
mainframe environments and offered for CMS for many years. This core
group of languages consists of Assembler, COBOL, PL/I, and FORTRAN.

You should be aware that almost any programming language is available for license under CMS. IBM offers languages as diverse as Pascal, LISP,
C, PROLOG, BASIC, RPG, and APL; other vendors add nearly all other
prominent languages to this list. The principles demonstrated in this chapter using the core group of languages are readily transferable to development in other languages. For example, Pascal program development is not
much different from preparing FORTRAN or PL/I programs. Look in the
vendor's language reference manuals for minor differences pertaining to
specific program language products under CMS.

Whatever languages are available on your computer are the result of
local purchasing decisions. All higher-level languages for CMS are separately purchased program products.

The Basics of Program Development

Assuming use of CMS's OS-oriented facilities for program development,
the developmental process consists of the same steps under CMS as under
any modern operating system. These steps include:

1. Enter the program source code into a CMS file.

2. Compile that program source into a relocatable object module (a TEXT file).

3. Identify input/output devices and files used by the program.

4. Link edit and load the program.

5. Execute the program.

These steps are depicted in flowchart form in figure 16-1. That diagram shows that programming is an *iterative process*. This means that program debugging is a repetitive procedure by which all compilation errors are removed from the original program source code. Then, all logical or run-time errors are removed through repeated testing. Both compilation errors and execution-time errors require re-editing of the original program source code and reiteration of the steps of program development.

Figure 16-1 is a simplified diagram. Depending on the situation, you may perform these steps in some modified fashion.

Figure 16-1
Program
Development
under CMS

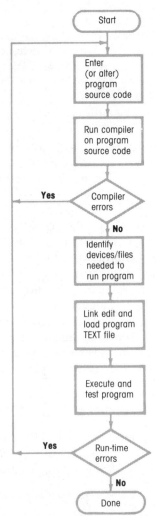

Running the Language Translators

You already know how to edit program source code through the CMS XEDIT editor. Under CMS, program source code is normally contained in CMS files. The filetype of the CMS file identifier indicates the language in which the code is written. Common CMS language processor filetypes are listed in table 16-1.

Table 16-1
CMS Language Processor Filetypes

Filetype	Contents
COBOL	COBOL source statements
PLI, PLIOPT	PL/I source statements
FORTRAN	FORTRAN source statements
ASSEMBLE	Assembler source statements
BASIC	BASIC source statements
VSBASIC	VS BASIC source statements
PASCAL	Pascal source statements

For example, you would enter source code for a COBOL program into a file name **MYPROG COBOL A1**. The filemode is usually **A1** for user-developed source code.

Once source code has been entered into an appropriately named file, it is processed by a programming language translator. CMS languages are invoked through single commands specific to the translator. Table 16-2 lists some of the more common programming language processors and the CMS commands that invoke them.

Table 16-2
Programming Language Processor Commands

Command	Invokes
COBOL	COBOL compiler
TESTCOB	Interactive COBOL Debugger
PLIOPT	PL/I Optimizing compiler
PLIC	PL/I Checkout compiler
FORTVS	VS Fortran 77 compiler
TESTFORT	Interactive FORTRAN Debugger
FORTGI, GOFORT, FORTHX	Other versions of FORTRAN
ASSEMBLE	Assembler
PASCALVS	Pascal compiler

Prior to running any particular compiler, you may wish to check with your system administrator. The compiler commands occasionally vary across systems according to version.

Examples of running programming language translators include:

```
COBOL   MYPROG
PLIOPT  SAMPLI
FORTVS  MYFILE    (NOTEST SOURCE)
FORTGI  TSTPRG    (SOURCE XREF PRINT)
```

The first example invokes a COBOL compiler against the COBOL source code contained in file **MYPROG COBOL A1**. In the second example, the **PLIOPT** command invokes the PL/I optimizing compiler on the PL/I source program contained in **SAMPLI PLIOPT A1**.

The last two commands show that different versions of the same programming language are invoked by different CMS commands. The **FORTVS** command runs the VS FORTRAN 77 compiler, while the **FORTGI** command runs a version of FORTRAN IV. Both these FORTRAN examples specify a list of compiler options in parentheses after the filename. Allowable options depend on the particular compiler.

Figure 16-2
Running CMS
Language
Translators
Produces Two Files

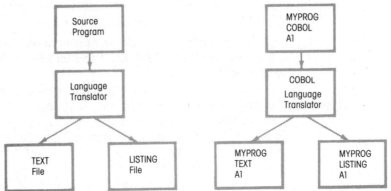

Typical CMS language processors produce two output files: a **TEXT** file and a **LISTING** file. The **TEXT** file is the object code (or "machine language") form of the source program. This file is ready to be link edited, loaded, and executed. The **LISTING** file is a printed listing of the input source code, along with compiler warning and error messages. Inspect this **LISTING** file to look for any errors the compiler encountered in your source code.

CMS language translators use **TEXT** and **LISTING** as the filetypes for these output files. The filename defaults to that of the input file. Assuming that the input source code resides on a writable disk, the filemode of these two output files will be the same as the input source file.

Figure 16-2 diagrams this situation. Running the COBOL compiler produces one **TEXT** and one **LISTING** file. The first file is the object code form of the source program, while the second lists any compiler-detected errors and compiler messages.

The second half of the figure shows that for an input source file named:

```
MYPROG COBOL A1
```

the output files produced are named:

```
MYPROG  TEXT  A1
```

and

```
MYPROG  LISTING  A1.
```

View MYPROG LISTING A1 via XEDIT in order to see if the source code resulted in compiler errors. Some CMS language translators will also list compiler messages on the terminal display. Correct errors in the input source file by editing with XEDIT (or any other CMS editor).

Defining Files for Program Use

After running the compiler on the program source code, define all input /output devices and data files needed by the program for its execution to CMS. Identify these devices and files to CMS via the CMS FILEDEF command.

Where an input/output device is allocated to the program, use this form of the CMS FILEDEF command:

```
FILEDEF  ddname  device
```

where ddname is the symbolic name used for the I/O device by the program, and device names the virtual device that the program uses. For example:

```
FILEDEF  OUTFILE  TERMINAL
```

associates the program's internal symbolic name of OUTFILE with the user's terminal. The CMS FILEDEF command thus links a device or file reference within a program to the proper resource controlled by the CMS operating system. In OS operating systems terminology, the CMS FILEDEF command performs the function of the TSO ALLOCATE command, or the DD card of OS batch Job Control Language (JCL).

Figure 16-3 shows how the CMS FILEDEF command establishes the relationship between internal program names for devices and the virtual devices controlled by CMS. While the examples shown are written in COBOL and PL/I, the principle involved applies to any programming language.

As another FILEDEF example:

```
FILEDEF  INFILE  READER
```

permits the program to refer to the virtual card READER via its own internal name of **INFILE**. Table 16-3 lists common keywords for the various CMS devices referred to in the CMS **FILEDEF** command.

Figure 16-3
FILEDEF Links
Internal
References with
Devices and Files

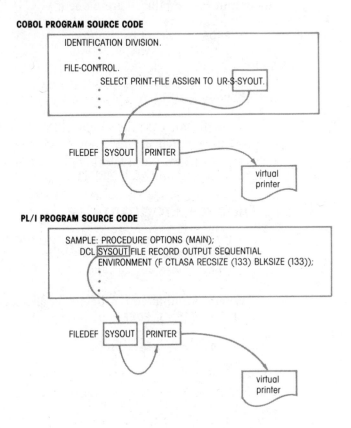

COBOL PROGRAM SOURCE CODE

IDENTIFICATION DIVISION.

FILE-CONTROL.
    SELECT PRINT-FILE ASSIGN TO UR-S-SYOUT.

FILEDEF SYSOUT PRINTER

virtual printer

PL/I PROGRAM SOURCE CODE

SAMPLE: PROCEDURE OPTIONS (MAIN);
    DCL SYSOUT FILE RECORD OUTPUT SEQUENTIAL
    ENVIRONMENT (F CTLASA RECSIZE (133) BLKSIZE (133));

FILEDEF SYSOUT PRINTER

virtual printer

Table 16-3
CMS FILEDEF
Keywords

FILEDEF Keyword	Virtual Device
TERMINAL	Data is input or output through a terminal display
PRINTER	Data is output to a printer
READER	Data is input via a card reader
PUNCH	Data is output to a card punch
DUMMY	No real I/O occurs
DISK	Data is input or output to disk
TAPn	Data is input or output to tape

Remember that under CMS, all devices are virtualized. For example, output sent to a **PUNCH** device goes through the usual CP virtualization process for spooled output.

The parameter **DUMMY** is used as a null device. That is, no real I/O is performed when **DUMMY** is specified.

Two of the above keywords, **DISK** and **TAPn**, require more complex forms of the CMS FILEDEF command. For example, in working with disk files, enter this general format to reference CMS files:

FILEDEF ddname DISK filename filetype filemode

The filename, filetype, and filemode provide the file name of the CMS disk file referred to by the program. The FILEDEF thereby links the symbolic name by which the program internally refers to the CMS file to the name of the CMS file itself. Here is an example:

FILEDEF INFILE DISK INPUT SCRIPT A1

The program now has access to a CMS file named INPUT SCRIPT A1, which it refers to internally as INFILE.

CMS support for OS-oriented programming permits programmers to access other kinds of files from their programs, in addition to the standard CMS files assumed thus far in this book. These kinds of files include *OS-simulated datasets* and *real OS datasets.*

OS-simulated datasets are CMS files that are kept on regular CMS disks, but in *OS-simulated format.* As CMS files, you can use all normal CMS file manipulation commands on them. For example, the CMS commands illustrated earlier in this book to copy, rename, print, and delete CMS files all operate properly on OS-simulated datasets. But, since these files are maintained by CMS in OS-simulated format, OS programs can use standard OS access methods on them, too. That is, an OS program processes OS-simulated datasets as fixed- or variable-length records, sequentially or directly, by such standard OS access methods as QSAM, BSAM, and BDAM. CMS emulates the standard OS file structures and access methods through its provision for OS-simulated datasets. (In technical terms, CMS provides the appearance of OS Data Control Block (DCB) characteristics to OS programs via OS-simulated datasets.)

OS-simulated datasets are identified by the use of a filemode number of 4. Thus, when you (or any program you run) refers to a CMS file with a filemode number of 4, you work with an OS-simulated dataset. Here is a CMS FILEDEF command that assigns an input file that is actually an OS-simulated dataset:

FILEDEF INNAME DISK INPUT DATA A4

The program uses its internal designation of INNAME to refer to a file called INPUT DATA A4. INPUT DATA A4 is an OS-simulated dataset maintained on a CMS disk that appears as a standard OS file to program processing.

The third kind of file CMS supports with its OS-oriented programming facilities is referred to as a real OS dataset. Real OS datasets are stored on *OS disks* (not CMS disks). OS disks may be defined in your virtual machine configuration as either entire disks or minidisks and may have on them both standard OS sequential datasets and PDS. Programs that process real OS datasets may read those datasets but not update them. Only a subset of CMS commands recognizes and operates on real OS disk datasets.

Use the CMS LISTDS command to display information about real OS datasets residing on real OS disks. LISTDS also displays information pertaining to free and allocated extents on OS disks, and can list PDS member names. (The LISTDS command also performs these services on real DOS disks.)

You specify real OS datasets for program processing in several ways. One way is to enter:

```
FILEDEF   ddname   filemode   DSN   ?   (options
```

Here, ddname is again the name by which the program refers to this file, filemode identifies the minidisk on which the file resides, the keyword DSN indicates that this is not a CMS file, and the question mark ? tells CMS to prompt for the OS file name. The options may include OS DCB information. Thus:

```
FILEDEF   INFILE   B1   DSN   ?   (RECFM   F   LRECL   80
```

associates a file on the B disk with the program's internal symbolic name of INFILE. The record format RECFM of this file is fixed unblocked F and its logical record length LRECL is 80 characters. After you enter this FILEDEF command at the terminal, CMS prompts you to enter the name of the dataset:

```
DMSFLD220R ENTER DATA SET NAME:
```

Respond by entering the standard OS dataset name of the dataset. For example:

```
OS.DATASET.NAME
```

The dataset name you enter must conform to OS standard dataset naming conventions. That is, the dataset name must consist of 1- to 8-character qualifiers separated by periods. The maximum total length of the name is 44 characters, including the periods.

Another way to handle a CMS FILEDEF for a real OS dataset is to enter the standard OS dataset name directly in the FILEDEF command. This method eliminates the question mark ? in the FILEDEF statement, and thereby foregoes CMS's prompt for entry of the OS dataset name:

```
FILEDEF  ddname  filemode  DSN  os  dataset  name  (options
```

In terms of the example:

```
FILEDEF  INFILE B1  DSN  OS DATASET NAME  (RECFM F LRECL 80
```

Note that the OS dataset name does not contain embedded periods. These are replaced by spaces.

Two options on the `FILEDEF` command should be mentioned. The `PERM` option retains file definitions until the end of your terminal session, or until you clear them or redefine them. This option is useful because the language translators otherwise clear outstanding `FILEDEF` commands, forcing you to redefine them continually during program development. The `PERM` option keeps file definitions in force when repeatedly compiling and testing programs.

The `DISP MOD` option of the `FILEDEF` command allows programs to add new records at the end of an existing file. As under the OS operating systems, writing to a file that is not identified as `DISP MOD` replaces that file with the new output. Here's an example that allocates a CMS output file:

```
FILEDEF  OUTFILE  DISK  APPEND DATA A1  (DISP MOD PERM
```

Any data written to the file named `APPEND DATA A1` is appended to the end of this file, due to the disposition of `MOD`. `PERM` means that this file definition is retained by CMS until explicitly cleared or redefined, or until logoff. Clear a file definition by the `FILEDEF` command, with the ddname and the keyword `CLEAR`. For example:

```
FILEDEF  OUTFILE  CLEAR
```

clears the above file definition for `OUTFILE`. Entering:

```
FILEDEF  *  CLEAR
```

clears all file definitions, except those declared with the `PERM` option. A `FILEDEF` entered with the `PERM` option must be cleared with an explicit ddname reference, as above.

The CMS `FILEDEF` command also identifies tapes for program processing. Under CMS, your virtual machine may use up to four tape drives at one time. These tape drives have the CMS virtual addresses of `181`, `182`, `183`, and `184`. In the `FILEDEF` command, you identify these tape drives by the keywords `TAP1`, `TAP2`, `TAP3` and `TAP4`, respectively.

In order to use a tape drive under CMS, you must first notify the operator to attach the tape drive to your virtual system and mount the tape. Use the CP `MESSAGE` command to do this:

```
CP  MESSAGE  userid   text of message
```

Here's an example that refers to the operator's special userid of **OPER-ATOR**, or **OP**:

```
CP  MESSAGE  OP  PLEASE MOUNT TAPE VOLUME SERIAL 19921 ON 181
```

In response, you receive a message such as this:

```
TAPE 181 ATTACHED
```

Now issue the **FILEDEF** command for the tape:

```
FILEDEF  ddname  TAP1
```

For example:

```
FILEDEF  INFILE  TAP1
```

associates the tape at virtual address 181 with your program's internal name of **INFILE**.

Loading and Executing the Program

After compilation of program source code and identification of devices and files required for execution of that program, you are ready to load the program for execution. The CMS **LOAD** command does this:

```
LOAD  filename
```

where **filename** is the name of the **TEXT** file to load. For example:

```
LOAD  MYPROG
```

loads a **TEXT** file named **MYPROG TEXT** into virtual storage and readies it for execution.

Issue the CMS **START** command to execute the program. Its simplest format is:

```
START
```

This command causes CMS to pass control to the program loaded into memory. If your program has more than one entry point, you may specify the entry point on the **START** command:

```
START  entry
```

This starts program execution at the entry point named by `entry`.

You may also use the `START` option on the `LOAD` command to execute the loaded object module immediately:

```
LOAD  MYPROG  (START
```

The above command has the same function as the `LOAD` and `START` commands issued separately.

Remember that you must have defined all files to be processed via CMS `FILEDEF` commands before issuing the `LOAD` command with the `START` option.

After your program has been debugged and tested, use the CMS `GENMOD` command to create a *program module.* Under CMS, a program module is a nonrelocatable, executable file, whose external references have been resolved. CMS modules have a filetype of `MODULE`.

In OS terminology, CMS modules are OS "load modules," whereas CMS `TEXT` files are OS "object files." Use the `GENMOD` command after the `LOAD` command to create the CMS module:

```
LOAD  MYPROG
GENMOD  MYPROG
```

The operand `MYPROG` on the `GENMOD` command specifies the name of the output module. Since its filetype is `MODULE`, the output file from this `GENMOD` command is named `MYPROG MODULE A1`. Now, to execute this program at any time, all you need to do is enter the assigned module name to CMS:

```
MYPROG
```

Remember that before executing a CMS module, you must first issue any necessary `FILEDEF` commands.

Pass run-time parameters to the program module merely by specifying them after the module name:

```
MYPROG  PARM1
```

`PARM1` is passed to the program at execution time. Look in the "CMS User's Guide" for your particular programming language to see how parameters are passed into your program.

The `GENMOD` command has an option that allows you to specify an entry point that represents the starting virtual storage location from which the nonrelocatable copy is generated. Only programs written in certain languages require explicit entry points. For FORTRAN programs, you use this entry option:

```
GENMOD  module-name  (FROM  MAIN
```

and for PL/I programs:

```
GENMOD  module-name  (FROM  PLISTART
```

These `ENTRY` options on the `GENMOD` command avoid what the reference manuals otherwise refer to as "unpredictable results."

Establishing Access to Libraries

CMS libraries are like OS partitioned datasets. That is, a CMS library has a directory and contains members. CMS libraries are of three types: *Macro, Text,* and *Loadlib.* Each contains members of a particular type. Since CMS libraries consist of members, CMS provides special sets of commands for creating, updating, and listing the members of its libraries.

Macro libraries contain either of two kinds of members: macro definitions and copy files. If you assemble a program that uses macro definitions, or, if you compile a program that refers to copy files, you specify the CMS macro library from which the language translator retrieves this information. Identify the libraries for the language processor to search via the CMS `GLOBAL` command. The `GLOBAL` command's general format is:

```
GLOBAL  library-type   library-name1 library-name2 ...
```

Where a `GLOBAL` command names more than one library as searchable, the order in which the libraries are listed in the `GLOBAL` command is the order in which they are searched. The library search order is important because it determines which member satisfies a search request when two or more members have the same member name. In retrieving a library member, functions retrieve the first member in the first library matching the search name.

A `GLOBAL` command applies throughout a terminal session, or until you issue another `GLOBAL` for the same type of CMS library. Thus, it is convenient to enter any required `GLOBAL` commands for CMS libraries immediately after logging onto CMS. Then, you do not have to issue further `GLOBAL` commands unless and until you want to alter the libraries named in the `GLOBAL` you entered earlier for that kind of CMS library.

For example, prior to compiling a COBOL program, you may wish to specify two macro libraries as searchable by the COBOL compiler:

```
GLOBAL  MACLIB  MYLIB  MYLIB2
COBOL  MYPROG
```

The `GLOBAL` statement specifies two macro libraries, with filetype of `MACLIB`, as searchable by the COBOL compiler. They are named `MYLIB MACLIB A1` and `MYLIB2 MACLIB A1`. When the `COBOL` command executes the compiler, `COPY` statements in the COBOL source program are resolved by retrieving the appropriate source statements from members in these two macro libraries.

As another example:

```
GLOBAL  MACLIB  MYLIB  PLILIB1
PLIOPT  MYPROG  (SOURCE XREF)
```

The `GLOBAL` command tells the PL/I compiler to search the macro libraries `MYLIB` and `PLILIB1` for macro or copy definitions. The compiler resolves any PL/I `%INCLUDE` preprocessor statements in the source by search of these MACLIBs. The `PLIOPT` command executes the PL/I optimizing compiler with reference to these libraries.

The second kind of CMS library, the text library, contains relocatable object programs. That is, CMS libraries having the `TXTLIB` filetype contain members which are `TEXT` files. Remember, `TEXT` files are files of machine code output from the CMS language translators.

`GLOBAL` commands referring to text libraries are issued immediately prior to the `LOAD` command. This allows the CMS loader to resolve external references by retrieving the appropriate object modules from the named `TXTLIB`. For example:

```
GLOBAL  TXTLIB  FORTLIB
LOAD    MYPROG
START   MYPROG
```

This series of commands defines the global text library named `FORT-LIB TXTLIB A1` to the CMS loader. The loader inspects the library called `FORTLIB` in resolving any external references when link editing the `TEXT` file `MYPROG`. Then, the link edited and loaded program is executed starting at entry point `MYPROG`.

Most higher-level programming languages require access to one or more language-specific link editing libraries. Identify these libraries by issuing a `GLOBAL` command prior to the `LOAD` command.

The third kind of CMS library, the `LOADLIB`, supports a load library similar in concept to an OS load module library. The CMS `LKED` command creates a `LOADLIB`. The `OSRUN` command causes CMS to load, relocate, and run a member of the `LOADLIB`.

Table 16-4 summarizes the kinds of CMS libraries, their filetypes, and their contents. CMS includes a special group of commands to create, update, and maintain CMS libraries. These are described in chapter 17.

The fourth kind of library, the Doslib, is the DOS executable phase library. Chapter 18, on DOS-oriented program development under CMS, discusses Doslibs.

Complete CMS and OS Program Development Examples

This section presents **several** complete examples in order to tie these CMS OS-oriented programming **commands** and concepts together.

Table 16-4
CMS Libraries

Type	Filetype	Input Members' Filetype	Contents
Macro	MACLIB	MACRO or COPY	Macro definitions and/or copy files
Text	TXTLIB	TEXT	Relocatable object programs (compiler output)
Loadlib	LOADLIB	TEXT	Link edit files (load modules)
Doslib	DOSLIB	TEXT	DOS executable phase library

Here is a basic example pertaining to the development of a COBOL program:

```
COBOL    MYPROG
FILEDEF  INFILE   TERMINAL
FILEDEF  OUTFILE  PRINTER
GLOBAL   TXTLIB   COBLIBVS
LOAD     MYPROG
START
```

In this example, the COBOL command runs the COBOL compiler on the input source file named MYPROG COBOL A1. Two FILEDEF commands establish the terminal and printer files as available to this program for its execution. The program refers to these devices by the ddnames of INFILE and OUTFILE, respectively.

The GLOBAL command establishes access to the required COBOL text library. The loader searches this library for missing subroutines when the MYPROG COBOL program is loaded. The name of this required COBOL library may vary by compiler version (and even by installation), so check with your system administrator for its name on your system.

Next, the TEXT file, or object module, produced by the COBOL command is loaded via the LOAD command. The START command initiates program execution.

This enhanced version of the same example illustrates several more points:

```
GLOBAL   MACLIB   COBOLVS
COBOL    MYPROG   (SOURCE XREF)
FILEDEF  INFILE   TERMINAL   (PERM
FILEDEF  OUTFILE  PRINTER    (PERM
GLOBAL   TXTLIB   COBLIBVS   COBOLVS   COBOLFIP
LOAD     MYPROG   (START
```

First, a GLOBAL command establishes the macro library named COBOLVS MACLIB for resolution of COBOL COPY statements in the source program during compilation. The COBOL command compiles the source code with two compiler options specified.

The FILEDEF commands include the PERM option. They apply throughout the terminal session, until explicitly cleared or redefined. This is useful during the repeated compiles and tests often required in the course of program debugging. (Note: some compilers clear all FILEDEF commands under certain conditions, even those declared with the PERM option.)

The GLOBAL TXTLIB command lists three object module libraries for the resolution of external references. The three libraries are searched in the order indicated on the command. This command remains applicable either until another GLOBAL TXTLIB statement is issued, or until logoff.

Finally, the LOAD command with the START option loads the program and initiates its execution.

Here is another example. In this case, a VS FORTRAN 77 program processes two disk files:

```
FORTVS    MYPROG
FILEDEF   10   DISK   INPUT  DATA  A1  (PERM
FILEDEF   20   DISK   OUTPUT DATA  A4  (PERM
GLOBAL    TXTLIB  VLNKMLIB   VFORTLIB
LOAD      MYPROG  (START
```

The FORTVS command compiles the source code from the input file named MYPROG FORTRAN A1. Two output files are produced: the compiler output listing, on the file MYPROG LISTING A1; and, the object code, in file MYPROG TEXT A1.

The FILEDEF commands allocate two disk files for this program's processing. The input file is a regular CMS-format file on a CMS disk. The output file is an OS-simulated dataset residing on a CMS disk. This is evident because the filemode number of this second file is 4. The two disk files are assigned to logical units 10 and 20 within the FORTRAN program's source code. Both file definitions stay in effect until they are explicitly cleared, redefined, or until the end of the terminal session.

The output file is always newly created by this program. In order to append output records to an existing file, use a file definition with the DISP MOD option:

```
FILEDEF   20   DISK   OUTPUT DATA A4     (PERM  DISP MOD
```

The GLOBAL TXTLIB command identifies required FORTRAN libraries that are searched for missing subroutines during link editing. FORTRAN usually requires more than a single subroutine library; different versions of FORTRAN require different libraries. Check with your system administrator to see which libraries are needed with your version of FORTRAN.

The LOAD command loads the TEXT file named MYPROG TEXT A1 and initiates program execution.

This last example shows use of the PL/I Optimizing Compiler:

```
GLOBAL  TXTLIB  PLILIB
PLIOPT  MYPROG
LOAD    MYPROG
START
```

The GLOBAL command identifies a required text library. The PLIOPT statement compiles the source program, and the LOAD and START commands load and execute the program.

As with all PL/I programs, the predefined PL/I default files of SYSIN and SYSPRINT are available to this program. Under CMS, both default to the terminal.

This is a more complete version of the PL/I example:

```
GLOBAL   MACLIB   MYLIB1   MYLIB2
GLOBAL   TXTLIB   PLILIB   MYTXT1
PLIOPT   MYPROG   (SOURCE XREF)
FILEDEF  INFILE   DISK   INPUT DATA A1
FILEDEF  OUTFILE  DISK   OUTPUT DATA A1
LOAD     MYPROG
GENMOD   MYPROG   (FROM PLISTART
START
```

In this example, two global macro libraries are declared. They are named MYLIB1 MACLIB and MYLIB2 MACLIB. The GLOBAL TXTLIB statement names a private TXTLIB as well as the compiler-required one used to resolve external references during link editing.

The PLIOPT command compiles the source program with the SOURCE and XREF options. Then the FILEDEF commands define two CMS files. These assignments are in addition to the PL/I compiler-provided default device assignments of SYSIN and SYSPRINT.

The LOAD command link edits and loads the MYPROG module into virtual storage. GENMOD produces a load module on disk. It is named MYPROG MODULE A1. START then runs the program.

Since a MODULE file has been created, the program can be run again at any time simply by entering its name:

```
MYPROG
```

This assumes that the two FILEDEF commands have been entered previously, since the program requires access to these files for execution.

Using the GENMOD command permits extension of the CMS operating system. It makes it possible to create programs that are executed by single statements, much like CMS commands. CMS includes several other features that conceptually provide for customization of the operating system.

For example, CMS's command procedure languages provide another technique of extending the operating system's suite of facilities. Most programmers use CMS command procedures in order to issue automatically the series of commands required during program compilation and testing. In practice, most programmers write command procedures to suit their programming development needs rather than manually re-entering the program preparation commands as shown in this chapter.

For Further Information

IBM publishes manuals generically called "CMS Compiler User's Guides" for each programming language. As description of specific compiler options requires knowledge of individual programming languages, refer to the vendor's "CMS Compiler User's Guide" for this information for the languages in which you are interested. These guides also contain any information unique to running a particular compiler. Here are several of these manuals and their reference numbers:

CMS User's Guide for COBOL, SC28-6469

OS COBOL Interactive Debug Terminal User's Guide, SC28-6465

PL/I Optimizing Compiler: CMS User's Guide, SC33-0037

PL/I Checkout Compiler: CMS User's Guide, SC33-0047

CMS User's Guide for FORTRAN IV, SC28-6891

FORTRAN Interactive Debug for CMS: Guide and Reference, SC28-6885

OS/VS-VM/370 Assembler Programmer's Guide, GC33-4021

VS/BASIC CMS Terminal User's Guide, SC28-8306

The self-study guide *CMS for Programmers: A Primer, SR20-4438,* contains a complete set of examples for translating and running programs written in Assembler language, COBOL, FORTRAN, PL/I, and APL. Further information on program development with the VS FORTRAN 77 compiler can be found in *VS FORTRAN Programming Guide, SC26-4118.* Information on other versions of FORTRAN and the slight differences they entail (for example, different GLOBAL TXTLIB commands) is contained in *CMS User's Guide for FORTRAN IV, SC28-6891.*

The *VM/SP CMS User's Guide, SC19-6210,* shows how to use the various CMS commands involved in readying and running CMS-based programs. The *VM/SP CMS Command and Macro Reference, SC19-6209,* contains complete reference information and an alphabetical listing of all CMS commands.

Test Your Understanding

List the basic steps of program development under CMS. Are these steps the same as those for program development for other operating systems with which you may be familiar?

For which steps in the program development process do you need to issue CMS GLOBAL commands?

Describe and define "CMS files," "OS-simulated datasets," and "real OS datasets." What are the differences between these three kinds of files in the CMS environment?

How can you tell if a CMS file is an OS-simulated dataset?

Describe how you allocate a tape file under CMS. What steps are involved?

List the kinds of CMS libraries. What are the purpose and contents of each?

Write a very brief program in any language with which you are familiar and have access to under CMS. Your program should read in one line of information from the terminal user and echo it back to the terminal. Compile and test your program under CMS.

CHAPTER 17

Additional CMS Programming Facilities

Support for Files

Chapter 16 mentions that, from the viewpoint of the CMS or OS programmer, CMS supports three important classes of files:

- CMS-formatted files, which reside on CMS minidisks
- OS-simulated datasets, which are CMS files with a filemode of 4
- real OS datasets, which reside on OS disks known to your virtual machine

CMS supports the access methods associated with these classes of files to varying degrees. Table 17-1 describes CMS's file support on an overview level. It shows that CMS fully supports CMS files. This means that programs can read and write CMS files, regardless of whether those files are CMS-formatted or OS-simulated datasets.

Table 17-1
CMS File Support

Read/Write Support	Read-Only Support	Unsupported
CMS files (both CMS-formatted and OS-simulated)	OS sequential files	DAM files (except for OS-simulated datasets)
VSAM files	DOS sequential files	ISAM files

CMS supports Virtual Storage Access Method (VSAM) files for both read- and write-access. (Chapter 20 describes CMS support for VSAM.) CMS also supports read-only access to real OS datasets residing on OS disks, and provides read-only support for real DOS datasets on DOS disks. Programs cannot directly update OS or DOS files on real OS or DOS disks attached to your virtual machine.

CMS only supports direct access methods (DAM) files through OS-simulated datasets on CMS disks. That is, CMS permits use of the Basic Direct Access Method (BDAM) only for CMS files having a filemode number of 4. CMS does not support direct access for real OS or real DOS disks, and does not support Indexed Sequential Access Method (ISAM) files.

Libraries

Chapter 16 discusses the three kinds of CMS libraries, Macro, Text, and Load.

For all three kinds of CMS libraries, the CMS GLOBAL command establishes the library reference prior to the compilation, loading, or running of the library member. The order in which libraries are named on the GLOBAL command establishes their search order. GLOBAL commands remain valid for the duration of a terminal session, until another GLOBAL command is issued for the same type of library, or until you reinitialize CMS (via the CP IPL command). You can check all searchable files at any time through the CMS QUERY command:

    QUERY librarytype

where librarytype is either MACLIB, TXTLIB, LOADLIB, or LIBRARY. LIBRARY lists the names of all the libraries of all kinds that are presently searchable. As an example:

    QUERY MACLIB

lists all MACLIBs presently searchable in their current search order.

The key to understanding CMS libraries is that they consist of a *library directory* and one or more *members*. The members represent individual macro or copy definitions, object modules, or load modules. CMS uses the directory to keep track of the members in the library. A CMS library is structured much like an OS partitioned dataset.

Since CMS libraries have a different internal structure than regular CMS files, they must be created, maintained, updated, and used differently.

MACLIB

CMS MACLIBs contain macro definitions and predefined source statements. These are input to MACLIBs from CMS files of filetypes MACRO and COPY. All CMS MACLIBs have the filetype of MACLIB.

The CMS MACLIB command supports the maintenance and manipulation of MACLIB members. Use it to:

create a MACLIB with one or more members

add, replace, or delete MACLIB members

compress the MACLIB

list the contents of the MACLIB

To create a new MACLIB, use the `MACLIB` command with the `GEN` (generate) function:

```
MACLIB GEN libraryname filename1 filename2 ...
```

where `libraryname` will be the filename of the newly created MACLIB, while its members are drawn from the files whose filenames are `filename1`, `filename2`, etc. Remember that these input files must be of filetypes `MACRO` and `COPY`.

Where a `MACRO` file is added to a MACLIB, the name of the member(s) added is taken from the macro prototype statement(s) in the input file. (In assembler language, each macro requires a macro prototype statement.) There may be one or more macros per `MACRO` input file.

Where a `COPY` file is added to a MACLIB, the name of the member added to the MACLIB is that of the `COPY` filename. Where more than one member is added to the MACLIB through a single `COPY` file, precede each member by this statement in the input file:

```
*COPY membername
```

The name of each member to add to the MACLIB is taken from this `*COPY` control statement in the input `COPY` file. Be sure to precede every member in the input file with this `COPY` control statement (including the first one in the input file), if there is more than a single copy definition in the file.

Here is an example:

```
MACLIB GEN MYLIB MYMACS MYCOPYS MYCOPY
```

Table 17-2 lists the partial contents of the input files.

Table 17-2
MACLIB Example

Filename	Contents
MYMACS MACRO A1	XGET macro prototype statement
	XPUT macro prototype statement
MYCOPYS COPY A1	*COPY XTERMIN
	*COPY XTERMOUT
MYCOPY COPY A1	(no *COPY statement is in file)

The `MACLIB` command creates a new macro library named `MYLIB MACLIB A1`. There are five members in this new MACLIB. Their member names are: `XGET`, `XPUT`, `XTERMIN`, `XTERMOUT`, and `MYCOPY`. Since the last input file referenced in the `MACLIB` command did not contain a

*COPY control statement, the default member name of the input filename is assumed.

Cautions are in order. First, if a macro library named MYLIB MACLIB A1 already exists, this command has the effect of erasing it and creating this new MACLIB of the same name. Secondly, the MACLIB command does not check for duplicate input member names. If more than one member is placed in the MACLIB with the same name, any retrieval attempt from the MACLIB retrieves only the first member of that name. It is strongly recommended that every member added to a MACLIB have a unique name.

Add new members to a MACLIB through the MACLIB command ADD function:

```
MACLIB  ADD  libraryname  filename1  filename2 ...
```

Similar to the function that generates a new MACLIB, the ADD function does not check for duplicate member names. It is the user's responsibility to avoid duplicate member names.

The REP (replace) function of the MACLIB command deletes the directory entries for input members in the specified MACRO and COPY files. It then appends new members to the macro library and creates directory entries for them.

The DEL (delete) function of the MACLIB command deletes the directory entries for one or more members and compresses the directory. It leaves the deleted macro or copy members themselves in the MACLIB, but those members cannot be retrieved because they have no entries in the MACLIB directory. Where duplicate members exist in the MACLIB, only the first one is deleted.

Repeated use of the replace and delete functions of the MACLIB command results in unused space within the MACLIB. The MACLIB COMP (compress) function eliminates this wasted space:

```
MACLIB  COMP  libraryname
```

where libraryname specifies the name of the MACLIB to compress. As an example:

```
MACLIB  COMP  MYLIB
```

compresses the MACLIB named MYLIB MACRO A1 by removing members that do not have directory entries.

The MACLIB MAP function creates a list containing the name of each member in the MACLIB, its size, and relative position within the library. Its format is:

```
MACLIB  MAP  libraryname
```

By default, the output of this command is sent to a disk file having the filetype of MAP and the same filename as that of the MACLIB itself. Thus:

```
MACLIB   MAP   MYLIB
```

creates a file named **MYLIB MAP A1** containing the member information. Use of the **PRINT** option spools a copy of the file to the printer:

```
MACLIB   MAP   MYLIB   (PRINT
```

Or, view the results directly on the terminal via the **TERM** option:

```
MACLIB   MAP   MYLIB   (TERM
```

Finally, certain CMS commands include a **MEMBER** option. This permits reference to MACLIB members. These CMS commands include: **TYPE** (display a member on the terminal); **PRINT** (print the member); **PUNCH** (punch a member). As an example:

```
TYPE   MYLIB   MACLIB   A1   (MEMBER   XTERMOUT
```

displays the **XTERMOUT** member of the macro library named **MYLIB MACLIB A1**, while:

```
TYPE   MYLIB   MACLIB   A1   (MEMBER   *
```

displays all the members of **MYLIB MACLIB A1** on the terminal.

TXTLIB

Text libraries have the reserved filetype of **TXTLIB**. Since they consist of object modules, inputs to text libraries are CMS files of filetype **TEXT**.

The CMS **TXTLIB** command creates, updates, maintains, and manipulates members in text libraries. Table 17-3 lists the uses and operands of the **TXTLIB** command.

Table 17-3
TXTLIB Command Operands

Function	Purpose
GEN	Create a TXTLIB having one or more members
ADD	Add member(s) to the text library
DEL	Delete member(s) from the text library
MAP	List members and member information for a specified text library

A statement such as:

```
TXTLIB   GEN   MYLIB   MYIN   MYTWO
```

creates a new TXTLIB named **MYLIB TXTLIB A1**. It contains members drawn from the input files named `MYIN TEXT A1` and `MYTWO TEXT A1`. The member names of the members in the TXTLIB are taken from the entry points or the CSECT names in the input `TEXT` files. (Entry points and CSECT names are places at which execution of a machine code module can begin.)

As with the `MACLIB` command, the `TXTLIB` command functions do not check for duplicate member names. Ensuring unique member names (or avoiding confusion if there are duplicate member names) is your responsibility.

The `TXTLIB` command has no replace function. A replace must be accomplished by deleting a member, then adding the new version of the member. Use the `DEL` and `ADD` functions of the `TXTLIB` command to do this.

The `TXTLIB` command also has no compress function. This makes sense because there is no replace function, and the `DEL` function automatically compresses the TXTLIB.

The `MAP` function lists the TXTLIB's members. For this example:

```
TXTLIB  MAP  MYLIB
```

the output file containing the list of members is named `MYLIB MAP`. The `MAP` function's default output is to disk. However, the options `TERM` and `PRINT` may be used to display the information on the terminal or route it to the printer. These options are used with `TXTLIB MAP` in the exact same manner illustrated earlier for `MACLIB MAP`.

As with macro libraries, members of text libraries can be referred to in CMS commands to display, print, or punch members. For example:

```
PUNCH  MYLIB  TXTLIB  A1  (MEMBER  PLISTART
```

punches member `PLISTART` of `MYLIB TXTLIB A1`, while:

```
PUNCH  MYLIB  TXTLIB  A1  (MEMBER  *
```

punches all the members of `MYLIB TXTLIB A1`.

LOADLIB

CMS load libraries provide a facility analogous to OS load libraries. Create a CMS LOADLIB through the CMS `LKED` command:

```
LKED  TESTTXT
```

creates a CMS load library named `TESTTXT LOADLIB A1` from the input object file named `TESTTXT TEXT A1`. The filetype of the input file is `TEXT`, while that of the output load library is `LOADLIB`. The resultant load library simulates an OS partitioned dataset containing the single member, `TESTTXT`.

Execute this LOABLIB member via the CMS `OSRUN` command. First, issue the GLOBAL command required to reference the load library for OS-RUN:

    GLOBAL LOADLIB TESTTXT

Then, enter the OSRUN command:

    OSRUN TESTTXT

The operand TESTTXT refers to the member within the referenced load library to load and execute.

You should be aware that CMS LOADLIBs are employed in a variety of ways in supporting OS practices. For example, the LKED command permits you to control link editing in several ways.

Alternate Ways to Prepare and Run Programs

CMS offers a wide variety of ways to develop programs. While all large, modern operating systems include similar facilities, CMS embodies a richer set of commands than most.

There are several other combinations of CMS commands that facilitate CMS and OS program development. This subsection concludes the discussion by demonstrating the simplest way to prepare and run programs. The CMS RUN command automatically takes appropriate actions in order to prepare and execute a program. The actions the RUN command assumes depends on the filetype of its operand. Here is an example:

    RUN MYPROG

The RUN command locates the file with filename of MYPROG. The action the RUN command takes depends on the filetype of MYPROG. For example, for a reserved filetype that indicates source code for a CMS command processor, the RUN command translates that source code with the appropriate language processor. If translation is successful, RUN then loads and executes that program.

RUN thus runs a FORTRAN compiler on files of type FORTRAN, the COBOL compiler on a file of type COBOL, the PL/I Optimizing compiler on files of type PLI and PLIOPT, etc. Following successful compilation, the RUN command loads and executes the program text.

The RUN command also handles files of types TEXT and MODULE. TEXT files are loaded via the LOAD command and then executed via START. For MODULE files, the CMS LOADMOD command loads the program module into storage and the START command begins program execution. When the START command is involved, program execution begins at the entry point named by the filename operand in the RUN command. In the example above, execution would begin at the label MYPROG.

The RUN command also properly executes CMS command procedure language files. These files have the filetype EXEC. Programming with the CMS command language processors is examined in section 6.

Use the RUN command when programming convenience is more important than machine efficiency. Remember that you need to enter any necessary FILEDEF or GLOBAL statements prior to issuing the RUN command.

Assembler Language Programming

Assembler language programming is beyond the scope of this book. However, it is useful to discuss CMS's facilities for assembler language programming on a conceptual level. Such understanding helps you comprehend the design of the CMS operating system.

There are several ways to write assembler language programs under CMS. First, one may code "native CMS" assembler language programs. These programs use programming conventions specific to the CMS environment (for example, for program linkage, parameter lists, etc.). They may also directly execute CMS commands.

A number of special assembler language macros are included in the CMS operating system for assembler programs written for execution specifically for CMS. These are contained in the macro libraries CMSLIB MACLIB and DMSSP MACLIB.

These two MACLIBs are both located on the system disk. The former contains the older VM/370 macros, while the latter consists of newer macros added or changed for the VM/SP releases of the operating system. Both libraries should be specified together with DMSSP MACLIB first in the library search order.

Together, these macro libraries include macros for: CMS disk file manipulation, terminal communications, unit record and tape input/output, and miscellaneous functions. Use the CMS GLOBAL command to identify these libraries to the assembler prior to assembling your program.

The second basic way to write assembler language programs in the CMS environment is to use the operating system's OS-oriented programming facilities. As described in chapter 16, these facilities permit development of code under CMS which runs compatibly under either CMS or OS.

CMS supports a subset of OS-oriented assembler macros. These reside in several CMS macro libraries on the CMS system disk, as listed in table 17-4.

The third basic way in which to write assembler programs under CMS is to use CMS's DOS-oriented programming facilities. CMS supports a subset of DOS assembly language macros for program assembly and execution. Similar to its support for OS macros, CMS also contains certain DOS macros that allow valid assembly (but *not* execution) of the assembled code under CMS. When using these macros in your programs, you may assemble your source code under CMS. But to run the assembled code with valid results, you must run the module in a DOS virtual machine running under VM, or on a DOS-based computer.

Library Name		Contents
OSMACRO	MACLIB	OS macros that CMS supports or simulates
OSMACRO1	MACLIB	OS macros that CMS does not support (You may only assemble programs using these macros under CMS, for later execution in an OS virtual machine or true OS computer.)
OSVSAM	MACLIB	Contains the subset of OS/VSAM macros CMS supports
TSOMAC	MACLIB	CMS-supported TSO macros

Table 17-4
CMS OS
Macro Libraries

Restrictions on OS-Oriented and DOS-Oriented Programming

File restrictions represent one general class of limitations on OS-oriented and DOS-oriented programming under CMS. CMS supports the kinds of files and access methods listed in table 17-1.

There are also various *execution-time restrictions* placed on programs run under CMS. The more important of these execution-time restrictions include:

- no multitasking support

- no use of multiple partitions

- no teleprocessing monitor support (IMS/DC is not available under CMS. A development-only program product is presently available for CICS.)

- timing-dependent programs will not work properly

These restrictions apply both to OS- and DOS-oriented programming under CMS.

In evaluating these restrictions, remember that the purpose of CMS's OS-oriented programming support is to provide a good development environment for OS programmers. CMS was *not* designed to provide a target machine exactly equivalent to that of the OS operating system itself. The virtual machine concept implemented in VM's CP component means that the OS operating system can run under VM. The solution to full OS programming compatibility under VM is therefore to run a separate OS virtual machine. The CMS single-user operating system thus offers a superlative environment to OS programmers for their program development, while a separate OS virtual machine provides an actual OS environment on the same computer.

In this manner, VM-based computers provide a rich program development environment (through CMS) and a compatible target machine (through OS running under CP). Programmers enjoy the benefits of two operating systems. They use CMS for its strengths in developmental activities and the OS operating system for production systems.

DOS-oriented program development is analogous to programming for OS systems in terms of CMS's role.

For Further Information

The *VM/SP CMS User's Guide, SC19-6210*, devotes several chapters to program development for CMS, OS, and DOS target machines. The *VM/SP CMS Command and Macro Reference, SC19-6209*, contains full summaries of all CMS commands relating to program development. These manuals give details concerning the degree to which CMS supports various file structures and access methods, and the specific rules any programmer must follow regarding CMS file usage. A comprehensive explanation of how CMS LOADLIBs simulate OS load module libraries is included. *SC19-6210* also contains precise lists of which OS and DOS macros are fully supported, and which ones are supported for assembly only.

The *VM/SP System Programmer's Guide, SC19-6203*, represents the final authority on such topics as CMS's support for files, assembler language programming under CMS, and restrictions on OS- and DOS-oriented programming under CMS.

Test Your Understanding

Does CMS support VSAM for read- and write-access? Does CMS support read- and write-access for real OS and real DOS datasets on real OS and DOS disks?

How can you tell what libraries you have assigned through CMS `GLOBAL` commands?

Create a CMS macro library with members that represent either assembly language macros or high-level language source statements. List the members through the MACLIB `MAP` function.

What happens if you attempt to add members with duplicate names to the sample MACLIB? How does CMS react to duplicate members within a macro or text library?

How do you reclaim lost space within a macro library? Compress your sample library.

Using the CMS `PRINT` command, print a listing of one member of your sample macro library. Now print a listing of all the members in the library.

What are the advantages and disadvantages of using the CMS `RUN` command compared to other ways of preparing and executing programs?

To what degree does CMS support standard OS and DOS assembly language macros?

What restrictions apply to OS- and DOS-oriented programming under VM/CMS?

CHAPTER 18

DOS Programming Facilities of CMS

CMS also provides broad-based support to DOS programmers to develop programs that run compatibly under various forms of the DOS operating system.

The default programming environment of CMS is OS-oriented. That is, no special CMS command must be entered in order to develop OS-oriented programs. This changes when developing DOS programs under CMS: in order to access the DOS-oriented facilities, you enter the *CMS /DOS environment*, which offers many of the same functions as a DOS operating system while retaining the interactive flavor of CMS. Various CMS commands issued under CMS/DOS embody functions that are analogous to those of the corresponding DOS/VSE control cards. If you are familiar with DOS, CMS/DOS is easy to learn.

Entering the CMS/DOS Environment

The CMS SET command allows you to turn on various functions in your virtual machine. You enter CMS/DOS by typing the CMS SET command with the DOS operand:

    SET DOS ON

Exit from the CMS/DOS environment by:

    SET DOS OFF

Re-initializing CMS via the CP IPL command also exits the CMS/DOS environment; the CMS default value is DOS OFF.

Once in the CMS/DOS environment, you still have access to CMS commands. You additionally use the CMS/DOS facilities described in this chapter. You cannot, however, develop and run programs that load and/or use OS-oriented macros. As an example, the `SCRIPT` command described in chapter 7 uses OS macros and would not run in the CMS/DOS environment.

Normally, you will want access to the DOS system residence volume (DOS SYSRES) during your session. This is necessary in order to use any of the DOS system libraries which reside on this volume. In this case, you need to make the minidisk that contains DOS SYSRES known and available to your virtual machine, prior to issuing the `SET DOS` command.

First, your virtual machine must be linked to the DOS SYSRES disk. This may have been done for you by virtue of the CP Directory entries defining your virtual machine to CP. Use the CMS `QUERY` command to see if the DOS SYSRES minidisk has been made available to your own virtual machine:

    QUERY DISK

If the DOS SYSRES disk is not among those listed, use the CP `LINK` command to associate the DOS SYSRES disk with your virtual machine.

As an example, if the DOS SYSRES minidisk is associated with the userid of `SYSUSR` at virtual address `390`, issue this `LINK` command:

    LINK TO SYSUSR 390 AS 390 R

The DOS SYSRES minidisk associated with user `SYSUSR` at virtual address `390` is associated with your virtual machine at its virtual address of `390`. The linking is specified as read-only mode `R`. If the disk is password protected, CMS prompts you for the read password.

Now issue the CMS `ACCESS` command to identify the DOS SYSRES volume to CMS and establish a filemode letter for the files on that disk. Assuming the above `LINK` command and a filemode letter of `G`, issue the `ACCESS` command this way:

    ACCESS 390 G

Indicate that DOS SYSRES is on your `G` disk by the `FILEMODE` parameter of the `SET DOS` command:

    SET DOS ON G

Issuing the `SET DOS` command with this `ON FILEMODE` parameter gives you access to the DOS SYSRES disk throughout your CMS/DOS session.

If you develop and run programs that read and/or write to VSAM datasets, or, if you use the VSAM Access Methods Services (AMS) utility program, add the `VSAM` parameter to the `SET DOS` command:

    SET DOS ON G (VSAM

This permits full use of DOS/VSAM during the terminal session.

Once in the CMS/DOS environment, a number of programming language translators may be available. Which ones you access depends on your installation's VM/CMS configuration. All higher-level programming language translators are separately ordered products. The most common language processors for DOS programmers under CMS are: COBOL, PL/I, RPGII, and Assembler.

The remainder of this chapter shows how to compile, debug, and execute programs written in these programming languages. Should you have access to other DOS-oriented language compilers, their use is similar in concept to these illustrative languages.

The Basics of Program Development

One follows the same generic steps for program development when using CMS/DOS as when using the OS-oriented programming facilities of CMS. These steps include:

1. Enter the program source code into a CMS file.
2. Compile that program source into a relocatable object module (a TEXT file).
3. Link edit and load the program.
4. Identify input/output devices and files used by the program.
5. Execute the program.

Certain of these steps may require identification of relevant libraries to CMS prior to their execution.

Running the Language Translators

As with the OS-oriented CMS programming languages, you invoke the CMS compilers for DOS programming by single commands referring to the individual language translators. The filetype of the source code program must be appropriate to each language processor, as shown in table 18-1.

Table 18-1
DOS Language Processor Filetypes

Command	Language Translator Invoked	Source Filetype
FCOBOL filename	COBOL	COBOL
DOSPLI filename	PL/I Optimizer	PLIOPT
RPGII filename	RPG II	RPGII
ASSEMBLE filename	Assembler	ASSEMBLE

Specify compiler options after a left parenthesis following the file name of the source code. Some compilers require specification of compiler options *before* running the language translator through the CMS OPTION command:

```
OPTION  option1  option2 ...
```

Simply list the required compiler options after the OPTION command, then run the appropriate CMS/DOS compiler. Table 18-2 lists the options of the CMS OPTION command; defaults appear in italics.

Table 18-2
OPTION Command Options

Option	Purpose
DUMP	Dump the registers and virtual partition in event of
NODUMP	abnormal program end
DECK/NODECK	Punch the output object deck (default specifies DECK to your CMS A-disk)
LIST/NOLIST	Write output listing to SYSLST device
LISTX/*NOLISTX*	Write Procedure Division map to SYSLST device
SYM/*NOSYM*	Write Data Division map to SYSLST device
XREF/*NOXREF*	Write symbolic cross-references to SYSLST device
ERRS/NOERRS	Write listing of all errors in source to SYSLST
48C/*60C*	Specifies 48- or 60-character set
TERM/*NOTERM*	Write compiler messages to the user's terminal

The CMS OPTION command is normally associated with IBM's DOS COBOL (FCOBOL) compiler. However, if you have questions concerning whether any particular compiler uses the OPTION command or expects its options as operands on its compiler command, refer to the "CMS User's Guide" for that compiler.

Another CMS command you may issue prior to invoking the program translator is the ASSGN command. ASSGN has the same function under CMS /DOS as it does under DOS; it identifies an input/output device for a system or programmer logical unit. It can be used to indicate the minidisk on which the source code input to the language translator resides.

Here are several examples of source program translation under CMS /DOS:

```
ASSGN   SYSIPT  A
DOSPLI  PLIPROG


ASSGN   SYSIPT  A
OPTION  XREF
FCOBOL  MYPROG


ASSGN  SYSIPT  A
RPGII  MYPROG  (LIST XREF
```

In the first example, the program source code resides in the file named PLIPROG PLIOPT A1. The CMS ASSGN command indicates that input to the compiler resides on the A disk. Similar to the OS-oriented CMS compilers, the compiler produces two outputs. One output is the **LISTING** file, named **PLIPROG LISTING A1**, the compiler printout of the source program and accompanying compiler messages and errors. The other compiler output is the **TEXT** file, or object code module, named **PLIPROG TEXT A1**. This is the machine code version of the source input which will later be link edited, fetched, and run. Both of these compiler outputs are placed on the same disk as the input source file (assuming the input source file resides on a read/write minidisk). The input to and outputs from the compiler are diagrammed in figure 18-1.

Figure 18-1
Running CMS/DOS
Language
Translators
Produces Two Files

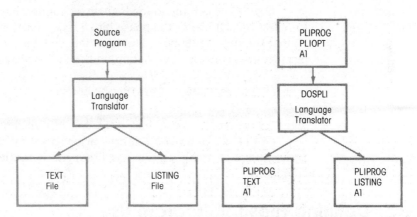

The second example shows the assignment of **SYSIPT** to the **A** disk. Then, the CMS **OPTION** command stipulates that the compiler output a symbolic cross-reference list. A version of the COBOL compiler processes the input file **MYPROG COBOL A1**.

The final example invokes an RPGII compiler. Check your RPG compiler's "CMS User's Guide" to see whether you should specify compiler options on the compiler command line, as in the example, or through the CMS **OPTION** command.

Creating an Executable Phase

Running a programming language translator on a source language input file produces an object module, or CMS **TEXT** file. The next step in program development is creation of an executable phase by link editing this **TEXT** file. Use the CMS **DOSLKED** command:

```
DOSLKED   filename   library-name
```

where **filename** is the filename of the input **TEXT** file, and **library-name** is the name of the CMS phase library in which to store the executable phase. This library is assigned a filetype of **DOSLIB** by CMS. For example:

```
DOSLKED   MYPROG   MYLIB
```

processes the input file named MYPROG TEXT A1 and outputs an executable phase in the library named MYLIB DOSLIB A1.

Loading the Program

After successfully link editing the object module, load the executable phase into memory. Use the CMS/DOS FETCH command to do this:

```
FETCH   phasename
```

The FETCH command loads the executable phase into virtual storage for execution. It brings the phase into a fixed location in virtual storage, at virtual address X'20000'. This location can be altered by specifying a hexadecimal address as an option on the FETCH statement. As an example:

```
FETCH   MYPROG   (ORIGIN   22000
```

loads an executable phase into storage at hexadecimal location 22000.

The FETCH command requires prior specification of the library containing the executable phase. The library is identified by a CMS GLOBAL command.

Defining Files for Program Use

After loading the executable phase into virtual storage, the last step prior to program execution is identification of the files and devices required for program processing. Use the CMS ASSGN and DLBL commands for this purpose. These commands are similar to their DOS counterparts.

The ASSGN command designates an input/output device or file for a system or programmer logical-unit. Here is its format for specifying devices:

```
ASSGN   logical-unit   device
```

Valid devices under CMS/DOS are listed in table 18-3.

Table 18-3
CMS/DOS Devices

Device	Function
TERMINAL	Data is input or output through a terminal display
PRINTER	Data is output to a printer
READER	Data is input via a card reader
PUNCH	Data is output to a card punch
TAPn	Data is input or output to a tape file (n can have a value of 1, 2, 3, or 4, representing virtual tape drive addresses of 181, 182, 183, or 184, respectively)

Valid programmer logical-units range from SYS000 to SYS241 under CMS/DOS. Thus:

```
ASSGN SYS010 TERMINAL
```

assigns the logical-unit SYS010 to the terminal.

The logical-unit parameter on the ASSGN statement can be assigned to one of a reserved set of system logical-units. These system logical-units are:

SYSIPT

SYSRDR

SYSIN

SYSPCH

SYSLST

SYSLOG

SYSCLB

SYSRLB

SYSSLB

The system logical-units have the same meanings as they do under DOS operating systems.

You can list all system and programmer logical-unit assignments at any time via the CMS LISTIO command:

```
LISTIO
```

The use of disk files mandates a slightly different form of the ASSGN command:

```
ASSGN logical-unit filemode
```

As an example:

```
ASSGN SYS010 A
```

assigns the logical-unit SYS010 to a file on your A disk. When this form of the ASSGN command is used, the CMS DLBL command must also be issued. The DLBL command has two forms. One form refers to CMS files. The other form of the DLBL command refers to DOS files residing on DOS disks. CMS/DOS supports read-only access to DOS sequential files residing on real DOS disks. This assumes that the DOS disks are properly defined to your virtual machine.

To refer to a CMS file, enter:

```
DLBL ddname filemode CMS filename filetype (SYSnnn PERM
```

The ddname is the symbolic name by which the file is referred to in the program, and filemode indicates the minidisk on which the file resides. The CMS keyword indicates that this is a CMS-formatted file, and filename and filetype provide the name of this file. SYSnnn indicates the logical-unit associated with the file. PERM is an optional operand that tells CMS /DOS that the DLBL is to remain in effect for as long as possible. Usually, this means until you terminate your session or IPL CMS again.

In the DLBL definition, the filemode and SYSnnn parameters *must* match their equivalents in the corresponding ASSGN statement. Here is the relationship between ASSGN and DLBL:

```
ASSGN  SYSnnn  filemode
DLBL   ddname  filemode  CMS  filename  filetype  (SYSnnn  PERM
```

As an example:

```
ASSGN  SYS010  A
DLBL   INDD    A  CMS  INFILE  DATA  (SYS010  PERM
```

This associates the programmer logical-unit SYS010 with the CMS file named INFILE DATA A1.

The second form of the CMS DLBL command refers to DOS files residing on real DOS disks defined to your virtual machine. The keyword DSN in the DLBL statement signifies a DOS file, just as the CMS keyword designates CMS files.

There are several ways to issue the DLBL command to identify DOS files; the simplest permits interactive entry of the DOS file name. For example, entering:

```
ASSGN  SYS010  D
DLBL   OUTDD  D  DSN  ?  (SYS010
```

results in this prompt from CMS:

```
ENTER DATA SET NAME:
```

to which you reply with the dataset name:

```
TEST.EXPLE.OUTPT
```

The DSN ? form of the DLBL is the most flexible form of this CMS statement in entering file names of DOS-disk resident files.

To clear a DLBL definition for any file, enter:

```
DLBL  ddname  CLEAR
```

as in:

```
DLBL  OUTDD  CLEAR
```

To see what `DLBL` definitions are outstanding, enter:

```
DLBL
```

without operands. Or, use the CMS `QUERY` command:

```
QUERY  DLBL
```

This query presents the ddname, filemode, logical-unit, dataset name, and other information on the terminal for each outstanding file definition.

CMS allows you to use a maximum of four tape drives at one time. These are referred to by their virtual device addresses of **181**, **182**, **183**, and **184**. As mentioned earlier, these are designated by the logical-unit names of **TAP1**, **TAP2**, **TAP3**, and **TAP4**, respectively.

Under CMS, you typically request attachment of a tape drive to your virtual machine and tape mounting by sending a message to the system operator. Do this by the CP command, `MESSAGE`. Its format is:

```
CP  MESSAGE  userid  text of message
```

Use the system operator's reserved userid of **OP** to send him this message to mount your tape:

```
CP  MESSAGE  OP  MOUNT TAPE VOLSER 17032 ON 181
```

A message such as this:

```
TAPE  181  ATTACHED
```

appears on your terminal when the requested tape has been mounted. Now enter the appropriate `ASSGN` command:

```
ASSGN  SYS010  TAP1
```

and the tape has been allocated.

The CMS `LABELDEF` command allows you to specify the tape label

description information required under CMS/DOS. It takes the place of the
TLBL card under DOS.

Running the Program

Here is a summary of the steps leading to program execution:

1. Enter the CMS/DOS environment.
2. Compile (or assemble) the program through a programming language translator.
3. Create an executable phase of the program.
4. Load the phase into virtual storage for execution via the FETCH command.
5. Define files and devices required for program processing via the ASSGN and DLBL commands.

Now, execute the program by the CMS START command. Simply enter:

```
START
```

An alternative way to run the program is to specify the START option on the FETCH command:

```
FETCH   phasename   (START
```

Be sure to identify all files needed for program processing (issue your ASSGNs and DLBLs) *before* entering the FETCH command with the START option.

Establishing Access to Libraries

In the program development process, there are several points when access to libraries may be needed. For example, immediately prior to assembly of a source code program, you can specify one or more libraries containing predefined macros for inclusion by the assembler.

You also need to specify a library immediately prior to issuing the FETCH command. In this case, you identify the library in which the executable phase resides.

In both cases, use the CMS GLOBAL command to identify the libraries to search. Use the GLOBAL command under CMS/DOS in the same manner described in the chapter on OS-oriented programming. The general format of the GLOBAL command is:

```
GLOBAL   library-type   library-name1   library-name2 ...
```

where library-type specifies the kind of library to search. For example, the macro library you identify as an input to the assembler is of filetype

MACLIB; the executable phase library you identify to the FETCH command is of filetype DOSLIB. (Note that the DOS COBOL and PL/I compilers obtain their copy files from a DOS source statement library rather than from CMS MACLIBs.)

One or more libraries are specified on the GLOBAL statement. The order in which they are listed is the order in which they will be searched. GLOBAL commands remain in effect for the duration of the terminal session, until you IPL CMS again, or until you cancel the effect of a previous GLOBAL command by issuing another GLOBAL for the same kind of library.

You create and maintain a MACLIB for use under CMS/DOS through the CMS MACLIB command.

You place executable phases into a DOSLIB through the CMS DOSLKED command, and you load phases from DOSLIBs through a FETCH command for which a reference has been established to the DOSLIB through the GLOBAL command. In addition, the CMS DOSLIB command aids in working with DOSLIBs. The DOSLIB command's functions are listed in table 18-4.

Table 18-4
DOSLIB Command Functions

Function	Purpose
DEL	Delete phase(s) from the DOSLIB
COMP	Compress the DOSLIB
MAP	List phase name, size, and relative location for each DOSLIB member

These functions are analogous to those illustrated earlier for the CMS MACLIB and TXTLIB commands.

Flexibility of DOSLKED and FETCH Commands

For the sake of clear discussion, we earlier simplified the discussion of the DOSLKED and FETCH commands. We assumed that both commands took their inputs from the CMS minidisks associated with your virtual machine. But in fact, both commands are highly flexible in the definition of their input sources.

For the DOSLKED command, CMS first searches for a specially named file on your CMS disks that contains linkage editor control statements. This file is assumed to have the same filename as the object program and a filetype of DOSLNK. The file may contain such linkage editor control statements as ACTION, PHASE, INCLUDE, and ENTRY. The INCLUDE statement refers to a CMS TEXT file, or a module in a DOS library. It can also immediately precede a CMS TEXT file as part of the input stream.

If a linkage editor control statement file is not found to direct the linkage editing process, then CMS searches the DOS private relocatable library. In order for this search to occur, you must have identified the DOS private relocatable library by appropriate `ASSGN` and `DLBL` statements. In these commands, use `SYSRLB` as the system logical-unit name for the private DOS library, and `IJSYSRL` as the ddname. Table 18-5 lists CMS/DOS-supported DOS libraries along with their reserved system logical-units and ddnames.

Table 18-5
CMS/DOS-supported DOS Libraries

System Logical-Unit	Contents	DDNAME
SYSCLB	Private Core Image Library	IJSYSCL
SYSRLB	Private Relocatable Library	IJSYSRL
SYSSLB	Source Statement Library	IJSYSSL

If a module is not found in the DOS relocatable library (or if the library was not identified to CMS), then CMS searches your minidisks for a `TEXT` file. This is the manner in which CMS located a module for link editing in the prior examples.

Finally, if a CMS `TEXT` file was not found, CMS searches the system relocatable library. This search only occurs if you specified a filemode letter when you originally entered the CMS/DOS environment through the `SET DOS ON` command.

Link editing occurs once the module(s) to link edit have been located. The executable phase is stored in the library named in the `DOSLKED` command.

The `FETCH` command similarly provides greater flexibility. CMS `FETCH` first searches a DOS private core image library on a DOS disk. This search occurs only if you have previously identified the library via the `ASSGN` and `DLBL` commands. Use the system logical-unit name of `SYSCLB` and its associated ddname of `IJSYSCL` to do this. This example defines this library, assuming it is known to your virtual machine as the `D` disk:

```
ASSGN   SYSCLB  D
DLBL    IJSYSCL D  DSN  ?  (SYSCLB
```

The second place the `FETCH` command searches for executable phases is your CMS minidisks. In order for this search to occur, you must have issued a `GLOBAL` command identifying the CMS DOSLIB to search. You can name up to eight CMS DOSLIBs on a single `GLOBAL` command for this search. If possible, limit the number of searchable DOSLIBs and the number of phases in each. This measurably improves your response time during CMS's search for executable phases.

Finally, the `FETCH` command searches the DOS system residence core image library. In order for this search to occur, you must have entered the

CMS/DOS environment with the DOS SYSRES identified by the filemode letter in the CMS **SET DOS ON** command.

The **DOSLKED** and **FETCH** commands, then, provide a great flexibility in their sources of input. You determine where these commands search for their input files through combinations of the **ASSGN**, **DLBL**, and **GLOBAL** commands.

DOS Libraries

CMS simulates the DOS librarian functions **SSERV**, **RSERV**, **PSERV**, **ESERV**, and **DSERV** through CMS/DOS commands of these names. These commands permit you to use, print, or display various kinds of files from DOS libraries and to create CMS files from DOS libraries.

For Further Information

Restrictions on DOS-oriented programming and CMS support for DOS assembly programming are described in chapter 17.

The *VM/SP CMS User's Guide, SC19-6210*, describes DOS-oriented programming under CMS in detail. This manual also provides information on the use of the DOS commands **SSERV**, **RSERV**, **PSERV**, **ESERV**, and **DSERV**. *VM/SP CMS Command and Macro Reference, SC19-6209*, provides reference summary information on all CMS/DOS commands.

CMS for Programmers: A Primer, SR20-4438, is an introductory manual for programming with CMS/DOS. It contains simple but complete development examples for DOS COBOL and PL/I programming.

Complete lists and explanations of the options for each language are contained in the "CMS User's Guides" for each programming language. These manuals include:

CMS User's Guide for COBOL, SC28-6469

DOS/PLI Optimizing Compiler: CMS User's Guide, SC33-0051

DOS/VS RPGII User's Guide, SC33-6074

OS/VS - VM/370 Assembler Programmer's Guide, GC33-4021

Test Your Understanding

List the basic steps of program development under CMS/DOS. For which steps in the program development process do you need to issue CMS **GLOBAL** commands?

List the CMS commands to carry out each of the basic steps of program development you cited in answering the question above. What is the function of each command?

For a CMS disk file named **MYFILE DATA A1**, write appropriate **ASSGN** and **DLBL** commands to access this file via the program ddname of **INPUT**.

What is the purpose of the CMS **DOSLIB** command? What are its functions?

Describe the manners in which the CMS **DOSLKED** and **FETCH** commands look for their inputs.

Write a very brief program in any language which you are familiar with and have access to under CMS/DOS. Your program should read in one line of information from the terminal user and echo it back to the terminal. Compile and test your program under CMS/DOS.

CHAPTER 19

Interactive Debugging under VM/CMS

One of VM/CMS's strengths as an operating system is the extensive facilities it provides for program development. Some of the reasons VM/CMS excels in this area are:

- Programs may be written and debugged under CMS for different target operating systems, including OS and DOS systems.
- Each user controls his own virtual machine, which he may tailor, configure, and direct as he sees fit for program development.
- All major programming languages (and several command procedure languages) are available under CMS.
- An extensive variety of add-on packages are available for VM/CMS. Many of these support program development.
- CMS was designed for interactive use.

Before describing the specific interactive facilities available within VM/CMS for program debugging, it is beneficial to analyze why interactive debugging leads to high productivity. In the *interactive environment*, programmers receive quick responses to questions they have about their programming errors. For example, you can speedily determine the nature of an error, the contents of storage, or the value in a register by entering an online command. In *batch mode* debugging, program listings and dumps are the only sources for this information. Unless you have a dedicated attached printer, batch debugging wastes time while you wait for printer output. In contrast, interactive CMS facilities answer debugging questions immediately. With interactive debugging, you can instantly correct programs and try them again. This quick response gives you the opportunity to test your program in different ways, using different approaches and techniques because there is no time penalty. The result is much higher programmer productivity.

VM/CMS features three classes of interactive debugging tools. The first set of facilities applies to programming in higher-level languages such as COBOL, PL/I, and FORTRAN. Remember, these programming languages are all separately purchased program products; which ones are available to you depends on your installation's purchasing decisions. Most of these third generation languages offer an interactive debugging package for CMS. For COBOL, this tool is called *COBOL Interactive Debug;* for FORTRAN, it is *FORTRAN Interactive Debug.* Both of these packages (and their equivalents for other programming languages) support similar capabilities. They allow you to halt program execution at predefined points in the program, interactively query and set values in program variables and memory, determine the nature of program exceptions, and perform related debugging activities.

Space limitation forbids illustration of all these capabilities for the many programming languages supported by VM/CMS; however, the COBOL Interactive Debug product is representative of the debugging facilities available for other languages. While the specifics of use are sometimes language-dependent, the principles of use are universal to the interactive debuggers available for most high-level programming languages.

A second method employed in interactive debugging under CMS is the CMS DEBUG command. The DEBUG command establishes the CMS Debug Environment, under which a dozen DEBUG subcommands are available. It provides functions similar to those of the COBOL and FORTRAN Interactive Debug products. However, the Debug Environment is oriented toward an assembly language view of the subject program. Its commands deal with program and variable addresses and assembler language instructions. For the most part, CMS DEBUG supports assembler programmers or others involved in low-level programming. It can be (and sometimes is) employed in debugging higher-level language programs. However, when debugging higher-level language programs it is simpler and more convenient to use the packages specifically designed for use with those programming languages because this sort of debugging is in keeping with the high-level nature of those languages. Thus, you could use the CMS Debug Environment when testing a COBOL program, and in fact you might prefer to in solving exceptionally difficult problems; but most of the time, the COBOL Interactive Debug package is both more convenient and more productive for debugging COBOL programs.

The CMS Debug Environment is similar to the assembly-level debuggers found in other operating systems. For example, the Debug Environment is quite similar to the MVS/TSO TEST command.

The third major VM/CMS facility for debugging programs consists of CP commands designed for virtual machine control and debugging. These commands allow you to perform functions highly similar to those of the CMS DEBUG subcommands. Similar to the Debug Environment, these CP commands assume some knowledge of addressing and machine-level operations. Whether you choose to use CMS DEBUG or the equivalent CP commands is a matter of personal preference. Most programmers find it easier to work with CMS DEBUG, rather than CP-level diagnostics.

Higher-Level Programming Languages

The underlying concepts and principles of the COBOL Interactive Debug tool apply to those available for other high-level programming languages. Outside of linguistic differences, COBOL Interactive Debug is representative of an entire group of interactive testing tools for third generation procedural programming languages.

COBOL Interactive Debug allows you to monitor, trace, and control execution of your program while it is executing. More specifically, you can:

- start and stop program execution
- display and alter program variables
- trace and alter the logical flow of program execution
- examine other aspects of program execution (for example, file status and program source statements)

The steps to using the COBOL Interactive Debug facility are as follows. First, you *must* compile the program source code using the TEST option. For example, for a program source file named MYPROG COBOL A1, you might enter:

```
COBOL  MYPROG  (TEST  SOURCE
```

If your program source includes COBOL COPY statements, specify the appropriate MACLIB prior to compilation via a GLOBAL command.

Next, issue the FILEDEF commands required by the program for input and output files. Recall that FILEDEF commands correspond to the files required by the COBOL SELECT statements in the program's source code. At this time, there are three additional FILEDEF commands you issue specifically for use with the COBOL Interactive Debugger. They are listed in table 19-1.

	File	Filetype	Purpose
Table 19-1 COBOL Interactive Debugger Files	Debug file	SYSUT5	Contains information required by the debugger so that you can refer to variable names and source statement numbers during debugging
	Compiler PRINT file	LISTING	Contains COBOL source listing (required if you display source statements at the terminal during debugging)
	Debug PRINT file	LISTING	Contains information you tell the debugger to print during the debugging session

Thus, in addition to any input/output files declared in the COBOL program SELECT statements, COBOL Interactive Debug requires these three additional FILEDEF commands. Here is an example:

```
FILEDEF  D        DISK  MYPROG  SYSUT5   A1
FILEDEF  MYPROG   DISK  MYPROG  LISTING  A1
FILEDEF  P        DISK  PRINTS  LISTING  A1
```

Three files are declared for use by the COBOL Interactive Debugger. The first is always required for use by the debugger. It contains data name and statement number information. The second file contains COBOL program source statements and is required if you intend to display COBOL source statements during the debugging session. The last file is where information you request the debugger to print for you is written. It is recommended that you routinely declare all three files whenever using the debugger. Then you won't encounter any restrictions during the debugging session due to lack of file allocation.

The Interactive Debugger routinely clears all FILEDEF commands upon completion, even those declared with the PERM option. Thus, you must reissue them every time you enter the facility.

Following file definition, declare any necessary GLOBAL libraries required for TEXT files. There is normally an installation-named library involved for COBOL programs, here called COBLIBVS. Additionally, if you have any TEXT modules that refer to your own TXTLIBs, they should be established too. In this example, the compiler output was a TEXT module not residing in a TXTLIB, thus only this statement is needed:

```
GLOBAL  TXTLIB  COBLIBVS
```

Now you are ready to enter the COBOL Interactive Debug test environment. Do this through the TESTCOB command. Once it is issued, you are in the TESTCOB environment. The TESTCOB environment consists of some two dozen subcommands to help debug the program. Enter it as shown in this example:

```
TESTCOB  MYPROG  (MYPROG D)  PRINT(P)
```

The TESTCOB command refers to the input TEXT module, here named MYPROG TEXT A1. This input could also be a text module within a TXTLIB, if a GLOBAL command were previously issued to identify the text module library.

The parameters in parentheses are the program name (from the PROGRAM-ID paragraph in the COBOL program source) and the name of the associated debug dataset (always of filetype SYSUT5). The keyword PRINT is followed by the name of the print output dataset defined earlier via a FILEDEF command.

Pass run-time information to your program by adding a question mark at the end of the TESTCOB command. The system prompts you to enter the character string parameter:

```
TESTCOB  MYPROG  (MYPROG D)  PRINT(P)  ?
```

Once you enter the TESTCOB command, you are in the Interactive Debug environment. The prompt:

```
TESTCOB
```

signals this.

Once under TESTCOB, you can establish program breakpoints, points at which program execution halts so that you can inspect program variables. The AT subcommand does this. For example, to halt program execution at statement 310, enter:

```
AT  310
```

Now enter:

```
GO
```

and your program executes until it reaches statement 310. Using the AT subcommand, you can establish multiple breakpoints within a program and thus control program execution. You can also specify a statement number from which execution begins with the optional statement-number operand of the GO subcommand:

```
GO  310
```

This initiates program execution at statement 310. Issuing the GO subcommand with a statement number provides one way to modify the logical flow of your program. But be careful not to skip parts of the program that are essential to proper execution of the remainder.

While the GO subcommand halts execution at the next breakpoint, you can ignore breakpoints altogether (and run until program completion or abend) through the RUN command. Like GO, RUN is entered with or without a statement number. Lack of a statement number means that program execution begins at the point at which it was last halted.

Once at a breakpoint, display the contents of program variables through the TESTCOB LIST subcommand. Typing:

```
LIST  VARIABLE-NAME
```

displays the contents of **VARIABLE-NAME**. List all variables, index names, and COBOL special registers by the **ALL** operand:

    LIST ALL

Print any variable, list of variables, or other data values to the print dataset specified by the **FILEDEF** prior to entry to **TESTCOB** through the **PRINT** operand:

    LIST (VARIABLE-NAME1, VARIABLE-NAME2) PRINT

Alter the value of variables through the **SET** subcommand. Entering:

    SET NUMERIC-VARIABLE = 72

sets the program variable **NUMERIC-VARIABLE** to the value 72. You can dynamically alter program variables by setting breakpoints and issuing **SET** subcommands. Of course, the values you move into program variables must be compatible with the data types of those variables.

Use the **TESTCOB LISTFILE** subcommand to display the status of files. **LISTFILE** displays (or prints) information like the file's dataset organization **DSORG**, name **DSNAME**, and other status information if the file is open. The additional information given for open files includes the record format **RECFM**, block size **BLKSIZE**, and logical record length **LRECL**. Enter the **LISTFILE** subcommand with the filename as its operand, optionally followed by the keyword **PRINT**:

    LISTFILE FILENAME

You can also display program source code statements at the terminal by entering the **SOURCE** subcommand. This assumes that you defined the source listing dataset as shown above in the **FILEDEF** commands prior to issuing the **TESTCOB** command. Thus:

    SOURCE 310

displays program source code statement number 310. Display a range of source code lines like this:

    SOURCE 310:390

This displays lines 310 through 390.

One of the most useful **TESTCOB** commands for analyzing logic errors is the **TRACE** subcommand. Issuing:

    TRACE PARA

displays the line number of each COBOL program paragraph or section at the moment execution of that paragraph or section begins, and:

TRACE NAME

displays the paragraph name and line number at the moment execution of each paragraph or section begins.

Redirection of this output is accomplished by adding the PRINT operand on the TRACE subcommand:

TRACE NAME PRINT

Cancel the effect of a previous TRACE subcommand through:

TRACE OFF

The TRACE subcommand helps you find errors in program logical flow very quickly.

Finally, to exit the TESTCOB environment, you enter:

DUMP

This dumps your virtual machine to the printer. Or, to exit without a dump input:

END

A third option is to enter the RUN subcommand, which runs the program until completion or abnormal end (abend).

In summary, this discussion presents only a subset of TESTCOB subcommands, and even then, it does not demonstrate all the operands of those subcommands. However, it does give you an idea of the nature of online debugging with the COBOL Interactive Debugger. This tool enormously increases programming productivity over other methods. Remember that although the specific commands are different in other higher-level language debugging packages, the capabilities of those packages and the underlying principles are the same.

CMS DEBUG

The CMS DEBUG command provides capabilities similar to those of the COBOL Interactive Debug facility. For example, you can:

- set breakpoints and control program execution
- inspect and alter contents of variables, storage, and the general registers
- trace and alter the logical flow of program execution
- dynamically apply temporary changes to a program and then continue with program execution

The main difference between a tool like COBOL Interactive Debug and the CMS **DEBUG** command is that in the CMS Debug Environment, you are more intimate with the machine architecture. You work with instruction and variable addresses and aspects of machine operation like registers and program status words. You do not work with symbolic names for variables or breakpoints unless you specifically establish these symbolic names through **DEBUG** subcommands.

To invoke the CMS Debug Environment, issue the CMS **DEBUG** command:

```
DEBUG
```

You generally do this after loading a program into storage, but prior to execution. At this time, you can establish breakpoints, for example.

We assume you have assembled a program for testing. Now enter:

```
LOAD   MYPROG
DEBUG
BREAK  0  200C0
BREAK  1  201B0
RETURN
START
```

In this sequence of commands, you first load the assembled **TEXT** module into virtual storage. The program is always loaded by CMS at virtual address X'20000', unless you specify otherwise.

Then, enter the Debug Environment by issuing the CMS **DEBUG** command. Set two breakpoints through the **DEBUG BREAK** subcommand. The breakpoints are assigned identifiers of 0 and 1, respectively, at addresses X'200C0' and X'201B0'. Notice that **DEBUG** subcommands that require address operands do not require the entry of leading zeroes in those addresses. X'200C0' is equivalent to X'0200C0'.

The **DEBUG** subcommand **RETURN** returns you to CMS. The CMS **START** command starts program execution. Program execution continues until it reaches the first breakpoint at address X'200C0'.

At this point, you may inspect the current settings of the Program Status Word (PSW), Channel Status Word (CSW), and Channel Address Word (CAW) by issuing these **DEBUG** subcommands:

```
PSW
CSW
CAW
```

None of these commands require operands. Responses to your commands are, of course, in hexadecimal.

You may also display the contents of the general registers, 0 through 15, by issuing the **GPR** subcommand:

```
GPR  0  15
```

Or, display the contents of a single register:

```
GPR  13
```

This displays the contents of general register 13.

The X subcommand allows you to examine virtual storage:

```
X  201B0  16
```

This example displays 16 bytes of storage beginning at hexadecimal location X'201B0'. You can display up to 56 bytes of storage through one X subcommand.

The DUMP subcommand prints all or part of your virtual storage on your virtual printer. Specify two addresses representing the range of storage to print:

```
DUMP  200C0  201B0
```

This sends a dump to the printer of locations X'200C0' through X'201B0'.

As well as inspecting values of areas in storage, you can alter them through DEBUG subcommands. For example, use the SET subcommand to alter the contents of control words and the general registers:

```
SET  GPR  1  00000000
```

sets general register 1 to binary zeroes. The operand representing the value is always in hexadecimal in the SET subcommand. To set the PSW, CSW, and CAW, use the operands PSW, CSW, and CAW, respectively, in place of GPR. For example, to alter the CAW to X'00004144', enter:

```
SET  CAW  00004144
```

Similarly, you use the STORE subcommand to store up to a dozen bytes of hexadecimal information starting at any valid virtual storage address. The general format of the STORE subcommand is:

```
STORE  hexaddress  hexinfo  hexinfo  hexinfo
```

where hexaddress is the starting virtual storage address where you store the hexadecimal values referred to by hexinfo. Each occurrence of hexinfo specifies four byte values in hexadecimal. For example:

```
STORE  200C0  00000000
```

stores X'00000000' at location X'200C0'. Setting twelve bytes to binary zeroes at the same address is accomplished by:

```
STORE  200C0  00000000  00000000  00000000
```

In all the examples above, you can refer to symbolic names instead of virtual storage addresses. To do this with DEBUG, you specifically establish symbolic names for storage locations during the debug session via the DEFINE subcommand. First, use the ORIGIN subcommand to serve as the base address for all locations you specify:

```
ORIGIN  20000
```

Now, instead of entering:

```
X   201B0
```

you may issue:

```
X   1B0
```

Once you've established an origin, it remains in effect until you issue another ORIGIN subcommand or obtain a new copy of CMS. The ORIGIN subcommand enables you to refer to instruction addresses relative to the beginning of your program, rather than to virtual storage addresses.

Assuming you issued the above ORIGIN subcommand, use the DEFINE subcommand to establish symbolic names:

```
DEFINE  NAME1  1B0  8
```

This DEFINE associates the symbolic name NAME1 with virtual storage address X'201B0' (X'1B0' from the origin point of X'20000'). The implied length of the symbolic name is 8 bytes. Now you can inspect the contents of this variable by this statement:

```
X   NAME1
```

You may use symbolic names you establish with the DEFINE subcommand with the DEBUG subcommands BREAK, DUMP, GO, ORIGIN, STORE, and X. Up to sixteen symbolic names may be defined at a time.

When you are done inspecting and altering program status words and storage contents, continue program execution with the GO subcommand. The operand on the GO subcommand is the hexadecimal address or symbolic name where you want execution to begin. For example:

```
GO   200C0
```

starts execution at address X'200C0'. Remember that if an ORIGIN is in effect, the address on the GO subcommand is relative to this point. If you entered:

```
ORIGIN  20000
```

issue the above GO subcommand as:

```
GO   CO
```

Program execution continues until the next breakpoint, program completion, program abend, or an external interrupt.

There are several ways to exit the Debug Environment. Entering the immediate command HX halts program execution entirely and returns you to CMS. You can also issue the DEBUG RETURN subcommand to return to CMS, if you entered the Debug Environment through the CMS DEBUG command. If you did not access Debug in this manner, the debugger responds to RETURN with the message:

```
INCORRECT   DEBUG   EXIT
```

Finally, the DEBUG subcommand GO returns you to CMS if your program runs to normal completion.

In summary, the CMS DEBUG command establishes the Debug Environment. In this environment, you issue DEBUG subcommands to inspect and alter the program status words, general registers, and locations in virtual storage. The work is accomplished via hexadecimal values and storage addresses. However, you can establish base addressing for the Debug session and symbolic names through the ORIGIN and DEFINE subcommands.

Enter the Debug Environment in one of two ways: either in the manner shown above, or by issuing the CMS DEBUG command immediately after receiving a program exception message from CMS. In this latter case, DEBUG retains the environment as it exists at the time of abend for your inspection.

CMS DEBUG provides a lower-level debugging tool than packages like COBOL Interactive Debug. It is used primarily with assembler language programs. However, you may find it a lifesaver in solving problems of such difficulty that they cannot easily be analyzed through higher level packages like COBOL Interactive Debug.

The CMS SVCTRACE Command

In addition to the CMS DEBUG command and the many subcommands of the Debug Environment, CMS contains the SVCTRACE command. To trace all supervisor calls occurring on your virtual machine, enter:

```
SVCTRACE   ON
```

To terminate this output to the spooled virtual printer file enter:

```
SVCTRACE OFF
```

The recorded trace information includes:

1. contents of general and floating-point registers before the SVC-called program is given control, after a return from that program, and when the SVC handling routine is finished processing
2. virtual storage location of the calling SVC instruction and the name of the called routine
3. normal and error return addresses
4. the parameter list passed to the SVC

CP Commands

Control Program has a variety of commands for the general user that duplicate many of the functions of the CMS Debug facility. These CP commands facilitate debugging on the virtual machine level. Most programmers prefer to work in the somewhat simpler CMS Debug Environment. For this reason, we only describe the functions of CP debugging commands on an overview level.

CP debugging commands include:

ADSTOP, establishes breakpoints at virtual addresses

BEGIN, restarts program execution at an address you specify

From the standpoint of user program debugging, the **ADSTOP** and **BEGIN** commands perform functions analogous to those of CMS **DEBUG** subcommands **BREAK** and **GO**.

To inspect the virtual storage locations and status words of your virtual machine use:

DISPLAY, displays virtual storage locations, storage keys, general registers, floating-point registers, control register(s), PSW, CSW, and CAW of your virtual machine

DUMP, prints contents of virtual machine's PSW, general registers, floating-point registers, control registers (EC mode only), storage keys, and virtual storage locations on the virtual printer

To alter storage and status words use:

STORE, alters virtual storage locations, general registers, floating-point registers, control register(s), and PSW.

Note that CP commands allow you to inspect and alter the floating-point and control register(s). The CMS **DEBUG** command does not.

Monitor program execution via these CP commands:

PER, traces all instructions, successful branches, register alterations, and instructions that alter storage

TRACE, traces instructions, branches, interrupts, and I/O and channel activity

Finally, CP commands allow you to simulate real computer console keys on your virtual console. These commands include:

ATTN, simulates the Attention key on a real computer console to your virtual machine

EXTERNAL, simulates an External Interrupt to your virtual machine

REQUEST, simulates the Request key on a real computer console to your virtual machine

SYSTEM, simulates the Reset and Restart buttons on a real computer console to your virtual machine

In summary, CP's commands for control of your virtual machine enable you to inspect and monitor the program activity of your virtual machine. They simulate the level of control over the virtual machine that you would expect to have if you were sitting at a real computer console. Since CP commands control the virtual machine, they represent the ultimate debugging tool set. For systems-level software development, this feature presents a major advantage for VM/CMS over other operating systems.

Command Procedures

Command procedures are programs written in one of the interpretive languages of CMS that allow you to direct execution of CMS and CP commands.

Command procedure *tracing* displays each EXEC statement immediately prior to its execution. It permits you to single-step through the command procedure and see how variables change.

The CMS command:

```
SET EXECTRAC ON
            OFF
```

turns the command procedure trace facility on or off prior to execution of an EXEC. The system default is OFF.

Once you are in a command procedure trace, turn it off at any time by entering:

```
TRACE  OFF
```

Two CMS immediate commands, TS (Trace Start) and TE (Trace End), also start and stop tracing for command procedure programs. Use TS to start the trace of an EXEC that has already started execution.

For Further Information

Further information on the COBOL Interactive Debug product is available in *OS COBOL Interactive Debug Terminal User's Guide, SC28-6465*. That manual contains complete explanation and examples of all **TESTCOB** subcommands for CMS users. It includes a sample terminal session that shows, step by step, how to use the interactive debugging facility to greatest advantage.

Other programming languages have interactive debugging guides analogous to that available for COBOL. These include *FORTRAN Interactive Debug for CMS: Guide and Reference, SC28-6885*, and *PL/I Checkout Compiler: CMS User's Guide, SC33-0047*.

The manual, *VM/SP CMS User's Guide, SC19-6210*, contains examples of the CMS **DEBUG** subcommands. That manual also explains how to use the CP debugging commands. The chapter entitled "CP Command Usage" in the *VM/SP CP Command Reference for General Users, SC19-6211*, provides more detailed examples of CP debugging commands.

The *VM/SP CMS Command and Macro Reference, SC19-6209*, formally summarizes the CMS **DEBUG** subcommands. The *VM/SP CP Command Reference for General Users, SC19-6211*, includes the equivalent information for the CP-level debugging commands.

As always, "hands-on" experience with the commands remains the best tutor. This is particularly true in that the system responses to your commands provide a more concrete understanding than that obtainable from books and manuals alone.

Test Your Understanding

Describe the three basic levels of program debugging under CMS. When is use of each level of debugging most appropriate?

What kinds of debugging activities can you perform with COBOL Interactive Debug? What are the essential differences between debugging with a product like COBOL Interactive Debug and the CMS **DEBUG** command?

Run a program under the control of the debugging tool equivalent of COBOL Interactive Debug for a language with which you are familiar and to which you have access. Use the package to inspect and alter program variables, the flow of program execution, and file status indicators. Can you examine source statements as they execute with your debugger?

If you are an assembly language programmer, run a program using the CMS **DEBUG** command. From the assembly listing, determine program addresses at which you can set breakpoints. Then start program execution. When you encounter a breakpoint, inspect status words by the **PSW**, **CSW**, **CAW**, and **GPR** DEBUG subcommands. Try setting these status words by the **SET** subcommand. You should also inspect and set storage values by the **X** and **STORE** subcommands.

If you are an assembly language programmer, run the same program as in the previous question, but this time, use the DEBUG **ORIGIN** and **DEFINE** subcommands to establish relative addressing and symbolic names. How does this alter the subcommand addressing references you entered in response to the previous question?

What are some of the differences and similarities between debugging with the CMS **DEBUG** command and the CP debugging commands? When would you use one approach or the other? Could you use these two approaches to debugging interchangeably?

CHAPTER 20

VSAM Storage and CMS Batch Execution

There are two other important CMS facilities available for use by CMS, OS, and DOS programmers. These are VSAM and the CMS Batch Machine Facility.

VSAM

VSAM supports sequential, direct, and indexed access to data records stored on disk. CMS's support for VSAM is based on the DOS/VSE operating system version of VSAM, referred to in the CMS manuals as VSE /VSAM.

With CMS's VSE/VSAM, you can:

- develop and test OS-oriented programs that read and write VSAM files

- develop and test DOS-oriented programs that read and write VSAM files

- execute VSAM's Access Methods Services (AMS) commands against VSAM datasets on both OS and DOS disks. The allowable AMS commands are those embodied in DOS VSE/VSAM.

CMS supports both read- and write-access to VSAM files on both OS and DOS disks. However, since CMS uses VSE/VSAM for all VSAM dataset processing, the disks used by CMS VSAM are all DOS disks. In other words, CMS services all VSAM requests by executing VSE/VSAM code (even those directed to OS disks).

CMS VSAM supports tape, so you can execute AMS commands that refer to tape files. To do this, you must have one or more tape drives attached to your virtual machine. Refer to tapes via their symbolic names of TAP1, TAP2, TAP3, and TAP4.

CMS VSAM's major limitation is that the facility works within the data sharing constraints of the operating system. Users share VSAM datasets on a read-only basis. CMS VSAM does not support shared write-access to VSAM datasets with data integrity.

CMS VSAM presents another limitation from the standpoint of the OS-oriented programmer: the functionality is based on VSE/VSAM. This means the allowable VSAM and AMS statements are those of VSE/VSAM. This command set comprises a subset of the commands familiar to the OS-oriented VSAM user.

CMS Commands

The basic mechanism for execution of AMS commands under CMS is the CMS **AMSERV** command. You create a file of filetype **AMSERV** and with a filename of your choice. For example, you might create a file containing AMS commands like **DELETE** and **DEFINE** to define a VSAM file, called **DEFINES AMSERV**.

Run AMS against this file by entering:

```
AMSERV  DEFINES
```

Output listings from the **AMSERV** command are directed to files of filetype **LISTING**. The output filename is the same as that listed on the **AMSERV** command. To spool output to the virtual printer instead, specify the **PRINT** option:

```
AMSERV  DEFINES  (PRINT
```

Any AMS commands acceptable to VSE/VSAM are run via the **AMSERV** command. Since CMS support is via the DOS/VSE version of VSAM, use CMS/DOS commands **ASSGN** and **DLBL** for file declarations to CMS.

When defining CMS VSAM datasets, the CMS **LISTDS** command is used to determine the amount of free space left on disks and current space utilization. Use **LISTDS** to keep track of CMS VSAM space utilization.

The CMS Batch Facility

The CMS Batch Facility provides a way to execute programs and job streams in batch mode within VM/CMS. It is useful for execution of long-running jobs in background. This avoids tying up your terminal and permits you to go on to other work while the CMS Batch Facility executes your batch job. The Batch Facility also allows you to submit jobs without access to a CMS terminal. An example of the utility of this feature is in an academic environment, where the campus does not have enough terminals to service all students. Students submit punched card decks to VM/CMS for batch execution through the CMS Batch Facility. Thus, users without terminal access can submit batch jobs to the VM/CMS system for processing.

As figure 20-1 shows, the Batch Facility is a CMS virtual machine specifically set up to process batch jobs. The VM/CMS administrators initiate and control this machine. The CMS command **CMSBATCH** sets up a CMS virtual machine as a batch job server.

Figure 20-1
CMS Batch
Machine Facility
Runs in Its Own
Virtual Machine

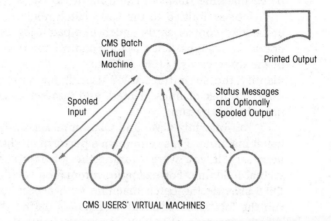

Batch Job Submission

Submit jobs to your installation's batch virtual machine by one of these two methods: reading real punched cards into the computer system's physical card reader; or spooling your virtual machine's virtual punch output to the virtual reader of the batch virtual machine.

When submitting real card decks to the computer systems card reader, the deck should be preceded by a single CP ID card. The format of this card is:

        ID   userid

ID starts in card column 1, and **userid** is the userid of the CMS batch machine. For example, if the batch machine is called **BATMON**, include this card as the first in the deck:

        ID   BATMON

If you are using CMS online, spool your virtual punch to the batch machine's virtual reader through the CP **SPOOL** command:

        CP   SPOOL   PUNCH   TO   BATMON

The parameter **BATMON** is the userid (system id) of the CMS batch machine. Your punch output is spooled to the virtual reader of the CMS batch machine.

Often, CMS users submit jobs to the CMS batch machine under control of CMS command procedures (or EXECs). If you punch individual lines to the batch machine from within an EXEC, be sure to release the spool punch file by the CP **CLOSE** command when you are done.

If you use the CMS `PUNCH` command to route input to the CMS batch machine, you should specify the `NOHEADER` option. The header card otherwise produced by `PUNCH` is unintelligible to the batch machine. The CMS batch machine flushes invalid input cards.

Jobs submitted to the CMS batch machine facility are controlled by embedded control cards, much like batch job control under OS and DOS operating systems. The CMS job control language is very simple. It consists of the three cards: `/JOB`, `/SET`, and `/*`. These cards serve to, respectively: identify the submitter's CMS userid; set maximum parameters for CPU time, number of lines printed, and number of cards punched; and terminate the job stream.

You intermix CMS and CP commands in the job stream to the CMS batch machine. These commands perform all the same tasks that would be necessary if you were running the job interactively, on your own CMS virtual machine. For example, commands such as CP `LINK` and CMS `ACCESS` provide the batch machine with access to the minidisks needed to run the job. CMS `FILEDEF` commands define the files for the batch program's execution. CP `SPOOL` commands route the program's printed output, which otherwise defaults to the batch machine's virtual printer with your own distribution code. You do not have to worry about cleaning up after your job has executed: the batch machine automatically resets itself by reloading CMS after each job completes.

The CMS Batch Facility communicates with you concerning batch jobs you submit for processing. You receive messages when:

execution begins on a job you submitted

execution completes on a job you submitted

a job you submitted abends

In summary, the CMS Batch Facility allows your VM/CMS system administrator to dedicate one (or more) CMS virtual machines to batch job processing. A CMS batch virtual machine processes batch jobs by *single-threading* (running one job after another). You take advantage of a CMS batch machine by spooling it a job from your virtual machine or by submitting a job on punched cards through a card reader. In either case, the batch job consists of batch job control cards and the CMS and CP commands necessary to execute the program(s) you desire.

For Further Information

The manual, *Using VSE/VSAM Commands and Macros, SC24-5144*, lists VSE/VSAM commands. In addition, there are certain incompatibilities between OS- and DOS-based VSAM. The *VSE/VSAM General Information Manual, GC24-5143*, enumerates these differences.

This book does not describe VSAM in detail because it devotes attention to the SQL/DS and IFS products instead. (See section 7.) Most sites purchase database management systems like SQL/DS that run in their own virtual machines to support record-oriented data access. In addition to the advantages associated with database management systems, these products overcome CMS restrictions to provide concurrent data update to multiple users.

The manual, *VM/SP CMS User's Guide, SC19-6210*, contains a full chapter on AMS and VSAM under CMS. For information on VSAM itself, refer to the appropriate VSE/VSAM manuals. The *VSE/VSAM General Information Manual, GC24-5143*, introduces VSE/VSAM and its capabilities. *Using VSE/VSAM Commands and Macros, SC24-5144*, lists VSE/AMS commands and describes their use. Detailed information concerning extents, **DLBL**, and **ASSGN** statement requirements are in the manual, *VSE/VSAM Programmer's Reference, SC24-5145*.

The *VM/SP CMS User's Guide, SC19-6210*, shows how to use the batch facility. It discusses control card formats and appropriate CMS and CP commands for directing batch job execution.

Many installations set up their own command procedures for use of their batch machine facility. These procedures range from useful to mandatory in using the local CMS Batch Facility. Contact your system administrator for access to this site-dependent information.

Test Your Understanding

What are the major advantages and limitations of VSAM under CMS?

Can you develop and test OS- and DOS-oriented VSAM programs under CMS?

In which manual are the allowable VSAM and AMS commands listed for VSAM for CMS?

What is the CMS command through which you define VSAM catalogs, data spaces, and clusters?

What are the two basic ways by which you submit batch jobs to the batch virtual machine facility?

What are the three cards (commands) of the CMS batch virtual machine facility and their functions?

Assuming you submit a background job from your terminal, at what times do you receive messages from the batch machine facility?

Why would you submit a background job to the CMS batch machine facility rather than running it directly online at your terminal?

SECTION 6

VM/CMS Command Languages

- Command Procedure Languages
- The REXX Language
- Essential Concepts of Command Procedures

CHAPTER 21

Command Procedure Languages

Command procedures are CMS files that issue CMS and CP commands. Often called EXECs, they are written in one of the three *command procedure languages* supported by the operating system. Since these languages include logical constructs, they enable you to direct selective execution of series of CMS and CP commands. Since command procedure languages are complete programming languages, you can also accomplish various kinds of programming tasks through their use.

Command procedures execute:

command procedure statements

CMS commands

CP commands

other command procedures

programs written in other languages available in CMS

For example, command procedures can:

- allocate files and execute CMS programs written in compiled programming languages

- perform programmable functions that might otherwise be written in compiled programming languages like COBOL or PL/I

- provide the user interface through which terminal users interact with programming applications. (The command procedures present the user interface and set up and execute programs to carry out the requested work.)

- issue series of commonly used CMS and CP commands. (This avoids re-entry of these commands and ensures accuracy.)

In general, command procedures allow you to develop what appear to be new CMS commands to the terminal user. Once you have written a command procedure, you execute it merely by entering its name to CMS. Thus, command procedures supplement the operating system commands.

EXECs are useful because they eliminate constant re-entry of CMS and CP commands. This greatly reduces typing errors, and also improves the operating system's user-friendliness. In effect, command procedures allow you to build upon and tailor CMS as you see fit. They often represent the only practical way to issue long or complicated series of operating system commands.

When do you use command procedure languages versus compiled programming languages like COBOL, PL/I, FORTRAN, or Pascal? There are no hard and fast rules in deciding which kind of language to use. However, command procedures are more appropriate for certain kinds of tasks. They:

- directly issue CMS and CP commands
- automate commonly used series of CMS and CP commands
- offer the interactive debugging capability inherent to interpretive languages
- are quick to write and easy to use
- are well-suited to the actions necessary to set up and execute compiled programs

One of the major disadvantages to command procedures versus separately purchased programming language translators is slower execution speed. A command procedure is reinterpreted every time it is executed. This means that procedures consume greater processor resources, especially in cases where a routine is run repeatedly. Many command procedure languages are less powerful for general- or special-purpose programming than specific alternative compiled languages. Finally, command procedure code is highly system-dependent.

These are not all the advantages and disadvantages of command procedures, but they do provide some idea of when their use is most appropriate.

CMS Command Languages

CMS offers three different command procedure languages. They are EXEC, EXEC2, and the "System Product Interpreter, REXX (REstructured eXtended eXecutor).

Command procedures written in all three of these languages are entered in CMS files of filetype **EXEC** and are popularly referred to as CMS EXECs. All three command interpreters are included in CMS as part of the VM/SP product license.

Figure 21-1 shows the historical relationship between these command processors. EXEC was originally the single command procedure language of the operating system. IBM later added EXEC2, and it became the interpreter of choice. More recently still, REXX was added to VM/CMS and declared the "System Product Interpreter." IBM considers REXX the primary command language for VM/SP.

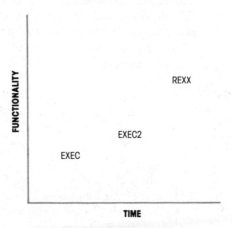

The EXEC2 and EXEC languages are very closely related. EXEC2 includes many of the same control statements and predefined variables and functions as the EXEC language. The languages appear so similar that if you are familiar with one of them, it is quite easy to learn the other.

Figure 21-2 diagrams the syntactical relationship between the EXEC2 and EXEC languages. While the two are highly similar, neither is a true subset of the other. Each has language elements unique to itself.

Figure 21-2
Syntactical
Relationship of
EXEC2 and EXEC

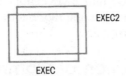

In terms of their relative functionality, EXEC2 and EXEC are so similar that it is difficult to declare one as clearly "better" than the other. However, VM/SP includes EXEC2 as the more modern, improved version of the EXEC language.

REXX is the newest command procedure language for VM/SP and is designated the System Product Interpreter. The linguistic elements that compose the REXX language are entirely different from those of the EXEC2 and EXEC languages. Figure 21-3 displays this syntactical dissimilarity.

Figure 21-3
Syntactical
Relationships of
REXX, EXEC2, and
EXEC

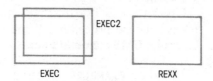

REXX also features much greater functionality than either the EXEC2 or EXEC languages. As a thoroughly modern command procedure language, REXX embodies many advantages over the older EXEC2 and EXEC languages. This is *not* to imply that EXEC2 and EXEC are not fully serviceable as command languages; both have been successfully employed for many years. However, for new applications, REXX is the command interpreter of choice for most VM/CMS installations. Figure 21-4 diagrams the greater functionality of REXX versus EXEC2 and EXEC.

Figure 21-4
Functional
Relationships of
REXX, EXEC2, and
EXEC

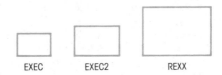

Tables 21-1 and 21-2 compare the relative levels of functionality in the three command languages by contrasting their language elements. Table 21-1 totals such language elements as control statements (or instructions), variables, functions, and operators. This table demonstrates the greater functionality of the REXX language over EXEC2 and EXEC. While there exist dimensions of programming language design that cannot be measured in this fashion, the chart does yield the valid conclusion that REXX is a more powerful language than the other CMS command interpreters.

Table 21-2 shows that REXX more fully supports structured programming than either EXEC2 or EXEC, due to its complete complement of logical constructs. REXX also provides for fixed and real numbers, while the other interpreters offer only integer arithmetic. Finally, while both EXEC2 and EXEC support character string manipulation, REXX renders text processing more convenient through its extensive string manipulation features.

CMS Selection of Command Processor

Whether you write command procedures in the REXX, EXEC2, or EXEC languages, the filetype of the command procedure is **EXEC**. For example, you might name a command procedure:

```
EXAMPLE  EXEC  A1
```

Assuming that the *implied EXEC function* is on (the CMS default), you merely enter:

```
EXAMPLE
```

to execute the procedure. If the implied EXEC function is off, you must enter the CMS command **EXEC** to run the command procedure:

```
EXEC  EXAMPLE
```

Table 21-1
Functional
Comparison of
CMS Command
Interpreters

Language Element	REXX	EXEC2	EXEC
EXEC, EXEC2 control statements		23	23
REXX instructions	24		
EXEC, REXX special variables	3 (see functions)		15
EXEC2 predefined variables		18	
EXEC built-in functions			6
EXEC2 predefined functions		16	
REXX functions	62		
EXEC, EXEC2 logical operators		6	6
REXX comparative operators	8		
Arithmetic operators	9	2	2
		(see functions)	
Boolean operators	4	0	0
Concatenation operators	3	0	0
		(see functions)	
Totals	113	65	52

Table 21-2
Qualitative
Comparison of
CMS Command
Interpreters

Language Element	REXX	EXEC2	EXEC
Logical constructs (support for structured programming)	excellent	poor	poor
Numeric data types support (support for fixed and real numbers as well as integers)	good	poor	poor
Character string manipulation	excellent	good	poor

Determine whether the implied EXEC function is on or off by the CMS command:

```
QUERY IMPEX
```

Pass any *parameters* or *arguments* to the command procedure simply by entering them after the command procedure name. If `EXAMPLE EXEC` requires two parameters, enter them like this:

```
EXAMPLE  ONE  TWO
```

where `ONE` and `TWO` are the parameter strings.

CMS selects the appropriate command processor to run the EXEC according to the contents of the first line of the EXEC file. If the first line of the file contains a REXX comment (bracketed by the symbols /* and */), then CMS runs the REXX interpreter against the EXEC. If the first line of the command procedure is the EXEC2 statement **&TRACE**, then EXEC2 processes the file. In all other cases, EXEC interprets the command procedure. Figure 21-5 diagrams CMS's command processor selection.

Figure 21-5
CMS Selection of
Command
Processor for EXEC
Files

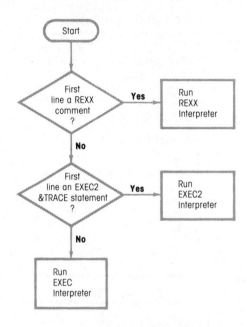

As an example, an EXEC containing this line as the first line in the code:

```
/*  This is the first line of a sample REXX Exec */
```

is passed to the REXX processor.

An **EXEC** file with this as its first statement:

```
&TRACE
```

is processed by EXEC2. If CMS does not recognize the first line in the EXEC file as a REXX comment or EXEC2 **&TRACE** statement, the EXEC interpreter processes the procedure.

Examples of Command Procedures

The first example command procedure links to another CMS user's A-disk for read-only access. The other user's logon id is **ZBPD01** and the disk is accessed as your E-disk at virtual device address **201**. Figure 21-6 contains the procedure.

Figure 21-6   Example Command Procedure

```
/*  This REXX EXEC links to user ZBPD01's A-disk as your  */
/*  E-disk at virtual device address 201.                 */

cp  link  to  ZBPD01  191  as 201  r
access  201  e
```

This REXX EXEC is stored in a file named **LINKTOB EXEC A1**. Assuming that the implied EXEC function is on, execute this command procedure by typing:

LINKTOB

After the procedure successfully executes, you receive the CMS ready prompt:

```
R;
```

In the EXEC listing, the first line is a REXX comment. This informs CMS that the program is written in the REXX language. Most programmers state the purpose of the program in several initial comments.

Following a blank line, the EXEC executes a CP command. REXX passes any statement that it does not recognize as part of the REXX language to the current CMS environment for execution. In this case, the procedure runs under CMS, and so the contents of the line are passed to CMS for execution. CMS recognizes that the command is directed toward CP because the letters **CP** precede the command. CP then executes the command.

The last line in the EXEC is a CMS command. Since REXX does not recognize the information on this line as part of the REXX language, the line is passed to CMS for execution.

As simple as this first command procedure may be, it presents several advantages to entering the two CMS and CP commands manually. First, the user merely types **LINKTOB** to execute the two commands. This shorthand saves typing effort. The longer the EXEC and the more frequently it is used, the greater the convenience of the command procedure.

Secondly, this command procedure limits typing errors. It's much easier to remember the name of the EXEC than the complex commands of which it might be composed.

The user executes the command procedure by typing its name, similar to any other CMS command. EXECs give you the power to develop new

"CMS commands," expanding the CMS environment and tailoring it to your needs.

Figure 21-7 contains an enhanced version of the same command procedure. This version prompts for entry of the first name of the user to which to link. If you enter **BERT** in uppercase or lowercase letters, the procedure links to the user **ZBPD01**'s A-disk. Otherwise, it links to the A-disk of user **ZHMF01**.

Figure 21-7   EXEC Prompt for Entry of First Name

```
/*   This REXX EXEC links to user ZBPD01's A-Disk if      */
/*   you enter 'BERT' in upper- or lower- case.  Otherwise */
/*   it links to ZHMF01's A-disk.                         */

say 'Enter the userid of the person to link to:'
pull username .

if  username  =  'BERT' then
     cp  link  to  ZBPD01  191  as 201  r
else
     cp  link  to  ZHMF01  191  as 201  r
access  201  e
```

This EXEC illustrates several additional command procedure features. First, procedures can perform input/output to all the same devices as programs written in compiled programming languages. In this case, the EXEC lists a line on the terminal through the REXX **SAY** instruction. The literal string:

```
Enter the userid of the person to link to:
```

appears on the terminal. Literal character strings are enclosed in either apostrophes ' or quotation marks ", which are equivalent in REXX. The EXEC also reads a word from the terminal user through the REXX **PULL** instruction. This input is placed into the variable named **username**. **PULL** translates the user's input into uppercase characters. The period . at the end of the statement discards any input the user may have entered beyond the single word expected.

This procedure also demonstrates control of the logical flow of execution. This example contains an **IF-THEN-ELSE** construct, which tests the value input in the variable **username** against the literal string **BERT**. If the two are equal, the first CP **LINK** command is executed. Otherwise, the command following the **ELSE** is executed. REXX contains a full complement of logical constructs including those supporting **IF**, **SELECT** (case), **CALL**, and **DO** logic.

Figure 21-8 contains the final version of this linking EXEC. In this example, the user runs the EXEC by entering:

```
LINKTO  userid  vaddr  diskletter
```

where `userid` is the CMS logon id to whose A-disk the link is to occur, `vaddr` is the virtual device address used for the linkage, and `diskletter` is the new disk letter. This sample execution of the `LINKTO` EXEC links to the A-disk of CMS user `ZBPD01`, giving this minidisk the virtual device address of `201` on your virtual machine, and making it your E-disk:

```
LINKTO  ZBPD01  201  E
```

Figure 21-8   Running the EXEC with Command Line Arguments

```
/*   This REXX EXEC links to another user's A-disk.      */
/*                                                        */
/*   Enter:     LINKTO   userid   vaddr   diskletter      */
/*   Example:   LINKTO   ZBPD01   201   E                 */

arg  userid  vaddr  diskletter  .

if  diskletter  =  ""  then
    say 'Wrong number of arguments, error!'
else do
    cp  link  to  userid  191  as  vaddr  r
    access  vaddr  diskletter
end
```

Thus, this EXEC expects that three arguments will be specified on the command line. The EXEC retrieves these three parameters via the REXX `ARG` instruction. With a format similar to that of the `PULL` instruction, `ARG` places the three parameters into three corresponding variables named `userid`, `vaddr`, and `diskletter`. The period following the three variables discards any additional parameters input by the user.

After retrieving the command line parameters, the EXEC tests the value of the third parameter, in variable `diskletter`. If this argument was not entered by the terminal user, it is equal to the null string, represented by two immediately adjacent quotation marks (or apostrophes). The `IF` instruction ensures an error message informs the user if he entered too few parameters on the command line. Otherwise, the CP `LINK` and CMS `AC-CESS` commands establish appropriate minidisk linkage.

Here are the CP and CMS commands:

```
cp  link  to  userid  191  as  vaddr  r
access  vaddr  diskletter
```

REXX scans these lines prior to passing them to the CMS environment for execution. During this interpretation process, REXX recognizes that `userid`, `vaddr`, and `diskletter` are program variables. It therefore replaces each variable with its current value *prior* to passing the commands to CMS. Assuming the above command line, REXX replaces these variables with their values of `ZBPD01`, `201`, and `E`, respectively. The two lines of code are thus dynamically transformed into these valid CP and CMS commands:

```
CP LINK TO ZBPD01 191 AS 201 R
ACCESS 201 E
```

There is one side effect of the translation of commands intended for CMS and CP. If this example statement were encoded within an EXEC:

```
QUERY DISK *
```

it fails execution because REXX recognizes the asterisk * as an invalid use of its multiplication operator. Enclose CMS and CP commands you do not want interpreted in apostrophes or quotation marks. REXX recognizes the command as a literal character string and does not attempt variable substitution. This form of the above command executes properly from within a REXX EXEC:

```
'QUERY DISK *'
```

The ability to interpret lines and replace variables in the code dynamically allows you to program EXECs with a high degree of generality. This principle renders command procedures useful for diverse tasks. Combined with the logic imbedded in EXECs through REXX IF, SELECT (case), CALL, and DO instructions, it allows you to alter dynamically the effects of your EXEC depending on user input and a wide variety of other conditions.

For Further Information

The manual, *VM/SP CMS User's Guide, SC19-6210,* is the primary source of general information on the CMS command processors. This manual tells what command procedures are and why they are useful. It discusses the concepts central to writing and using command procedures under CMS.

That manual contains an appendix that describes the CMS EXEC language. This appendix is the sole source of information on the older EXEC processor in the current manual set.

The primary source of information on the EXEC2 language is *VM /SP EXEC2 Reference, SC24-5219.* As a reference manual, this guide contains complete details on the EXEC2 language. An appendix provides an easy-to-read "EXEC2 Primer for New Users."

Several of the vendor's manuals introduce REXX, the current System Product Interpreter. The *VM/SP CMS User's Guide, SC19-6210,* presents basic concepts common to all the EXEC processors and uses REXX in its coding samples. The manual, *VM/SP CMS Primer, SC24-5236,* offers a brief and simple tutorial introduction to why command procedures are useful. It includes a few short REXX EXECs as examples.

The primary manual for learning to write REXX command procedures is *VM/SP System Product Interpreter User's Guide, SC24-5238.* This volume is designed quite differently from most reference manuals. Its tutorial on REXX programming is organized according to a three-pass reading scheme. During your first, second, and third readings of this manual, read only the portions marked for that reading. Each part of the tutorial describes different parts of the REXX language, amply supported by in-text examples. This manual comprises an excellent learning tool for beginning REXX programmers, regardless of their previous levels of programming experience.

The *VM/SP System Product Interpreter Reference, SC24-5239,* constitutes the complete reference manual on the REXX language. It alphabetically describes all parts of the language and includes complete instruction and function formats.

As a new command procedure language embodying modern principles of command language design, REXX has received attention outside of the vendor's manuals. Michael F. Cowlishaw presents an overview of the language in his paper entitled "The Design of the REXX Language," published in *IBM Systems Journal* (23:4, 1984). Mr. Cowlishaw also wrote a book entitled *REXX Language* (Prentice-Hall, 1985). R.P. O'Hara and D.R. Gomberg have also written an introductory book entitled *Modern Programming Using REXX* (Prentice-Hall, 1985).

Test Your Understanding

What are command procedure languages? How can they be used?

Why would you use a command procedure language instead of a compiled programming language? What are the relative advantages and disadvantages of command procedure languages versus high-level programming languages like COBOL, PL/I, Pascal, and FORTRAN?

What kinds of statements do command procedures contain?

Name the three command procedure languages available under CMS. Are these languages syntactically related? Which offers the greatest functionality? Which is the preferred command procedure language for CMS?

When you execute a command procedure, how does CMS know which command processor to invoke?

Write a REXX EXEC that issues either a CP **QUERY TERMINAL** or a CP **QUERY SET** command, depending on the user's input parameter. Name your command procedure **MYQUERY EXEC**. You should be able to invoke your EXEC with one of these two statements:

```
MYQUERY TERMINAL
```

or

```
MYQUERY SET
```

CHAPTER 22

The REXX Language

The REXX command procedure language is a rich and powerful general-purpose programming language. Although only the bare essentials are presented here, the purpose is to render you functional with REXX as quickly as possible.

This "minitutorial" assumes you have knowledge of at least one other programming language. However, the example programs are all quite short and should be of interest to anyone desiring further information on the uses of command procedures.

REXX Design

The primary design criteria for the REXX language was ease of use. Programs written in this language are highly readable, in that they may be encoded in both uppercase and lowercase characters. REXX is a free-format language that limits punctuation to only that which is absolutely necessary.

In addition, REXX takes full advantage of the potential of interpreters for debugging. It features a comprehensive execution tracing facility. Finally, the language supports structured programming through a complete set of instructions for implementing structured logical constructs.

REXX is unusual among command procedure languages in that it is as powerful and yet as easy to use as any compiled programming language; REXX has only two dozen instructions. The language adds over 60 functions to this core of instructions, covering the whole gamut of character string manipulation, arithmetic, conversion, and environmental control primitives. Within a simple command structure, REXX gives programmers great power and flexibility.

Elements of REXX

As with other programming languages, REXX employs the concept of program *variables,* objects whose values may be altered during program execution.

Variables are represented in REXX programs by *symbols,* essentially variable names. While REXX supports several kinds of symbols, the only rules for creating simple symbols is that they must not contain any periods, nor start with digits.

Example symbols in figure 21-8 are `userid`, `vaddr`, and `diskletter`. An example symbol in figure 21-7 is `username`.

Program variables are altered by either one of two events: an input instruction, or an assignment statement. Input instructions include `PULL` and `ARG`. Figures 21-7 and 21-8 demonstrate these instructions. Recall that these instructions read input from the keyboard and retrieve an EXEC's command line parameters, respectively.

REXX assignment statements follow the same format as assignment statements in other programming languages:

```
symbol = expression
```

where `expression` represents an expression that the interpreter resolves and assigns to the variable named by symbol. For example:

```
string = 'Sample One'
```

assigns the variable named `string` the value of `Sample One`.

Blanks or spaces within character strings are characters the same as any others. Note that the literal character string on the right side of the assignment symbol `=` is *not* translated to upper case. The interpreter never alters values within literal character strings.

Variables are not *typed* within the REXX language. They are not declared before usage as required by compiled languages. Like many interpreters, REXX treats all data in variables as typeless strings. Another way to consider this is to say that the data type of a variable is determined by its assignment and usage.

In REXX, character strings are denoted by their enclosure in apostrophes or quotation marks. The interpreter does *not* perform variable substitution or case translation within these literal strings. Numbers consist of digits, optionally preceded by a plus or minus sign, and optionally containing a period representing a decimal point. Numbers may also be expressed in scientific or engineering notations. Here are example valid numbers:

```
3
17742
1454.03
12E3
```

REXX supports whole numbers, numbers having a decimal point, and numbers expressed in scientific or engineering notations. Often these kinds of numbers are referred to as *integers, fixed point numbers,* and *floating-point* or *real numbers,* respectively. Numeric precision defaults to 9 digits. It may be altered via the REXX **NUMERIC** instruction.

REXX includes a full variety of arithmetic operators, which are listed in table 22-1.

Table 22-1
REXX Arithmetic
Operators

Operator	Meaning
+	Add
–	Subtract
*	Multiply
/	Divide
%	Divide and return integer portion of result
//	Divide and return remainder
**	Exponentiation (raise a number to a whole-number power)
(prefix) –	Negate the number following this prefix
(prefix) +	A positive number follows this prefix

As with any programming language, REXX has its own operator *order of precedence.* That is, where an expression contains multiple operators, it is resolved in a predetermined order. REXX's precedence order is that used in algebra and most other programming languages.

It is easiest to remember that expressions in parentheses are always resolved first. If you are uncertain concerning the order in which an expression is evaluated, dictate this order by using parentheses.

Thus, you can write expressions like this:

```
variable = (3 * (-1 + 2)) ** 2
```

with confidence that the variable is assigned the value 9. You needn't be concerned with precedence order in most cases.

REXX also has several operators for string concatenation, as shown in table 22-2.

Table 22-2
REXX String
Concatenation
Operators

Operator	Meaning
(blank)	Concatenate strings with one intervening blank
||	Concatenate without an intervening blank
(abuttal)	Concatenate without an intervening blank

In this table, (blank) means that the two strings are encoded adjacent one another in the REXX statement, separated by a single blank, while (abuttal) means that variables are encoded immediately adjacent one another with no intervening space.

Figure 22-1 contains a REXX program that shows concatenation operations and sample program output. Since REXX EXECs are easy to write and do not require compilation, you can quickly encode and test short EXECs such as this one in order to test how the language works.

Figure 22-1   REXX Concatenation Operators

```
/*  REXX sample to illustrate concatenation operators.    */

say  'This is an' || 'example.'     /* uses concatenation operator */
say  'This is an' 'example.'        /* concatenation with blank    */

what  =  'example.'
say  'This is an'what               /* concatenation by abuttal    */

numberone  =  1
numbertwo  =  2.3
say  numberone || numbertwo         /* uses concatenation operator */
say  numberone numbertwo            /* concatenation with blank    */
say  numberonenumbertwo             /* symbol not initialized,      */
                                    /* REXX displays its name       */
say  1 2.3                          /* concatenation with blank     */
say  1 || 2.3                       /* uses concatenation symbol     */




         SAMPLE PROGRAM OUTPUT:


This is anexample.
This is an example.
This is anexample.
12.3
1 2.3
NUMBERONENUMBERTWO
1 2.3
12.3
R;
```

Logical Constructs

REXX contains a complete set of *logical constructs* that fully support structured programming. Logical constructs are REXX instructions that direct the program's logical flow of control. Table 22-3 lists these instructions and their keywords.

These logical constructs work much as you would expect. Their operation is quite similar to these constructs in the PL/I language.

The IF Instruction

The basic formats of the IF instruction are:

```
IF  expression  THEN  instruction
```

and

```
IF  expression  THEN  instruction
    ELSE  instruction
```

For example:

```
IF  (input  =  1)  THEN  say 'The input is 1'
    ELSE  say  'The input is not 1'
```

Where more than a single instruction executes as a result of the determination of the conditional expression, that group of instructions should be denoted by a DO instruction. Bracket multiple instructions within the DO-END keywords.

For example:

```
IF  (input  =  'YES')  THEN
    DO
    say  'The input is YES'
    say  'Please enter your next input'
    END
ELSE
    nop
```

Here, the two SAY instructions are executed if input compares equally to the string YES. The ELSE branch is executed if input does not equal the string YES, according to REXX's rules for character string comparison.

If the ELSE branch of the IF instruction is taken, the REXX instruction NOP ("no operation") is executed. The NOP instruction has no effect; it is useful in implementing a null instruction as part of an IF THEN or ELSE clause. Its use is similar to the semicolon ; as the null action in the PL/I programming language, or the ELSE NEXT SENTENCE phrase in COBOL. Of course, since the NOP instruction has no effect, both it and the ELSE clause

Table 22-3 REXX Logical Constructs	

Instruction	Keywords
IF	THEN, ELSE
DO	END, TO, BY, FOR, WHILE, UNTIL, FOREVER
SELECT	WHEN, THEN, OTHERWISE
CALL	

could be eliminated from this example IF statement with no change to its effect.

Since REXX is a free-format language, indentation is largely up to the programmer. We suggest indenting in a style that accurately reflects the program's logical structure. Such a style is employed in the examples in this book. Notice also that upper and lower case may be mixed freely throughout the program. This is because REXX recognizes instruction keywords and symbols regardless of their case. Some REXX programmers use this fact to their advantage in emphasizing program structure by encoding all REXX instruction keywords in upper case and the rest of their program in lower case. In these in-text examples, the uppercase instruction keywords highlight their use.

In the IF instruction:

```
IF  expression  THEN  instruction
    ELSE  instruction
```

the expression is evaluated and resolves to 0 or 1. This tests the truth of the condition and determines whether the THEN branch or the ELSE branch (if any) executes.

REXX provides a full set of comparative operators that may be used in conditional expressions for IF instructions. Use them also in the conditional portions of DO and SELECT instructions. The REXX comparative operators are listed in table 22-4.

Table 22-4
REXX Comparative Operators

Comparative Operator		Meaning
=		True if the comparators are equal
= =		True if the comparators are identical
¬=	/=	True if the comparators are not equal
< >	> <	Greater than or less than (same as not equal)
¬= =	/= =	True if the comparators are not identical
>		Greater than
<		Less than
> =	¬<	Greater than or equal to; not less than
< =	¬>	Less than or equal to; not greater than

REXX makes numeric comparisons if both comparands involved are numeric. In numeric comparisons, leading zeroes are ignored and the numeric values are compared. For string comparisons, both leading and trailing blanks are ignored and the character-by-character comparison is made. The comparative operators dictating *identical string comparison* represent the exception to the string blank-padding rule. For example, in this series of statements:

```
IF  (input = 'YES')  THEN  say  'We have equality'
IF  (input == 'YES')  THEN  say  'We have identical strings'
```

If input contains the character string YES with leading or trailing blanks, only the first SAY instruction executes. Only if input is the exact character string YES, without leading or trailing blanks, does the second SAY instruction execute as well.

REXX's logical (or *boolean*) operators, listed in table 22-5, are also useful in condition testing.

Table 22-5
REXX Logical
Operators

Boolean Operator	Logical Operation	Meaning
&	AND	Returns 1 if both terms are true
¦	OR	Returns 1 if either term is true
&&	EXCLUSIVE	Returns 1 if either (but not both) terms are true
(prefix) ¬	LOGICAL NOT	Returns 1 for 0 and vice versa

With these boolean operators, you can construct compound conditions in comparisons:

```
IF  (input = 'YES' ¦ input = 'Y')
    THEN  say  'You are a very agreeable person'
```

The statement displays if either of the comparisons evaluates to 1. In this instance:

```
IF  (input = 'YES' & second_input = 'YES')
    THEN  say  'You are still agreeable, I see'
```

both of the expressions must be true for the SAY instruction to execute.

The DO Instruction

The REXX DO instruction implements a looping construct. Its keywords TO, BY, FOR, WHILE, UNTIL, FOREVER, and END enable you to construct DO loops that repetitively (and, optionally, conditionally) execute a group of instructions. The general format of the DO instruction is:

```
DO  repetitor  conditional
    instruction
        .
        .
        .
END
```

Figure 22-2   REXX DO Loops

```
/*  In this example, the simple DO group allows both SAY     */
/*  instructions to execute since the IF statement is true.   */

input  =  'YES'
IF  input  =  'YES'  THEN
     DO
     say  'The input is YES'
     say  'This displays too as part of the DO group'
     END


/*  In this example, the statements within the DO group are   */
/*  unconditionally executed three times.                     */

DO  3
     say  'This statement displays three times'
     say  'and so does this one  -  DO loop #1'
END


/*  In this example, the statements within the DO group execute */
/*  three times.  TO and BY work as in many other programming   */
/*  languages, for example, PL/I.                               */

DO  I  =  1  TO  6  BY  2
     say  'This statement displays three times'
     say  'and so does this one  -  DO loop #2'
END


/*  In this example, the statements within the DO group execute */
/*  conditionally three times.  WHILE and UNTIL work as in many */
/*  other programming languages, for example, PL/I.             */

loop_counter  =  1
DO  WHILE  loop_counter  <=  3
     say  'This statement displays three times'
     say  'and so does this one  -  DO loop #3'
     loop_counter  =  loop_counter + 1
END


/*  This example shows a compound condition which must hold     */
/*  true for execution of the DO loop.  WHILE implements a top- */
/*  driven loop (while UNTIL tests the conditional at the       */
/*  bottom of a loop).  The SAY statements execute twice here.  */

loop_counter  =  1 ;  input  =  'YES'
DO  WHILE  (loop_counter  <=  3  &  input  =  'YES')
     say  'This statement displays while both conditions hold true'
     say  'and so does this one'
     IF  loop_counter  =  2  THEN  input  =  'NO'
     loop_counter  =  loop_counter + 1
END


/*  This displays a character string until the user enters      */
/*  'COOKIE' in upper- or lower- case.  The LEAVE instruction    */
/*  transfers control to the instruction following the END      */
/*  clause.                                                      */

DO  FOREVER
     say  'give me cookie'
     pull  input .
     IF  input  =  'COOKIE'  THEN  leave
     say  'I SAID, GIVE ME COOKIE!'
END
say  'Thank goodness I got OUT!'
```

Figure 22-2 (cont.)

```
The input is YES
This displays too as part of the DO group
This statement displays three times
and so does this one  -  DO loop #1
This statement displays three times
and so does this one  -  DO loop #1
This statement displays three times
and so does this one  -  DO loop #1
This statement displays three times
and so does this one  -  DO loop #2
This statement displays three times
and so does this one  -  DO loop #2
This statement displays three times
and so does this one  -  DO loop #2
This statement displays three times
and so does this one  -  DO loop #3
This statement displays three times
and so does this one  -  DO loop #3
This statement displays three times
and so does this one  -  DO loop #3
This statement displays while both conditions hold true
and so does this one
This statement displays while both conditions hold true
and so does this one
give me cookie
no
I SAID, GIVE ME COOKIE!
give me cookie
Cookie
Thank goodness I got OUT!
R;
```

REXX's **DO** loops operate in a manner similar to the same construct in PL/I, FORTRAN 77, or Pascal. The comparative and boolean operators summarized in tables 22-4 and 22-5 apply to the **DO** instruction as well.

Figure 22-2 shows several sample **DO** loops and describes the manner in which they execute. The figure also includes sample program output.

The SELECT Instruction

The REXX **SELECT** instruction implements the "case" construct. Here is its general format:

```
SELECT
      WHEN   expression   THEN   instruction
      WHEN   expression   THEN   instruction
        .          .        .          .
        .          .        .          .
        .          .        .          .
      OTHERWISE   instruction
END
```

The **SELECT** instruction evaluates expressions and executes the instruction(s) associated with the first expression that results in **1** (true). If none of the expressions is true, then the instruction(s) associated with the OTHERWISE keyword execute.

Like the IF instruction, you must use a DO-END construct to associate a group of instructions with a single WHEN or OTHERWISE keyword. You may use the NOP instruction for a "no operation" branch.

Figure 22-3 contains an example SELECT instruction. The EXEC is named the PIZZA EXEC, and it asks the terminal user if he wants to have a pizza party. The REXX PARSE instruction reads the single word response to the question, in exactly the same manner as the PULL instruction illustrated

Figure 22-3   EXEC with SELECT Instruction

```
/*  This EXEC uses a SELECT statement to determine when      */
/*  tonight's pizza party starts.  It displays one of several */
/*  alternative party times depending on the user's input.    */

say  'Hey project team, are we going for pizza tonight?'
parse pull input .    /* Like PULL, but no uppercase translation */

SELECT
        WHEN  input  =  'YES'  THEN  say  'Meet at 6 PM'
        WHEN  input  =  'yes'  THEN  say  'Meet at 7 PM'
        WHEN  (input  =  'no'  |  input  =  'NO')  THEN
            DO
            say  'You entered a negative response'
            say  'Please log off or be logged off'
            END
        OTHERWISE
            DO
            say  'What is going on out there?'
            say  'Can''t you answer a simple question?'
            END
END   /* SELECT */


    pizza
    Hey project team, are we going for pizza tonight?
    YES
    Meet at 6 PM
    R;
    pizza
    Hey project team, are we going for pizza tonight?
    yes
    Meet at 7 PM
    R;
    pizza
    Hey project team, are we going for pizza tonight?
    no
    You entered a negative response
    Please log off or be logged off
    R;
    pizza
    Hey project team, are we going for pizza tonight?
    maybe
    What is going on out there?
    Can't you answer a simple question?
    R;
```

earlier, but without translating the input to upper case. If the user enters **YES** as an uppercase string, it is assumed he is enthusiastic, and so the EXEC sets party time for 6 PM. If the user enters a lowercase **yes**, it is assumed he wants pizza but that his enthusiasm is not as great. In this case, the pizza party starts at 7 PM. Entry of either a lowercase or uppercase negative response is interpreted as poor team spirit and results in a logoff message. Finally, if the user enters none of the above responses, none of the **WHEN** expressions evaluates as true. In this case, the **SELECT** instruction executes the instructions associated with the **OTHERWISE** keyword. Since more than one instruction is involved, all are enclosed within a **DO-END** pair. In this last instance, the user receives a "wake up call."

The second part of figure 22-3 shows repeated interaction with the **PIZZA EXEC**.

In **SELECT** instructions, the instruction(s) associated with the **OTHERWISE** keyword are only executed if none of the **WHEN** expressions are true. If this were the case, and the **OTHERWISE** clause were omitted, an error results.

The CALL Instruction

Last among the structured logical constructs is the **CALL** instruction. This instruction passes control to a routine it names. Following completion of that subroutine, execution continues with the instruction following the **CALL**.

REXX **CALL** instructions refer to *internal routines, external routines,* or *built-in functions.* Internal routines are REXX routines whose code resides in the same file as that of the calling routine. The code for external routines exists in a file separate from that of the calling routine. Built-in functions are routines provided by REXX that return a value to their point of invocation. They are similar in concept to the functions of such languages as PL/I, C, Pascal, and FORTRAN.

The format of the **CALL** instruction is:

```
CALL   routine  expression1 ,  expression2 ...
```

The expression(s) are the argument string(s) passed to the subroutine.

For internal routines, all variables known to the caller are accessible to the subroutine. The REXX **PROCEDURE** instruction permits you to limit the availability of variables to internal routines.

Figure 22-4 contains an example REXX program that calls an internal routine. The calling routine passes the variable **a** to the internal routine **double_string** through the **CALL** instruction parameter list. The **PROCEDURE** instruction on the subroutine ensures that it can only access this single variable from the calling routine, which it retrieves via an **ARG** instruction. The subroutine passes a result to the calling routine through the **RETURN** instruction. The caller manipulates this value through the REXX *special variable* named RESULT. A REXX special variable is a variable that is set by the interpreter under the proper conditions. The special variable RESULT is set by the execution of a RETURN instruction in a CALL subroutine.

The EXEC displays this output:

```
Other:  OTHER_VAR
11
```

The procedure displays 11 as output for the concatenated string. Since its subroutine cannot access the variable other_var, it displays the variable name. (When unassigned, the value of a symbol is its own name translated to upper case).

This sample program shows only one way to call other routines and handle the scoping of variables between REXX routines. REXX provides facilities in this area as extensive as those of almost any language.

Other Instructions Affecting Logical Flow

Figure 22-4 illustrates both the REXX RETURN and EXIT instructions, while figure 22-2 demonstrates the LEAVE instruction. Table 22-6 lists other REXX instructions that affect the flow of control within REXX EXECs.

Figure 22-4   REXX Program CALLing an Internal Routine

```
/*  This illustrates the CALLing of an internal routine.      */
/*  The CALL instruction invokes the subroutine, and makes    */
/*  variable "a" accessible to that routine.  The sub-routine's */
/*  RETURNed value is accessible to the caller through the     */
/*  REXX special variable named RESULT.                        */

other_var = 'This variable is not accessible to the subroutine'
a = 1
call  double_string  a        /* call the subroutine          */
say  result                   /* print returned result        */
exit


/*  Here is the internal routine named 'DOUBLE_STRING'.        */
/*  It can only access the variable "a" due to the PROCEDURE   */
/*  instruction.  It returns a single value via the RETURN     */
/*  instruction.  The caller gets ahold of this value thru     */
/*  the REXX special variable named RESULT.                    */

double_string:  procedure
  arg  a                      /* access passed variable        */
  say  'Other: '  other_var   /* inaccessible, shows its name  */
  return  a  ||  a            /* return concatenated string    */
```

Functions

REXX includes a minimal set of some two dozen instructions. The power of the language is embodied in its 60 or so built-in functions. Remember, built-in functions are routines provided as part of the REXX language that return a value to their point of invocation.

Table 22-6
REXX Instructions
Affecting Flow of
Control

Instruction	Meaning
RETURN	Returns control (and optionally a result) from a REXX program or internal routine to its caller at the point of invocation
EXIT	Unconditionally leaves a procedure and optionally returns a return code to the caller
LEAVE	Causes immediate exit from a DO loop to the statement following the loop
ITERATE	Causes control to be passed from the current statement in the DO loop to the bottom of the loop
SIGNAL	Provides exception trapping (also can be used to unconditionally transfer control to a specified label, like a GOTO instruction in other programming languages.)

REXX also embodies the concept of *function packages,* groups of functions that act just like built-in functions from the viewpoint of the REXX programmer. You encode them like built-in functions, and they return a single value to their point of invocation like built-in functions. IBM provides a function package containing four functions as part of the REXX language. Your installation may also develop or purchase other function packages. Function packages are important vehicles through which the power of the language is enhanced. This chapter describes only functions supplied as part of the REXX language with CMS; this consists of some 58 built-in functions and 4 functions from the RXSYSFN function package provided by IBM.

The REXX functions can be classified according to what they do. We classify them into these categories:

string manipulation

conversion

arithmetic

environmental control

miscellaneous

String Manipulation

With over 30 functions, this comprises the largest single category of REXX built-in functions. These functions make it easy for you to handle the kinds of text manipulation tasks that are so often required in interpretive command procedures, and make REXX an excellent language for character string processing.

Functions may be defined as routines that return a result right back into the expression in which the function was encoded. Once the value of a function has been determined, it replaces the encoding of the function call.

As an example, look at this use of the SUBSTR function:

```
/* Example of the SUBSTR string manipulation function */
pull  input  .
one_letter  =  substr(input,1,1)
if  one_letter  =  'Y'  then
    say  'We assume your answer was YES'
```

The SUBSTR function returns the substring of the variable INPUT, starting at the first position within INPUT and having a length of one character. The 1,1 in the function encoding thus stand for the starting character position in the returned substring and the number of characters in that substring.

The substring calculated via the SUBSTR function effectively replaces the function call in the code. The assignment statement moves this value into the variable one_letter. The IF instruction thus verifies whether the first character of the user's input was a Y or y.

A more compact way to write this same code is:

```
/* Example of the SUBSTR string manipulation function */
pull  input  .
if  substr(input,1,1)  =  'Y'  then
    say  'We assume your answer was YES'
```

Given this understanding of how functions work, the procedure in figure 22-5 illustrates several string manipulation functions in verifying its input parameters. An input editing routine such as this is often a required part of larger EXECs.

This EXEC retrieves its parameters via the REXX PARSE ARG instruction. This ensures that the input parameters to the procedure are not translated to uppercase letters. The procedure then uses the string manipulation functions ABBREV, DATATYPE, INDEX, POS, LENGTH, TRANSLATE, and VERIFY to ensure that its input parameters meet the criteria specified in the EXEC documentation. The EXEC documentation explains how these string functions work.

There are far too many REXX string manipulation functions to demonstrate them all in this book. What is important is that you under-

Figure 22-5 REXX String Manipulation Functions

```
/****************************************************************/
/*  This EXEC illustrates various string functions through      */
/*  verification of user-input parameters.  These tests are:    */
/*                                                              */
/*       PARAMETER:               TEST:                         */
/*       ----------     ---------------------------------------  */
/*        first         Must be valid abbreviation for TESTSTRING */
/*                        and consist only of letters a-z and A-Z */
/*        second        Must be numeric and under 5 bytes long   */
/*        third         This string must occur within the       */
/*                        first parameter                       */
/*        fourth        After translation to upper-case, must   */
/*                        consist of only the letters A, B, C    */
/*                                                              */
/*  It is assumed that all parameters are entered.              */
/****************************************************************/

parse  arg  first  second  third  fourth  .

/*  See if first parm is valid abbreviation for TESTSTRING      */

if  abbrev('TESTSTRING',first,4)  =  0  then
     say  'First parm must be valid abbreviation for TESTSTRING'


/*  Check that first parm contains only letters a-z and A-Z     */

if  datatype(first,m)  =  0  then
     say  'First parm can only contain letters a-z and A-Z'


/*  Ensure second parm is numeric, and under 5 byte length      */

if  datatype(second)  ¬=  'NUM'  then
     say  'Second parm is not numeric'
if  length(second)  >  4  then
     say  'Second parm is more than 4 bytes long'


/*  Return character position of third parm in the first        */

position  =  index(first, third)
if  position  =  0  then
     say  'third parm does not occur within first, error'
else
     say  'third parm occurs in first at position:' position
/*  Return character position of third parm in the first        */
/*  but this time use the POS function instead of INDEX         */

if  pos(third,first)  =  0  then
     say  'third parm does not occur within first, error'
else  do
     say  'third parm occurs in first at position:'
     say  pos(third,first)
end


/*  Translated fourth parm must contain only letters A, B, C    */

uppercase  =  translate(fourth)
if  verify(uppercase,'ABC')  >  0  then
     say  'fourth parm contains letter other than A, B, C'
```

stand how built-in functions work. Table 22-7 provides a quick reference to the built-in string functions.

Table 22-8 supplies a list of the *word-oriented* string manipulation functions of REXX. REXX defines a *word* as a string of characters delimited by blanks. REXX's word-oriented functions compose a subset of the string manipulation functions that support word-oriented text processing. Their addition to the string functions gives REXX exceptional string handling capabilities.

Table 22-7
REXX String
Manipulation
Functions

Function	Meaning
ABBREV	Tests if a string is a valid abbreviation
BITAND	Logically ANDs two strings
BITOR	Logically ORs two strings
BITXOR	Logically exclusively ORs two strings
CENTER	Centers a string within another
COMPARE	Compares two strings
COPIES	Returns concatenated copies of a string
DATATYPE	Verifies contents of a string by data type
DELSTR	Deletes a substring
INDEX	Locates one string within another
INSERT	Inserts a string within another
JUSTIFY	Margin-justifies a string
LASTPOS	Returns position of the last occurrence of a string
LEFT	Returns a leftmost substring
LENGTH	Returns the length of a string
OVERLAY	Overlays one string within another
POS	Locates one string within another
REVERSE	Returns a string with characters swapped end for end
RIGHT	Returns a rightmost substring
STRIP	Removes leading and trailing blanks from a string
SUBSTR	Returns a substring
TRANSLATE	Translates characters within a string
VERIFY	Verifies character composition of a string
XRANGE	Returns a string of a hexadecimal byte range

Conversion

Another class of built-in functions offered by REXX are those for conversion. These functions aid in the conversion of strings that represent data of types character, decimal, and hexadecimal. With them, you pass in a variable containing one kind of data and receive in return the representation of that string in another data type.

Table 22-8
REXX Word-oriented String Manipulation Functions

Function	Meaning
DELWORD	Deletes word(s) from a string
FIND	Locates words or phrases in a string
SPACE	Formats the words within a string
SUBWORD	Returns a substring of word(s)
WORD	Returns the Nth word from a string
WORDINDEX	Returns the relative position of a word in a string
WORDLENGTH	Returns the length of a word within a string
WORDS	Returns the number of words in a string

For example, the `C2X` function converts a character string to its hexadecimal equivalent. This example:

```
say  'Hex form of character 14 is: '  C2X('14')
```

displays:

```
Hex form of character 14 is: F1F4
```

Table 22-9 lists the REXX conversion functions. In the names of these functions, C stands for character, X for hexadecimal, and D for decimal.

Table 22-9
REXX Conversion Functions

Function	Meaning
C2D	Character to decimal
C2X	Character to hexadecimal
D2C	Decimal to character
D2X	Decimal to hexadecimal
X2C	Hexadecimal to character
X2D	Hexadecimal to decimal

Additional Built-in Functions

REXX contains a variety of arithmetic functions. Table 22-10 lists these functions.

Table 22-10
REXX Arithmetic
Functions

Function	Meaning
ABS	Returns absolute value of a number
FORMAT	Rounds and formats a number
MAX	Finds the largest number of a list
MIN	Finds the smallest number of a list
RANDOM	Returns a random number
SIGN	Tells whether a number is positive, negative, or zero
TRUNC	Returns the integer portion of a number

Finally, a very important class of functions enables the EXEC to interrogate various aspects of its environment. For example, the ADDRESS function returns the name of the environment to which host commands are passed. The EXECs in these chapters direct their commands at CMS, and so their environment is CMS. As another example, the TRACE function returns the EXEC tracing options currently in effect. A final example is the CMSFLAG function. (This function is not built-in, but is part of the RXSYSFN function package that comes with REXX.) With CMSFLAG, an EXEC determines whether the implied EXEC and implied CP functions are on as well as the status of several other indicators in the CMS environment.

Table 22-11 lists REXX's environmental functions as well as several miscellaneous functions.

Arrays

Simple symbols do not contain periods or start with a digit. REXX supports arrays (sometimes called tables) through its concept of the *compound symbol*. A compound symbol contains at least one period, and has characters on each side of any periods. It may not start with a period or digit.

Examples of valid compound symbols are:

```
checkers.4
table.i.j
table_position.sub
```

The first character(s) of the compound symbol, up to and including the first period, are known as the *stem*. Before the compound symbol is used, any internal simple symbols are replaced by their values. This substitution effectively implements subscripting with collections of variables that have a common stem. Moreover, since subscripts are not necessarily numeric and they are variables, you may simulate a content addressable data structure.

	Function	Meaning
Table 22-11 REXX Environmental and Miscellaneous Functions	ADDRESS	Returns the name of the host environment for commands
	ARG	Returns information about the command arguments
	CMSFLAG	Returns CMS SET command information
	DATE	Returns the date
	DIAG	Communicates with CP through a dummy DIAGNOSE instruction
	DIAGRC	Communicates with CP through a dummy DIAGNOSE instruction
	ERRORTEXT	Returns the error message text of an error number
	EXTERNALS	Returns the number of elements in the terminal input buffer
	LINESIZE	Returns the current terminal line width
	QUEUED	Returns the number of lines in the program stack
	SOURCELINE	Returns a line from the command procedure source code
	STORAGE	Returns virtual machine storage size or memory data (also, can change virtual storage memory values)
	SYMBOL	Tests for valid REXX symbols
	TIME	Returns the time
	TRACE	Returns current TRACE options
	USERID	Returns the user identifier
	VALUE	Returns the value of a REXX symbol

The command procedure of figure 22-6 shows a simple example use of compound symbols in the initialization and use of a table. This EXEC sets PF key definitions for keys 1 through 12 by repeatedly issuing the CP SET PFn command.

Figure 22-6   Command Procedure with an Array

```
/*  REXX EXEC that sets PF key functions.  Multiple REXX  */
/*  assignment statements occur per line by use of the    */
/*  semi-colon to indicate the end of the clauses.        */

key.1  =  'retrieve';          key.2  =  'xedit' ;
key.3  =  'immed ispf';        key.4  =  'immed query disk';
key.5  =  'immed query time';  key.6  =  'immed query reader';
key.7  =  'immed query punch'; key.8  =  'immed query prt';
key.9  =  'immed query files'; key.10 =  'immed query all';
key.11 =  'immed set msg on';  key.12 =  'immed set msg off';

DO  keyno  =  1  to  12
    stringvalue  =  key.keyno
    'cp  set  pf'keyno  stringvalue
END
```

In this procedure, the dozen assignment statements initialize values in the KEY array to various operating system commands. Note that more than one REXX statement can be placed on each program source line when semicolons separate them. The DO instruction then issues a CP SET PFn command for each value in the KEY table, thereby setting PF keys 1 through 12.

For Further Information

The paper, "The Design of the REXX Language," by Michael F. Cowlishaw, describes the design criteria and major features of the REXX language. It appeared in *IBM Systems Journal* (23:4, 1984).

We recommend the tutorial manual, *VM/SP System Product Interpreter User's Guide, SC24-5238*, as an outstanding source for learning REXX programming. This book presents a completely self-contained, self-taught approach to learning the language.

The manual, *VM/SP System Product Interpreter Reference, SC24-5239*, is the comprehensive reference manual for REXX.

Test Your Understanding

Describe the general characteristics of REXX as a command language and its advantages over other command languages.

List the categories of REXX functions. Describe how REXX built-in functions operate. What does the REXX interpreter do when it encounters a function reference within a REXX program?

Write your own command procedure to set your terminal's PF keys to whatever CMS and/or CP commands you like. Your procedure should set either 12 or 24 function keys, depending on your terminal model.

Write a simple command procedure that prompts the user to input two numbers and returns the sum of these two numbers. Your command procedure must **CALL** an internal routine to perform the addition.

Write a command procedure that prompts the user to input two character strings, and then determines if the first string is a substring of the second. Your main procedure should perform all input/output to the terminal user while an internal routine handles the substring determination.

Write a command procedure that prompts the user to input a single character string. Your procedure should analyze the input and write a message stating whether the input string is numeric. If the string is numeric, the procedure should state whether it is a whole number or a valid hexadecimal number. If the input string is not numeric, the procedure should write a message stating whether the input consists of lowercase or uppercase alphabetic letters, or whether it is mixed case. (Hint: refer to the REXX **DATATYPE** function.)

Write a command procedure called **ANY EXEC** that converts a user-input string into its character, decimal, or hexadecimal equivalent.

CHAPTER 23

Essential Concepts of Command Procedures

This chapter covers fundamental concepts for writing command procedures. While examples in this chapter are written in REXX, the concepts apply to command procedures written in the EXEC2 and EXEC languages as well.

Return Codes

One key concept in EXEC writing is that of the *return code*. When a command procedure issues a CMS or CP command, the return code provides feedback concerning the success or failure of the command. A zero return code means the command succeeded, whereas any other number indicates failure of the command. Depending on the intent of the EXEC in issuing the command, you may wish it to take action in response to failed commands.

REXX's special variable RC makes the return code available to your programs. The system sets the value of RC to the return code issued by CMS and CP commands.

In the EXEC2 and EXEC languages, the predefined variables &RC or &RETCODE capture command return codes.

Figure 23-1 contains an example REXX program that captures the return code resulting from the CMS STATE command. The STATE command verifies the existence of a file on an accessed disk. The program accesses the return code in the special variable RC and displays a message appropriate to the status of the user's file.

Since other CMS and CP commands reset the return code in special variable RC, many programmers immediately move the return code to another variable where they can retain it regardless of subsequent commands.

In writing EXECs, you should normally check the return codes from all CMS and CP commands. If you need to know the return codes issued by any CMS or CP commands, an easy way to find out is simply to try them out online with CMS or look in the online "HELP" file.

Figure 23-1   REXX Program That Inspects Return Codes

```
/*
This EXEC determines the existence of a file, as based on
the return code issued by the CMS STATE command.

To use this EXEC, enter:  EXIST  fn  ft  fm
You are required to enter the filename and filetype.
If you donot enter the filemode, it defaults to '*'.
*/

arg  fn  ft  fm  .

/*  This code uses the SOURCELINE built-in function to         */
/*  display the documentation at the top of this EXEC          */
/*  when the user does not enter appropriate parameters.       */

if  ft  =  ''  then  do
    do  line  =  1  while  sourceline(line)  ¬=  '*/'
        say  sourceline(line)
    end
    exit  1
end

if  fm  =  ''  then  fm  =  '*'

/*  This code issues the CMS STATE command and checks the      */
/*  return code that results from it.                          */

state  fn  ft  fm
if  rc  =   0  then
    say  'This file exists on an accessed disk'
else  do
    if  rc  =  28  |  rc  =  36  then
        say  'The file doesnot exist on an accessed disk'
    else
        say  'Error, return code is:' rc
end

exit
```

PROFILE EXEC

CMS recognizes a special command procedure with the file name of **PRO-FILE EXEC** and always executes this procedure whenever you IPL CMS. Whether you explicitly issue the CP **IPL CMS** command, or automatically initiate CMS via your CP directory entry, CMS executes the **PROFILE EXEC** as part of its initialization process.

The **PROFILE EXEC** is an extremely useful command procedure in that it automatically issues any commands required to tailor the CMS environment to your use. With the **PROFILE** command procedure, you can:

- set CP spooling options (for example, establish appropriate distribution and routing information for your virtual printer)

- access disks (in addition to those in your CP Directory entry)
- access any libraries required for programming during your session (through the CMS **GLOBAL** command)
- set PF key definitions
- issue CP and CMS **SET** commands to establish other aspects of the environment
- set virtual console (terminal) characteristics as appropriate
- invoke your synonym table

Figure 23-2 contains an example **PROFILE EXEC**. It performs several of the tasks listed above. The EXEC contains comments that explain its operation.

Figure 23-2   PROFILE EXEC Command Procedure

```
/*  This PROFILE EXEC  establishes a tailored CMS environment.  */
/*  CMS always executes this command procedure when IPL'd.      */

/*  Set proper CP spooling options                              */

'cp  spool  console  dist  ornl1220'
'cp  spool  printer  route ornl0002  dist  ornl1220'
'cp  spool  punch    dist  ornl1220'

/*  Access appropriate CMS libraries                            */

global  txtlib  plilib
global  maclib  cmslib


/*  Set up Program Function (PF) keys, through CALLing a        */
/*  external REXX command procedure routine that sets them.     */

call  keys


/*  Invoke my synonym table                                     */

synonym  mysyns


/*  Conclude with miscellaneous environment commands            */

set  rdymsg  smsg
'query disk *'
```

Create or change your **PROFILE EXEC** at any time through any editor. Execute the **PROFILE EXEC** procedure explicitly to place any new options into effect, or IPL CMS again.

One function the **PROFILE EXEC** can *not* do is issue CP commands that reset the virtual system. For example, do not issue the CP **DEFINE STORAGE** command from your **PROFILE EXEC**. Attempting to reset the system during IPL through the **PROFILE EXEC** halts the IPL and hangs up your virtual machine.

Tracing

All the CMS command procedure languages offer a comprehensive tracing facility. In REXX, this can be controlled from within an EXEC by the **TRACE** instruction. This instruction provides several alternatives in the degree of tracing. For example, you can trace: all clauses before execution; commands resulting in nonzero or negative return codes after execution; or program labels passed during execution.

Figure 23-3 shows how the trace appears when the command procedure of figure 23-1 is executed with the additional statement:

TRACE   R

added after the initial comments in that program. The **R** option traces all clauses before their execution, results of expression evaluation, and values assigned during **PULL**, **ARG**, and **PARSE** instructions. **TRACE R** is recommended as the normal debugging mode.

Figure 23-3   Example TRACE Output

```
R;
exist   nofile   nowhere
    10 *-* arg   fn   ft   fm   .
       >>>    "NOFILE"
       >>>    "NOWHERE"
       >>>    ""
       >.>    ""
    12 *-* /*  This code uses the SOURCELINE built-in function to        */
    13 *-* /*  display the documentation at the top of this EXEC         */
    14 *-* /*  when the user does not enter appropriate parameters.      */
    16 *-* if   ft   =   ''
       >>>    "0"
    23 *-* if   fm   =   ''
       >>>    "1"
       *-* then
       *-* fm   =   '*'
       >>>    "*"
    25 *-* /*  This code issues the CMS STATE command and checks the     */
    26 *-* /*  return code that results from it.                         */
    28 *-* state   fn   ft   fm
       >>>    "STATE NOFILE NOWHERE *"
DMSSTT002E FILE 'NOFILE NOWHERE *' NOT FOUND.
       +++ RC(28) +++
    29 *-* if   rc   =   0
       >>>    "0"
    31 *-* else
       *-* do
    32 *-*    if   rc   =   28   |   rc   =   36
       >>>       "1"
       *-*    then
    33 *-*    say   'The file doesnot exist on an accessed disk'
       >>>        "The file doesnot exist on an accessed disk"
The file doesnot exist on an accessed disk
    36 *-*    end
    38 *-* exit
R;
```

In the trace output of figure 23-3, the symbols *-* indicate statements within the source procedure. The line numbers preceding these symbols identify the relative position of these source statements within the EXEC file.

Lines preceded by the symbols >>> show the results of expression evaluation. And, lines that are flush on the left margin (that are indented left) are those that display on your terminal even if you have the trace disabled.

Remember that you can also control command procedure tracing from outside the EXEC code through the CMS **SET EXECTRAC** command and the CMS immediate commands **TE** and **TS**. These CMS commands provide for interactive setting of the trace without altering the source code of your command procedures.

The control statements in the EXEC2 and EXEC languages that set the command tracing options are **&TRACE** and **&CONTROL**, respectively.

Exception Trapping

Exception trapping enables you to transfer control to a specific portion of your command procedure when exceptional conditions occur. The REXX **SIGNAL** instruction, listed in table 23-1, allows you to go to a specific point in the command procedure code when these conditions occur.

Table 23-1
REXX SIGNAL
Instruction

Condition	Meaning
ERROR	A host command returns a nonzero return code
HALT	An external interrupt occurs (for example, through the CMS immediate command HI (halt interpretation)
NOVALUE	Use of an uninitialized variable
SYNTAX	A syntax error occurs during interpretation

A REXX EXEC *label* is a simple symbol followed by a colon. After you enable an exception condition through the **SIGNAL** instruction, if that condition is raised, control passes to a program label that has the same name as the exception condition. Figure 23-4 contains an example that traps a nonzero return code from a CMS **STATEW** command. The **STATEW** command verifies the existence of a file on a write-accessible minidisk.

In figure 23-4, the statement:

```
signal  on  error
```

designates that control **passes to** the program label:

```
error:
```

if a nonzero return code results from the CMS `STATEW` command. If transfer of control to this label occurs because of the `SIGNAL` condition, the EXEC displays the return code raising the exception. It also displays the number of the procedure source line raising the condition through use of the REXX `SIGL` special variable. The `SIGL` special variable provides the line number of the clause currently executing when the transfer of control occurs.

Figure 23-4   Command Procedure with Exception Trapping

```
/*  This procedure traps any non-zero return code issued      */
/*  by the CMS STATEW command.  That command checks for        */
/*  existence of a specified file on a write-access disk.       */

arg   fn   ft   fm   .

signal   on   error

statew   fn   ft   fm
say   'The file exists on a write-accessed disk, rc is:' rc
exit   rc

error:
say   'STATEW command failed, rc was:'   rc
say   'Source line number executing was:'   sigl
exit   rc
```

Edit Macros

An *edit macro* is a command procedure invoked from within XEDIT. The edit macro allows you to expand the basic set of XEDIT subcommands and tailor the XEDIT environment to your own specifications. Edit macros bring the same benefits associated with execution of command procedures under CMS to the XEDIT editor. They expand the subcommand set of XEDIT while eliminating the typing that results from repetitive tasks.

You issue an edit macro in the same manner as any other XEDIT command. That is, you type it into the command line. You may also write edit macros that become prefix commands and are entered in the editor's prefix area (over the equal signs on the left side of the editor screen).

Edit macros typically contain:

XEDIT subcommands

command procedure statements

CMS and CP commands

Edit macros determine the success or failure of XEDIT subcommands in the exact same manner as CMS and CP commands: through the return code. This enables edit macros to react intelligently to their environment.

Edit macros may be written in the REXX, EXEC2, or EXEC command procedure languages. The filetype of all edit macros is `XEDIT`. Writing edit macros is not much different than writing other command procedures, except that they primarily issue XEDIT subcommands.

PROFILE XEDIT

The **PROFILE XEDIT** file is a command procedure having a special name, similar to the **PROFILE EXEC**. The **PROFILE XEDIT** procedure automatically executes upon issuance of the CMS **XEDIT** command (or editor's **XEDIT** subcommand). Analogous to the **PROFILE EXEC**, the **PROFILE XEDIT** establishes and tailors the XEDIT environment to your personal specification.

Like most edit macros, the **PROFILE XEDIT** procedure issues various XEDIT subcommands. In the XEDIT profile, many of these are **SET** subcommands that tailor the XEDIT environment.

Figure 23-5 contains a simple example XEDIT profile written in REXX. This command procedure could also have been developed in the EXEC2 or EXEC languages. The procedure is self-documenting.

Figure 23-5   PROFILE XEDIT Command Procedure

```
/*  This PROFILE XEDIT command procedure tailors XEDIT    */
/*  upon entry.  First, set XEDIT options:                */

set autosave 5
set scale off
set cmdline top
set nulls on
set curline on 3
set tofeof off
set trunc 73
set case mixed

/*  Set program function keys as desired beyond defaults */

set pf3 FILE
set pf15 FILE
'set pf22 -11'
set pf23 11
```

If you have a **PROFILE XEDIT** command procedure, and do *not* wish it to be executed upon entry to the editor, enter the **XEDIT** command with the **NOPROFILE** option:

```
XEDIT  filename  filetype  filemode  (NOPROFILE
```

Recall that in the introduction to the XEDIT editor in chapter 4, we issued the **XEDIT** command with this option. This prevented inadvertent execution of a system-dependent **PROFILE XEDIT** procedure that might have tailored your editor so that its screen would have appeared vastly different from the editor examples in chapters 4 and 5.

The Stack

Perhaps one of the most important (and misunderstood) command procedure concepts is that of the *stack*.

The *console stack* is a series of several input/output buffers. A *buffer* is a place in computer memory used to hold information.

Figure 23-6 shows that the CMS console stack consists of two parts: the *program stack* and the *terminal input buffer*. The program stack normally consists of one or more buffers. Each holds information for communication between programs within CMS. The *terminal input buffer* is the place where the lines typed at the terminal are placed prior to their execution by CMS.

Figure 23-6
The Console Stack
and Its
Components

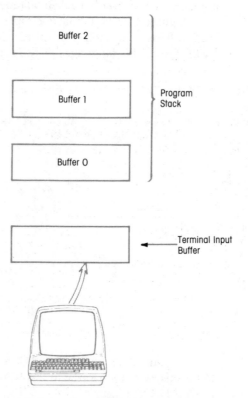

The program stack is of especial importance to command procedures. It is used to pass data to certain CMS commands, and to retrieve information from them.

The program stack is thus a generalized facility for inter-program communication. For example, when command procedures issue certain CMS commands, they can direct the output of these commands to the program stack. The procedure then reads the program stack data and, in this manner, accesses information output from CMS commands.

Conversely, certain other CMS commands prompt the terminal user for input. You can preempt these CMS requests for user-entered input by placing the relevant responses in the program stack. The command procedure must place the desired responses into the program stack *before* issuing the CMS command that requests input.

CMS commands that optionally place output information into the program stack are listed in table 23-2.

Table 23-2
CMS Placing
Output onto the
Stack

Command	Function
EXECIO	Read lines from disk or virtual reader into the program stack; execute CP commands and collect their resulting output in the stack
IDENTIFY	Get the userid and node id, date, time, etc.
LISTFILE	Retrieve file information
NAMEFIND	Retrieve communication information from the names file
QUERY	Retrieve information about CMS status
RECEIVE	Read communicated files and notes
RDR	Retrieve virtual reader status information

Table 23-3 lists some of the CMS commands that can take their input information from the program stack.

Table 23-3
CMS Accepting
Input from the
Stack

Command	Function
EXECIO	Writes lines from the program stack to disk, virtual printer, or virtual punch
COPYFILE	With SPECS option, reads stack information specifying how the copy should occur
FORMAT	Requires input for formatting a minidisk
SORT	Requires input information in sorting a file

Figure 23-7 contains a simple EXEC that shows how to capture information output by a CMS command to the program stack. The command procedure issues the CMS IDENTIFY command. This command supplies such data as the userid of the virtual machine, the node id, the date, time, and other information. The STACK option on the IDENTIFY command directs CMS to place this command's output on the program stack. The EXEC then displays this information formatted for the user.

The command procedure retrieves the line output from the IDENTIFY command through normal input instructions. In REXX, these instructions are PULL and PARSE PULL. How does this occur?

The standard input or "read" instructions in CMS command procedure languages read from the parts of the console stack in this order:

Figure 23-7 Program Stack with CMS IDENTIFY Command

```
/*  This procedure directs output from the CMS IDENTIFY       */
/*  command to the program stack.  It then reads that         */
/*  information by the PULL instruction and displays it.      */

'identify (stack lifo'

pull userid at node via rscsid date time zone day

say  'The virtual machine userid is:' userid
say  'The RSCS node is:' node
say  'The userid of the RSCS virtual machine is:' rscsid
say  'The date, time, and day are:' date time day
exit
```

1. from the program stack

2. if the program stack is empty, from the terminal input buffer

3. If the terminal input buffer is empty, the program waits while the CMS status indicator in the bottom right-hand corner of the screen displays the words **VM READ**. The program resumes execution after the terminal user types information and presses the **ENTER** (or other) terminal input key.

The process by which the REXX **PULL** and **PARSE PULL** instructions read information is therefore from the top down in terms of figure 23-6. It is very important to understanding the use of the stack that you remember the search order followed by CMS through the stack. The fact that reading the information in the console stack occurs in a known order means that EXECs can manipulate stack information in a predictable fashion. You can control the console stack from your command procedures because the stack always works in the same way.

One fundamental aspect of the program stack's operation as a communication vehicle between EXECs and CMS commands is that the term "program stack" is misleading. In terms of computer data structures, the program stack, in fact, functions either as a stack or a *queue*. Figure 23-8 illustrates the difference between a stack and a queue as data structures. One commonly speaks of *pushing* a line of data onto a stack, and of removing the information from the stack by *pulling* it. The key concept that underlies this terminology is that the most recent line of information entered into the stack is also the first retrieved. This is referred to as a *Last In, First Out* (LIFO) data structure. A queue, on the other hand, retrieves information in a different order than a stack. It is a *First In, First Out* (FIFO) data structure. The first line of information placed in a queue is also the first retrieved from the queue. The CMS program stack serves as either a LIFO or FIFO structure.

REXX commands to remove data from the program stack are **PULL** and **PARSE PULL**. These search through the components of the console stack as described above.

The REXX **PUSH** instruction places lines of information on the pro-

Figure 23-8
The Program Stack
Functions as Stack
or Queue

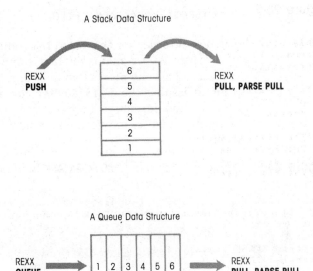

A Stack Data Structure

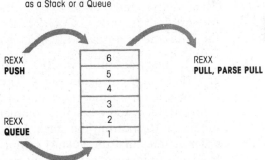

A Queue Data Structure

The CMS Program Stack Can Function Either
as a Stack or a Queue

gram stack in LIFO order. The REXX QUEUE instruction places information
on the program stack in FIFO order. The EXEC2 and EXEC languages use
the &STACK and &BEGSTACK control statements to perform these same functions, with the options FIFO and LIFO dictating whether the data structure
functions as a queue or stack (FIFO is the default).

The CMS commands that place information into the program stack
have options specifying whether they place lines into the program stack in
FIFO or LIFO order. Most CMS commands use the program stack FIFO
unless directed otherwise. However, there are exceptions: look up any
particular command prior to using it.

As an example, the CMS IDENTIFY command in figure 23-7 uses the
program stack for LIFO output. The command procedure could have also used
the program stack as a queue by issuing IDENTIFY with the FIFO option:

```
IDENTIFY (STACK FIFO
```

The default order for the IDENTIFY command is FIFO.

Figure 23-9 contains another command procedure that manipulates the stack. This one places two lines of information into the program stack, prior to issuing the CMS FORMAT command. In this way, the program acquires and formats a temporary minidisk for terminal users without bothering them for any terminal input beyond that which starts the EXEC itself.

Figure 23-9   Program Stack with CMS FORMAT Command

```
/*   This procedure acquires a temporary 3380 minidisk.      */
/*   It places responses to the CMS FORMAT command in the     */
/*   program stack prior to issuing that command.             */
/*                                                            */
/*   Enter:  XDISK cyls vaddr diskletter                      */
/*   Example:  XDISK  3  201  E                               */

arg  cyls  vaddr  diskletter  .

if  diskletter = '' then exit 10

cp  define  t3380  as  vaddr  cyls
if  rc  ¬= 0  then exit 20

queue  'YES'
queue  'TDISK'
format  vaddr  diskletter
if  rc  ¬= 0  then exit 30
exit
```

In this procedure, two REXX QUEUE instructions place the words YES and TDISK in the program stack. Thus, when the CMS FORMAT command asks whether to format the acquired minidisk, it retrieves the answer YES from the stack, and when this command needs a minidisk label, it retrieves the name TDISK from the stack. In both cases, the console stack retrieval order dictates that the FORMAT command retrieve this queued information from the program stack without reading input from the terminal input buffer or from the terminal user himself. In this way, this EXEC issues the CMS FORMAT command without forcing terminal users to enter responses to the FORMAT command themselves.

This technique of automating interaction between the EXEC and CMS without user intervention is quite common. Use it to avoid unnecessarily bothering the terminal user for input, or when you want to dictate what the user's responses should be.

CMS EXEC

In addition to the PROFILE EXEC and the PROFILE XEDIT, another command procedure with a special name is the CMS EXEC. It is created as a result of executing either the CMS LISTFILE or CMS/DOS LISTIO commands with the EXEC option.

To take an example:

```
LISTFILE * DATA A1 (EXEC
```

creates a file named **CMS EXEC A1**. This file contains one line per each file of filetype **DATA** on your A-disk, each of which is in the form:

```
&1  &2  filename  filetype  filemode
```

The **&1** and **&2** are significant because in the EXEC2 and EXEC command procedure languages, parameters passed to the procedures are automatically assigned these names within the procedures. For example, if you execute an EXEC2 procedure named **TEST EXEC A1**:

```
TEST  FIRST  SECOND
```

The string **FIRST** is automatically assigned to the procedure variable named **&1**, **SECOND** is captured in **&2**, and so on for other command line parameters.

This means that the output from the **LISTFILE** command with the **EXEC** option is a ready-to-execute CMS command procedure written in the EXEC language.

Once this **CMS EXEC** file has been created, you manipulate the files in it as a group by issuing the **CMS EXEC** with appropriate parameters as input. For example, to print all the files that are output as a result of the **LISTFILE** command above, enter:

```
CMS  PRINT
```

PRINT becomes **&1** in the **CMS EXEC**, and the files are printed. Since **&2** was not entered on the command line, it defaults to the null string and has no role in the command procedure.

Figure 23-10 contains a REXX command procedure that takes advantage of the CMS **LISTFILE** command to create a **CMS EXEC** file. First, the procedure executes a **LISTFILE** command with the **EXEC** option to build a **CMS EXEC** file that lists all the user's **SCRIPT** files on the A-disk. The **LISTFILE** command includes the **DATE** option, which outputs disk label information to the **CMS EXEC** file as well.

Next, the EXEC issues the REXX **PUSH** instruction. This sends the two numbers shown to the program stack **LIFO**. These numbers will be the response to the CMS **SORT** command, which is subsequently issued to sort the files listed in the **CMS EXEC** file by file size. The file size information is contained in positions 47 through 51 in each **CMS EXEC** file record (the numbers pushed onto the stack). The sorted list of files is then displayed on the terminal through the CMS **TYPE** command. Figure 23-11 shows how sample output from this procedure might appear. Note that the EXEC did not remove the **&1** and **&2** parameters from the start of each line of the output file.

Figure 23-10   Using a CMS EXEC File

```
/*  This procedure lists script files sorted by size,       */
/*  smallest to largest.                                     */
/*                                                           */
/*  Enter:     LISTSCR                                       */

makebuf

'listfile  *  script  a  (exec  date'

push 47 51

set  cmstype  ht
sort  cms  exec  a  sortlist  exec  a
set  cmstype  rt

type  sortlist  exec  a

dropbuf
exit 0
```

Figure 23-11   Sample Output from LISTSCR EXEC

```
&1 &2 LEARNING SCRIPT   A1 F        80          3      1 10/21/85  7:22:32
&1 &2 GMLTEST  SCRIPT   A1 F        80          5      1 10/24/85  7:02:38
&1 &2 MFSLIB   SCRIPT   A1 F        80         39      1 10/10/85 14:14:47
&1 &2 MAN      SCRIPT   A1 F        80         63      2 12/06/85 15:35:38
&1 &2 BSPREPT  SCRIPT   A1 F        80         90      2  6/14/84 13:30:34
&1 &2 DB2NOTE  SCRIPT   A1 F        80         91      2 10/31/85 14:05:47
&1 &2 DB2LIBS  SCRIPT   A1 F        80        104      3  1/14/86 10:53:01
&1 &2 BSPDEFS  SCRIPT   A1 F        80        303      6  2/24/84  8:26:24
```

In the code of figure 23-10, the EXEC issues the CMS command SET CMSTYPE HT immediately prior to the CMS SORT command. This prevents the SORT command from prompting the terminal user to input the sort positions used in sorting the CMS EXEC file. The SET CMSTYPE RT command immediately after the SORT command resumes output to the terminal and is essential if the subsequent CMS TYPE command is to display the sorted output file properly on the terminal user's screen. Use these SET CMSTYPE options to turn terminal output on and off at will from within command procedures.

One other feature of interest in this command procedure is its use of the CMS MAKEBUF and DROPBUF commands. The former creates an additional buffer in the program stack, while the latter eliminates the buffer. It is not necessary to create a new buffer just for the use of this program. However, in complex environments, where another command procedure or program also uses the program stack, these CMS commands help ensure that the procedure only works with its own buffer(s).

CMS commands that aid in controlling the program stack and its buffers are listed in table 23-4.

The REXX QUEUED built-in function also aids in the process of controlling the program stack by returning the number of lines already on the program stack. Use this line from within a REXX program:

```
number  =  queued()
```

and number tells how many entries are already on the program stack. This function helps you determine whether a subsequent read (through PULL or PARSE PULL) reads from the program stack or results in a physical read to the virtual console.

File Processing

The CMS EXECIO command is the basic mechanism through which EXECs perform input and output to and from disk files, the virtual reader, the virtual printer, and the virtual punch.

Figure 23-12 contains a command procedure that writes lines to a disk file, then reads the file and displays its contents on the user's terminal. The figure also shows a sample interaction with the program.

In the code of figure 23-12, this statement:

```
'execio 1 diskw' fn ft a '(string' line
```

writes lines to the disk file. The 1 indicates a single line is written, while the DISKW operand denotes the disk write operation. The fn, ft, and a represent the filename, filetype, and filemode of the disk output file, respectively. Any information following the STRING option (here supplied by the variable line) is treated as an output data string by the EXECIO command. Notice the use of apostrophes to direct REXX where variable substitution is not permitted (as in the unalterable portions of the EXECIO command itself), and where substitution is desired (as in the file name and line of output information).

This procedure statement reads lines from the disk file:

```
'execio 1 diskr' fn ft a
```

Again, the EXECIO command affects a single line of data, this time in a DISKR (disk read) operation. The location of the apostrophes indicates that the filename and filetype are substituted for the parameters fn and ft.

	Command	Function
Table 23-4 CMS Program Stack Buffer Control Commands	MAKEBUF	Create a new buffer within the program stack
	DROPBUF	Eliminate the most recently created buffer from the program stack
	SENTRIES	Determine the number of lines currently in the program stack
	DESBUF	Clear the console and program stack input and output buffers
	CONWAIT	Synchronize input/output to/from the terminal by waiting until all pending terminal I/O completes

Figure 23-12   Command Procedure with EXECIO Command

```
/*  This writes lines you enter to a disk file.  It          */
/*  displays all lines of the file on the terminal.          */
/*                                                            */
/*  Enter:    INOUT   fn  ft                                  */
/*  Example:  INOUT   NEWFILE  DATA                           */
/*                                                            */
/*  If the file exists, data entered is appended to it.       */

arg  fn  ft  .

desbuf  0

/*  Access terminal input lines and write them to the file    */

say  'Enter lines of data, enter a null line when done'
parse  pull  line
do  while  line  ¬=  ''
    'execio  1  diskw'  fn  ft  a  '(string'  line
    if  rc  ¬=  0  then say 'Bad RC on file write:' rc
    parse  pull  line
end

finis  fn  ft  a

/*  Read the file lines and write them to the terminal        */

say  'The following is typed courtesy of EXECIO reads:'
'execio  1  diskr'  fn  ft  a
do  while  rc  =  0
    parse  pull  line
    say  line
    'execio  1  diskr'  fn  ft  a
end

if  rc  ¬=  2  then  say  'Bad RC on file read:' rc

finis  fn  ft  a
exit

R;
inout newfile data
Enter lines of data, enter a null line when done
This is the first line of data.
This is the second line of data.
This is the third and final line of data.
The following is typed courtesy of EXECIO reads:
This is the first line of data.
This is the second line of data.
This is the third and final line of data.
R;
```

Two other aspects of the procedure are worthy of comment. First, notice the use of the CMS **FINIS** command to close the disk file. Use **FINIS** whenever your program needs to close a file. Should you issue this command on a file that is not open, you receive a nonzero return code. Second, this program issues the CMS command **DESBUF** to clear the console stack input and output buffers. You should normally clear these buffers only when you are quite certain as to what you are eliminating, since they communicate information between programs. This procedure includes DESBUF simply for purposes of illustration.

As well as facilitating disk input/output, the CMS EXECIO command can also retrieve replies from CP commands issued from within an EXEC, or suppress messages issued by CP commands. To retrieve replies from CP commands, encode this EXECIO statement:

```
'EXECIO * CP (STRING' cp-command
```

where cp-command is the CP command you want to issue. The CP replies are stacked FIFO in the program stack. As an example, encode:

```
'EXECIO * CP (STRING' QUERY TIME
```

to stack time information. The apostrophes are important because they prevent the command procedure language interpreter from analyzing this statement and concluding that the asterisk implies a REXX multiplication operation.

Suppress messages from CP through specifying 0 lines of CP output information on the EXECIO command:

```
'EXECIO 0 CP (STRING' cp-command
```

As before, cp-command is any CP command.

Figure 23-13 shows an example of a procedure that issues the CP QUERY DASD command and collects its output in the stack. The program uses this information to produce the formatted minidisk analysis shown in the second portion of figure 23-13.

After this task, the procedure issues the CP QUERY TIME command and suppresses its output. This statement achieves this:

```
'execio 0 cp (string' query time
```

with the 0 suppressing the output from the CP command.

Two other features of the procedure require comment. First, notice the use of the CMS MAKEBUF and DROPBUF commands to create (and then eliminate) a new buffer in the program stack for this programs's use. The return code from MAKEBUF is the number of the program stack buffer created. Second, note the use of the REXX built-in function QUEUED to return the number of lines remaining in the program stack. This helps ensure that the program only operates on lines it caused to be placed in the program stack.

Special CMS Commands for EXECs

This chapter demonstrates many CMS commands that are either particularly or primarily useful when employed in command procedures. Table 23-5 lists a few more CMS commands of special interest to those developing command procedures.

Figure 23-13   Command Procedure That Captures CP Command Output

```
/*  This procedure captures output from the CP QUERY DASD   */
/*  command in the program stack.  It displays the disk     */
/*  types and the number of cylinders for each minidisk.    */
/*  It outputs the total number of accessible cylinders.    */
/*  It then issues the CP QUERY TIME command and suppresses */
/*  output from this command.                               */

say 'Disk      Number of'
say 'Type:     Cylinders:'        /* initialize, write headers */
total_cyls  =  0

already_stacked  =  queued()    /* determine stack condition */

makebuf                          /* issue CP QUERY DASD cmd.  */
'execio * cp (string' query dasd


/*  pull CP QUERY DASD output lines from stack and display  */

do  while  queued()  >  already_stacked
    pull dasd vaddr  disk_type  disk_name  access_type  cyls  .
    say  disk_type '           ' cyls
    total_cyls  =  total_cyls  +  cyls
end

say 'Total Number of Cylinders:'  total_cyls


/* issue CP QUERY TIME command and suppress terminal output */

'execio 0 cp (string'  query  time
if  rc  =  0  then
    say  'CP QUERY TIME command issued, output was suppressed'

dropbuf
exit

Disk      Number of
Type:     Cylinders:
3380         30
3380         27
3380         5
3350         50
3380         10
3380         20
3380         30
3350         35
3350         30
Total Number of Cylinders: 237
CP QUERY TIME command issued, output was suppressed
R;
```

Writing EXECs with Style

The CMS command procedure languages, especially REXX, represent a CMS feature that significantly increases productivity. In order to maximize the benefits of using them, consider these simple guidelines in writing command procedures:

Command	Meaning
EXECOS	Cleans up after running OS and VSAM programs (used in EXECs that run more than one OS or VSAM program)
GLOBALV	Saves command procedure variables globally across command procedures and from one invocation to the next
IMMCMD	Establishes or cancels CMS immediate commands from within an EXEC
SET	Options like ABBREV, IMPEX, and IMPCP modify the CMS command search procedure; CMSTYPE controls output to the screen; EXECTRAC controls EXEC tracing

Table 23-5
CMS Commands for Command Procedures

1. Check for error conditions to make your EXECs "leakproof." Always check the return code from CMS and CP commands.

2. Show your program's logical structure with indentation.

3. Some programmers capitalize REXX instruction keywords to distinguish them from the rest of the code.

4. Always document your code. REXX forces you to enter one comment line. If you use several to describe the purpose of every program you write, your procedures become more intelligible. We highly recommend liberal use of commentary as this is so useful and so infrequently done.

5. Don't nest functions too deeply because it renders command procedures unintelligible.

6. Check to see that the user enters appropriate parameters to the EXEC. If not, your procedure should display "HELP" information to the user.

Observance of these simple suggestions greatly increases the utility of the command procedures you write.

For Further Information

For information on CMS commands, look in the *VM/SP CMS Command and Macro Reference, SC19-6209,* under the command name.

See the manuals on the System Product Editor for details and examples of how to write edit macros. These manuals are *VM/SP System Product Editor User's Guide, SC24-5220,* and *VM/SP System Product Editor Command and Macro Reference, SC24-5221.* Also, the *VM/SP System Product Interpreter User's Guide, SC24-5238,* contains a simple tutorial on XEDIT macro writing using REXX.

The *VM/SP CMS User's Guide, SC19-6210,* contains a chapter that demonstrates the CMS commands that have particular importance in command procedures. That chapter illustrates each command with programs written in the REXX language.

The *VM/SP CMS User's Guide, SC19-6210,* also covers many of the concepts presented in this chapter. The manuals on the command procedure languages cited at the conclusion of chapter 21 also illustrate several of these concepts.

Test Your Understanding

When are `PROFILE EXEC` and `PROFILE XEDIT` executed? What are the functions of these two special command procedures? What kinds of tasks does a `PROFILE EXEC` typically perform?

What is the purpose of the console stack and what are its components? What is the order in which CMS attempts to retrieve information from the console stack components?

What's the difference between a stack and a queue? What REXX instructions do you use to employ the program stack in each of these roles? A *dequeue* is a data structure from which you can insert and retrieve data from both ends. How would you implement a dequeue using REXX instructions?

Write a command procedure that creates a `CMS EXEC` consisting of all the files on your A-disk of a particular filetype, and then erases those files through execution of the `CMS EXEC`.

Write a command procedure named `CPSILENT` that issues any CP command you enter and ensures that no output from the CP command displays on your terminal.

Modify the command procedure you wrote in response to the previous question so that it keeps a running log of all CP commands and the corresponding responses in a CMS file.

Write a command procedure that sorts a file of data records on any particular input column. The beginning and ending column numbers for the sort field should be entered with the `EXEC` command, and the procedure should place this information in the stack prior to issuing the CMS `SORT` command.

Write a command procedure that reads lines of text from an input file and copies them to an output file. Translate all lowercase input text into uppercase text in the output file. Use the CMS **EXECIO** command to perform all file input/output.

The messages issued by the CMS **RDR** command are not always intelligible to new CMS users. Write a command procedure that issues the CMS **RDR** command and, based on the return code from the **RDR** command, displays an easy-to-understand interpretation of the **RDR** response on the user's terminal.

Write a general-purpose program stack buffer manipulation **EXEC**. Under the direction of the terminal user, the procedure should create and destroy buffers in the program stack, push and pop lines of terminal input onto/off of the stack, and determine the number of lines currently in the stack. In writing this procedure, you might use the CMS **SENTRIES** command and the REXX **QUEUED** built-in function. Is there a difference between the values these commands return?

SECTION 7

VM/CMS Software

- PROFS, ISPF, IPF, and DMS
- Additional Software Products

CHAPTER 24

PROFS, ISPF, IPF, and DMS

PROFS

The Professional Office System (PROFS) automates the tasks performed in business offices, providing comprehensive computer-based support.

PROFS is a separately licensed application marketed by IBM Corporation, and has become widely popular at VM/CMS mainframe installations. IBM also markets a PC-based PROFS product that ties into the mainframe VM version of the software.

Design

PROFS is designed for use by typical office workers, including managers, secretaries and receptionists, business professionals, technical professionals, executives, and clerical personnel.

PROFS features, such as selection menus, prompting panels, predefined program function keys, easy-to-understand online "help" screens, and user-friendly error messages, orient the system toward use by people with little or no prior computer experience.

PROFS enables office workers to perform typical office tasks more quickly and efficiently, with a minimum of training. It complements traditional office technologies like telephones and internal and external mail services.

Capabilities

PROFS' capabilities facilitate: formal and informal communication; information storage, retrieval, and dissemination; and scheduling.

With PROFS' primary menus, you may:

- process schedules
- open the mail

- search for documents
- process notes and messages
- prepare documents
- process documents from other sources
- process the mail log
- check the outgoing mail
- add an automatic reminder

In processing schedules, PROFS helps you maintain your personal calendar. PROFS assists in arranging meetings more quickly and easily, and it automatically verifies your choice of meeting date and time to ensure that it complements those of the participants you have named. This PROFS function eliminates the telephone calls otherwise required in scheduling meetings.

For incoming mail, PROFS provides an electronic "in-basket." You can select from the letters, notes, memos, and documents in your "in-basket" to process them in whatever order you wish. This PROFS function eliminates unnecessary paper in the office through a complete *electronic mail* system.

PROFS's ability to search for documents simulates an electronic filing cabinet. Since PROFS works with documents in electronic form, you can search for documents using a variety of criteria. These include the unique number PROFS assigns each document, the author of the document, its date, the subject, and the person to whom the document was sent. PROFS's document search capability cuts down on the need to file and index paper documents manually.

PROFS's ability to process notes and messages means that you can send and receive notes and messages to and from other PROFS users, a form of electronic mail. It reduces the dependency on traditional sources of communication such as telephones and company mail services.

PROFS's document preparation feature is based on the XEDIT editor program described earlier in this book. PROFS bundles extra features along with XEDIT, including spelling verification, a spelling aid, a word usage aid, a synonym aid, an awkward phrase detector, and a phrase aid. These enable you to write more clearly, accurately, and concisely. PROFS harnesses computer power to provide you with a personal proofreader.

PROFS's mail log is a chronological record of all documents that you have sent, received, or otherwise filed. It keeps track of your incoming and outgoing mail. The mail log function replaces the manual control of your mail in a traditional office.

Finally, PROFS can send you an automatic reminder for meetings or other important tasks. You tell PROFS the date and time of a future event and the system automatically reminds you of that event. Of course, you have to be logged onto PROFS in order to receive the reminder. This PROFS function provides a useful adjunct to the PROFS calendaring and scheduling features.

Summary

PROFS represents one of IBM's premier office automation products. It supplements (and to some extent replaces) traditional office technologies for communication and information storage and retrieval. PROFS is a strategic IBM office product and the company has recently released products that allow personal computers to participate in VM/CMS-based PROFS systems.

ISPF

The Interactive System Productivity Facility (ISPF) is an IBM program product designed to aid application developers in creating interactive applications. It enables programmers to develop full-screen applications that have the sophisticated features one associates with carefully designed on-line systems in much less time than might otherwise be required.

Services

Applications developers create *dialogs* through ISPF. A dialog is a system of programs and predefined display screens put together so as to present the terminal user with a meaningful sequence of screens in order to accomplish work. User-developed dialogs run under control of ISPF, so ISPF represents a *dialog manager*. ISPF is therefore sometimes referred to as the ISPF Dialog Manager or the Dialog Manager, as well as ISPF.

Since dialogs run under control of the ISPF Dialog Manager, programs in the dialogs make use of a wide variety of ISPF services, invoking them through the CALL facility of the programming language. The following list includes ISPF services accessible from dialog programs.

Display services. These permit full-screen presentation of information to the dialog user as well as full-screen data entry. Display services include automatic input editing of user-entered data.

Variable services. ISPF includes a comprehensive capability for handling variables from within user-developed dialogs. For example, dialogs can associate variables with particular terminal users, save such information across terminal sessions, and retrieve system-provided environmental information.

Message services. Dialogs use these services to display context-sensitive informational and error messages to users. ISPF also supports a complete system of "help" and tutorial screens accessible from within user dialogs.

Table services. Dialogs can direct ISPF to store data within two-dimensional tables. This data can be stored permanently on disk and is accessible to other dialogs.

File tailoring services. These services allow dialogs to tailor input "skeleton" files dynamically by substituting dialog variables into appropriate places within those files. Tailored output is thus produced, for example, to create batch jobs dynamically for submission to the batch virtual machine facility.

Library access services. These services permit access to and management of datasets managed through ISPF.

Miscellaneous services. ISPF supplies a wide variety of miscellaneous services, including, for example, dialog-transparent "split screen" capability, a log file of ISPF and dialog messages, and access to editor programs from within dialog programs.

Creating Dialogs

Developing ISPF dialogs requires creating various dialog components and placing them into ISPF-accessible libraries. Creating a dialog involves developing *dialog functions, dialog panels, dialog messages,* and *file tailoring skeletons.*

Dialog functions, or programs, represent the logic and processing of the dialog. These may be written in almost any programming language, including COBOL, FORTRAN, PL/I, Pascal, APL, and others. Remember that it is through a **CALL** from these programs that dialogs invoke the ISPF services listed above. ISPF also supports the CMS command languages REXX and EXEC2.

Dialog panels, or screen display definitions, are defined in a simple panel definition language unique to ISPF for display of information to the dialog user, for data entry, for selection of a processing option in the case of a menu panel, or for display of "help" or tutorial information in the case of an ISPF tutorial system panel.

Dialog messages are the messages that display to the dialog user through ISPF's message services. Like ISPF panels, they are written in a simple notation unique to ISPF.

File tailoring skeletons are processed via ISPF's file tailoring services to tailor output files dynamically. These output files can be used for a variety of purposes: one common use is to create background jobs dynamically which are then submitted to the batch machine facility.

If you have installed a separately purchased IBM program product, ISPF/PDF, you have complete dialog development and testing facilities available through ISPF/PDF.

Summary

In summary, ISPF enables programmers to develop sophisticated online dialogs using a wide variety of ISPF services. Programmers develop applications with ISPF in a fraction of the time previously required.

It is IBM's stated direction to expand ISPF as the common dialog manager for all new and existing products wherever feasible. At the time of writing, over 70 IBM program products and 65 software products from independent vendors utilize ISPF as their dialog manager.

ISPF's strategic role as a program development tool is underscored by the fact that it is a *cross system product*. That is, ISPF is also available under IBM's other strategic operating systems including MVS/TSO, DOS/VSE, SSX/VSE, VM/PC, and PC-DOS (in an adapted form called the EZ-VU Development Facility). This leads to many advantages to program development with ISPF, including the transferability of programmer skills across operating systems and the transportability of code written in compiled programming languages. ISPF occupies a central role in IBM's software strategies, and is widely used for program development under VM/CMS.

ISPF/PDF

The Interactive System Productivity Facility/Program Development Facility (ISPF/PDF) is an IBM program product designed to aid programmers in the design, debugging, and testing of programs; the editing of files; and the performance of operating system tasks. ISPF/PDF is a menu-driven interface to CMS. It allows you to issue many CMS commands and perform the same functions you would under CMS, but to do so through a series of explanatory menus. Also, ISPF/PDF contains a complete set of tutorial or "help" menus that are accessible at any time merely by issuing the ISPF HELP command, or by pressing a program function key that issues this command (normally PF1). ISPF/PDF thus represents a programmer-friendly menu interface built on top of CMS.

Like PROFS and ISPF, ISPF/PDF runs as an application under CMS. PROFS, ISPF, and ISPF/PDF are all separately purchased IBM program products.

Functions

Figure 24-1 shows what the ISPF/PDF master menu looks like. The menu at your site may look slightly different, since installations often tailor this menu to meet their own requirements. Figure 24-1 shows those functions minimally accessible from ISPF/PDF.

You reach the ISPF/PDF master menu by entering ISPF or PDF to CMS. (Some installations tailor their products so that you enter them through locally written command procedures. Contact your system administrator for the command through which you access the product in this case.)

Figure 24-1 indicates that you browse files by selecting menu option 1, and edit them by selection menu option 2. From ISPF/PDF, you can use either the XEDIT editor or ISPF's own editor. The ISPF editor is functionally equivalent to XEDIT and is the main editor used under the MVS/TSO operating system. It has different editor commands than XEDIT.

The ISPF/PDF option for "Utilities" permits the user to perform such tasks as copying files, moving files, and displaying information about files. Thus, ISPF/PDF issues CMS commands on your behalf as you direct it through the task-oriented, menu interface.

The next two options in figure 24-1 allow you to compile and link edit programs in foreground or through the CMS batch virtual machine facility.

Figure 24-1   The ISPF/PDF Primary Option Menu

```
-------------------- ISPF/PDF PRIMARY OPTION PANEL --------------------
OPTION ===>
                                               USERID   - ZHMF01
   0  ISPF PARMS   - Specify terminal and user parameters   TIME     - 07:37
   1  BROWSE       - Display source data or output listings  TERMINAL - 3278
   2  EDIT         - Create or change source data    PF KEYS  - 24
   3  UTILITIES    - Perform utility functions
   4  FOREGROUND   - Invoke language processors in foreground
   5  BATCH        - Submit to batch for language processing
   6  COMMAND      - Enter CMS command or EXEC
   7  DIALOG TEST  - Perform dialog testing
   8  LM UTILITIES- Perform library management utility functions
   T  TUTORIAL     - Display information about ISPF/PDF
   X  EXIT         - Terminate using console, log, and list defaults


Enter END command to terminate ISPF.
```

The programs may be written in any of several programming languages, depending on which are installed on your system. Again, the options represent an alternative to issuing the CMS commands directly to perform these tasks.

The "Command" option enables you to enter CMS commands directly from within ISPF/PDF. This is useful because it is faster and more convenient than exiting and re-entering ISPF/PDF when you want to issue CMS commands.

The "Dialog Test" option contains a complete facility for the development and testing of ISPF dialogs. This option helps you trace dialog execution, conditionally write messages to the ISPF log, set breakpoints at which dialog execution is temporarily suspended, and inspect the value of dialog variables during dialog execution. You can also test dialog panels, functions, and messages. Dialog Test is a comprehensive and effective facility in interactively developing ISPF dialogs.

Lastly, the "Tutorial" option of figure 24-1 contains a complete system of tutorial panels on the use of ISPF/PDF. These may be accessed from anywhere within ISPF/PDF to provide context-appropriate "help" information, or they may be read sequentially as a self-contained tutorial system. The tutorial system is effective in that you rarely need to look up ISPF/PDF information in the product manuals since the tutorial system supplies the same information online.

In addition to these menu options, many installations bundle other functions on the ISPF/PDF master menu or a submenu. In this way, these sites provide easy, menu-oriented access to local utilities and other program products they may have installed.

Summary

ISPF/PDF is an ISPF dialog vended by IBM. Its use requires installation of ISPF.

Like ISPF, ISPF/PDF is available under IBM's other strategic operating systems including MVS/TSO, DOS/VSE, SSX/VSE, VM/PC, and PC-DOS (in the adapted form called the EZ-VU Editor). For this reason, ISPF/PDF is considered a *shell;* that is, a program product which surrounds the operating system and gives it a new software personality. Using ISPF/PDF under CMS renders the use of CMS quite similar to MVS/TSO, for example, where one uses ISPF/PDF with TSO. Thus, ISPF/PDF along with ISPF renders IBM's various mainframe operating systems similar to terminal users. Together, ISPF and ISPF/PDF provide such advantages as transferability of user and programmer skills across operating systems, code transportability, and a common program development interface. For these reasons, both products have become de facto standards in the marketplace.

IPF

The VM/Interactive Productivity Facility (IPF) is a menu-driven facility which allows users to interact with CMS and issue CMS commands through full-screen panels. Like ISPF/PDF, IPF allows users to forego direct interaction with CMS and instead take advantage of full-screen displays in performing common operating system tasks.

Applications

Similar to ISPF/PDF, entry to IPF is accomplished by a single command to CMS. You enter this command yourself, or it may be issued for you as part of the logon procedure.

Once in IPF, the panels you see and the work that can be accomplished depend on your IPF-recognized user class. IPF addresses three classes of users:

general VM/CMS users

VM/SP system administrators

VM/SP system operators

Each class of user interacts with a set of IPF panels designed to accomplish work appropriate to that class. In all cases, IPF makes full use of program function keys, menu-driven selections, and a full tutorial system of "help" panels. IPF is similar to ISPF/PDF in these design characteristics, since both products are actually ISPF-based dialogs.

A unique feature of IPF is its Problem Control Facility (PCF). PCF panels permit online entry of problem reports concerning the VM/CMS system. Problem reports are automatically generated and routed to the appropriate person within the system.

Comparison of IPF and ISPF/PDF

IPF is similar in many ways to ISPF/PDF. Both act as front-ends to CMS in the form of menu-driven dialogs. This renders CMS simpler to use because the user does not have to remember CMS commands or their formats. IPF and ISPF/PDF embody similar design characteristics because both are ISPF dialogs.

One major difference between IPF and ISPF/PDF is that IPF is specifically designed for the VM/CMS environment. IPF does not run under other operating systems. ISPF/PDF, on the other hand, is a cross system product designed to run under a wide variety of operating systems.

IPF is therefore more tailored to CMS users, particularly for system operators and system administrators. ISPF/PDF provides the advantages of a cross system product (such as applicability of the acquired skills across operating systems). It also enjoys a strategic role among IBM software products.

Another major difference between IPF and ISPF/PDF is in their intended audiences. IPF serves general CMS users, VM/SP system administrators, and system operators; ISPF/PDF is a programmer's development facility. While these categories of users are not mutually exclusive, the result is that the two products exhibit some differences in their design and functionality.

In the final analysis, IPF and ISPF/PDF are similar products in many ways. Nonetheless, their differences in design criteria give each a slightly different role within the VM/CMS environment.

DMS

Display Management System (DMS) for CMS is a programmer tool that allows you to define full-screen displays easily for terminal input/output. DMS enables your programs to take advantage of mainframe full-screen terminals. DMS is designed so that you quickly define screens used by your programs through a simple "screen painting" technique.

Applications

DMS functions group into three basic categories:

- interactive panel formatting
- panel management from compiled and interpreted programming languages
- "write full-screen" capability for assembler language programs

Interactive panel formatting means that you use DMS to design interactively your screens, called *panels,* under DMS. You enter the CMS command:

PANEL

to enter the DMS panel formatter selection screen. (Some installations tailor their products so that you enter them through locally written command procedures. Contact your system administrator for the command through which you access the product in this case.)

Once in DMS, you assign the panel you wish to design a name and identify the terminal device type and screen size for which it is created. At this point, you access the panel "layout format" screen by pressing a PF key. This screen looks similar to that shown in figure 24-2. Using this screen, you design a panel such as the sample illustrated in figure 24-3. As demonstrated in that diagram, DMS employs a simple set of attribute characters which define how each field in the panel layout format is to be treated. DMS also has a set of editing commands which help in designing the panel layout. Throughout the panel definition process, a program function key gives access to a DMS context-sensitive "help" function.

Figure 24-2 DMS Panel Layout Format Screen

```
            1    5   10   15   20   25   30   35   40   45   50   55   60   65   70
            !...!....!....!....!....!....!....!....!....!....!....!....!....!....!....!
  1 - :  _
  2 - :
  3 - :
  4 - :
  5 - :
  6 - :
  7 - :
  8 - :
  9 - :
 10 - :
 11 - :
 12 - :
 13 - :
 14 - :
 15 - :
 16 - :
 17 - :
 18 - :
 19 - :
 20 - :
 21 - :
 22 - :
 23 - :
 24 - :


    ===>                         PF7-HELP   PF8-MENU
DELIMITERS: TEXT= ¬ OR ! , DATA= _ , SELECT= %      FILL: BLANK= @ , NULL= #
```

When you have finished designing your panel layout format, you view this screen by entering the DMS DISPLAY command. Figure 24-4 shows how the panel of figure 24-3 appears.

Pressing PF keys allows you to alter the default formats (or attribute characters) for fields within the panel definition.

After you finish the panel layout and field definition processes, you save the panel you have created. This panel definition is now usable for full-screen data input and output from within programs you write.

Figure 24-3   Defining a DMS Panel

```
           1   5   10   15   20   25   30   35   40   45   50   55   60   65   70
           !...!....!....!....!....!....!....!....!....!....!....!....!....!....!....!
  1 - :          !THIS IS A DMS EXAMPLE PANEL DEFINITION
  2 - :
  3 - :
  4 - :          ¬EMPLOYEE...........@@@@@@@@@@@@@@@@@@@@@@
  5 - :
  6 - :          ¬STATUS.............@@@@@@
  7 - :
  8 - :          ¬EMPLOYEE NUMBER...._@@@@@@@@_
  9 - :
 10 - :
 11 - :
 12 - :
 13 - :
 14 - :
 15 - :
 16 - :
 17 - :
 18 - :
 19 - :
 20 - :
 21 - :
 22 - :
 23 - :
 24 - :

    ===>                              PF7-HELP   PF8-MENU
DELIMITERS: TEXT= ¬ OR ! , DATA= _ , SELECT= %      FILL: BLANK= @ , NULL= #
```

Figure 24-4   DMS Panel Display

```
THIS IS A DMS EXAMPLE PANEL DEFINITION

EMPLOYEE........... _

STATUS.............

EMPLOYEE NUMBER....
```

The *panel management* function of DMS refers to your ability to use the panel layout format you have defined from your programs. Programs display DMS panels and use them for terminal input/output through a standard CALL to the DMS interface routine. With DMS, programs perform such panel management functions as sounding the terminal alarm, controlling the cursor, reading data from panel input, moving data to the terminal for display, and displaying messages at the bottom of panels.

DMS supports a variety of programming languages including COBOL, PL/I, RPGII, and assembler language. You can also use panels through command procedure languages like REXX and EXEC2.

Programs refer to DMS panels through a CALL to the DMS panel management routine. Use of DMS requires you to issue appropriate CMS `GLOBAL` commands to reference the DMS product libraries.

Finally, the *write full-screen* function of DMS enables your assembler language programs to request the basic full screen I/O communication used by DMS directly through an assembler language macro.

Comparison of DMS and ISPF

DMS provides a facility for program screen handling that is similar to that offered by ISPF. However, DMS is a much more narrowly targeted product. It functionally duplicates only ISPF's display services: it does not provide any of the other ISPF services.

Another difference between DMS and ISPF is that, whereas ISPF uses its own, code-oriented panel definition language, DMS users define panels interactively. DMS's pictorial approach to screen design is variously called *screen painting* or *WYSIWYG* (What You See Is What You Get).

Earlier, ISPF was described as IBM's cross system product for screen management. It is available for all strategic IBM operating systems and it interfaces with all major programming languages. This leads to advantages such as the wider applicability of programmer skills across operating systems and programming languages, as well as IBM's special designation of ISPF as its strategic dialog manager. In contrast, DMS runs only under CMS. DMS represents a narrowly targeted product that only supports panel management for user-written CMS programs.

For Further Information

The manual, *VM/SP Introduction,* briefly describes the nature and purposes of PROFS, as well as many of the other program products discussed in this section of this book. The order numbers for this manual depend on your version of VM/SP. Refer to chapter 8 for a list of the order numbers for this manual. The manual, *Using the Professional Office System, SH20-6797,* contains a complete tutorial that includes examples and pictures of how the PROFS panel appears to the user.

The book, *Using IBM's ISPF Dialog Manager,* by H. Fosdick (Van Nostrand Reinhold, 1987) provides a comprehensive introduction to the use of ISPF. It includes complete programming examples in COBOL. The newsletter of the GUIDE ISPF Project tracks the number of software products that employ ISPF as their product manager. The manual, *ISPF and ISPF/PDF General Information, GC34-4036,* describes the purpose and functions of ISPF and ISPF/PDF on an overview level. *ISPF Dialog Management Services, SC34-4010,* is the basic programmer's reference manual for ISPF. (The manual set for the ISPF and ISPF/PDF products is under revision. Manual numbers may be changed.)

The manual, *VM/IPF General Use Guide, SC24-5233,* describes interaction with IPF and use of this product from the viewpoint of the IPF general user. System operators and system administrators locate the equivalent information for their use of IPF in the manuals, *VM/IPF Operation, SC24-5229,* and *VM/IPF Administration Guide, SC24-5230,* respectively.

Further information on DMS is found in the manual, *DMS/CMS Guide and Reference, SC24-5198.* This single manual includes all the information necessary to the understanding and use of this product.

Test Your Understanding

Who are the potential users of PROFS? What basic office functions does PROFS provide?

What is a dialog? What is a dialog manager? What groups of services does the ISPF Dialog Manager provide user programs?

What dialog components do you develop when writing an ISPF dialog?

Describe the advantages of developing online applications with a cross system product like ISPF.

What is the basic purpose of ISPF/PDF? What is the relationship between ISPF/PDF and ISPF?

What is the function of IPF? For what classes of users is IPF designed? What are the major similarities and differences between IPF and ISPF/PDF?

What are the three basic functions of DMS for CMS? What is the major advantage of screen design with DMS versus ISPF? What are the advantages of ISPF versus DMS?

Of the program products described in this chapter (PROFS, ISPF, ISPF/PDF, IPF, DMS) which are designed for end-users and which represent development tools for programmers?

CHAPTER 25

Additional Software Products

IFS

VM/Interactive File Sharing (IFS) is a separately purchased program product designed to support commercial interactive data processing. IFS permits multiple users concurrent write access to the shared data which it controls. IFS stores its data within VSAM data sets. It represents a separate shared data VSAM product which provides VSAM support above and beyond that included in the VM/SP license as part of CMS.

IFS is one of the record-processing systems for shared access to data mentioned in chapter 13. IFS's advantage in controlling shared access to data over that possible through the CP `LINK` and CMS `ACCESS` commands is that it manages shared data access to ensure data integrity in cases of concurrent update. IFS can do this because it runs in its own virtual machine.

IFS's locks operate on the *record level*. When one program locks a record for update, other programs can write-access any other record in that file. Other programs can also read-access the record locked for update. However, IFS prevents two programs from updating the same record at the same time. IFS thereby ensures data integrity.

Data Manager

IFS runs in its own virtual machine. The IFS *data administrator* or *data manager* has responsibility for starting and administering the IFS virtual machine and the shared files it controls. The data manager handles these tasks through a small group of IFS commands and subcommands. The IFS subcommands logically divide into two groups: those for *system control* and those for *file management*.

The system control subcommands help the data manager control the IFS virtual machine. These five subcommands also permit the data manager to control authorization of users and application programs in their access to specific shared IFS VSAM files.

The file management subcommands allow the data manager to control the creation and maintenance of the underlying KSDS VSAM (indexed) files and their data spaces. There are 18 file management subcommands and they are based on VSE/VSAM. Table 25-1 lists the IFS file management subcommands.

Table 25-1
IFS File Management Subcommands

Subcommand	Function
AIX	Creates a VSAM alternate index on a file
ALTERSEC	Updates file passwords
DEFINE	Defines a file
DEFLOAD	Combines DEFINE and LOAD subcommands
DELETE	Deletes a file
DETACH	Removes a volume from VSAM space management
DISPLAY	Displays file passwords
DUMP	Dumps catalog entries and data in recovery area
EXPORT	Transfers catalog entries and file to disk/tape
IMPORT	Transfers catalog entries and file from disk/tape
LISTCAT	Lists contents of VSAM master catalog
LISTVOL	Prints or transfers catalog recovery area data
LOAD	Loads disk/tape file into IFS VSAM file
PRINT	Prints IFS VSAM file
RENAME	Changes file name
RESTORE	Restores catalog entries from previous DUMP command
UNLOAD	Creates disk/tape file from IFS VSAM file
VERIFY	Updates master catalog to reflect file status

Issuing the IFS command engages the data manager in an interactive script. This dialog assists data managers in their definition and maintenance of the IFS VSAM files by prompting for AMS parameter values. IFS thus presents a user-friendly front-end to AMS. This interaction is line-oriented (rather than full-screen).

Program Development

The role of the data manager is: to activate, prepare, and control the IFS virtual machine; to create and maintain VSAM file definitions for the shared VSAM files on that virtual machine; and to authorize users and programs for access to specific shared files on that virtual machine. It is the role of applications programmers to develop programs in programming languages such as COBOL, PL/I, RPG II, and assembler language that access the shared data on the IFS virtual machine. These programs provide appropriate functionality to end users in their manipulations of the shared data.

Figure 25-1 diagrams the IFS system. It shows that the IFS virtual machine is administered by the IFS data manager, who issues IFS commands and subcommands to control the virtual machine and its shared VSAM files. The *IFS File Maintenance System* is that part of IFS that provides the simplified interface to AMS. AMS and VSAM control the shared files on this virtual machine.

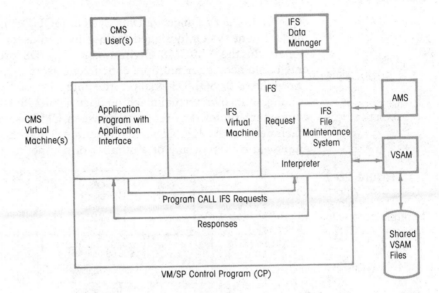

Figure 25-1
Diagram of IFS
System

Figure 25-1 also shows that programs access the shared VSAM files on the IFS virtual machine through a standard **CALL** to an application interface. As a result of this **CALL**, a request for an IFS service is shipped through VM/SP's CP component to the IFS virtual machine. The *IFS Request Interpreter* takes the appropriate action against the shared IFS VSAM files. The Request Interpreter services program requests with record locking and security checking. After IFS has taken appropriate action, it sends a response back to the application program.

In the encoding of the application program, communication with IFS occurs through a program communications block (PCB), the record I/O area, and a two-byte status code returned by IFS. A program **CALL** to IFS appears similar to a DL/I (or IMS) program **CALL**, with segment search arguments (SSA) specifying search keys. Valid **CALL** function requests are also similar to those used by DL/I and include **GHN** (Get Hold Next), **GHU** (Get Hold Unique), **GN** (Get Next), **GU** (Get Unique), **ISRT** (Insert), **DLET** (Delete), and **REPL** (Replace).

Summary

IFS represents one of a number of separately purchased program products that addresses CMS's shared data access restrictions for programmed applications. For meeting these requirements, most installations choose full-fledged DBMSs over IFS, which offer additional functionality in the areas of data backup and recovery, interrecord relationships, data integrity, and database security.

SQL/DS

Structured Query Language/Data System (SQL/DS) is a relational database management system designed for use by end-users and computer professionals. In the VM/CMS environment, SQL/DS provides for record-oriented data access for multiple concurrent users.

Like IFS, SQL/DS ensures the integrity of the data it controls by running in its own virtual machine. Figure 25-2 illustrates how VM/SP's CP component routes data requests between CMS users in their own virtual machines and the SQL/DS virtual machine. This scheme is the same as that employed by IFS or any of a number of competing DBMS products.

Figure 25-2
CMS Virtual
Machines
Communicate with
SQL/DS

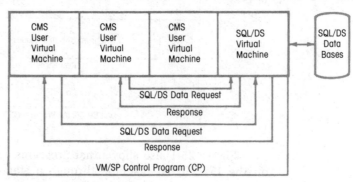

SQL and Relational DBMS

As a *relational DBMS*, SQL/DS stores all data in two-dimensional tables, a simple row and column format, as shown in the example table in figure 25-3.

Figure 25-3
An Example
SQL/DS Table
Named
EMP__TABLE

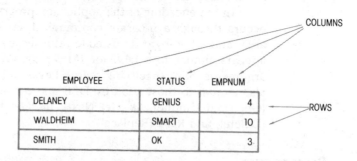

Structured Query Language manipulates data within SQL/DS tables. Among its many features, three deserve special note. First, SQL is exceedingly simple to learn and to use. Second, a single SQL statement can manipulate groups of records, rather than merely a single record. Third, the same SQL language is used interactively, or from within programs written in languages like COBOL, PL/I, and FORTRAN. Use of SQL from within programs is called *embedded SQL*.

Here are samples of the four basic SQL statements to query, insert, delete, and update records:

```
SELECT  *  FROM  EMP_TABLE  ;
INSERT  INTO  EMP_TABLE  VALUES('NEWGUY','OK',2)  ;
DELETE  FROM  EMP_TABLE  WHERE  EMPNUM = 3  ;
UPDATE  EMP_TABLE  SET  STATUS = 'FIRED'  WHERE  STATUS = 'OK'  ;
```

These four SQL commands represent the entire SQL data manipulation language. Each operates on zero, one, or more rows of information in a table. The statements can be embedded directly into the code of application programs written in traditional programming languages, or they can be interactively issued against the databases through the SQL/DS facility called Interactive SQL (ISQL).

The SQL language also encompasses complete facilities for relational DBMS definition and administration. Use these commands to perform such functions as creating and dropping tables, indexes, and logical tables (called *views*).

The SQL language further includes facilities for security authorization, database administration, database recovery, and operations control. All of these features are implemented as an integrated part of the SQL language.

SQL/DS's collection of internal tables called the *catalog* is accessible via the same SQL language. Depending on your security authorization, you can interrogate the catalog tables to find out almost anything about the SQL/DS system. The SQL/DS catalog represents an active data dictionary.

A few SQL commands are only useful from within application programs. You use these commands when manipulating a set of records from within programs.

Finally, ISQL includes another group of commands. These enable you to make better use of the ISQL interface. For example, with ISQL commands you can store an SQL command for later use. You can also format query results to your own output specification. ISQL commands provide the flexibility of human interface required when issuing SQL commands online.

The DBS Utility

The Data Base Services (DBS) Utility is an application program provided as part of the SQL/DS program product. Normally run as a batch program, it performs two important services. First, it allows you to execute SQL commands in batch mode. Second, it is the most convenient way to run database utilities to load, unload, reload, backup, and recover SQL/DS tables. SQL/DS provides complete transaction-oriented database management facilities for data backup, recovery, and logging. Capabilities such as these distinguish a true database management system from an indexed file manager such as IFS.

QMF

The Query Management Facility (QMF) is a separately purchased program product that provides an end-user interface to SQL/DS databases. The QMF interface allows you to interact with SQL/DS either through the SQL language or through the Query-By-Example (QBE) facility.

The QBE interface is graphically oriented. In order to use it, access QMF by issuing a single command to CMS. (At most installations you enter **QMF.**) Then press a PF key to enter the QBE query panel. Once in the query panel, you enter the QBE **DRAW** command to request that QBE display a skeletal table. Assuming a table with data such as that contained in figure 25-3, this command is entered as shown in figure 25-4. Figure 25-5 pictures the skeletal table QBE displays in response to the **DRAW** command. Now, you enter QBE commands directly into the table in order to request a report. Figure 25-6 illustrates entry of QBE commands such as **p.** (to include a column in the query report) and **ao.** (to sort the report in ascending order on the indicated column) into the skeletal table. This query results in the report depicted by figure 25-7.

Figure 25-4   The Query-By-Example Query Panel

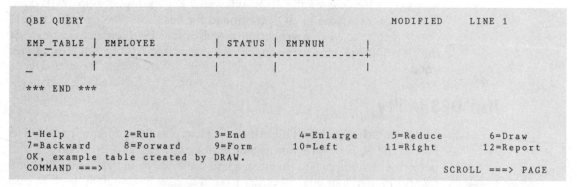

```
QBE QUERY                                                        LINE 1

*** END ***



1=Help          2=Run          3=End         4=Enlarge      5=Reduce        6=Draw
7=Backward      8=Forward      9=Form        10=Left        11=Right        12=Report
OK, QUERY is displayed.
COMMAND ===> draw emp_table_                              SCROLL ===> PAGE
```

Figure 25-5   A Query-By-Example Skeletal Query Table

```
QBE QUERY                                          MODIFIED    LINE 1

EMP_TABLE | EMPLOYEE            | STATUS | EMPNUM         |
----------+--------------------+--------+----------------+
   _      |                    |        |                |

*** END ***



1=Help          2=Run          3=End         4=Enlarge      5=Reduce        6=Draw
7=Backward      8=Forward      9=Form        10=Left        11=Right        12=Report
OK, example table created by DRAW.
COMMAND ===>                                              SCROLL ===> PAGE
```

QMF, then, offers a choice of two languages for working with SQL/DS tables. SQL and QBE are nonprocedural, fourth generation languages that support full query, reporting, and update capability on SQL/DS databases.

Figure 25-6   Entering the Query-By-Example Query

```
QBE QUERY                                               MODIFIED     LINE 1

EMP_TABLE | EMPLOYEE           | STATUS | EMPNUM       |
----------+-------------------+--------+--------------+
          | p.ao.             | p.     | p._          |

*** END ***




1=Help          2=Run          3=End        4=Enlarge    5=Reduce      6=Draw
7=Backward      8=Forward      9=Form       10=Left      11=Right      12=Report
OK, example table created by DRAW.
COMMAND ===>                                            SCROLL ===> PAGE
```

Figure 25-7   Query-By-Example Query Result

```
REPORT                                          LINE 1       POS 1     79

  EMPLOYEE               STATUS      EMPNUM
++--------------------++-------++-----------+++++++++++++++++++++++++++++++++++++


  EMPLOYEE               STATUS      EMPNUM
  --------------------   ------      -----------
  DELANEY                GENIUS          4
  SMITH                  OK              3
  WALDHEIM               SMART          10


*** END ***




1=Help          2=             3=End        4=Print      5=           6=Query
7=Backward      8=Forward      9=Form       10=Left      11=Right     12=
OK, this is the REPORT from your RUN command.
COMMAND ===> _                                          SCROLL ===> PAGE
```

Summary

SQL/DS is a full-fledged relational database management system that brings the benefits of DBMS to VM/CMS. These benefits include the high productivity possible through the use of nonprocedural languages like SQL, the graphic interface of QBE, and the underlying relational data model. As a DBMS, SQL/DS offers advantages over traditional file management in the areas of security, data backup and recovery, space management, and data integrity.

SQL/DS is the most popular of a large group of database management systems such as RAMIS, FOCUS, INQUIRE, ADABAS, ORACLE, and NO-MAD2, available for VM/CMS systems in the 1980s. These products are significant because of their high-productivity, fourth generation, database languages. However, their greatest impact on the VM world is that they bring true transaction-oriented processing to the VM/CMS environment. This processing requires applications to share data across different CMS virtual machines with full-featured data backup and recovery. These database products compose the key component in the evolution of VM /CMS into an operating system capable of supporting production transaction processing systems.

VM/Pass-Through

The VM/Pass-Through Facility implements a simple form of networking for VM (and other) systems. VM/Pass-Through allows you to log onto and use another computer defined in the network as though your terminal were directly attached to that computer. An important feature of Pass-Through is its transparency to existing programs. Thus, you use programs remotely, via Pass-Through, without any changes either in the programs or your interaction with them.

VM/Pass-Through can be considered a simple, transparent, terminal switching mechanism. Pass-Through provides users full access to any VM /CMS systems in the network. It also allows users to access non-VM systems (like OS and DOS systems running products like IMS and CICS) as "terminal nodes" in the network because Pass-Through will not run on these operating systems. Figure 25-8 illustrates how you access other nodes in the network via Pass-Through. While you are physically connected to a VM/CMS computer in Chicago, you can access machines in Denver, Houston, and Austin as well (assuming each runs VM/Pass-Through). You can also access the OS-based system in Dallas; you cannot "pass-through" the Dallas node to other computers since it is not a VM/CMS machine.

Figure 25-8
Accessing Other
Systems through
VM/Pass-Through

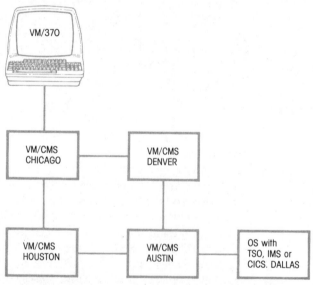

Pass-Through does not support other networking features, such as electronic messaging, file transfer, or remote batch job submission. Sites typically use RSCS for these functions within VM/CMS environments.

IBM's SNA also embodies a higher level of network functionality than Pass-Through.

VM/Pass-Through runs in a CMS virtual machine on each VM/CMS computer participating in the network. Each Pass-Through virtual machine contains a network directory called the *configuration file*. The configuration file gives Pass-Through the necessary information for supporting the routing function. Users may access Pass-Through either through CMS or directly under CP.

GDDM

Graphical Display Data Manager (GDDM) is a separately purchased program product that supports other IBM program products in their graphics output. These graphics may be produced for terminal display or printing. GDDM also supports applications that require a mixture of graphic and alphanumeric information. GDDM is a graphics access method for general use under VM/CMS.

GDDM includes three interactive utilities that aid in producing charts and symbols. The *Interactive Chart Utility* is a tool for the design of various kinds of charts, such as bar graphs and line charts. The *Image Symbol Editor* enables users to add symbols of their own definition to existing character sets. Using the Image Symbol Editor, you define new symbols by specifying dot positions within a matrix that represents an oversized version of the new symbol. The *Vector Symbol Editor* allows you to define vectorized symbols by specifying vector end points.

GDDM can also be used as a graphics access method from application programs encoded in such languages as COBOL, PL/I, FORTRAN, BASIC, APL, and assembler language. GDDM's *Interactive Map Definition* feature aids in screen design for user-developed programs.

Like ISPF, GDDM is a cross system product. Its availability under a wide variety of operating systems gives it an important role as a basic graphics product for VM/CMS.

CICS for CMS

Customer Information Control System (CICS) is one of IBM's premier program products for transaction processing. IBM recently introduced a version of the product for VM/CMS systems.

The CICS product for VM/CMS is currently a development facility. This means that programmers can use the extensive array of CMS development tools in designing and developing CICS applications for production execution under other operating systems. CMS's heavily interactive nature provides major benefits in developing CICS applications. In addition, the program isolation feature inherent in the virtual machine concept prevents a single programmer from bringing down an entire CICS test region. This lack of program isolation is a problem on many CICS systems that the VM

/CMS version overcomes. Finally, the CICS/CMS facility provides an appropriate testing interface to DL/I, IMS, and VSAM data.

An especially significant aspect of the product is that it runs under the personal computer version of VM/CMS, VM/PC. Availability of the CICS development facility on the VM/PC personal computer is significant because it opens up a new world of programmer workstations, offering much better response times than available on mainframe computers while simultaneously offloading excessive work from the mainframe. This portends a new and expanding role for the VM/CMS operating system on personal computers.

CSP

Cross System Product (CSP) is an application generator available under VM/CMS as well as many other IBM operating systems. It enables application developers to create applications in a fraction of the time and effort required when programming in third generation programming languages like COBOL or PL/I. The goal of CSP is to reduce application development time and cost.

CSP presents programmers with a series of screens containing options and fill-in-the-blank questions. Within this design structure and its specialized language, programmers generate applications.

CSP consists of three components: CSP/Application Development (CSP/AD), CSP/Application Execution (CSP/AE), and CSP/Query. CSP/AD is the interactive application generator through which you define, test, and generate application programs, while CSP/AE executes those programs within the production environment. CSP/Query provides a query and report capability for users with little or no experience in data processing.

CSP is important to VM/CMS users for two reasons. First, it is a strategic application generator product for IBM. Second, CSP offers extensive cross system compatibility and portability. CSP brings together IBM hardware as diverse as the 4300, 9370, 3000, and 8100 series of processors, and operating systems and subsystems as diverse as VM/CMS, MVS/TSO, DOS/VSE, SSX/VSE, CICS/DOS/VSE, CICS/OS/VS, DOS/VS, DMS/DPCX, and DMS/DPPX. CSP also works with a variety of data storage software including SQL/DS, VSAM, DL/I for DOS/VS, and DB2.

Programming Languages

As mentioned in section 5 of this book, while almost any programming language is available for purchase for VM/CMS, the VM/SP license only includes the system assembler.

The following discussion lists a few of the more common programming languages used under VM/CMS, and the kinds of tasks for which each is most appropriate. Note that the programming languages can all be used (sometimes quite effectively) in ways not mentioned here.

Although the descriptions do not explore such subleties as different versions of the languages, nor is the list comprehensive, here is a brief sketch of the most common:

APL and APL2. APL is a matrix-manipulation language that is popular under VM/CMS in application to scientific, engineering, and mathematical programming. The language's greatest advantage is that you can write enormously powerful programs in only a few lines of code. Unfortunately, deciphering someone else's code later is a real chore. APL is easily recognizable because of its extensive use of special symbols.

APL has surprising application to data processing. It supports A Departmental Reporting System (ADRS II), a separate program product which creates customized business reports quickly and easily and includes a graphics option. Users do not need to know APL to use ADRS II. The APL Data Interface (APL/DI) is another program product that provides a general-purpose interactive data inquiry facility based on APL functions.

Assembler. A version of the 370 assembler language is the only programming language included as part of the VM/SP license. Assembler language programming requires greater programming expertise and time in exchange for programs that are more efficient in terms of execution time and memory requirements. The primary reason for using assembler is that systems-level programming often requires the level of control one gains over the machine with assembler language.

BASIC. IBM BASIC supports a complete programming environment for BASIC language programming. BASIC's strength is that it is one of the easiest general-purpose programming languages to learn and to use. IBM's implementation offers users both the debugging ease of an interpreter and the efficiencies of a compiler. The availability of BASIC gives VM/CMS users an important link to what remains the most popular microcomputer programming language.

C. C is distinguished by its low-level language capabilities embedded within the structure of a high-level language. C is also known for its portability and association with the UNIX operating system. With an appropriate function library, you can write programs in C that would otherwise require assembler programming. There are several implementations of C for VM/CMS available both from IBM and independent vendors.

COBOL. COBOL is by far the most popular language for data processing applications. Relatively easy to use and largely self-documenting, it interfaces with almost any program development tool available. To a greater or lesser extent, traditional COBOL applications are being displaced by the kinds of fourth generation database languages described in the subsection on SQL/DS.

FORTRAN. FORTRAN is primarily identified with scientific, engineering, and mathematical applications, although as one of the first major programming languages, it has been applied to almost every other kind of programming problem as well. Newer versions of FORTRAN comply with structured coding techniques and facilitate interactive debugging.

LISP. LISP is an older programming language which can be used for a wide variety of nonnumeric and symbol-manipulation problems. Under VM/CMS it has found use particularly in artificial intelligence applications and in the academic community.

Pascal. Pascal is a general-purpose programming language that is employed on a variety of computers for many kinds of programming applications. The language is fully structured, easy to learn, and popular for teaching programming. A significant difference among Pascal compilers has to do with their extensions to the ISO (and other) standards. ISO-standard Pascal lacks string manipulation and input/output capabilities and most compilers address these defects through language extensions.

PL/I. PL/I is a large and powerful general-purpose programming language. Many experienced mainframe programmers prefer PL/I as a language that flexibly combines the best features of COBOL and FORTRAN. Like C and Pascal (and the newer versions of BASIC, COBOL, and FORTRAN) PL/I is a fully structured language.

PROLOG. PROLOG is a newly popular programming language for artificial intelligence applications, and especially for expert systems. The availability of this language (along with LISP) gives VM/CMS an important role among IBM operating systems in research and development in natural language processing, symbolic manipulation, theorem proving, deductive reasoning, and dynamic relational databases. IBM's version of PROLOG can use SQL/DS as its DBMS.

RPG II. RPG is representative of the report generator languages invented during the 1960s and is widely used for data processing on IBM minicomputers. The availability of RPG under VM/CMS gives VM users an important link to business minicomputer systems.

SNOBOL. SNOBOL is a special purpose string processing language. It is widely used in linguistic and text processing applications. Both interpreted and compiled versions of the language are offered by independent vendors for use under VM/CMS.

Systems Products

While the program products described in this book are used by end-users and programmers, the software described in the next two subsections is often familiar only to systems programmers. Nevertheless, we include discussion of VM Assists and the VM/Directory Maintenance software because knowledge of these products proves useful to managers, analysts, and system planners in the VM/CMS environment.

VM Assists

While VM/SP has many strengths as an operating system, one criticism to which it has historically been vulnerable is its inefficiency. Running one operating system under another necessarily incurs overhead. For example, when running an OS operating system like MVS/SP under VM/CMS, inefficiency results because both operating systems perform their own virtual storage management. This effects a dual level of demand paging (called *shadow paging*). Other inefficiencies result because the guest operating system issues privileged instructions that must be intercepted by CP, which then issues its own privileged instructions. This produces a long instruction path length for critical internal MVS functions.

The inefficiencies inherent in VM/SP when running guest operating systems have long been recognized. Over the years, IBM has introduced a number of hardware and software solutions to these problems. While each has its own name, we refer to them generically as *VM assists*. The purpose of these assists is to render VM/SP more efficient in running guest operating systems.

Many of the VM assists introduced over the years are technical in nature and it is not our intent to cover them here. It is only important to understand the concept and role of VM assists. If you run one or more guest operating systems under VM/SP, you should be aware of the available assists and their potential impact on your system's performance.

VM/Directory Maintenance

The VM/Directory Maintenance program is a separately purchased program product that aids in online update of the CP Directory. This program renders the update task easier and more accurate than through manual updating of directory entries.

The Directory Maintenance program recognizes two groups of users: general users and VM system administrators.

Each class of user has commands at his disposal to update appropriate aspects of the CP directory. For example, general users can update their own password through this product, but not other users' passwords. Directory updates that require special authorization are restricted to the system administrators who access privileged classes of commands for that purpose.

Internally, the Directory Maintenance program requires two virtual machines: DIRMAINT, the directory manager; and DATAMOVE, which performs copying and formatting functions.

For Further Information

Further information on IFS is available in the manual, *VM/Interactive File Sharing General Information, GC24-5195.* Complete information on using the product is found in *VM/Interactive File Sharing Guide and Reference, SC24-5196.*

SQL/DS General Information for VM/SP, GH24-5064, and *SQL/DS Concepts and Facilities for VM/SP, GH24-5065,* are the two basic introductory manuals on the SQL/DS product. The *Query Management Facility: General Information, GC26-4071,* contains an equivalent introduction for QMF.

Further information on VM/Pass-Through is available in *VM /Pass-Through Facility General Information, GC24-5206,* and *VM/Pass-Through Facility Guide and Reference, SC24-5208.* An article in the *IBM Systems Journal* also summarizes the product and its history: N. Mendelsohn, M.H. Linehan, and W.J. Anzick, "Reflections on VM/Pass-Through: A Facility for Interactive Networking," *IBM Systems Journal* (22:1-2, 1983).

The manual, *GDDM General Information, GC33-0100,* introduces the functions and capabilities of GDDM.

Further information on CICS for CMS is available in the *CICS /CMS General Information, GC33-0284,* documentation.

The general information manual on CSP for VM/CMS users is *Cross System Product/Application Development and Cross/System Product /Application Execution General Information Version 3, GH23-0500.* The introductory manual for CSP/Query is *Cross System Product/Query General Information, GH24-5048.*

The major programming languages and their characteristics are described in *Programming Languages* by Allen B. Tucker (McGraw-Hill, 1986) and *Programming Languages: History and Fundamentals* by J. E. Sammet (Prentice-Hall, 1969). The manual, *VM/SP Introduction* discusses many of the IBM programming language products available for purchase for VM/CMS.

The *VM/SP Introduction* manual describes the concept of VM assists and mentions several VM assist options. That manual also introduces the VM/SP High Performance Option (VM/SP HPO). More detailed information on VM/SP HPO is found in *VM/SP High Performance Option General Information, GC19-6221.*

An overview of the VM/Directory Maintenance program product is available in *VM/Directory Maintenance General Information, GC20-1836.* The *VM/Directory Maintenance Guide for General Users, SC20-1830,* describes how to use the program from the viewpoint of general users.

Test Your Understanding

What are the essential differences between IFS and VSAM (as included with CMS in the basic VM/SP license)?

What are the components of IFS and their functions? How do application programs request IFS services?

What is a relational database management system? How do the basic SQL commands for data retrieval and update reflect the relational DBMS philosophy?

What are ISQL, the DBS Utility, QMF, and QBE? How do these components relate to SQL/DS? What are the functions and roles of these components relative to one another?

Why do installations purchase software products like IFS and SQL/DS? What are the needs these products fulfill within the VM/CMS environment?

What are the purpose and benefits of VM/Pass-Through? What features do RSCS and SNA offer that VM/Pass-Through lacks? What advantages does VM/Pass-Through offer over RSCS and SNA networks?

What basic functions does GDDM provide terminal users? What benefits does it provide programmers?

Why is the advent of CICS important for CMS users? Why would it be beneficial to develop CICS programs under CMS for production use on target DOS- or OS-based computers?

Is CSP a: fourth generation language; application generator; database language; or all three? Can CSP applications replace basic COBOL programs for retrieval and update of data?

Which programming languages are identified with the following applications (Note: each has more than a single answer)

artificial intelligence

mathematical programming

data processing

engineering applications

character string and textual processing

list processing and symbolic programming

What are VM assists? Why are they important in the VM/SP environment? What benefits do installations expect from a product like VM/SP HPO?

What are the benefits of the VM/Directory Maintenance program product?

SECTION 8

VM/CMS and the Future

- ◼ Virtual Machine/Personal Computer
- ◼ Summary of VM/CMS

CHAPTER 26

Virtual Machine/Personal Computer

VM/CMS distinguishes itself among IBM's mainframe operating systems in that it is the most interactively oriented. VM/CMS also spans the greatest range of machine sizes, running on entry-level mainframes through the largest machines IBM vends. Finally, with its ability to run guest operating systems, VM/CMS represents an important part of IBM's compatibility strategy.

With the rise of microcomputers, it is natural that IBM should select VM/CMS from among its mainframe operating systems to transport to microcomputers. The company has accomplished this migration in the form of a VM/CMS variant called Virtual Machine/Personal Computer (VM /PC). VM/PC runs on standard IBM personal computers such as the XT and AT that have been adapted by the insertion of special circuit boards. Those particular models are called the XT/370 and AT/370; generically, we call these machines the PC/370.

VM/PC is an extremely significant development because it is the first appearance of the VM/CMS operating system on microcomputers. Thus, while many implementation details are specific to the PC/370 computers and this first version of VM/PC, much can be learned about how VM/CMS and microcomputing are evolving.

PC/370 Hardware

VM/PC hardware consists of a standard model Personal Computer, such as the XT or AT models, with the addition of three circuit boards. These cards are referred to as the PC/3277EM (or PC/3278EM), PC/370-P, and PC/370-M. The first card emulates a full-screen mainframe computer terminal (a 3277-2 or a 3278). This card enables the PC/370 user to access a System /370-architecture mainframe computer as a remote host.

The PC/370-P and PC/370-M cards work together and are connected by a ribbon cable. The PC/370-M card provides memory. The PC/370-P card contains three microprocessors: a custom-developed System/370 Subset microprocessor that performs many System/370 commercial instructions; a custom-developed floating-point processor that executes System/370 extended precision instructions; and a Motorola MC68000R microprocessor that emulates many remaining System/370 instructions. The result is that these cards enable the PC/370 to execute a substantial subset of the instruction set of IBM System/370 architecture mainframe computers. This capability underlies the PC/370's ability to run many System/370 mainframe computer programs unaltered. Programs that run without alteration include many user programs, and also include support programs like editors (XEDIT), output formatters (SCRIPT), language processors (COBOL, PL/I, and others), and other CMS applications.

Basic Features

VM/PC is a variant of the VM/SP operating system adapted as necessary to run on the PC/370 hardware. The goal of the VM/PC system is to allow many System/370 mainframe programs to run unaltered on the personal computer. This is achieved through the combination of the underlying hardware supporting the 370 instruction set and the operating system environment supported by VM/PC.

VM/PC is based on VM/SP Release 2. While it looks very much like VM/SP Release 2, certain aspects of the operating system have been adapted to the unique environment of the personal computer. VM/PC supports subsets of the VM/SP Release 2 CP and CMS commands, some of which have different options and formats than in VM/SP Release 2.

Table 26-1 lists the CP commands in the initial release of VM/PC; table 26-2 lists the CMS commands. Among the latter, two are new with VM/PC. The **IMPORT** and **EXPORT** commands permit the copying of files between the two operating systems that run on the PC/370, VM/PC, and PC-DOS.

Table 26-3 enumerates the VM/SP Release 2 commands that VM/PC does not support. Here is a high-level summary of the differences between VM/PC and VM/SP Release 2:

- VM/PC does not support tape I/O, virtual readers, and virtual punches since the personal computer does not include the underlying hardware.
- VM/PC does not support CMS/DOS.
- VM/PC necessarily presents slight differences in the display and keyboard mapping due to the personal computer hardware.

Additional differences between VM/PC and VM/SP Release 3 and later include:

- VM/PC has no HELP facility.

Table 26-1
VM/PC CP
Commands

Command	Function
*	A comment (ignored by CP)
#CP	Execute a CP command while remaining within CMS
ATTN	Generate attention interruption pending at virtual console
BEGIN	Continue virtual machine execution
CHANGE	Alter attributes of a closed spool file
CLOSE	Terminate spooling activity on a spooled virtual device
CP	Execute a CP command while remaining within CMS
DEFINE	Reconfigure your virtual machine
DETACH	Detach a device from your virtual machine
DISPLAY	Display virtual machine storage and status words
DUMP	Print virtual machine storage and status words
EXTERNAL	Generate external interrupt to the virtual machine
IPL	Initial program load of the virtual machine
LINK	Access a minidisk for the virtual machine
LOGOFF	Log off and terminate the virtual machine session
ORDER	Order closed spool files
PURGE	Delete closed spool files
QUERY	Query virtual machine status and configuration
REQUEST	Generate attention interruption pending at virtual console
SET	Set functions in the virtual machine
SPOOL	Dictate spooling control parameters
STORE	Set virtual storage and status word values
TAG	Associate information with spool files
TERMINAL	Set virtual console characteristics
TRACE	Trace virtual machine activity

- VM/PC supports the EXEC2 and EXEC command interpreters but not REXX.
- The manual set for VM/PC is largely that used for VM/SP Release 2.

While there may appear to be many differences between VM/PC and VM/CMS as presented in this book, in fact, the two systems are highly similar and moving between them is easy. VM/PC faithfully reproduces the mainframe VM/CMS environment to the extent that many programs and their users require no significant adjustment in the transition between systems. The PC/370 running VM/PC successfully grafts the VM/CMS mainframe environment onto desktop computers.

Multiple Session Capability

The PC/370 system supports up to four independent terminal sessions concurrently. Some of these sessions are *local,* meaning that they occur on the PC/370 processors; others are *remote,* or connections to a System/370 architecture mainframe which views the PC/370 as a terminal. You can run all four sessions concurrently. You switch your terminal between sessions

Table 26-2
VM/PC CMS
Commands

Command	Function
ACCESS	Access a minidisk for the CMS virtual machine
CMDCALL	Convert EXEC2 extended PLIST function calls
COMPARE	Compare two CMS files
COPYFILE	Copy CMS files
CP	Enter CP commands from CMS environment
DEBUG	Enter DEBUG subcommand environment
DEFAULTS	Set/display default options for several CMS commands
DROPBUF	Drop most recently created program stack buffer
ERASE	Erase CMS files
ESTATE	Verify existence of CMS files
ESTATEW	Verify existence of CMS files on read/write disks
EXEC	Execute command procedures
EXECIO	Perform I/O between devices and the program stack, or execute CP commands and recover their output
EXPORT	Copy a CMS file to a PC-DOS file
FILEDEF	Define a device and relate it to an OS DDNAME
FILELIST	Full-screen list of CMS files
FINIS	Close files
FORMAT	Format CMS minidisks
GENDIRT	Fill in auxiliary module directories
GENMOD	Generate executable MODULE files
GLOBAL	Specify searchable CMS libraries
GLOBALV	Manipulate named variables globally from EXECs
IDENTIFY	Display user, date, and time information
IMPORT	Copy PC-DOS files to CMS
INCLUDE	Load and link TEXT files
LISTFILE	List information about CMS files
LOAD	Load TEXT files for execution
LOADMOD	Load MODULE files into storage
MACLIB	Create or modify CMS macro libraries
MAKEBUF	Create new buffer(s) within the program stack
MODMAP	Display the load map of MODULE files
NUCXDROP	Delete nucleus extensions
NUCXLOAD	Load nucleus extensions
NUCXMAP	Map nucleus extensions
PRINT	Spool files to the printer
QUERY	Query CMS virtual machine status indicators
RELEASE	Release minidisks
RENAME	Rename CMS files
SENTRIES	Query the number of lines in the program stack
SET	Set CMS virtual machine characteristics
SORT	Sort CMS files
START	Initiate execution of loaded programs
STATE	Verify existence of CMS files
STATEW	Verify existence of CMS files on read/write disks
SYNONYM	Establish synonyms for CMS and user-written commands
TXTLIB	Create or modify CMS text libraries
TYPE	Display CMS files on the virtual console
UPDATE	Change program source files
XEDIT	Enter the XEDIT editor
HT, HX, RT	CMS immediate commands

Table 26-3
VM/SP CMS
Commands Not
Supported
by VM/PC

AMSERV	ESERV	NOTE	RSERV
ASSEMBLE	FETCH	OPTION	RUN
ASSGN	HELP	OSRUN	SENDFILE
CMSBATCH	LABELDEF	PEEK	SETPRT
DDR	LISTDS	PSERV	SSERV
DISK	LISTIO	PUNCH	SVCTRACE
DLBL	LKED	RDR	TAPE
DOSLIB	LOADLIB	RDRLIST	TAPEMAC
DOSLKED	MOVEFILE	READCARD	TAPPDS
DSERV	NAMEFIND	RECEIVE	TELL
EDIT	NAMES		

by a single keystroke. The four sessions are:

1. *Local 3270 Session.* The personal computer display and keyboard act as the virtual console to the CMS session on the PC/370 processor card.

2. *Local PC/370 Processor Control Session.* A special session that permits access to the registers, memory, and status words of the PC /370 processor card.

3. *Remote 3270 Session.* The personal computer emulates a 3270 family terminal coaxial-attached to a System/370 architecture mainframe.

4. *Remote 3101 Session.* The personal computer emulates a 3101 terminal attached to the remote mainframe. (This session requires purchase of the IBM 3101 Emulation Program Product.)

The fact that these sessions run concurrently gives the PC/370 user tremendous flexibility (and productivity). For example, you could run a CMS application on the local 3270 session, while running another application on the remote VM/CMS mainframe through the remote 3270 session, while sustaining an ASCII communications link via the remote 3101 session. This concurrency renders the VM/PC-based PC/370 an excellent workstation. Such a workstation is of great value to both computer professionals and end-users.

Remote Services

VM/PC Remote Services support a variety of services for accessing the resources of the remotely attached mainframe VM/CMS computer. Use of VM/PC Remote Services requires installation of the remote server program (named VMPCSERV) on the remote mainframe computer. The VMPCSERV software is installed via the PC/370.

VM/PC Remote Services support these features:

Remote 3270 Session

remote minidisks

remote files

remote printers

Access to remote minidisks means that you issue the CP LINK and CMS ACCESS commands to access minidisks on the remote VM/CMS mainframe exactly as if those minidisks were resident within your own local PC /370 system. VM/PC knows to search for minidisks on the attached mainframe if they are not within the local PC/370 system. The access to remote files means that you refer to and use the files on those remote linked and accessed minidisks exactly as if they were resident on your local PC/370.

VM/PC Remote Services access to remote minidisks and files supports totally transparent access to mainframe disk and file resources. Neither you nor programs you run on the local PC/370 must know that these resources actually reside on the remote VM/CMS mainframe.

With the remote minidisk and file services, it is easy to upload or download files from the local PC/370 computer to the remote VM/CMS mainframe. Merely use the CMS COPYFILE command as you always do to copy files. The minidisk letters specified in the filemode portion of the two file names indicate the residency of the files involved in the copy.

Remote printer services are similar in concept to remote minidisk and file access. You direct a file to a remote VM/CMS mainframe printer merely by issuing a CP SPOOL command to spool the printer to the proper CLASS. As always under VM/CMS, the printer CLASS dictates how the printer spool files are handled, and in this case the CLASS identifies an attached mainframe printer. Now, enter the CMS PRINT command to print the file. As in the cases of remote minidisks and files, access to the remote mainframe resource is fully transparent.

In summary, the VM/PC Remote Services comprise a very strong networking package between the PC/370 and a remote VM/CMS mainframe because it implements access to the mainframe resources totally within the context of unaltered VM/CMS commands. This is achieved in a manner transparent to users and their programs.

Local PC/370 Processor Control Session

The local processor control session supports a control and debug facility similar to that encountered in the operator console of System/370 architecture mainframes. Remember that this session runs concurrently with the other three sessions on the PC/370 and that you switch into and out of it at will. With the local processor control session, you can:

- start and stop the PC/370 processor
- *single-step* the PC/370 processor (execute a program instruction by instruction under your direction)
- externally interrupt, reset, and clear reset the PC/370 processor
- full-screen edit the PC/370 registers and storage (general-purpose,

floating point, and control registers; program status word (PSW); real and virtual storage; page address table).

The local processor control session provides a superlative debugging facility that renders the PC/370 an effective programmer workstation.

Summary

VM/PC represents an important part of the future of VM/CMS; the adaptability of VM/CMS to microcomputers gives it a critical future role among operating systems.

The existence of VM/CMS-based computers spanning the spectrum of computers from desktop to large mainframes represents a major step forward in intersystem compatibility. VM/PC means that personal computers run mainframe software without requiring program changes.

VM/PC is an early version of VM/CMS for microcomputers that will certainly evolve, as will the underlying PC/370 hardware. Nonetheless, even the VM/PC-based product described here shows tremendous capabilities. On the PC/370, VM/PC:

- runs most VM/CMS mainframe user and purchased programs without alteration
- deviates minimally from "true" mainframe VM/CMS
- accesses remote VM/CMS mainframe minidisks, files, and printers in a manner that is totally transparent and within the framework of the VM/CMS operating system
- supports several concurrent sessions with great flexibility
- provides an outstanding level of local processor session control

Given the evolution of the supporting hardware, VM/PC has the potential to spawn workstations of outstanding productivity. A microcomputer-based form of VM/CMS could fulfill an important role among operating systems.

For Further Information

The article, "System/370 Capability in a Desktop Computer," by F.T. Kozuh, D.L. Livingston, and T.C. Spillman appeared in *IBM Systems Journal* (23:3, 1984). It describes the PC/370's purpose and its architecture on an overview level.

The basic manual for VM/PC is *VM/PC User's Guide, SC24-5254.* This manual contains the information needed to operate the system and summarizes the differences between VM/PC and VM/SP Release 2. The other manuals documenting usage of the VM/PC product are the same as those supporting mainframe VM/SP Release 2. The *VM/PC User's Guide* lists the manual names and order numbers.

Test Your Understanding

What are the major differences between VM/PC and VM/SP Release 2? To what extent are these differences based on differences between mainframe and microcomputer hardware?

What sessions operate concurrently on the PC/370? Describe how you could use these multiple sessions to your advantage if you were an applications programmer.

Describe how the VM/PC user accesses remote minidisks, remote files, and remote printers. Is it necessary to copy a file from an attached mainframe in order to use it under VM/PC?

What is the Local PC/370 Processor Control Session? What kind of computer user would employ this feature most frequently?

What are the premier features of the PC/370 running VM/PC? What are the implications of VM/CMS for personal computers and desktop mainframes?

CHAPTER 27

Summary of VM/CMS

For what applications and environments is VM/CMS most appropriate? What criticisms have been directed at this operating system?

Different operating systems, like different programming languages, each have their own unique strengths and areas of best application. No single operating system is superior across the board and for all tasks.

With VM/CMS experiencing growth of over 50% per year on smaller mainframes and over 100% for larger mainframes, the directions it assumes are of great importance. (And these growth statistics do not not mention the potential of VM/PC or similar systems on desktop computers!)

Strengths

The strengths of VM/CMS have been enumerated and explained throughout this book. It is worthwhile to reiterate several of them here.

VM/CMS is strongly interactive. From online editing to electronic communications, to interactive program development, to its exceptional debugging environments, to its comprehensive online HELP facility, CMS is an interactive system.

VM/CMS can support large numbers of interactive users. On an identical computer, VM/SP with CMS as its teleprocessing monitor supports significantly more terminal users than does MVS running TSO, for example.

VM/CMS provides a good program development environment. An underlying principle of the VM/CMS environment is that it supports program development for other operating systems. These target operating systems may be of any variety, including those of the OS and DOS families. The target systems may run as VM/SP guests on the same physical computer as the CMS development system or on a different computer in native mode.

There is an important distinction between VM/CMS and the UNIX operating system, which also offers an exceptional program development environment. Development in UNIX and C language yields its highest degree of portability to other machines running UNIX and C. VM/CMS, on the other hand, is designed for porting applications to machines running either VM/CMS or one of a variety of other operating systems. This portability encompasses the several mainframe operating systems and their "traditional" programming languages including COBOL, FORTRAN, RPGII, PL/I, and assembler language. While this comparison simplifies the capabilities of both VM/CMS and UNIX, it points out an important difference between the two systems that marketing claims often blur.

Two other particularly strong points of VM/CMS as a software development environment should be mentioned. First, the virtual machine philosophy can be employed to advantage as programmers configure and customize their virtual machines to fit their requirements. Second, control of your own virtual machine especially aids in machine-level debugging.

VM/CMS offers many purchasable program development tools. There are a vast array of program-support tools available for VM/CMS, including ISPF, ISPF/PDF, IPF, DMS, GDDM, CICS for CMS, CSP, SQL/DS, and QMF.

VM/CMS offers many purchasable applications. VM/CMS has been a mainstream, general-purpose operating system for years. One can purchase products for almost any application or business function. The product birth rate in the add-on market has increased dramatically in the past few years, as software vendors and users grasp the central role of VM /CMS in IBM's plans and in the marketplace.

VM/CMS is the ONLY major operating system designed to run guest operating systems. This premier feature of VM/SP underlies many of the system's advantages as an operating system and is partially responsible for the important role the system has today in its vendor's plans and the marketplace. While some operating systems offer a degree of coexistence with another operating system, VM/CMS is specifically designed so that it can concurrently run any operating system capable of running on the same physical computer. The implications for compatibility between operating systems are tremendous. This is one reason industry analysts tout VM/SP as a solution to the incompatibilities between operating systems on computers ranging from the largest general-purpose mainframes down to desktop microcomputers. We leave prediction to the soothsayers but urge you to consider VM's unique properties in this respect.

VM/CMS represents a key link between IBM's diverse OS offerings, including OS, DOS, and UNIX systems. This is true both in terms of VM/CMS's support of program development for alternate operating environments and in terms of VM/CMS's likely future role among operating systems.

VM/CMS facilitates conversions between operating systems. VM/CMS's ability to run more than one guest operating system lends it a special role in reducing "conversion trauma," as well as in the testing of new releases and fixes. This is just one example of benefits resulting from VM's ability to run different guest operating systems.

VM/CMS provides compatibility between mainframes and microcomputers. VM/PC allows the porting of programs between personal computers and mainframes with full compatibility. VM/PC's remote services and multiple concurrent terminal sessions form another part of this micro-mainframe compatibility.

VM/CMS has a unique role among mainframe operating systems in the transition to the powerful microcomputers of the future. IBM's porting of VM/CMS to personal computers in the form of VM/PC is likely only the first implementation of VM/CMS on microcomputers. While VM/CMS's future on microcomputers is not known at this time, the operating system clearly has great potential on desktop systems. Part of this potential lies in the inherent VM ability to coexist with other operating systems like PC-DOS and UNIX, as well as the prerequisite fit between its interactive nature and the demands of microcomputing.

VM/CMS supports office automation. Most office automation experts advise that discrete office workstations are more cost-effective in automating the office than "shared-logic" mainframe-based solutions. Nevertheless, VM/CMS and its office support applications represent a key part of IBM's office automation strategy. PROFS is a well-designed and functionally robust product. A VM/CMS mainframe with office support software is especially practical in that one automates the office merely by adding software to an existing mainframe system. Developments such as VM-based microcomputers, PROFS products for personal computers, and the continued development of SNA indicate that the VM/CMS environment is evolving in such a way as to ensure its future in the office automation marketplace.

VM/CMS supports end-user computing and Information Centers better than other mainframe operating systems. Both the interactive nature of CMS and the large number of end-user oriented packages available for the VM/CMS have rendered it the leading operating system for this purpose.

CMS is widely considered easier to learn and to use than other mainframe teleprocessing monitors (such as MVS's TSO). Adding front-end packages like IPF or ISPF/PDF makes CMS even more user-friendly because of their full-screen panels, menus, programmed function keys, and tutorial screens.

VM/CMS enhances computer science education. VM/CMS has long been associated with computer science research in a way that many other mainframe operating systems have not. This has led to its popularity in academic circles and the availability of software products for VM/CMS that facilitate research. For example, VM/CMS is unusual today among mainframe operating systems in its suitability for research in artificial intelligence. But with its LISP and PROLOG translators and the several expert systems that run under VM/CMS, this should not be surprising.

VM/CMS is also particularly appropriate for educational purposes because of its virtual machine concept. Having control of one's own virtual machine, the DEBUG environment, and CP-level debugging make CMS a "visible machine," the educational ideal. Since the start of the 1980s the rise of microcomputing has diminished the significance of this role for VM/CMS.

VM/CMS requires less systems support than other mainframe operating systems. Sites running VM typically require fewer systems programmers and operators. This strength renders VM/CMS especially appealing on smaller computers, departmental processors, and in support of office automation.

VM/CMS is highly configurable. Because of the virtual machine philosophy, individual CMS users can have their own virtual machines configured appropriate to their needs. Different virtual machines may control different virtual devices and offer different hardware configurations. Virtual machine configurations can be established statically (through CP Directory entries) and modified dynamically, through CP commands issued through the virtual console.

Moreover, CMS itself presents a tailored user interface. Users may modify the command search order, add command procedures and programs to extend CMS capabilities, rename commands through `SYNONYM` files, set defaults for various CMS commands through the CMS `DEFAULTS` command, alter terminal characteristics, and set program function keys. Command procedures represent an important mechanism for customizing CMS. `PROFILE EXEC` file(s), `PROFILE XEDIT` file(s), and edit macros all comprise part of the power of command procedures in tailoring CMS userids.

While such a judgment must be subjective, we feel that VM/CMS supports one of the most customizable of all operating system environments.

Weaknesses

Over the years, VM/CMS has received its share of criticism. Analyzing these shortcomings is surely as important as discussing the operating system's strengths.

VM/CMS is weak as a batch operating system. Although VM/CMS offers its Batch Machine Facility, if you need a batch architecture, this assertion has merit. CMS is clearly oriented toward interactive computing. VM/CMS is not a batch-oriented architecture in the same sense as operating systems in IBM's OS and DOS families and it is less efficient in running batch jobs.

VM/CMS is inefficient. One must first determine what is meant by inefficiency. As stated in the list of VM/CMS strengths, VM/SP with CMS as its teleprocessing monitor supports many more interactive users than does MVS/TSO, for example, on the same model of computer. VM/CMS is highly efficient for interactive computing. Questions of efficiency are usually directed at VM/CMS when the system runs guest operating systems. For example, running MVS/SP under VM/CMS was for many years much less productive than running MVS/SP in native mode (on its own computer without VM/SP as host). This relative inefficiency is inherent in VM's ability to run virtual machines, and it forms the basis for the many different VM assists released over the years. Interestingly, these improvements have resulted in a situation where running guest operating systems no longer extracts the price it once did. In fact, under certain conditions, some operating systems run more efficiently under VM/SP with assists than in native mode. Running DOS/VSE under VM/SP is especially widespread and yields well over 90% efficiency for most users. If you intend to run guest operating system(s) under VM/SP, obtain current statistics before making any assumptions or adopting foregone conclusions concerning performance.

VM/CMS is too "mainframe," i.e., *too big, too complex, and too difficult to learn.* The several hundred CMS and CP commands reflect the evolution of VM/CMS over a twenty-year period so this statement contains more than a little truth. To some extent, CMS's "HELP" Facility ameliorates this criticism. Many operating systems do not offer an integrated, menu-oriented, comprehensive "HELP" system online like CMS.

VM/CMS lacks design integrity. In one sense, VM/CMS has much greater design integrity than most operating systems. It is based on the virtual machine philosophy, which is carried through the entire architecture. In another sense, however, VM/CMS's evolutionary growth has obscured this design integrity. For example, the CP and CMS commands designed for interuser communication have overlapping and duplicate functions. The VM/CMS manuals merely present these commands without any perspective on when their use is most appropriate.

VM/CMS only offers a traditional "mainframe" user interface. This criticism is as true of VM/CMS as it is of any other mainframe operating system. One does not tend to associate VM/CMS systems with mice for cursor control, voice input/output, touch screens, and other new forms of person/machine interface. VM/CMS evolution will likely progress in these areas to at least the same degree as any other mature operating system, and possibly much more rapidly, depending on the future of VM/PC.

VM/CMS is weak for networking. VM/CMS offers communication commands that use RSCS, and also the simple-to-use, yet highly effective and widely popular VM/Pass-Through product. Why then, have some talked of VM/CMS as being "weak for networking"? The answer is that VM/CMS traditionally supported IBM's SNA only in the most rudimentary fashion: by requiring users to run a guest operating system that supported SNA. The SNA support issue is critical because SNA is IBM's official blueprint for networking all of its diverse computing products. IBM is bringing VM/CMS into the SNA fold. A major improvement in VM/CMS Release 4 is its Group Control System (GCS) software for supervising a virtual machine dedicated to SNA and communications products. GCS and associated products amelieorate criticism concerning VM/CMS's SNA capabilities.

VM/SP has also been enhanced in Release 5 to support Ethernet, TCP/IP, and other communications protocols for the 9370 series of computers. The result of these enhancements is that VM/CMS has evolved from IBM's weakest into its strongest operating system for networking.

VM/CMS is not good as a "production environment" for transaction-oriented processing. This criticism, too, has more basis in historical than current reality. Prior to the advent of many of the current DBMS for VM

/CMS shops, this criticism was valid. However, today properly configured VM/CMS machines support production environments quite adequately. The author has worked with production applications (written in languages like PL/I and COBOL, in combination with ISPF for screen control, and SQL/DS for database management) and has found VM/CMS as reliable as MVS/TSO (with comparable software) for production systems. While one could argue concerning the transaction volume VM/CMS handles, today VM/CMS readily supports production systems.

VM/CMS does not support shared file access with data integrity for up-dates for CMS users. Shared file locks are an assumed feature of most multi-user computer operating system environments. For example, under MVS /TSO terminal users routinely edit files in a multi-user environment with full assurance that the operating system's locks prevent any possibility of data destruction due to updates.

The virtual machine architecture of VM/CMS gives CMS users a very different situation. Individual CMS users each have their own virtual machines, so they cannot edit each other's files across virtual machines with data integrity assured by the operating system.

The VM/CMS architecture dictates that CMS users share data differently than under most multi-user operating system environments. VM /CMS operating system communications features and products such as IFS and SQL/DS address many of the deficiencies associated with CMS's lack of shared file integrity for updates. Nevertheless, the environment's lack of built-in shared file integrity represents a defect in situations where you require the kinds of update locks provided by most multi-user operating system environments.

The Future

The strengths and weaknesses of VM/CMS suggest many possible future directions for this operating system: as an agent for operating system compatibility between large mainframes, superminicomputers, and desktop computers; as a general-purpose interactive operating system; as a link between microcomputers and traditional business computer systems; and as a host for a wide variety of applications packages.

VM/CMS can be used to support program development, end-user computing, information centers, office automation, scientific/engineering environments, academic computing, software engineering, vendor package development, business data processing, and other functions too numerous to mention.

The coincidence of VM/CMS's technical strengths, the evolution of computing needs, marketplace demand, and IBM's own interests ensure continued explosive growth for this flexible operating system.

Test Your Understanding

What do you think are the major strengths of VM/CMS as an operating system? Compare these strengths to how well other operating systems fare in these areas.

What are some of the major strengths of other operating systems with which you may be familiar? How does VM/CMS compare in these areas?

What kinds of software must a VM/CMS site install in order to perform transaction processing? What software packages described in this book would be most suitable for the VM/CMS installation that develops and runs transaction-oriented data processing programs?

VM/CMS sales are soaring. Given that the operating system has been for sale for over 15 years, why is the VM/CMS boom occurring now?

Appendices

APPENDIX A

Roadmap to the VM/CMS Manual Set

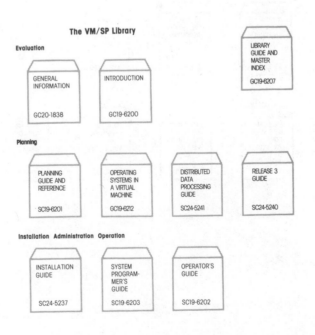

The VM/SP Library

Evaluation

GENERAL INFORMATION — GC20-1838

INTRODUCTION — GC19-6200

LIBRARY GUIDE AND MASTER INDEX — GC19-6207

Planning

PLANNING GUIDE AND REFERENCE — SC19-6201

OPERATING SYSTEMS IN A VIRTUAL MACHINE — GC19-6212

DISTRIBUTED DATA PROCESSING GUIDE — SC24-5241

RELEASE 3 GUIDE — SC24-5240

Installation Administration Operation

INSTALLATION GUIDE — SC24-5237

SYSTEM PROGRAMMER'S GUIDE — SC19-6203

OPERATOR'S GUIDE — SC19-6202

(con't on next page)

End Use

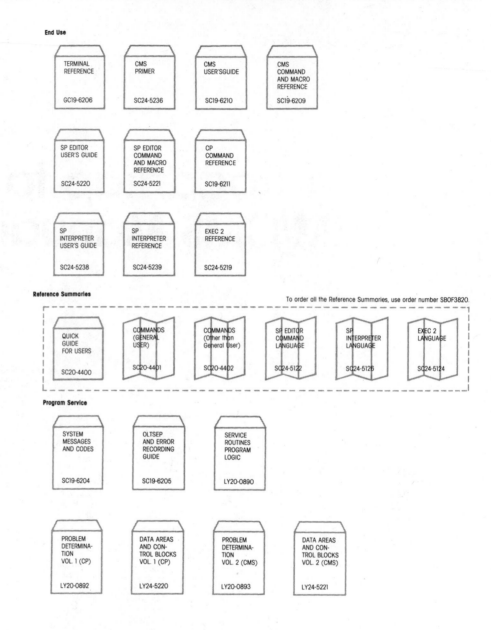

TERMINAL REFERENCE	CMS PRIMER	CMS USER'S GUIDE	CMS COMMAND AND MACRO REFERENCE
GC19-6206	SC24-5236	SC19-6210	SC19-6209

SP EDITOR USER'S GUIDE	SP EDITOR COMMAND AND MACRO REFERENCE	CP COMMAND REFERENCE
SC24-5220	SC24-5221	SC19-6211

SP INTERPRETER USER'S GUIDE	SP INTERPRETER REFERENCE	EXEC 2 REFERENCE
SC24-5238	SC24-5239	SC24-5219

Reference Summaries

To order all the Reference Summaries, use order number SBOF3820.

QUICK GUIDE FOR USERS	COMMANDS (GENERAL USER)	COMMANDS (Other than General User)	SP EDITOR COMMAND LANGUAGE	SP INTERPRETER LANGUAGE	EXEC 2 LANGUAGE
SC20-4400	SC20-4401	SC20-4402	SC24-5122	SC24-5126	SC24-5124

Program Service

SYSTEM MESSAGES AND CODES	OLTSEP AND ERROR RECORDING GUIDE	SERVICE ROUTINES PROGRAM LOGIC
SC19-6204	SC19-6205	LY20-0890

PROBLEM DETERMINATION VOL. 1 (CP)	DATA AREAS AND CONTROL BLOCKS VOL. 1 (CP)	PROBLEM DETERMINATION VOL. 2 (CMS)	DATA AREAS AND CONTROL BLOCKS VOL. 2 (CMS)
LY20-0892	LY24-5220	LY20-0893	LY24-5221

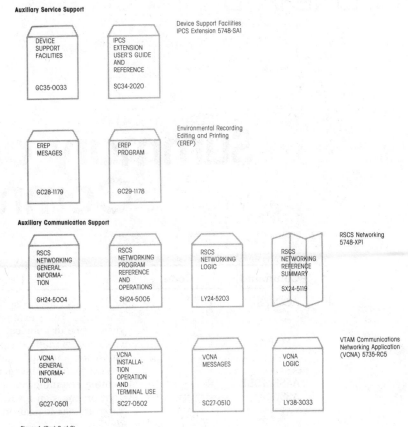

Auxiliary Service Support

DEVICE SUPPORT FACILITIES
GC35-0033

IPCS EXTENSION USER'S GUIDE AND REFERENCE
SC34-2020

Device Support Facilities
IPCS Extension 5748-SA1

EREP MESAGES
GC28-1179

EREP PROGRAM
GC29-1178

Environmental Recording Editing and Printing (EREP)

Auxiliary Communication Support

RSCS NETWORKING GENERAL INFORMATION
GH24-5004

RSCS NETWORKING PROGRAM REFERENCE AND OPERATIONS
SH24-5005

RSCS NETWORKING LOGIC
LY24-5203

RSCS NETWORKING REFERENCE SUMMARY
SX24-5119

RSCS Networking 5748-XP1

VCNA GENERAL INFORMATION
GC27-0501

VCNA INSTALLATION OPERATION AND TERMINAL USE
SC27-0502

VCNA MESSAGES
SC27-0510

VCNA LOGIC
LY38-3033

VTAM Communications Networking Application (VCNA) 5735-RC5

Figure 1 (Part 2 of 2).
The Virtual Machine/System Product Library

APPENDIX B

Summary of CMS Commands

Command	Code	Usage
ACCESS		Identify direct access space to a CMS virtual machine, create extensions and relate the disk space to a logical directory
AMSERV		Invoke access method services utility functions to create, alter, list, copy, delete, import, or export VSAM catalogs and data sets
ASSEMBLE		Assemble assembler language source code
ASSGN		Assign or unassign a CMS/DOS system or programmer logical unit for a virtual I/O device
CATCHECK		Allows a CMS VSAM user (with or without DOS set ON) to invoke the VSE/VSAM Catalog Check Service Aid to verify a complete catalog structure
CMDCALL		Converts EXEC 2 extended plist function calls to CMS extended plist command calls
CMSBATCH		Invoke the CMS batch facility
COMPARE		Compare record in CMS disk files
CONWAIT		Causes a program to wait until all pending terminal I/O is complete
COPYFILE		Copy CMS disk files according to specifications
CP		Enter CP commands from the CMS environment
DDR		Perform backup, restore, and copy operations for disks
DEBUG		Enter DEBUG subcommand environment
DEFAULTS		Set or display default options for the commands: FILELIST, NOTE, RDRLIST, RECEIVE, PEEK, SENDFILE, and TELL
DESBUF		Clears the program stack and the terminal input buffers
DISK		Perform disk-to-card and card-to-disk operations for CMS files

Command	Code	Usage
DLBL		Define a VSE filename or VSAM ddname and relate that name to a disk file
DOSLIB		Delete, compact, or list information about the phases of a CMS/DOS phase library
DOSLKED		Link-edit CMS text decks or object modules from a VSE relocatable library and place them in executable form in a CMS/DOS phase library
DOSPLI	VSE PP	Compile DOS PL/I source code under CMS /DOS
DROPBUF		Eliminate a program stack buffer
DSERV		Display information contained in the VSE core image, relocatable, source, procedure, and transient directories
EDIT		Invoke the VM/SP System Product editor in CMS editor (EDIT) compatibility mode to create or modify a disk file
ERASE		Delete CMS disk files
ESERV		Display, punch or print an edited (compressed) macro from a VSE source statement library (E sublibrary)
EXEC		Execute special procedures made up of frequently used sequences of commands
EXECIO		Do I/O operations between a device and the program stack
EXECOS		Resets the OS and VSAM environments under CMS without returning to the interactive environment
EXECUPDT		Produces an updated executable version of a System Product Interpreter source program
FCOBOL	VSE PP	Compile DOS/VS COBOL source code under CMS/DOS
FETCH		Fetch a CMS/DOS or VSE executable phase
FILEDEF		Define an OS ddname and relate that ddname to any device supported by CMS
FILELIST		List information about CMS disk files, with the ability to edit and issue commands from the list
FINIS		Close an open file
FORMAT		Prepare disks in CMS fixed block format
GENDIRT		Fill in auxiliary module directories
GENMOD		Generate nonrelocatable CMS files (MODULE files)
GLOBAL		Identify specific CMS libraries to be searched for macros, copy files, missing subroutines, LOADLIB modules, or DOS executable phases
GLOBALV		Set, maintain, and retrieve a collection of named variables
HELP		Display information about CP, CMS, or user commands, EDIT, XEDIT, or DEBUG subcommands, EXEC, EXEC 2 and System Product Interpreter control statements, and descriptions of CMS and CP messages

Command	Code	Usage
IDENTIFY		Display or stack userid, nodeid, rscsid, date, time, time zone, and day of the week
IMMCMD		Use the IMMCMD command to establish or cancel immediate commands from within an EXEC
INCLUDE		Bring additional TEXT files into storage and establish linkages
IOCP	IOCP UG	Invoke the Input/Output Configuration Program
LABELDEF		Specify standard HDR1 and EOF1 tape label description information for CMS, CMS/DOS, and OS simulation
LISTDS		List information about data sets and space allocation on OS, DOS, and VSAM disks
LISTFILE		List information about CMS files
LISTIO		Display information concerning CMS/DOS system and programmer logical units
LKED		Link edit a CMS TEXT file or OS object module into a CMS LOADLIB
LOAD		Bring TEXT files into storage for execution
LOADLIB		Maintain CMS LOADLIB libraries
LOADMOD		Bring a single MODULE file into storage
MACLIB		Create or modify CMS macro libraries
MAKEBUF		Create a new program stack buffer
MODMAP		Display the load map of a MODULE file
MOVEFILE		Move data from one device to another device of the same or a different type
NAMEFIND		Display/stack information from a NAMES file. (default 'userid NAMES')
NAMES		Display a menu to create, display or modify entries in a 'userid NAMES' file (The menu is available only on display terminals.)
NOTE		Prepare a 'note' for one or more computer users, to be sent via the SENDFILE command
NUCXDROP		Delete specified nucleus extensions
NUCXLOAD		Load a nucleus extension
NUCXMAP		Identify existing nucleus extensions
OPTION		Change the DOS/VS COBOL compiler (FCOBOL) options that are in effect for the current terminal session
OSRUN		Load, relocate, and execute a load module from a CMS LOADLIB or OS module library
PEEK		Display a file that is in your virtual reader without reading it onto disk
PRINT		Spool a specified CMS file to the virtual printer
PSERV		Copy a procedure from the VSE procedure library onto a CMS disk, display the procedure at the terminal, or spool the procedure to the virtual punch or printer
PUNCH		Spool a copy of a CMS file to the virtual punch
QUERY		Request information about a CMS virtual machine

Command	Code	Usage
RDR		Generate a return code and either display or stack a message that identifies the characteristics of the next file in your virtual reader
RDRLIST		Display information about files in your virtual reader with the ability to issue commands from the list
READCARD		Read data from spooled card input device
RECEIVE		Read onto disk a file or note that is in your virtual reader
RELEASE		Make a disk and its directory inaccessible to a CMS virtual machine
RENAME		Change the name of a CMS file or files
RESERVE		Use the RESERVE command to allocate all available blocks of a 512-, 1K-, 2K-, or 4K-byte block formatted minidisk to a unique CMS file
RSERV		Copy a VSE relocatable module onto a CMS disk, display it at the terminal, or spool a copy to the virtual punch or printer
RUN		Initiate series of functions to be performed on a source, MODULE, TEXT, or EXEC file. SCRIPT control words in the document file
SENDFILE		Send files or notes to one or more computer users, attached locally or remotely, by issuing the command or by using a menu (display terminal only)
SENTRIES		Determine the number of lines currently in the program stack
SET		Establish, set, or reset CMS virtual machine characteristics
SETPRT		Load a virtual 3800 printer
SORT		Arrange a specified file in ascending order according to sort fields in the data records
SSERV		Copy a VSE source statement book onto a CMS disk, display it at the terminal, or spool a copy to the virtual punch or printer
START		Begin execution of programs previously loaded (OS and CMS) or fetched (CMS/DOS)
STATE		Verify the existence of a CMS file
STATEW		Verify a file on a read/write CMS disk
SVCTRACE		Record information about supervisor calls
SYNONYM		Invoke a table containing synonyms you have created for CMS and user-written commands
TAPE		Perform tape-to-disk and disk-to-tape operations for CMS files, position tapes, and display or write VOL1 labels
TAPEMAC		Create MACLIB libraries directly from an IEHMOVE-created partitioned data set on tape
TAPPDS		Load OS partitioned data set (PDS) files or card image files from tape to disk
TELL		Send a message to one or more computer users

Command	Code	Usage
		who are logged on to your computer or to one attached to yours via RSCS
TXTLIB		Generate and modify text libraries
TYPE		Display all or part of a CMS file at the terminal
UPDATE		Make changes in a program source file as defined by control cards in a control file
VSAPL	OS PP	Invoke VS ASPL interface in CMS
XEDIT		Invoke the VM/SP System Product Editor to create or modify a disk file

APPENDIX C

Summary of Selected CP Commands

Command	Usage
#CP	Execute a CP command from within the virtual machine environment
ADSTOP	Halt execution at a virtual machine address
ATTACH	Attach a real device to a virtual machine (Privilege Class B command)
ATTN	Generate attention interruption pending at virtual console
BEGIN	Continue virtual machine execution
CHANGE	Alter attributes of a closed spool file
CLOSE	Terminate spooling activity on a spooled virtual device
CP	Execute a CP command from within the CMS virtual machine environment
DEFINE	Reconfigure your virtual machine
DETACH	Detach a virtual device from your virtual machine
DISPLAY	Display virtual machine storage and status words
DUMP	Print virtual machine storage and status words
EXTERNAL	Generate external interruption to the virtual machine
IPL	Initial Program Load of the virtual machine
LINK	Access a minidisk for a virtual machine
LOGOFF	Log off CP and terminate a virtual machine session
LOGON	Log on to CP
MESSAGE	Send a message to another user
ORDER	Order closed spool files
PER	Trace virtual machine events
PURGE	Delete closed spool files
QUERY	Query configuration and status information
REQUEST	Generate attention interruption pending at virtual console
RESET	Clear pending interruptions and reset virtual device
REWIND	Rewind tape and ready tape drive
SCREEN	Set virtual console display attributes
SET	Set functions for your virtual machine
SPOOL	Dictate spooling control parameters
STORE	Set virtual storage and status word registers

Command	Usage
SYSTEM	Simulate RESET, CLEAR STORAGE, and RESTART buttons on a real system console on your virtual console
TAG	Associate information with spool files
TERMINAL	Set virtual console characteristics
TRACE	Trace virtual machine activity
TRANSFER	Transfer input files to/from other users' spooling queues